WILLIS DUKE WEATHERFORD

WILLIS DUKE WEATHERFORD

RACE, RELIGION, AND REFORM IN THE AMERICAN SOUTH

ANDREW McNEILL CANADY

UNIVERSITY PRESS OF KENTUCKY

Copyright © 2016 by The University Press of Kentucky

Scholarly publisher for the Commonwealth,
serving Bellarmine University, Berea College, Centre College of Kentucky, Eastern Kentucky University, The Filson Historical Society, Georgetown College, Kentucky Historical Society, Kentucky State University, Morehead State University, Murray State University, Northern Kentucky University, Transylvania University, University of Kentucky, University of Louisville, and Western Kentucky University.
All rights reserved.

Editorial and Sales Offices: The University Press of Kentucky
663 South Limestone Street, Lexington, Kentucky 40508-4008
www.kentuckypress.com

Cataloging-in-Publication data is available from the Library of Congress.

ISBN 978-0-8131-6815-9 (hardcover : alk. paper)
ISBN 978-0-8131-6816-6 (epub)
ISBN 978-0-8131-6817-3 (pdf)

This book is printed on acid-free paper meeting the requirements of the American National Standard for Permanence in Paper for Printed Library Materials.

Manufactured in the United States of America.

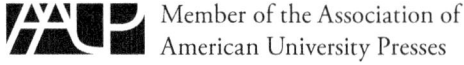 Member of the Association of
American University Presses

In Memory of D.R.C.

Contents

Introduction   1

1. The Making of a Southern Liberal   11
2. A Respectable Religious Message   37
3. Sowing the Seeds of Southern Liberalism   71
4. Professionalizing the Southern YMCA   115
5. A Liberal but Never an Activist   149
6. Bringing a Revival to the Mountains   187

Conclusion   215

Acknowledgments   219

Notes   223

Bibliography   307

Index   321

Introduction

In 1894 an eighteen-year-old white Texan traveled to a national YMCA student conference in Lake Geneva, Wisconsin.[1] There he met an African American student, roughly ten years his senior, from the Iowa State College of Agriculture and Mechanic Arts.[2] It is very likely this interaction was the first time the former had ever encountered an African American man of such education and stature. In fact, a meeting like this one in the South in this period, and for the coming decades, would have been very unusual considering how segregated that world was. This event was indeed such a striking moment for the younger man that over forty years later he still remembered it. To an acquaintance in the late 1930s he recalled the following about that conference and this man: "I remember that he was rather popular, that he was the only Negro on the grounds and that those of us from the South at the time thought it a little queer that there should be a Negro delegate present."[3] As it turns out, the Iowa student was George Washington Carver, just nearing the completion of his undergraduate work. Within a few years he would take a master's degree as well, and then move on to a faculty position at the well-known Tuskegee Institute in Alabama, where he would make quite a name for himself. Though the Texan's recollections indicate a measure of prejudice he harbored at this time toward African Americans, this meeting was part of a series of experiences that helped transform his perspective. In the coming years his views on race and many other subjects broadened, and he became one of the most prominent and important southern white liberals of the early twentieth century.[4] The young man was Willis Duke Weatherford, and his long and dynamic career of reform in the South was soon to begin.[5]

Born in 1875, Weatherford matured as Jim Crow came of age, yet his life would go on to surpass the latter's. Indeed, living for almost a century (he died in 1970), Weatherford would see the collapse of segregation, witnessing the *Brown* decision and the passage of the 1964 Civil Rights and 1965 Voting Rights acts. In his long career Weatherford stood out as a leader promoting improvement and change in the South. On June 4, 1962, nearly seventy years after his initial meeting with Carver, Weatherford received an honorary doctor of laws degree from the University of North Carolina at Chapel Hill. It was a fitting tribute for his life's work in race relations, religion, education, and the Appalachian region.[6]

In the first half of the twentieth century, Weatherford was not the typical white Southerner. As the region faced enormous challenges in terms of race relations, poverty, education, labor, and agriculture, few whites there made any effort to change the nature of these things. But Weatherford was always different from the majority of his peers. An extremely energetic, driven, and, indeed, prideful man, he committed his life to improving conditions in the South. Coming from fairly humble circumstances, he had a strong desire to make something of his life, and he felt a deep responsibility to try to help others. At times he was not easy to get along with, as he could get frustrated with those who did not share his own drive, social conscience, and way of doing things.[7] But for the poor, and those who faced racism and prejudice, he tried to be their champion as best he knew how.

To get some sense of Weatherford's personality and outlook, a literary comparison may be helpful. One of his favorite writers was the English novelist George Eliot, and while completing his master's thesis on her work in his mid-twenties, he read all her novels. He thus must have come across the character of Tertius Lydgate in Eliot's masterpiece *Middlemarch*. At the start of this lengthy story set in the early 1800s, this young, energetic, and idealistic medical doctor arrives in the fictional town of Middlemarch, hoping to change and improve his profession and make a prosperous career. At times his ways and practices alienate the established physicians and surgeons of the area for being too progressive and unorthodox, but he nevertheless pushes on despite their criticisms. Weatherford similarly came onto the scene in the South at a young age, trying to improve his region's conditions, his conscience being pricked by his education, interaction with African Americans, and his Christian faith. Indeed, taking his religious beliefs very seriously, he came to recognize that the reality of southern life was inconsistent with how things should be. Through his vocation as a minister (in many forms), he sought to improve this region and, like Lydgate, endured criticisms for his unconventional attitudes and actions in his own time. While Weatherford never seems to have lost his idealism and hope, he, like Eliot's character, also had to face how the circumstances of life and things out of one's control can constrain one's ambitions. Debt, family responsibilities, and town gossip eventually drive the young Lydgate to leave Middlemarch for a practice in London. Even though Weatherford, while having several promising offers outside the South, never departed his own region, he too had to make concessions to his ideals at times. Thus, this study is the story of Weatherford, his dreams for the South and his contributions there, and an exploration of the compromises he made along the way and the limits of his efforts. It is an experience with striking parallels to those of the other white liberals (a small group) who operated in the South at this time.

Weatherford had good reason to have an interest in and understanding of the South's problems, as his own life started in this region and he spent his adult life there. Raised in the small town of Weatherford, Texas (named after a distant relative), Weatherford attended his local junior college before going to Vanderbilt University, where he ultimately received his Ph.D. in literature in 1907. While completing his dissertation in 1902, he became a YMCA secretary, traveling throughout the South, speaking and working with college students. In this period the YMCA was a very vibrant institution, particularly serving as the key campus ministry in colleges and universities. In these years the Y played on a trend of "muscular Christianity" prominent at this point, which emphasized the importance of faith, personal fitness, and health.[8] As an ordained Methodist minister, athlete, and vigorous man, Weatherford fit very much into this mode. For him, the Y would prove to be the chief institution through which he worked during most of his career. In the wake of the violent Atlanta Race Riot of 1906, and reflecting on his own early experiences in the South, Weatherford began directing his attention increasingly toward improving race relations between southern whites and blacks. Initially his work fell largely along the lines of educational efforts, through books he wrote for YMCA study programs.[9] Weatherford, however, soon went on also to take an active role in the emerging interracial organizations of this period, working with the Southern Sociological Congress from its beginning in 1912 and helping found the Commission on Interracial Cooperation (CIC) in 1919. For this era he was at the cutting edge of southern white liberalism.

In 1912 Weatherford also began operating a YMCA conference center (Blue Ridge) to serve white southern college students. While similarly styled YMCA retreat centers existed in other parts of the country in this period, Weatherford thought it important to have a meeting place in the South focused on this region's specific issues—particularly the "race problem," as it was called at that time. Blue Ridge became a unique space where this subject could be discussed and even—to a limited degree—where whites and blacks could meet in these tense years. Indeed, beginning in 1919, Blue Ridge hosted African American speakers (Carver being one of them who made repeated trips) for its summer conferences and included a small number of black YMCA student delegates, a very unusual thing for the time. Moreover, the center became the site of important conferences on lynching.[10] While the Blue Ridge approach was gradualist, it was then one of the few places in the South where such events and conversations could occur. Despite this organization's own limits in the early twentieth century, the YMCA as a whole was an important force in promoting progressive causes in the South.[11] Most state and private higher education institutions had college YMCAs on their campuses in this period. Weatherford's varied work in the Y would prove to have a significant influence on those persons who came of age in the 1910s, 1920s, and 1930s and who began to address racial and labor problems in the coming years. Noted figures such as Frank Porter Graham, Howard A. Kester, Katharine Du Pre Lumpkin, Myles Horton, Don West, Clarence Jordan, and Martin England all became important southern liberals (and some even radicals) in the 1930s, 1940s, and 1950s, and they all had roots in the southern YMCA and contact with Weatherford.[12]

In the midst of Weatherford's work at Blue Ridge, he was also involved in a series of other ventures. In 1915 he joined the board of trustees of Berea College in Kentucky. This school had a long heritage of religious and interracial education, manual labor, and attention to the Appalachian region dating back to the school's founding in 1855. Weatherford remained involved with this school until the end of his life, and his son, Willis Jr., eventually became president there in 1967.[13] In 1919 Weatherford created and began operating a graduate school for the professional training of southern YMCA leaders. The Southern College of the YMCA (later renamed the YMCA Graduate School) stood adjacent to Vanderbilt University, having an intimate relationship with that institution as well as connections to Scarritt College for Christian Workers, George Peabody College for Teachers, and the African American Fisk University—all in Nashville. The YMCA Graduate School also was tied to Blue Ridge, holding its summer quarter at that location through the 1930s. Weatherford remained the school's president until 1936, when it closed because of financial problems. Besides these fiscal issues, its failure was also related to the growing decline the YMCA experienced in this period. Attaining its peak around 1921, membership in the student YMCA reached approximately 94,000, representing roughly 33 percent of all collegiate male students.[14] By 1934, however, the number had fallen to 8 percent, and by 1940 (even as college population numbers rose) membership had slipped to 51,000.

After the YMCA Graduate School closed, Weatherford turned his attention to Fisk University from 1936 to 1946. At this historically black liberal arts school in Nashville he worked as a professor in its Department of Religion and Humanities and also as a fund-raiser, having close interaction with African American staff, faculty, and students. Leaving Fisk in the mid-1940s, he shifted his efforts full-time to Berea, working to help with student recruitment and institutional development. Moreover, he increasingly labored to improve the Appalachian region as a whole—a section of the country gaining national attention at the time for its poverty and underdevelopment. Weatherford also wrote several books about this area and its religious traditions and contributed to a major survey of the region financed by the Ford Foundation.[15] Throughout his life and at the various institutions of which he was a part, he cultivated friendships and contacts with a number of important southern white and black leaders and reformers, including Booker T. Washington, Robert Russa Moton, John Hope, Will W. Alexander, Jessie Daniel Ames, Mary McLeod Bethune, George Washington Carver, Frank Porter Graham, Howard A. Odum, Benjamin Mays, Charles S. Johnson, Arthur F. Raper, and Rupert B. Vance. As a result of these contacts and his prominent place in addressing southern social issues, it is clear that examining Weatherford provides a window into understanding the subjects of race, religion, education, and Appalachian reform in the South in this dynamic period of the twentieth century.

Weatherford's approach to improving the South is most adequately defined as liberal. From the time he entered YMCA work at the turn of the twentieth century to the end of his life, he always remained optimistic about the future and believed in progress. In the concern of race relations he was a gradualist, and he came to denounce segregation explicitly only after 1957. For the most part, before that time he was interested in alleviating the faults of that social system and eliminating the violence that occurred within it. In these years he worked to expose white college students (mainly young men) to leading African Americans and knowledge about black culture and living conditions. His general philosophy was that education and personal experience would change individual lives. These young white men and women would become future southern leaders who would effect change in their own communities, which in turn would improve the South as a whole.

Weatherford had a good deal of optimism about people, believing that if they just knew more, they would act better. It was a view heavily tied to his Christian faith. But perhaps he had too much confidence in this approach; the reality may be that some people, even with education and knowledge, still will not change their opinions or act differently. As a result, there are some things, in terms of fairness, that government and law must compel people to do.

Weatherford's interest in reform in the South put him among a small group of like-minded white progressives in this region at this time. These "southern liberals" were largely middle- and upper-class whites in the late nineteenth and first half of the twentieth century—many of them religiously motivated—who sought to improve their section of the country, the key issue they confronted being race.[16] Along with Weatherford, other southern liberals included such figures as Edgar Gardner Murphy, Lily Hardy Hammond, William Louis Poteat, Howard A. Odum, Will W. Alexander, Jessie Daniel Ames, William T. Couch, Lillian Smith, Frank Porter Graham, and Arthur F. Raper. Still, it is important to recognize that before the 1950s he and many of these other whites stopped short of truly denouncing Jim Crow segregation. Yet what makes Weatherford different from most of his contemporaries was that his career spanned such a wide breadth of time, from roughly 1900 to 1965. And as the years passed, his views on racial issues continued to evolve. Indeed, in his 1957 book, *American Churches and the Negro,* he called for churches to be at the forefront of desegregation.[17] Living through so many political and social changes, Weatherford strikingly was able to advance on this issue. In the end, the extent to which Weatherford worked to improve race relations—and later the conditions of the southern Appalachian region—reveals much about the limits of southern liberalism at this time.[18]

Weatherford has received some attention from scholars and popular writers for his importance to twentieth-century southern history. They have generally agreed that—while a forward-thinking white Southerner for his time—he was essentially a moderate, benevolent paternalist.[19] In fact, most historians have focused primarily on Weatherford's work from the first decade of the 1900s through the 1920s, much of his later efforts being overlooked. While their assessment is generally correct, in many ways it is also too simplistic, considering Weatherford's long career and evolving views on race and other social issues during his life. To truly understand him, one needs to see him in the context of southern liberalism and grasp how religious faith drove and limited those like him. Thus, this study provides the first comprehensive examination of his life that situates him among southern liberals of his era and explores the limits of their reform activities and what remained possible at the time.

This analysis also emphasizes that the overriding factor that tied Weatherford's life together was his Protestant Christian faith. His religious beliefs motivated his actions in all areas he entered, be it race, education, or the Appalachian region. Indeed, it is fair to say that he directed more of his attention to correcting the problems of society than to converting people. Such an approach was not the norm for most religious white Southerners. Without a doubt he wanted people to be Christians, but it was more important that they live what he considered to be "Christian" lives—which he envisioned to include personal activities as well as social.

As a result of Weatherford's religious emphasis and broad concern about society, some scholars have placed him among the social gospel tradition of this period.[20] Nevertheless, such a characterization has some problems. Historians and religious specialists have generally agreed that the social gospel was a distinctively American movement that developed in the late nineteenth century when theologians and ministers began offering a new critique of society in the midst of rapid industrialization and urbanization.[21] Figures like Walter Rauschenbusch, Washington Gladden, and Josiah Strong all criticized the existing economic order, particularly the excesses of capitalism that led to the laboring classes' deplorable living and working conditions in these years. Writing in 1907, Rauschenbusch—whom nearly all historians credit as more "fully represent[ing]" this movement than anyone else—noted the sense of crisis that urban areas of the United States were in as a result of unbridled capitalism.[22] In this period Rauschenbusch recognized the tremendous advances that had been made in "the control of the natural forces" in the nineteenth century, and he envisioned that the twentieth century might be able to do the same for "control of social forces."[23] He and other social gospelers of these years imagined that Jesus's call for the Kingdom of God was not an otherworldly affair, but a goal that people should actively work to bring about on this Earth. These spokesmen were, in general, liberal Christians, very optimistic about the power of their faith tradition to affect the world in the here and now. Their belief in progress, however, was greatly tempered by World War I, as several important historians of this movement generally declared it over by the late 1910s. Thus, a traditional interpretation of this movement defines it as mainly a northern urban phenomenon, typified by a theological critique of society's economic and social structures, that was most powerfully manifest from roughly 1880 to 1920.[24]

Working from such a definition, it is not appropriate to consider Weatherford a social gospeler. Weatherford certainly recognized and sought to alleviate problems in the South, particularly in respect to race relations and poverty, but he never leveled a critique of the structures that created these concerns. For most of his life he did not seek to end Jim Crow segregation, nor did he strongly question America's capitalist economy. Instead, he remained a gradualist throughout, relying most heavily on the belief that education would bring change over time. While he did work with institutions, and to a very limited degree get involved in politics, his real focus always remained with individuals. Weatherford largely tried to change the attitudes of ambitious and bright white Southerners, hoping they would transform the region through their lives and future leadership. As for the sense of crisis so evident in Rauschenbusch's writings, Weatherford never displayed such a tone.[25] And though the Kingdom of God was something Weatherford seems certainly to have desired on this Earth (and in many ways worked toward), the urgency of this hope was not as manifest in him as it was in Rauschenbusch.[26] In his Appalachian religious work Weatherford did not advocate overthrowing capitalism; rather, he wanted mountain congregations to be more socially engaged in their region. Rather than conceptualizing Weatherford in terms of the social gospel, it is better to view his activities as a form of socially engaged Christianity, where his religious beliefs led him into societal concerns. One of Weatherford's comments toward the end of his life reveals this truth about his approach. He remarked, "The Lord almighty does not need the things you and I can do except he needs to have them done for one of his children."[27] In short, Weatherford was much more interested in how people lived out their Christian faith than in simply saving their souls.

Understanding how Weatherford's religion influenced him is also central to appreciating the limits to his liberalism. Throughout Weatherford's career his Christian faith both propelled his social engagement and constrained it. For him, the religious message included a concern for personal faith and salvation as well as an interest in social problems. Being true to Jesus's example (as he understood it) and active in society was just as important as—or more important than—particular beliefs. Yet how far Weatherford would go in making changes was always limited. He would not sacrifice his overall Christian emphasis for any particular social issue. Weatherford was guided by a particular religious philosophy that held that each individual, regardless of status or skin color, had worth, an idea he expressed time and again in the phrases "the sacredness of personality" and "the dignity of all persons." These views helped bring him to address injustice to African Americans as well as Appalachian poverty. Yet in some ways Weatherford's emphasis on the individual prevented him from tackling larger structural issues.

Weatherford's liberalism was also restricted in other ways. His religious faith and intellectual development moved him into progressive directions and causes, but he was at the same time constrained by the past. The South had no major social gospel tradition for him to draw on, which perhaps prevented him from thinking in terms of structural critiques.[28] Weatherford was also unable to escape the times in which he lived, particularly where race was concerned, and, in his desire for pragmatic results, he made compromises. His southern birth, his sentimentality about the Old South and Appalachia, the financial issues he faced as director of several institutions, the climate of white supremacy in the South, and his religious focus all kept him within certain boundaries, limiting how far he pushed for equality and the fair treatment of African Americans and the people of the Appalachian region. Because the constraints he worked under were similar to those of other leading liberals of this section of the country, his life reveals much about southern liberalism and its limits from 1900 to 1965.

1

The Making of a Southern Liberal

"I was never a drifter—I have steered not drifted."[1] In 1964 Weatherford wrote these words as he pondered nearly ninety years of living. Yet even during a life so directed and focused, numerous changes did take place. Perhaps the most dramatic transformation occurred in the first third of his life, as his formal education and life experiences shaped how he understood the world. In this period he moved from holding a provincial, small-town worldview to becoming a "southern liberal" for his time.[2] Weatherford's liberalism was evident not only in his progressive views on race—a central point that defined Southerners who fit this label in this era—but also in his more modern religious views. Weatherford's gradual awakening was brought on by his intellectual curiosity and development, urban living, interaction with African Americans, and questioning of religious faith.

Weatherford was born December 1, 1875, in Weatherford, Texas, a small town about thirty miles west of Ft. Worth.[3] Weatherford was the seventh of the eight children of Samuel Leonard and Margaret Jane Turner Weatherford.[4] His father (born November 9, 1829) came from Virginia before moving on to Tennessee and finally settling in Texas.[5] His mother was born January 20, 1837, in the small mountain community of Crawfish Springs, Georgia.[6] In her youth her family also moved to Texas, where at some point she met Samuel, and the two were married in 1856 or 1857.[7]

The early years of their marriage were not easy. The young couple moved several times, first living for two years in Tarrant County near Ft. Worth and then heading west to the vicinity of Ft. Griffin.[8] Samuel Weatherford worked in the cattle business during this period, at times leaving his young wife to drive the animals to market.[9] In these years they were living on what was the Texas frontier, at the farthest edges of white settlement. For such newcomers this setting was harsh and, at times, dangerous. Conflicts developed between whites and Native Americans as the former pushed farther west. During the Civil War, Samuel Weatherford served as an "Indian fighter to protect his own family and the frontier settlements," probably in the Second Frontier District of Texas.[10] Little is known of his activities with this group, other than family reports that he fought in the "Battle of Concho Creek."[11] Therefore, in the first decade of Samuel and Margaret's marriage, Samuel was often away from his wife for extended periods. According to other family memories, his wife faced several Indian raids during these absences. These events—along with frequent pregnancies, the loss of several children, and the fear of other impending conflicts—placed a heavy burden of stress on Margaret in these years. Her first pregnancy, within two years of their nuptials, had ended in a premature birth.[12] Following that misfortune, according to later recollections from her daughter Flora, Margaret "bore children very rapidly—too rapidly for any woman's health."[13] In 1861 her third child, Samuel Leonard Jr., died in his first year owing to complications from being burned.[14] Thus, these personal tragedies, intensified by the dangerous and isolated living conditions of the frontier, put such a strain on Margaret that she had a "nervous breakdown" in the mid-1860s.[15] Seeking to provide greater safety and more stability, the Weatherfords purchased a home and began farming in the recently organized town of Weatherford, Texas, sometime between the fall of 1866 and spring of 1867.[16]

When the Weatherfords arrived there, the town was in its first decade of existence and still remained the "principal frontier settlement in North Texas."[17] Changes took place in the coming years, however, that shifted the character of this town as well as that of so many others across America. In 1880 the Texas and Pacific Railway came to the city, and the Santa Fe line arrived in 1887.[18] These railroads, along with local extensions, helped connect Weatherford with larger markets and the greater world. They also helped build Weatherford into a hub for farmers and cattlemen as well as for local businesses. By the 1890s three newspapers, three banks, four hotels, several churches and schools (including Weatherford College), and roughly one hundred businesses served this thriving small city of five thousand people. Thus, by the time Weatherford was in his teenage years, the town, while still relatively small and provincial, was growing and vibrant.

Racially, Weatherford, like the rest of Parker County, was made up mostly of whites in the late 1800s. The county had been created in 1855, and a limited number of slaves remained there between its founding and the end of the Civil War.[19] In 1860, 300 slave owners in the county held 341 African Americans in bondage, the latter making up roughly 8 percent of Parker County's total population.[20] In 1870, following emancipation, 293 African Americans lived in the county, accounting for 7 percent of the entire population of 4,186.[21] Thus, W. D. Weatherford probably had only a small degree of exposure to African Americans in his youth and would have had little, if any, contact with college-educated or professional blacks.[22] In short, his background was not conducive to a progressive stance on race, and the negative stereotypes that many white Southerners applied to this group would have been easy for him to accept.

As the Weatherfords were settling into this small Texas town, the South was in the midst of Reconstruction, and images of the Civil War still lingered in the minds of many white Southerners. This was a time of readjustment. Since Weatherford's father had fought with the frontier forces rather than with those of the Confederacy, however, it is likely that the war did not hold such a prominent place in his memory or in his family's. Nevertheless, Texas, like the rest of the South, was in this period in the process of rebuilding and accepting slavery's end. With the addition of railroad networks in the town and the growth of business in these years, Weatherford was also entering the New South. Along with the economic changes taking place, important alterations in the political and social spheres were also occurring. By the time of Weatherford's birth in 1875, Reconstruction was nearing its formal end (1877), and over the coming years whatever flexibility African Americans had had in this small town and across the South had begun to tighten.[23] Laws increasingly restricted the lives of this minority group and narrowed their political participation. Indeed, as W.D. grew, so too did the spread of segregation laws. By the time Weatherford was twenty years old, violence against blacks was rising in the South, and the region was truly entering the "nadir of race relations."[24] Thus, Weatherford matured in a segregated world, and this context, along with his limited interaction with African Americans in his youth, deeply affected how the young man initially viewed the status and potential of this group.

The intellectual and religious world in which Weatherford developed was also largely circumscribed. For the most part in his early years his life was sheltered, his family focusing on religion, hard work, and respectability. The Weatherfords were Methodist, and W.D. would maintain this denominational affiliation throughout his lifetime. From this tradition Weatherford certainly gained a sense that progress could be made and that the world could be improved. During his childhood and teenage years, Weatherford was active in the Methodist Church, attending Sunday school and worship services, and was largely insulated from life's more worldly aspects.[25] He later recalled a story from his adolescence that indicates some sense of this limited exposure. Weatherford noted that at one Sunday service the preacher's daughter fainted in the choir, adding, "I well remember one of the older women in the congregation cried out loosen her corset. That shocked me for I don't think I had ever seen a corset in my life and to have it talked about in public was a little too much for me."[26] Overall, Weatherford's experience growing up provided him with a rather narrow worldview, one that was certainly provincial and traditional, and also tinged with racism. It would take leaving this setting for Weatherford to expand his outlook.

Yet no evidence exists that Weatherford traveled outside Texas before his later teenage years. It is safe to assume he spent most his early life in the local setting of his hometown. His family lived on the edge of Weatherford and farmed during his first years, but later his father left agriculture to become a store owner.[27] Samuel Weatherford had been unsuccessful in several business ventures over the years, and as an adult W. D. Weatherford's memories showed that his childhood was stamped by a sense of poverty and lack of opportunities; he recalled that his father had been "a poor man and a little farmer."[28] At best his family was middle-class—but only barely—for the time, owning its own home and approximately twenty acres of farmland.[29]

Weatherford's relationship with his father appears to have been strained. As an adult Weatherford mentioned him very few times, recalling primarily his memories of working on the farm in his childhood and as a cashier in the merchandise store in his youth.[30] Weatherford described his father as "an exacting man" who "never talked much" and also as a "kindly man but rigidly stern and demanding."[31] Something Weatherford never articulated, but which undoubtedly affected his life, was the fact that his father apparently was an alcoholic and at some point in the marriage left the family. The exact details of this breakup are unclear because neither Weatherford nor other members of his family ever talked of this deep family secret.[32]

Weatherford resolved at a young age to be different from his father and to make something more of his life. Thinking back on this period in later years, he remembered that at age eight "I determined I would not use tobacco—although my father and two older brothers smoked. . . . I have never drawn a puff of pipe, cigarette, or cigar—I am and have always been a tetoller [sic] on tobacco and whiskey. At 12 I decided I would go to college. My father discouraged me, but I set my mind on getting a real education. At about 15 I determined to go into religious work."[33] Samuel Weatherford's problem with alcohol probably explains why W.D. became such a strong critic of drink for the rest of his life.[34] After Weatherford left Texas in 1897 for his studies at Vanderbilt University, he revealed only one time when he and his father met again.[35]

Of his parents, Weatherford's mother was undoubtedly the more important force, and this was particularly evident in her support of his education. Before entering the fourth grade at age eight, Weatherford had received no formal schooling, until that time being tutored at home by his mother.[36] Weatherford attended his local school until he was twelve.[37] He then sat out a year, working at his father's store.[38] At age fourteen he enrolled in Weatherford College, an institution founded in 1869 and connected to the Methodist Episcopal Church, South, during this period.[39] Between two hundred and four hundred students made up the student body in these years, and it offered programs from the elementary level through all four years of college.[40] It was served by approximately ten faculty members, and according to one of the instructors at the time, the institution "was almost a part of the local Methodist Church," which perhaps explains some of its strict discipline.[41] In 1894, at eighteen years of age, Weatherford graduated from Weatherford College as his class's valedictorian, earning his B.S.[42]

Two stories from his years at Weatherford College and immediately thereafter reveal something of Margaret Weatherford's devotion to her son's education and ambitions. The first occurred just before his junior year. One of his teachers insisted that Weatherford consider taking Greek if he intended to enter the ministry, as this subject would be needed if he sought further higher education.[43] Following this suggestion, Weatherford gathered with his parents and older brothers and sisters for a family conference to discuss the issue. His father did not think it necessary for his son to take up this subject because he did not expect W.D. would "pursue [his] studies through college, certainly not through graduate study or theological training."[44] Moreover, his father did not consider education crucial to being a good preacher, citing a recent example of a minister with less training than Weatherford already had delivering an outstanding sermon at a Methodist conference. While Weatherford's mother sat silently listening to this discussion, his brothers and sisters tacitly agreed with their father, and it was

Willis Weatherford (far right) as a young man with his brothers, Robert, John, and Felix. (Courtesy of Weatherford Family Papers)

implicitly accepted he would not take Greek. Yet Weatherford later recalled that as everyone started to leave, his "mother nudged [his] elbow and said: 'If you want to take Greek—you take it.'"[45] Weatherford did take it, and his study of the language not only boosted his confidence in this period but also proved important for his future studies at Vanderbilt.

The other story that illustrates his mother's dedication occurred after Weatherford graduated from the local college. By this time he had taught and served as a principal for two years in small Texas schools and was planning to begin Vanderbilt in the fall of 1897.[46] Weatherford hoped to enter the Nashville school with standing as a junior because of his earlier academic work. To achieve this advanced status, however, he would have to pass a series of examinations. Over the previous years, while working as a teacher and paying off his local college debt, he had continued to read widely, apparently by an oil lamp at night. As a result of these not-so-favorable reading conditions, his "eyes broke down," and his doctor insisted he rest them in the summer months before starting at Vanderbilt.[47] These instructions exasperated Weatherford because he had hoped to study extensively in the fields of history, economics, and sociology in preparation for his entrance tests. His mother, who was with him on this occasion, vowed to read the material to him. Weatherford avers that over the next months she "read thousands of pages" on these subjects, helping him pass his oral examinations when he arrived at Vanderbilt, and thus giving him junior status.[48] He never forgot her sacrifice and encouragement of his education.

Weatherford's experience at his hometown college introduced him to some intellectual and religious concerns that foreshadowed later important interests in his life. While the school was by no means outstanding—Weatherford remarked at one point that although it granted bachelor's degrees in the arts and sciences, it "really should not have for it did not have adequate resources to give degrees"—it did provide him with the basic fundamentals of learning. Moreover, his schooling at Weatherford College prompted him to begin thinking through his religious commitments and how they squared with his studies.[49] One course that proved particularly influential was an introduction to philosophy. The instructor, Fannie Whitsell, while probably not the "greatest student of philosophy," according to Weatherford, often let him and another student, Jim Wilson, debate major philosophical problems in class.[50] Thus, in this setting Weatherford had the opportunity to defend the Christian and religious perspective, while Wilson, the "sceptic or doubter," took the "materialistic view" of things.[51] Looking back on this experience Weatherford observed he

> was already turning in [his] thought to what [he] later learned to call "Personalism." Personalism according to Dr. Borden Browne [*sic*] of Boston University means that neither materialistic mechanism nor abstract forms of idealism will enable us to move forward in the explanation of our universe. Personality is the real and only principle of philosophy which will enable us to take any rational steps whatever. . . . This thought has made concrete and real the meaning of religion to me, for it is the relationship between a human person and a divine person. It is not simply emotion. It has an emotional content because all personal relations have an emotional content, but it is a real and definite relationship between persons. To be a Christian is to be a friendly son of God—and that has real content or to put it another way Christian experience is right relationship between a human personality and a divine personality and that has both reality and power in it.[52]

This experience helped Weatherford slowly begin to develop a more systematic theological grounding for his faith and, furthermore, pushed him to try to make a rational argument for religious belief, a key theme that would follow him for the rest of his life. Indeed, the field of philosophy of religion would remain very important for Weatherford, being for him, as he called it, "the queen of all the studies."[53]

Of equal importance to those courses that affected his intellectual growth at this time was Weatherford's involvement in an extracurricular activity, the YMCA. While at Weatherford College he joined this student organization, becoming its president by the time he was sixteen.[54] This proved to be a very important decision in his life, since he would devote most of his career to this institution. What would have drawn him to this group? W.D. was Methodist, but it is unlikely there was a campus ministry representing that denomination at the school. College YMCAs were common in this period, often being the only religious organization on a campus.[55] Besides the obvious social advantages of such a group, the Y's largely Protestant constituency and outlook, as well as its stance on purity issues, would have meshed well with Weatherford's religious background and his early vow to abstain from alcohol and tobacco. For a religious youngster like Weatherford, it was a logical fit.

The YMCA proved very influential in broadening Weatherford's worldview and fostering his budding leadership abilities. Specifically, it exposed him to new and more learned religious figures, provided him opportunities for travel, and pushed his ambitions. In 1893 Fletcher Brockman, the YMCA's southern student secretary, stopped at Weatherford College on one of his tours through southern institutions.[56] Weatherford, as the school's YMCA representative, met Brockman at the railroad station and escorted him to campus. In a letter to Brockman over thirty-five years later, Weatherford still remembered this visit, declaring that it was "one of the high spots in [his] life."[57] After this initial encounter, Brockman's influence on Weatherford continued as the two crossed paths in future years.

As a result of his involvement in the YMCA at his hometown college, Weatherford traveled as a student delegate to a national Y conference in Lake Geneva, Wisconsin, in 1894. This trip proved to be a very important moment in his life. Here Weatherford met George Washington Carver, who would later become a friend and important coworker in southern interracial efforts. Carver, a student at Iowa State College of Agriculture and Mechanic Arts at the time, was also a participant in the National Students' Summer School that Weatherford was attending.[58] Weatherford must have harbored some prejudice toward blacks at this time, and he hinted at this feeling in a letter to Carver in 1932. Thinking back about their initial meeting, he wrote, "You were from Iowa and I was from a small college in Texas—yes, Texas—the state of wide prairies, but narrow prejudices at the time. So you and I were as widely separated personally as were our educational institutions separated physically."[59] Meeting Carver at this conference seems to have begun a slow awakening process for Weatherford in terms of his racial views. Here was an African American man of learning and faith, and it is likely that the conscientious and religious Weatherford had to begin rethinking how this man—and others of his race—were also his "neighbors" in the biblical sense.

This YMCA event was also important because it put Weatherford once more in touch with Brockman. Brockman was in his mid-twenties at the time and had been working as a YMCA secretary since 1892.[60] He was also a recent graduate of Vanderbilt University. Weatherford probably identified with this man because of his age, and Brockman's ambition and education similarly would have impressed him, making YMCA service appealing. Indeed, at the conference the two discussed the possibility of Weatherford's entering the YMCA secretaryship in the coming years in a capacity similar to Brockman's.[61] Weatherford also talked to him about his intent to pursue further education, specifically the prospect of going to Vanderbilt.[62] Thus, Brockman's influence helped nudge Weatherford in two important directions that would be defining for him: Vanderbilt for additional studies and the YMCA as a career.

Other factors probably played a role in Weatherford's decision to choose Vanderbilt. In many ways it would have been the logical decision for a southern Methodist and ambitious young man at the time (particularly for someone interested in the ministry), as it was that denomination's flagship university in the South.[63] Moreover, there was already some precedent in his family for pursuing higher education in Nashville. One of his older sisters had graduated from Peabody College in that city.[64] This connection would have provided him with some basic understanding of the area and possibly some contacts there to aid in the transition. Another experience in his early teenage years may also have played a part in his ambition to attend Vanderbilt.[65] The story goes that while Weatherford was working at his father's store, a man came to request a donation for Weatherford College. But Samuel Weatherford did not have money to offer at the time. With a condescending tone the man commented that his son did not even intend to matriculate at Weatherford College, but was going instead to the more prestigious Vanderbilt. He went on to add that Samuel Weatherford would certainly want to give to the local school to ensure its survival because W.D. probably would go there, if he went anywhere. Apparently this event affronted the young Weatherford's sense of pride, pushing him to set his sights on the Tennessee university. Whatever the exact reasoning, in the fall of 1897 Weatherford made his way to Nashville to begin his education at Vanderbilt. This decision reveals much about Weatherford's ambitious nature and his willingness to step out of his comfort zone. It would also prove to be a pivotal point in the course of his life and his entry into reform efforts.

This move undoubtedly was a major transition for the young man from west Texas. At this time Nashville's population was roughly 80,000, African Americans making up nearly 40 percent of that total.[66] Thus, the city was very different in size and racial makeup from his hometown. Vanderbilt itself had been open for a little more than twenty years, and it was just beginning to develop into the high-quality institution of which its founders had dreamed.[67] In its first matriculating class in 1875 there were 167 students; by the time Weatherford began in 1897, attendance had risen to over 200.[68] While the size of the university would not have been particularly imposing in terms of its student body, socially it would have been a different story. Vanderbilt catered to the mid-South's more well-to-do, drawing most of its students from families in business and the professional classes.[69] According to Paul Conkin, the university's historian, students who went to Vanderbilt "saw themselves as an elite, as the ablest young men of the South" who "were clearly the future leaders and shapers of a new South."[70] As academic standards rose through the 1880s and 1890s, the preparation required to gain admission had led to a decline in the number of Methodists attending the school; fewer than 50 percent claimed this church affiliation in 1900.[71] Instead, Episcopalians and Presbyterians—denominations often associated with more affluence—increasingly came to make up a higher percentage of the students. Thus, while Weatherford certainly identified with the ambitious nature of the school's students, his small-town and humble family background probably made him feel socially inferior at the time.

Despite Vanderbilt's growing standing in the 1890s and the esteem in which its students held the university, the years during which Weatherford attended were marked by some setbacks.[72] One of the chief reasons for this decline was the economic depression of the 1890s, which put financial pressure on the college.[73] The school had already extended itself in building projects, and a small yield from its endowment strained it further. These issues contributed to low faculty salaries, which led many of the ablest professors to seek positions at better-paying institutions.[74] Further adding to the decline in excellence of Vanderbilt's faculty was the death and retirement of several key professors in this period.

Amid these circumstances Weatherford entered Vanderbilt in 1897. Because he was expecting to enter the ministry, he initially intended to study philosophy, but there he found the department head to be "quite dogmatic" and "not as up to date."[75] Instead of majoring in that field, he shifted to English literature, studying under the highly regarded William M. Baskervill, a man whom Weatherford described as "one of the grandest men in the university."[76] Weatherford's transcript reveals that he did well in these courses in his two undergraduate years, posting grades in the middle to high nineties for all four semesters—his highest averages for each term being in this subject.[77] In his other classes Weatherford performed admirably, his poorest performance coming in his two semesters of English philology, in which he received grades in the low eighties. Overall, his marks proved strong enough to win him a Phi Beta Kappa key, a source of intense pride that he wore the rest of his life.[78] Academic achievement and learning always remained critical indicators of success for Weatherford. It is likely that his memory of his father's discouragement about collegiate studies never left him, and Weatherford sought continually to prove himself and his abilities.

Weatherford's time at Vanderbilt was also taken up by activities other than his studies. Since Weatherford did not have the financial means to pay up front for college, he had to take out loans and work during his student years to pay his way. Like most undergraduates intending to enter the ministry at this point, he lived in the Biblical Department's building, Wesley Hall, for his first year.[79] Here he helped pay his room costs by being responsible for handling the gas lighting, but Weatherford still began accumulating debts (over $1,900 by the end of his graduate education).[80] During his second year he secured an assistantship as a gym instructor and moved into a private home, where he also took his meals. Weatherford also continued his YMCA involvement after entering Vanderbilt. Moving on to graduate school at the university, he became more occupied in the leadership of the school's YMCA, serving as president for two years.[81] In addition to those activities, Weatherford joined a fraternity, Alpha Tau Omega, and became the president of the Graduate Club. To help provide for his school and living costs in these later years, he served as an assistant in the History Department and as head instructor in physical education. In the latter position he coached Vanderbilt's first basketball team, in 1900.[82] These athletic activities placed him well into the "muscular Christian" image of the time that he embraced.

Of considerable importance in broadening Weatherford's worldview in this period was the exposure to African Americans that he experienced at Vanderbilt and in and around Nashville. The sizable black population in the city was much greater than he had been accustomed to in Weatherford, Texas.[83] Still, Weatherford's closest interactions would probably have been with the staff at Vanderbilt (almost entirely black) who took care of much of the arduous and less pleasant work around the campus, such as the cooking, groundskeeping, and janitorial services.[84] In this period the white students on campus generally seem to have held a pessimistic view about the potential of African Americans, considering "social equality" virtually "impossible."[85] At best, the most progressive of the students were gradualists.

Weatherford probably came to Vanderbilt with a similar outlook, but his interactions with blacks in Nashville proved to be crucial for his views on race. In 1932, as he reminisced with George Washington Carver about their initial meeting in 1894 and his narrow views at that time, he went on to add, "But when I went to Vanderbilt I had the opportunity to serve a number of colored workers, so my sympathies were broadened enough and my eyes opened."[86] In particular, Weatherford had contact with two African American men who were campus institutions. In his first year of graduate school Weatherford lived on Westside Row, a series of dorms that each housed roughly sixteen students.[87] Here Robert Wingfield served as the cook for these residents and was known for having a special annual Christmas dinner for a select group of his favorites, usually inviting six to eight of them.[88] In 1899 Weatherford was one of these chosen few, and he later remembered Wingfield as "one of the finest Negro men in the laboring class I ever knew."[89] Not only was this invitation an honor, but it also put Weatherford in touch with other blacks at the school and gained their respect. As he noted, "From that time on I stood tops with all the colored help on the campus."[90] Weatherford also got to know John E. Fulton, who lived in the basement of Wesley Hall.[91] Fulton had been a longtime servant of the Club IV, a group of bachelor professors at Vanderbilt that had included Chancellor James H. Kirkland, William Dudley, John T. McGill, William T. Macgruder, and Austin H. Merrill.[92] Fulton became rather famous around campus for posting the pictures of former Vanderbilt students on the walls of his room and for his reading of Joel Chandler Harris's Uncle Remus tales, which gained him the nickname "Uncle Remus."[93] Weatherford later

Weatherford as a graduate of Vanderbilt University. (Courtesy of Weatherford Family Papers)

recalled that Fulton "became a friend" of his and that the latter invited him to his room "often to meet people so I came to know many who were sympathetic toward the Negro."[94] Weatherford considered it "almost providential" that he had such "favorable contact with quite a company of Negro people," and he credited these experiences with contributing to his preparation for his "work on behalf of the Negro of the South."[95] In short, Weatherford's personal relationships with these men and other African Americans around the campus made him aware of the humanity of blacks and the inequality of existing conditions.

Weatherford's growing understanding of racism occurred as he continued to develop intellectually. As he excelled under Baskervill in the English Department, he was also exposed to this professor's more "cosmopolitan" worldview and broader outlook on race.[96] After completing his bachelor's degree, Weatherford chose to remain at Vanderbilt for his graduate work, pursuing the field of English literature for his master's and doctorate.[97] Weatherford followed this path because of his success in this field already and his belief that a Ph.D. would give him a "broader education" than a theological degree.[98] Also, since he was considering YMCA work as a possible career, he believed the Ph.D. would give him more credibility and a wider audience than seminary training would. In the end, this study of literature still allowed him to pursue many of the theological questions weighing on his mind.

Also highly influential in Weatherford's decision to follow this route was the presence of a new English professor, Richard Jones, who replaced Baskervill after the latter's death in 1899.[99] Jones, born in 1855 in Berlin, Wisconsin, was the son of a minister.[100] He had attended Grinnell College and studied at Oxford and Munich before receiving his doctorate from Heidelberg in 1893.[101] Jones specialized in the literature of Alfred Tennyson and John Ruskin, and by the time Weatherford took his class, Jones was in his mid-forties, still a relatively young professor. As Weatherford made plans for the beginning of his master's work, he was attracted to this new teacher who had a "keen social conscience" and who was planning to offer a course titled "Philosophical Aspects and Ideals of Literature," paying particular attention to the works of Robert Browning, John Carlyle, Ruskin, Tennyson, and Dante.[102] Just as Weatherford desired, this course would allow him to grapple with fundamental issues and concerns in religion and philosophy, matters in which he was deeply interested. Jones's mentorship and the overall experience of graduate school proved to be very significant in Weatherford's life. Weatherford later described Jones as "thoroughly alive and passionately interested in people," adding, "I owe him a great debt of gratitude for what interest I have had in human welfare."[103] On his advanced training as a whole, Weatherford, looking back more than sixty years later, credited this education as passing to him three "great" gifts: "a passionate love for great literature," "a sense of social mission in the world," and "a method of study which has dominated my life."[104] Graduate school, in short, solidified Weatherford's already basic love of learning while helping him direct his knowledge toward social improvement.

Over these years of study Weatherford gained an appreciation for a relatively wide range of literature. He developed a great respect for British and American writers, but he also came to admire classical authors as well. Weatherford considered Browning's *The Ring and the Book,* Tennyson's *In Memoriam,* and Dante's *Divine Comedy* the great poems he had read, Dante's "perhaps" being the "greatest of the three."[105] His favorite poet was a Southerner from Georgia, Sidney Lanier, whose work attracted Weatherford so much that Lanier's volume of poems was the only one that Weatherford "committed to memory" in his student days at Vanderbilt.[106] Weatherford also admired the work of Rabindranath Tagore and Thomas Carlyle, particularly the latter's *Sartor Resartus.*[107] Moreover, Weatherford respected the writing of Nathaniel Hawthorne and George Eliot; his master's thesis compared their philosophies of life (Puritanism versus positivism), and he later would assert that the latter "wrote the greatest novels" he had ever read.[108] His high esteem for Eliot is somewhat surprising in that he would have found several aspects of her personal life objectionable, particularly that she espoused a nontheistic philosophy and lived with a married man for many years. Perhaps his admission reveals that Weatherford's personality was less rigid than it often seemed to be, and that he could separate the art from the artist.

Weatherford maintained his interest in literature in future years, but other concerns left little opportunity for returning to these great works. Near the end of his life, in one of the more moving revelations Weatherford ever made, he commented, "If I were not so overwhelmed with social problems, such as race, the Appalachian problems, poverty, ignorance and evil, poetry would be my great passion—but I find little time to go back to Browning, Tennyson, Shakespeare, Dante or Lanier. I do occasionally go back to Tagore—when the pressure gets too great. (Forgive me for revealing quite so much of my heart.)"[109] Though literature nurtured some of Weatherford's deepest needs, the life of the mind would always remain secondary to pragmatic action for him.

Weatherford completed his master's and doctoral work (1900, 1907) under the program Vanderbilt had developed in the 1890s.[110] It was the beginning of a modern system that included specialized graduate-level seminars and a more directed course of study, a trend drawing on the German educational model already followed in advanced institutions around the United States.[111] Yet the rigor of Vanderbilt's program undoubtedly would not have matched that at top-notch institutions such as Johns Hopkins University and the University of Chicago.[112] For his master's Weatherford had to complete six hours of graduate coursework, take a five-hour exam, and write a thesis; and for the Ph.D. he needed to prepare for and take exams in three fields of study, produce a "typed or published dissertation," and pass a final exam.[113] Weatherford quickly finished his M.A. by 1900.[114] His thesis does not survive, but other records reveal that this project was essentially an extension of Weatherford's interest in wrestling with the existence of God. In the process of reading Eliot's works, Weatherford came to study Auguste Comte's positivism, the philosophy underlying Eliot's approach. This system denied the existence of a personal God and declared humanity to be the "ultimate reality."[115] While it is unclear what Weatherford's precise thoughts on Hawthorne's beliefs were, Comte's approach apparently did not satisfy him, as he noted, "I am bold to say this school of thought carried little conviction with me."[116] Secular humanism in no way squared with Weatherford's understanding of the world.

Weatherford's undergraduate and graduate school years, however, did prompt a questioning of his Christian faith. In the midst of his master's work in 1900 he experienced a period of deep doubt that would extend throughout the rest of his coursework.[117] Weatherford later recalled that in this time "the spirits of E. B. Taylor and Herbert Spencer—the earliest sociologists were walking the American campus and troubling the souls of youth."[118] Weatherford's exposure to new knowledge had made him uncertain of the foundation of his beliefs. By this point in his studies, he had already had a basic introduction to the sciences through undergraduate courses in chemistry, physics, botany, and biology, and as he began his advanced work in literature, he also was taking a course in geology. Though he would later be unable to recall any particular aspect of that discipline that created doubt in him, he insisted that "the whole general atmosphere of inquiry so characteristic of the time and of the university forced me to ask whether there was any reality in this experience we called religion, or, whether it might just be something put over on me from the past, simply a superstition handed down through my parents, or through the church."[119] Within this context, Weatherford began a searching process, probing the meaning of religion. He noted that he received guidance in this quest from "an English professor" (presumably Richard Jones) who helped him "raise all the questions" and encouraged him "never to rest until [he] had answered some of them at least tentatively."[120] This teacher also introduced his student to classic works of literature that showed how others had struggled with these great questions, having him study the book of Job, Dante's *Divine Comedy,* Milton's *Paradise Lost,* Carlyle's *Sartor Resartus,* Tennyson's *In Memoriam,* and Browning's *Le Saisiaz.* Weatherford's problem was one that many serious-minded believers at the time were likely to face if they wanted to reconcile their knowledge of the world with their faith.

As Weatherford wrestled with various explanations for the origin of religion, he repeatedly came back to one particular point: Why were people "drawn to worship"?[121] Weatherford believed that there was a profound need within all people for something greater than themselves and that their souls longed for "fellowship" with this entity.[122] Working from this basic idea, he regarded humanistic philosophies as inadequate because they could not account for this deep need. Weatherford wrote, "If there was no superhuman but only humans, why should man be drawn to worship at all?"[123] He also gained crucial guidance in his quest while studying Tennyson's *In Memoriam* during his second year of graduate school. In this text the writer struggled with the death of a close friend, and Weatherford connected with this piece because it seemed to consider for him all the concerns "that were troubling [his] soul" at the time.[124] In the end, Weatherford settled his crisis of faith through a version of the ontological argument for God, which asserts that because there is an idea of an infinite being within us, then there must be some reality corresponding to it.[125] As he contemplated Tennyson's poem, he came to the following conclusion: "If in one's deepest nature there is a great need, then there must be some provision for meeting that need—else this world is not a rational world. Hence this longing for fellowship with a power like ourselves but infinitely beyond ourselves, could mean nothing except that such a power did exist. So argued Tennyson, and his reasoning met a deep response in my troubled soul."[126] Weatherford went further to conclude that religion was basically about a relationship, specifically "the response of the soul of man to the soul of God."[127] Weatherford's line of reasoning reveals two basic assumptions he held: first, that all people have a longing for something greater than themselves and, second, that the world should make sense. Like most people of this era, he worked from a beginning position that there was meaning and purpose in life. Weatherford was unable to entertain the notion of the alternative, and thus he settled his faith predicament working from this premise.

Weatherford went on to confront other timeless religious questions in his doctoral work and while writing his dissertation. He finished the coursework for this degree by 1902, but it took him until 1907 to complete the written document and finally earn his Ph.D.[128] Weatherford chose to focus on Robert Browning in his dissertation, exploring the author's underlying religious beliefs through a close reading of his poetry. Like Weatherford's master's thesis, his dissertation no longer exists, but it can be assumed that his first book, *Fundamental Religious Principles in Browning's Poetry* (1907), is virtually the same as his dissertation.[129] Weatherford must have passed along to the Methodist publishing house in Nashville the completed document soon after he finished the requirements for the degree. The book lists "W. D. Weatherford, Ph.D." on the title page, and the foreword by Gross Alexander—formerly a professor in Vanderbilt's Biblical Department—was written in May 1907.[130] Since Weatherford was granted the Ph.D. in that year—even if it was a January conferral—it is likely few changes were made before publication. In short, it is safe to assume the dissertation and book varied little, if at all.

The book was not exactly the epitome of rigorous scholarship. Weatherford basically read through Browning's poetry, pulling together his interpretation of the author's thoughts about God, Christ, and the meaning of evil and suffering in the world; there was little other research. The outcome of his study runs just over 150 pages (typeset in a rather large font) and contains only fifty-one footnotes. Yet more disquieting than the length or level of research is that Weatherford's analytical skill is at times lacking. For example, as he made his argument for how he would determine Browning's religious views from his poetry, Weatherford noted, "Passages glowing with fervor may be considered as representing the poet."[131] This approach is not a very precise method, particularly for the reader who is unfamiliar with Browning. How one is to determine which parts "glow with fervor" is never made clear, and Weatherford provided no examples that illustrate such passages. At another point in the book Weatherford asserted that "real poetry"—which he described as "verse which glows with passion"—is the "expression of the truth of a writer's soul."[132] Again, Weatherford did not present instances in which Browning's words "glow." He went on to assert that his ability to understand if Browning wrote a section "sympathetically" came from "a sense which must be acquired by much reading and a deep love of Browning's poetry."[133] Weatherford's contention may well be true, but this is hardly the way to make an argument in a scholarly work. Overall, though Weatherford certainly seems to have studied Browning's work closely, he did not do an effective job of illustrating his points, relying too much on the reader's simply accepting his opinions because of his supposed expertise.[134]

Weatherford's style of writing leads one to suspect that his own religious beliefs were roughly the same as those he attributed to Browning. Weatherford's basic argument was that Browning believed in a personal and loving God, and that despite the existence of evil and suffering in this world, life has purpose.[135] Since Weatherford made the point that Browning did not believe in a literal manifestation of evil (the devil), or in eternal punishment (hell), it was necessary for Weatherford to explain the existence of pain and suffering in the world.[136] Weatherford insisted that Browning worked from the assumption that humanity was "in a state of progress," moving slowly closer toward perfection.[137] Within this framework, the presence of evil was apparently necessary to life because it helped direct humankind toward this goal. Specifically, its purpose was to "teach knowledge of good by contrast; to arouse the feeling of sympathy; and to serve as a means of development."[138] In the end, Weatherford acknowledged, "God is entirely responsible for the possibility of moral evil."[139] Weatherford's understanding of this phenomenon reveals an interpretation highly abstract in nature and seemingly divorced from personal experience. Absent from Weatherford's study, however, is how one makes the move from the belief in a personal God to proving this is the God of Christianity.

Fundamental Religious Principles in Browning's Poetry is in keeping with Weatherford's later books. Rather than being works of rigorous scholarship, these volumes were written with a key purpose in mind that formed his argument. They were not simply about adding another brick of information to a wall of knowledge. He often wrote his later books on race relations not so much with a highly analytical style but, rather, with the intention of providing information that would change and, he hoped, improve conditions for African Americans. While possessing an interest in ideas and research, Weatherford was not a professional scholar. His books were always works of advocacy of one sort or the other, not disinterested inquiry.

In the case of his study of Browning, Weatherford was essentially asserting his belief in the validity of personalism as a philosophy of life. A close reading of Weatherford's study shows the growing influence that the philosophical school of thought had on him at this time.[140] As noted earlier, Weatherford was beginning to move toward an acceptance of this way of thinking even in his junior college days, despite the fact that he would not have applied this term.[141] Personalism holds that personality is the "irreducible, ultimate reality."[142] The father of this philosophy, Borden Parker Bowne, defined personality as "selfhood, self-consciousness, self-control, and the power to know."[143] The central starting point of this philosophy is that God is personal and is the "first cause" of all existence; therefore, all life and matter is to be considered as "the ongoing of the conscious activity of God."[144] For example, a rock—which may be thought to be only a physical object and, thus, impersonal—is actually the "experience or activity of personality" in the sense that God created it.[145] Personalism is a form of idealistic philosophy and stands in opposition to materialism, which asserts that only matter truly exists. Materialism would explain the existence of personality as simply the interaction of various physical elements, specifically atoms and molecules, working together to produce the mind. Yet personalism insists that matter exists only insofar as one's personality interprets it through one's senses. Personality organizes and gives meaning to the material world, and the ultimate person (in the form of God) is responsible for all reality.

While some of the idealistic elements in personalism had existed throughout the history of philosophy, the particular strand Weatherford connected with was that which flourished at Boston University beginning in the late 1800s, when Bowne led that institution's philosophy department.[146] Bowne's efforts went against the prevailing trends in his discipline and among intellectuals. This was an age when religious belief (specifically Christianity) had been seriously undermined by science (particularly by new knowledge in geology and biology) and through higher criticism of the Bible. Biblical miracles became harder and harder for the highly educated to accept. Charles Darwin's theories, beginning with *On the Origin of Species* (1859), further challenged belief in the supernatural, as his ideas disputed the existence of a purposeful world with a God active in life and human affairs. Intellectuals increasingly questioned whether humanity held a special and unique place in the world and if life had purpose. For these thinkers, as Bowne put this viewpoint, "The truth about man had been found out, and the truth was that instead of being a child of the Highest he is merely the highest of the animals, having essentially the same history and destiny as they,—birth, hunger, labor, weariness, and death. Man was viewed as simply an incident in the condensation of dispersed matter, or the cooling of a fiery gas."[147]

Bowne, of course, disagreed with this assessment, and he labored to provide a basis for theistic belief (specifically Christianity) while still accepting advancements made in science. Through personalism he tried to reinstate the uniqueness of humankind, emphasizing that self-consciousness not only made humans special among all animals but also connected them to God. Moreover, personality gave meaning to the material world; as Bowne insisted, "The world of space objects which we call nature is no substantial existence by itself, and still less a self-running system apart from intelligence, but only the flowing expression and means of communication of those personal beings."[148] In essence he asserted that while science can explain the physical aspects of the world by reducing everything to the interplay of atoms, there is still much left to account for—and personalism alone provides the explanation. For Bowne and his followers, the intangible was the truly real. Matter, the visible, was actually an extension of the ultimate personality (God). Humans and God share consciousness, yet the complete form is found only in God. Bowne's ideas helped Weatherford reconcile his faith with the new knowledge he had acquired in his Vanderbilt years. Weatherford would go on to laud Bowne's *Personalism* (1908) as the "greatest piece of philosophical writing that America has produced," synthesizing the philosopher's argument down to one sentence: "A world of persons with a supreme person as the head is the conception to which we came as the result of our critical reflection."[149] For Weatherford this became "the summation of [his] philosophy of religious life."[150] After Bowne's death, in 1910, the Boston University philosophers A. C. Knudson and Edgar Sheffield Brightman took up Bowne's mantle, and in later years Weatherford developed a close connection to Brightman.

Weatherford's acceptance of personalism was almost certainly due to his time at Vanderbilt, where he undoubtedly came under the influence of this school of thought. Wilbur F. Tillett, professor of theology and dean of the Biblical Department during Weatherford's years at the school, was a promoter of this philosophy.[151] Since Weatherford first began his studies in this field, it is likely he encountered these ideas through Tillett. Moreover, personalism was a philosophy that would have appealed to intellectuals at the time trying to maintain faith in the divine; thus, it probably had numerous followers at a Methodist school like Vanderbilt, where religion still remained important. For Weatherford it would have been a logical fit as he tried to preserve his religious beliefs in the face of the increasing knowledge to which he was being exposed.

Weatherford's adherence to personalism is crucial for understanding his later involvement in race relations and other reform efforts. Specifically, it provided him with an intellectual basis for asserting that all persons have value. Since all human beings—regardless of their race, class, or sex—have "personality" and the ability to commune with the ultimate person (God), then they are important and have worth. Weatherford went on to merge this idea with the long-held biblical assertion that all people were made in the image of God, which gave further weight to his conviction.[152] From this foundation, together with Weatherford's personal experiences with African Americans and the intellectual prodding by his Vanderbilt professors on social questions, Weatherford came to recognize that blacks deserved respect and fair treatment. Moreover, something had to be done about this group's situation in the South at the time. As a result, Weatherford began cautiously to move into a more public concern for race relations in the early 1900s. Yet at this time Weatherford would go only so far, being unwilling to use political measures to confront Jim Crow. It was a stance he would share with almost all other white southern liberals of the time.[153]

Just as Weatherford's racial views slowly moved leftward over the course of this period, so did his religious views, making the label "liberal Christian" an appropriate description of him in the context of the early twentieth century. In the historian Paul Conkin's perceptive history of the secularization of American intellectuals, he argues that this term applied to "those Christians who rejected narrow interpretations of creeds or doctrinal statements, were generous and inclusive in setting standards of membership, and, most important, were open and responsive to the need for rethinking or reformulating doctrines in the light of new biblical and scientific knowledge."[154] Another marker circulating in this period, sometimes assumed proudly by those who claimed it and at other times leveled by more conservative Christians as an epithet, was "modernist." In actuality the term represented a subset of liberals, a smaller and more radical faction of this broader category. In Conkin's delineation of these concepts, what distinguished the modernist was that rather than "struggling to accommodate new knowledge" as the liberal did, the modernist "avidly greeted it."[155]

Working from these definitions, "liberal" is more suitable for Weatherford because he begrudgingly worked to adjust his Christian beliefs to fit with modern understanding. Certainly this is true if one compares Weatherford to an exemplar of modernism in this period, the University of Chicago divinity professor Shailer Mathews.[156] For example, whereas Mathews would have found biblical miracles unbelievable at this time, Weatherford maintained a view that they were still possible.[157] Weatherford's identification with liberal Christianity became even more evident in the coming years as he came to define his stance on such issues as evolution, biblical literalism, the Virgin birth, the Crucifixion, and premillennialism.[158] Thus, considering Weatherford's openness toward modern knowledge and his flexibility in reading the Bible, he certainly qualified as a liberal Christian.[159] His stances and perspective would have been unsettling to the vast majority of southern Protestants.

Even as Weatherford was developing into a racial and religious liberal for his time, he continued to maintain many of the traditional notions dominant in southern culture of the late nineteenth and early twentieth centuries. This was not unusual for men and women of the South whose education and status were similar to Weatherford's. Certainly his involvement in the YMCA, an organization that emphasized purity, self-control, respectability, and faith, contributed heavily to this attitude. Moreover, Weatherford also aspired to a life of culture, refinement, and status. He demonstrated these ambitions in his formal dress and conduct, and throughout the rest of his life he held to such standards.[160]

Weatherford also developed a strong identity as a Southerner and a sentimental view of the Old South.[161] Throughout Weatherford's writings from the early 1900s onward he expressed deep pride in being a "southern man" and often noted he was "born and educated in the South."[162] Weatherford played up such qualifications over the years to give him credibility with his southern audience as he called for reforms, particularly when dealing with the issue of race. In the early 1930s he was still extolling the virtues of the Old South when he wrote the following lines for an article regarding the Natchez, Mississippi, Garden Club: "The old South is rapidly passing. The glory and culture of that era is in great danger of being lost to the new generations. If it is lost, the future will be much impoverished. One does not need to lose sight of the shortcomings of a past age to be able to appreciate it. The old South had weaknesses of course, but it also had values that few of the present generation really understand."[163]

Interestingly, Weatherford's respect for the South does not seem to have grown out of his Texas childhood and youth. He was not from an Old South family. Indeed, his father was no Confederate, and Weatherford, Texas, was certainly not an old southern town. Ironically, Weatherford's southern identity was formed to a greater extent by his time outside his hometown, the same experiences that had also pushed him in a more progressive direction on race and religion. Think back to his 1894 trip to Wisconsin for the national YMCA conference. There he met George Washington Carver, an event that probably brought him his first contact with a college-educated black man. While this encounter helped open his eyes to the potential of African Americans, the fact that Weatherford was outside the South and among people from all across the country also made him define himself as southern.

Weatherford's time at Vanderbilt and around Nashville also had an effect on his connection to the South. In his years at the university he interacted and associated with upper-class southern students and professors. Many of them would have had families tied to the Old South. Coming from his modest background, Weatherford probably envied some of those more affluent students who had had greater opportunities and advantages than he. In Nashville he would have had more exposure to this region's past and its culture than he had in Weatherford, probably developing some respect for them. His professors, particularly Baskervill—Weatherford's undergraduate English adviser—also would have contributed to Weatherford's respect for the South. Baskervill specialized in southern literature and had published a study of these writers, including one book on Weatherford's favorite poet, Sidney Lanier.[164] Thus, Weatherford's contact with these authors' works may have also inspired a longing for this bygone era.

One more connection to Nashville almost certainly influenced Weatherford's nostalgia for the Old South: his first marriage. On December 1, 1903 (his twenty-eighth birthday), Weatherford wed Lula Belle Trawick.[165] She was a native of Nashville and a college graduate, and her father, Andrew Marcus Trawick, was a medical doctor.[166] Dr. Trawick—though not from an aristocratic southern family—had served in the Confederacy and later developed a successful medical practice in Nashville, a city he had moved to in 1889 to provide better educational opportunities for his children.[167] Considering Weatherford's own family history, he was marrying up. As he worked to fit into his new lifestyle, he would have become more aware of southern high culture, of which an appreciation for some of the Old South's

Weatherford's first wife, Lula Belle Trawick (right), with Mrs. Arch Trawick. (Courtesy of Weatherford Family Papers)

refinements would have been a part. Weatherford's future daughter-in-law, Anne Weatherford, later recalled a story that provides some sense of how his relationship with the Trawick family affected Weatherford. She noted that Weatherford at some time, presumably early in his relationship with Lula Belle, visited the Trawick home for dinner.[168] Apparently Weatherford was not dressed as suitably for the occasion as Lula Belle's father expected. Dr. Trawick told the young Weatherford not to come to dinner in the future without proper attire. In later years Weatherford always dressed for the nightly meal in coat and tie, and Anne Weatherford regarded this earlier experience as contributing to this tradition. This sense of social inadequacy, along with perhaps other events he faced in his first years at Vanderbilt, proved significant in shaping Weatherford's early life. These experiences also probably explain why status and appearance became so important to Weatherford.

Sadly, Weatherford's marriage to Trawick lasted for only a brief time. In 1907 he faced another crisis, this one more real and personal than his struggle with faith in 1900. Since December 1903 Weatherford and Lula

Belle had been making their lives together as he worked for the YMCA. But in June 1907 tragedy struck. Just as Weatherford was completing his doctoral work on Browning and his book was coming out, Lula Belle died while giving birth to their first child, a daughter.[169] The baby did not survive either, and their deaths left Weatherford devastated. As he worked through this terrible misfortune, he no longer was facing the meaning of suffering in the abstract, as he had during his graduate work. Though he never recorded how he came to peace with this event (perhaps he never did), one wonders if he reevaluated his earlier understanding of the purpose of evil. Near the end of his own life Weatherford would remember this signal event and recall that it was the start of "eight of the loneliest years any young man ever had."[170] In this period of struggle Weatherford would throw himself into his YMCA work, the issue of race relations in the South, and the development of a new project, the creation of the Blue Ridge Association for Christian Conferences and Training. He would also spend time traveling the world. In the midst of these activities, he again would find a partner. Yet the death of his first wife and daughter remained a powerful and painful memory that he hardly ever commented on, and this tragedy would sadly foreshadow another personal struggle he would face with his second wife.

Overall, Weatherford's move from Texas to Tennessee represented a shift in both geography and perspective. His time in Nashville put him in touch with a world that was far removed from that of his small-town Texas upbringing. His own background, together with his Vanderbilt experience and marriage into the Trawick family, cemented a respect and nostalgia for the Old South, intense pride in his native region, and a drive to adopt many of the prevailing white, southern, middle-class cultural conventions. Nevertheless, Weatherford came to hold other values as well that made him different from most white Southerners. Through his higher education, urban living, analysis of his religious beliefs, and exposure to African Americans, he became a particular sort of liberal on matters of race and religion for this time, that of the southern variety.

2

A Respectable Religious Message

From 1901 to 1919 Weatherford enmeshed himself in the YMCA student movement, working as the Association's secretary for colleges of the southern region of the United States. Weatherford held a deep interest in the philosophical foundations of Christianity, an outgrowth of his graduate school experience, and he felt a need to help college students who, like himself, struggled to reconcile faith and learning. Indeed, he considered this duty particularly important in light of the fact that "evolution, higher criticism," and certain "phases of psychology" had shaken faith in this era.[1] It became Weatherford's goal as a YMCA leader to "present a religion which had genuine intellectual content."[2] Weatherford started with that key theme, while also incorporating an emphasis on muscular Christianity. But by the end of the first decade of the twentieth century, he began to expand his message to include social issues by participating in interracial organizations and publishing race-related texts. Overall, in these years Weatherford sought to make Christian faith intellectually respectable and engage the South's major social issue of the time, race. Along the way he would become the most prominent figure in the southern collegiate Y and one of the most important white southern liberals of the time.

When Weatherford entered YMCA service at the beginning of the twentieth century, the organization was much more explicitly Christian than the institution it has become since. Today the Y—as it has come to be called—usually brings to mind a workout facility with a vaguely Christian foundation that provides a gymnasium and pool and sponsors recreational activities and swimming lessons. But the agency in 1900 put faith at its center. Originating in London in 1844, the YMCA by the late 1800s had made its way across the Atlantic and was thriving on American soil.[3]

Indeed, by that point numerous branches were serving young men in a variety of venues, including cities, the armed services, rural areas, railroads and industrial organizations, and colleges.[4] These YMCAs offered a host of activities and programs, such as prayer groups, Bible studies, libraries and reading areas, athletic facilities, educational courses, and boarding spaces.[5] Indeed, by 1900 on American college campuses it proved particularly influential, serving as the largest ministry group, encompassing nearly 32,000 student members in 559 YMCAs at a time when there were only 237,592 undergraduates.[6]

This process of taking root on American university and college campuses (both public and private) had begun as early as the late 1850s.[7] Between 1857 and 1859 undergraduates at the University of Michigan organized the Students' Christian Association.[8] On October 12, 1858, University of Virginia students established a YMCA.[9] The network of YMCAs continued to expand to other higher learning centers in the 1860s, including the University of North Carolina, Grinnell College, Olivet College, Cornell University, University of Mississippi, College of the City of New York, Washington College (which became Washington and Lee), and Howard University.[10] The early college YMCAs featured programs similar to those at local city branches as well as Sunday school outreach ministries and religious lecture series.[11]

Collegiate YMCAs proved successful for a variety of reasons. For one thing, even though the YMCA had a Protestant focus, it was still rather ecumenical and could accommodate a variety of Christian practices and beliefs. Moreover, the YMCA, with its international organization, connected college chapters and students across the country and in other nations.[12] Thus, these young men gained opportunities for fellowship with one another along with opportunities to hear well-known speakers and Christian figures. The latter was true because the extensive network of Associations made it easier to secure such visitors.[13] Protestant and evangelical, and with a well-established structure, the YMCA was broad enough theologically and organizationally to suit the religious and social interests of a wide variety of American college students.

The collegiate movement also proved successful because of support provided by the larger organizing body of the YMCA, the International Committee.[14] Over time this entity increasingly gave attention to building and nurturing collegiate programs. Several early YMCA leaders in the late 1860s, Robert Weidensall and Luther Wishard in particular, proved pivotal in promoting and fostering this work.[15] Weidensall was the first traveling secretary of the International Committee, and his responsibilities included a number of activities in city and state YMCAs.[16] His duties also extended to student work; he visited colleges, set up chapters, and revived and reorganized declining Associations. In 1877 what was known as "the student movement" of the YMCA became officially recognized by the larger North American international body; at the time there were twenty-six Associations at the collegiate level.[17] With this pronouncement came the creation of the office of a secretary for taking "care of the general work of the Associations in Colleges, and other higher educational institutions."[18] These activities had been a component of Weidensall's responsibilities in the previous year, but Wishard (a recent Princeton graduate) was hired to conduct this work exclusively, becoming the first YMCA student secretary. Serving part-time while pursuing further studies at Union Theological Seminary in New York, Wishard helped build the student organizations through written correspondence, personal trips to schools, and the publication of a student-oriented periodical, the *College Bulletin*.[19] In 1879 Wishard's post became full-time, and he intensified his activities by writing fifteen hundred letters, distributing twenty thousand copies of the eight issues of his magazine, and meeting with students at thirty-one colleges in the United States and Canada. At the end of that year his efforts proved fruitful; membership in college YMCAs rose to over 4,000 students in 96 chapters. More than a decade later, in 1891, the total student movement had grown to 345 organizations with more than 22,000 members.[20] Wishard's traveling work among colleges was the type of position Weatherford would later occupy when he became the YMCA secretary for the South and Southwest regions.

Southern college YMCAs had a strong presence in the early student movement. Indeed, nine of the original twenty-six Associations in 1877 were in the South, and there is some evidence that an additional eleven southern schools also had Ys.[21] Part of the organization's success in this region was due to an intentional outreach effort on the part of the International Committee following the Civil War.[22] Though this conflict had divided northern and southern Associations, there had never been a formal separate "southern federation" created, as had been the case with some of the major Protestant denominations.[23] Yet southern YMCAs in all forms, including college branches, were "virtually wiped out" by the end of the war, "there being only two or three that kept up some shadow of existence."[24] Some of the specific efforts made to reestablish fellowship between the two sections included New York YMCA members giving money in 1867 to enable Southerners to attend the international convention in Montreal and the decision to hold the 1875 convention in Richmond, Virginia.[25] Beginning intensely in 1872, Weidensall spent a large portion of his time trying "'to bring the Southern folks into practical alliance' again" through his work in city and college branches (black and white) and state organizations, and by encouraging participation in international YMCA gatherings.[26] These efforts brought results, particularly among student Associations: thirty-four chapters were active by 1880, making up roughly one-third of the ninety-six existing ones at the time across the United States and Canada.[27] By the end of the nineteenth century the collegiate YMCA in the South had become, as was the case in the American movement overall, the predominant campus ministry organization.[28] The Y was thus positioned to play an influential role among this region's students.

With the rise of the student movement, the YMCA's college leaders increased their attention and specialized their work among this constituency. Beginning in 1883 state conferences were created, and regional and national meetings would soon follow, all devoted exclusively to student needs and issues.[29] Before this time, when the North American YMCAs' international convention met, specific departments of YMCA outreach—in this case student work—were given only limited attention as part of the larger program. Wishard concluded that collegiate Associations, though they should continue their involvement in these international gatherings, needed their own assemblies to allow more focused attention to their particular needs and interests. Railroad Associations had already taken a similar step in 1877, and so Wishard moved in 1883 to begin state meetings of college YMCAs. Then, in 1886, the first national summer student conference was held under the leadership of Wishard and the evangelist Dwight L. Moody at the Mount Hermon School, near the latter's home in Northfield, Massachusetts.[30] This event brought together 235 students from ninety-six college YMCAs, many from outside the Northeast.[31] The conference included Bible study, worship services, recreational activities, lectures, and discussions of YMCA programs and procedures. Following this gathering's apparent success, organizers began planning a similar one for the next year, to be held at Northfield, where more ample accommodations could be provided.[32] In subsequent years this location became the annual destination.

The Northfield idea expanded in later years and led to the development of new conference sites serving various other U.S. regions. The need for additional locations was probably due largely to travel time and costs that students faced if they lived far from Massachusetts. Furthermore, as the movement grew, it is likely that different parts of the country confronted particular regional issues that might be better solved through their own meetings. The first extension took place in 1890 as students from the midwestern and western colleges met at Lake Geneva, Wisconsin.[33] In the coming years this location would become a permanent fixture for that section of the country's students, and it was at this gathering in 1894 that Weatherford (while still a student at Weatherford College) met George Washington Carver.

The South soon followed with its own student conference. In 1892 southern leaders put on their first region-wide gathering at the University of Tennessee in Knoxville.[34] This meeting was under the direction of Fletcher S. Brockman, who in the previous year, after finishing his undergraduate studies at Vanderbilt, had become the first "student secretary set aside for a specific region."[35] Apparently in this period the student movement in the South was in the midst of a "struggling" phase, and there remained a number of schools still untouched by it.[36] Despite Brockman's evident enthusiasm, the South was slow to find its own permanent meeting place. Indeed, in 1893 and 1894 no conference was held in this region, its students having to attend those in either Northfield or Lake Geneva.[37] In the coming years what became the Southern Student Conference met in a variety of settings in the mountains of North Carolina, in or within a short distance of Asheville. This arrangement included gatherings at Bingham School (1896–1901); the Asheville School for Boys (1902, 1903, and 1905); Haywood White Sulphur Springs Hotel in Waynesville (1904); Farm School (later Warren Wilson College) in Swannanoa (1906–7); and Montreat (1908–11). Finally, in 1912 the South's summer assembly found its longtime home at a place called Blue Ridge near Black Mountain, North Carolina, an institution of Weatherford's creation.[38]

Blue Ridge's development began in 1906. At this time Weatherford was frustrated with the southern YMCA's chaotic selection of gathering locations.[39] He was vitally interested in making the YMCA in the South strong and respectable, and he wanted this region to have its own place comparable to the other Y centers at Northfield and Lake Geneva.[40] Weatherford's idea for Blue Ridge sprang up after the summer of 1904, when he and Lula Belle vacationed along the North Fork of the Swannanoa River in western North Carolina.[41] Apparently during this time Weatherford developed an affin-

Montreat Student Conference faculty and secretaries, 1910. Weatherford is in the bottom row right; William Louis Poteat is behind him and John R. Mott is to Weatherford's left. (Courtesy of YMCA Blue Ridge Assembly)

ity for that area, considering it a fitting location for a future YMCA conference center. Moreover, there was already precedent for having it in the North Carolina mountains, as the Southern Student Conference had gathered there since 1896. As Weatherford tried to find a suitable site, he considered the Montreat property; however, because this place was already an established area with over thirty residences, he thought there might be too much "social life which would be detrimental" to his purposes.[42] Weatherford seems to have had in mind a place of natural beauty and seclusion where students could meet and discuss important Y concerns. As he continued to search, an Asheville judge who was aware of Weatherford's interest advised him of another tract of land near the town of Black Mountain that he thought would be "an ideal location."[43] Thus, on October 6, 1906, A. L. Phillips, a friend of Weatherford's who worked with the Presbyterian Sunday School Board in Richmond, Virginia, accompanied Weatherford to view this site, and they determined it to be nearly perfect for the purpose. In the end the land was bought and the building project soon proceeded.

How the entire Blue Ridge venture was financed is unclear, but in 1906 Weatherford did secure $50,000 for the project from John D. Rockefeller Sr. Weatherford probably raised the rest of the money from business leaders and philanthropic organizations in the North and South, as he continued to do over the years. From the beginning, as Weatherford noted, "a basic purpose of Blue Ridge . . . was to give to religious life in the South intellectual respectability."[44]

Weatherford's activities in the YMCA had begun at Weatherford College, and his involvement intensified during his studies at Vanderbilt University. After serving as president of the latter's campus Y for two years while a graduate student, Weatherford went on to paid employment in the organization. In 1901, in the midst of his doctoral coursework, he took a part-time position as the YMCA state student secretary of Tennessee.[45] In September 1902 he worked full-time for the Y, becoming the secretary for the entire southern region under the employment of the YMCA's International Committee.

Because of the student movement's growth in this period, college YMCA secretarial work underwent expansion at all levels—local, state, regional, and national. Significant changes in the YMCA's high administrative levels also took place. In 1888 Wishard left the student movement for foreign missions, and a recent Cornell University graduate and rising star in the YMCA, John R. Mott, took an associate secretary position under Charles Kellogg Ober, who had replaced Wishard as senior student secretary.[46] In 1890 Mott moved into Ober's role as the head of the student movement, an office he would hold until 1915.[47] Mott, who became a critical figure in the YMCA in these years (he later would receive a Nobel Peace Prize in 1946 for his efforts in the Y), was skillful at developing this organization. Indeed, he recognized his own limited capabilities and created more supervisory positions to help in this process.[48] In 1891 he began preparing small teams of students to work with the schools in their states, effectively producing state student secretaries. At the regional level, he strove to increase the number of secretaries serving the eastern, western, and southern parts of the country.[49] In 1901 Weatherford worked at the state level for Tennessee. His next step, in 1902, was regional employment.

The complete story behind Weatherford's quick rise in the YMCA is not fully known. Weatherford originally entered Vanderbilt in 1897 with the intention of preparing himself to be a minister. Even at that time—he would have been twenty-one—it is likely he had already been ordained a Methodist pastor, perhaps by his local Texas conference.[50] Yet something changed Weatherford's mind, and he shifted his sights to the YMCA. Considering his financial struggles in school, perhaps he needed the extra money in graduate school initially, and then as his involvement with this organization increased, it seems fairly logical that he would have considered full-time work there, perhaps expecting this to be only a temporary setup. We should remember that in 1902 he was in the midst of completing his doctoral coursework; he had only his dissertation to write before he would have his Ph.D. Therefore, Weatherford may have planned to work with the YMCA only while he was finishing this final degree requirement. On March 1 of that year Weatherford received a wire from Mott asking him not to accept any employment before his assistant, Hans P. Anderson, could speak with him in person.[51] Weatherford met with Mott's representative soon thereafter and was offered the International Student Secretaryship for the Southern and Southwestern States. Weatherford agreed to take the assignment for three years with only one condition, that he would "not have to raise money."[52] As it turned out, his term extended much longer, for he stayed in this role for nearly seventeen years. His sole stipulation also ultimately proved unrealistic, as he "soon found things [he] knew should be done, but could not without money to back them."[53] Actually, Weatherford turned out to be quite good at fund-raising, estimating near the end of his life that he had secured over $10 million in donations for the various organizations with which he was associated. While working as a traveling secretary, Weatherford remained ABD (all but dissertation) until 1907, when he finally completed his Browning study. In the end, instead of following the traditional path of being a church pastor, the ministry Weatherford chose for his life's work was with the Y.

Weatherford would have had good reason to stay with this profession because the career was a promising one at the time. Indeed, he was entering the YMCA in its heyday. In 1902, across the United States, 681 college branches existed with a membership of nearly 42,000.[54] Combined attendance at the regional summer conferences (Northfield; Lake Geneva; Bingham School near Asheville, North Carolina; and Pacific Grove, California) in the previous year totaled more than 1,400 students.[55] At the movement's height, in 1920 (just one year after Weatherford left the secretaryship), 764 American colleges and universities had YMCAs with a membership exceeding 80,000.[56] In the period during which Weatherford worked for the YMCA, between 25 and 30 percent of male students in higher education were involved in the Y.

Weatherford's position as the traveling college secretary for the South included a variety of responsibilities. Chief among these was visiting approximately two hundred public and private institutions in fourteen states across the region.[57] Each year his work took him to as many as fifty colleges, from Virginia in the Upper South, down to Florida, and as far west as Texas and Oklahoma.[58] Over time he also would visit colleges outside this region, including the University of Iowa, University of Nebraska, Northwestern, Oberlin, University of Pennsylvania, Pennsylvania State, University of Washington, and University of Wyoming, "in fact in practically every state in the Union."[59] The majority of his focus was on the white colleges, but he apparently did visit some African American schools, mainly in the years after 1910, when he began to turn more attention to the issue of race relations.[60] Collegiate black YMCAs were the responsibility of the Colored Work Department in these years, not the student department of the YMCA.[61] Spending as many as four days at the largest of these institutions, Weatherford met personally with faculty and students and also made addresses (sometimes as many as four per day) to larger gatherings of YMCA groups and, at times, even to the general student body.[62] According to Weatherford's later memories of these years, he lectured on a variety of concerns, noting, "I spoke on honesty, real study and what it meant, Christian life, life dedication or calling, on what religion could do for students and was hard on college evils such as cheating, drunkenness etc."[63] In general his addresses were appeals for religious living with an emphasis on personal conduct, all strongly influenced by his own southern middle-class and traditional perspective.

In the early period of his service Weatherford focused primarily on changing individual lives. He believed strongly in anyone's ability, through personal effort and willpower, to overcome weaknesses in character and develop a deeper Christian faith. Yet Weatherford's concentration came at some cost. It resulted in his giving less attention to social matters and the structural causes underlying these problems.[64] Even as Weatherford became more interested in public issues in the coming years, he maintained this emphasis on the individual, which perhaps inhibited him from examining the root cause of societal dilemmas where solutions lay beyond character reformation.

In the first decade of his student YMCA employment, Weatherford also concentrated heavily on presenting religion in a rational manner. Basically, he tried to defend Christianity at a time when this faith was being challenged by new scientific knowledge. Evolutionary theories, and particularly the application of the historical critical method to the Bible, seem to have gathered real strength in southern colleges and universities after 1900, obviously later than had been the case in Europe and even the northern United States.[65] Weatherford attempted to engage with, rather than ignore, these competing truth claims. He believed that "a religion that is not rationally based cannot stand up under the strain of modern life."[66] At this time Weatherford himself was not far removed from his own crisis of faith, and it seems he also wanted to help other serious-minded religious students undergoing similar doubts. Weatherford's approach was to appeal more to their heads than to their hearts.

To aid him in this task Weatherford devoted himself to further studies of his own in this period. Indeed, it appears he was very intentional in this process, choosing specific subjects to cover each year and then gathering relevant readings. The fields of comparative religions, philosophy of religion, and psychology of religion were the first "themes" he chose, and these "consumed most of [his] time for the first ten years" of his student work.[67] Since he was traveling, usually by train, he also apparently made it his habit to try to read a book each week.[68] This devotion to reading, while perhaps not at this same intense level, continued in later years as he expanded his interests to include some of the most current works in religion, history, and literature.[69]

Several stories from Weatherford's early years as secretary for the South and Southwest exemplify how his interest in intellectual concerns affected his appeal and gained students' attention. The first comes from a visit he made to the University of Iowa. Here three Hindu students "challenged [Weatherford's] claim that Jesus was the greatest religious leader that ever lived," insisting Weatherford had no basis for comparison since he had not read their "great religious books."[70] Weatherford countered that indeed he had studied some of their sacred texts, including the Bhagavad Gita and the Upanishads. According to Weatherford's memory of this incident, the students on hearing this news were "amazed—and willing to listen."[71] Weatherford noted, "Almost every state university I visited had one or more of Asia's choicest minds and they could only be reached by a fair evaluation of their religious leaders and thought in comparison with Biblical Prophets and Jesus."[72] To what extent Weatherford was able to give these other religions a sympathetic and open-minded reading in the context of his time and with the scholarly materials he had available is unclear, but his efforts at least to familiarize himself with these traditions was probably an unusual step for a southern YMCA secretary in the early twentieth century.

Another episode exemplifying Weatherford's effort to defend Christian belief involves his encountering a religious skeptic at the University of Arkansas. Henry Ingersoll, the nephew of the famous American agnostic Robert Ingersoll, was then a student at the state school. In Weatherford's telling of the story, Ingersoll was poised for an argument about religion and God when Weatherford visited there in the early 1900s.[73] As Ingersoll engaged Weatherford in debate, the latter shifted the conversation to allow the young man to list the key issues with which he objected. Weatherford himself then became the critic, pointing out to Ingersoll what he considered to be other "more basic and important" points that Ingersoll had overlooked.[74] Weatherford went on to raise additional questions to the young man and then offered a list of books that addressed these concerns. A year later Weatherford returned to Arkansas to visit and met Ingersoll again. To Weatherford's inquiry "How does your thinking respond to my books?" Ingersoll replied, "I cannot say I am a Christian but it seems to me the books are true."[75] Weatherford took this as a good sign. Engaging students with a rational argument for belief remained a key goal throughout Weatherford's traveling work.

Weatherford's YMCA responsibilities also extended beyond college students to include professors and college administrators. He later recalled numerous occasions when he discussed religious matters with these teachers and officials, who also had been affected by scientific challenges to their beliefs. Overall, it is clear Weatherford believed Christianity was the best religion to follow, and he tried to lead people to this faith through a more rational approach rather than an emotional one. In truth, this appeal was never a highly analytically rigorous one, but he labored with a decided bent in that direction.

Weatherford went on to become something of a legend in southern YMCA circles in this period. He came to consider his work with students highly successful, and in later years many of them attested to his influence on their lives.[76] Beyond his regional travels, Weatherford added to his reputation through the publication of two devotional studies, *Introducing Men to Christ* (1911) and *Christian Life, a Normal Experience* (1916). In both works Weatherford targeted college students and YMCA leaders, outlining why they should believe in Christianity and how they should live a Christian life. Moreover, he used numerous anecdotes from his YMCA travels to illustrate his points and connect with his audience. The books exemplified his interest in making religion intellectually respectable, particularly in the pages where he engaged with the challenges the field of psychology had made to faith and also in those that compared Christianity with other religions and philosophies of life.[77] Apparently more than 15,000 students studied *Introducing Men to Christ; Christian Life, a Normal Experience* built on the earlier text and provided a guide for "more mature workers," presumably graduate students and YMCA secretaries.[78] Overall, these published works helped make Weatherford a well-known figure in southern YMCA work. They added to his visibility and prestige as a secretary, and they probably also helped meet Weatherford's personal need to prove himself. By 1913 Weatherford had one more feather in his cap to attest to his prominent place in the southern Y: his name had found its way into the chorus of the official Southern Student Conference song of that year.[79]

Other factors also explain his success as a Y secretary. Certainly his youth in the early years of his career probably played a part by making it easy for students to identify with him. Moreover, Weatherford had a fraternity background, and he directed many of his appeals in colleges toward fraternity groups. Members of these orders were likely to be campus leaders and influential in social circles, which made them an attractive group for the YMCA to reach. Weatherford was also aided by his "high energy."[80] Contemporary sources and later testimonies attest repeatedly to this quality.[81] Frank Porter Graham, a United States senator (1949–50) and president of the University of North Carolina at Chapel Hill (1930–49), as a Chapel Hill undergraduate encountered Weatherford around 1909. Graham later described Weatherford in the following terms: "There were no bounds to [his] energy and his devotion as he went from state to state and college to college. He had no patience with sloth, complacency, or low standards in religion, personal life, scholarship, athletics, and campus citizenship."[82] Weatherford's vigor and drive helped him be an effective and engaging speaker and also gave him the ability to invest himself in many projects and cultivate countless relationships.

Weatherford's active lifestyle and approach also fit with a trend flourishing in American Protestantism and particularly manifest in the YMCA at the time: muscular Christianity. The historian Clifford Putney has described this movement, at its height between 1880 and 1920, as a "Christian commitment to health and manliness."[83] Proponents of this religious philosophy essentially emphasized that the body was the temple of God and that physical health was a vital part of being a Christian.[84] Indeed, the body had a "higher purpose," which "instead of just being a tool for labor" could also be "a tool for good, an agent to be used on behalf of social progress and world uplift."[85] Muscular Christianity gained strength in part as a reaction to the supposed feminization of the church. With the advent of more bureaucratic and managerial jobs owing to the urban-industrial transformation, some religious leaders thought that men's separation from physical labor lessened their masculinity. In short, proponents of muscular Christianity assumed that there were appropriate gender roles for Christian men, and personal fitness and "manliness" were central components of their ideal role. Only an intentional effort to cultivate a vigorous way of life could help Christian men regain their masculinity and revive their faith.

Weatherford personally embodied this conception and also sought out this characteristic in the students with whom he came in contact. One episode in his travels illustrates particularly well Weatherford's idea of muscular Christianity. Early on in his role as southern student secretary, Weatherford traveled to Emory College in Georgia.[86] He had been given time to speak at the chapel meeting that day, but the school's president insisted that Weatherford need not plan for an evening session because he did not expect a good student turnout. As the story goes, Weatherford found this assumption unsatisfactory and devised a strategy to interest the undergraduates in attending his lecture. Weatherford went to the college's gym, outfitted himself in exercise attire, and "challenged" some of the school's "best athletes" to a workout.[87] Weatherford apparently was in good physical shape at the time, having recently left his graduate school post working in Vanderbilt's Physical Education Department and serving as basketball coach there. This incident caught the attention of a number of students from around the campus. As Wilma Dykeman notes, "Students and faculty discovered that if Weatherford could give them a strenuous work-out on the gym floor, he could give them no less an energetic work-out from the platform."[88] Accordingly, Weatherford's evening speech was well attended, as were his future visits to the Methodist school.

Weatherford developed an interest in another issue in this period—one that initially posed the threat of alienating him from his southern constituency—but in time actually proved to attract many students. This concern

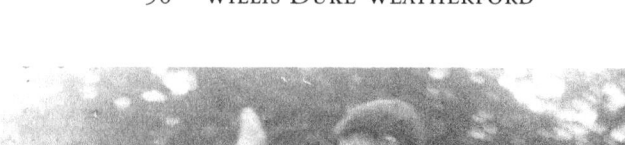

Weatherford the athlete (on bottom), with Tom West and Fred Hume. (Courtesy of Weatherford Family Papers)

was the condition of African Americans in the South, and on this subject Weatherford recognized there needed to be some things said and changes made. Later reflecting on this time, Weatherford commented, "I spoke out boldly for justice for the Negro. Yes, some people caricatured me as carrying a Negro child—but I do not believe I lost the respect of any real student or professor because I spoke out boldly for the Negro."[89] Along with making religion "intellectually respectable," Weatherford considered that his "second great task" of these years was "to give the Negro people a new sense of dignity and make better relations between white and black."[90] It is revealing that Weatherford did not think of this work in terms of bringing full political and social equality to blacks but rather improving the conditions of the time. In truth, Weatherford at this point did not wholly accept the idea that blacks and whites were completely equal. Like most other white Southerners of this time—even some of the most liberal ones—Weatherford was unable to wrap his mind entirely around this concept. Growing up in a region so pervaded by notions of white supremacy and in a period when segregation laws increasingly restricted the lives of African Americans, it was difficult for him to think differently. Yet given his exposure and personal connections to blacks in his Vanderbilt years, he had developed a growing interest in race relations. His travel throughout the South as a student secretary further contributed to this concern because these activities put him in close touch with the Jim Crow world of this region (particularly on the trains, his main source of travel) and the injustice under which blacks lived.[91] His YMCA work also gave him a very good sense of the racial attitudes of the South's white students. From these experiences he determined that southern white college men largely had no understanding of black life and culture and practically no contact with middle- or upper-class African Americans. Perhaps, as Weatherford met these young white men, he saw himself in them, as he was before attending Vanderbilt. He wanted to share his own enlightenment with them, and in the process help bring a change to the South.

Weatherford's concern with racial issues involved him in a wider trend of reform that characterized this era. The movement, broadly termed Progressivism, affected western Europe as well as the United States and gained increasing strength in the South at the beginning of the twentieth century.[92] In general, Progressivism, much like the YMCA, was a response to a world changed by industrialization and urbanization. A number of Progressive initiatives were aimed at protecting citizens from the excesses of capitalism. In the United States this movement was initiated largely by a "new middle class" as this group harnessed the power of government to enact legislation to provide new services and securities for the populace.[93] Even as the South remained largely rural in this period—despite the growth of cities such as

Atlanta—reforms also began touching this region. Here, as one historian of this movement has described, "bureaucratic intervention in education, public health, child welfare, and public morality replaced traditional governance, which had relied on voluntarism and community control."[94] Child labor laws, work safety standards, clean water and food regulations, prohibition campaigns, and public education provisions represent only a few of the reforms enacted in this period. Yet the results these reformers brought were beneficial "mostly for whites."[95] Voting requirements enacted in the late nineteenth century—including poll taxes, literacy tests, and grandfather clauses—had largely disenfranchised African Americans in the South. Jim Crow laws that supposedly allowed for "separate but equal" facilities and accommodations seldom lived up to their claim. In this context a small group of southern Progressives began directing more attention to racial issues, most confronting the problem from a Christian faith perspective. Weatherford, with his religious emphasis and his middle-class outlook, fit into this group.

In 1908 Weatherford publicly entered the field of race relations. Sometime after his 1903 marriage he and his wife, Lula Belle Trawick, moved from Nashville to Atlanta (probably because of his YMCA work), making their home there until her death in June 1907.[96] In the midst of the painful period that followed, Weatherford returned to Nashville to set up his headquarters and share a home with his late wife's sister Bess and her husband, James Marvin Culbreth.[97] Weatherford was probably still living in Atlanta when the violent Atlanta Race Riot of 1906 occurred.[98] Such an event and the generally deteriorating race relations at the time prompted him to take action. In April 1908 Weatherford gathered together a small group of educators, clergymen, and YMCA secretaries at a "Y building" in Atlanta "to discuss the present race question, with special reference to what the college men of the South might do to better conditions."[99] Along with the conference's subject, what made this event particularly extraordinary for its time was its interracial nature; the gathering consisted of four African American men and three white men.[100] It notably included John Hope, the first black president of Atlanta Baptist College and a later significant figure in interracial movements, along with key leaders of the African American YMCA department.[101] As a result of this one-day conference, the group decided that Weatherford should prepare a textbook on southern black culture and living conditions to be used in study groups among this region's student YMCAs. The finished product, published in 1910, was *Negro Life in the South*.

In this book Weatherford balanced his adherence to southern tradition with a challenge for white Southerners to treat African Americans more justly. Addressing white southern YMCA college men as his central audience, he essentially argued that they should take an interest in African Americans, specifically learn more about their religious, economic, and home lives, and help in definite ways to elevate blacks and improve their condition. By today's standards the book seems hardly progressive but rather condescending and paternalistic in its tone at many points. Yet for its time and in the context of the segregated southern world, it would have been considered liberal. The fact that such a volume elicited some backlash against Weatherford reveals much about this era's deep-seated racism.

In this text Weatherford made a number of appeals to his readers that clearly would have been seen as forward thinking for the time. Indeed, early in the book he "challenge[d]" the widely held belief of white Southerners that they "knew" their African American neighbors.[102] He argued that though this group probably did "know much more of real negro life than men of other sections can possibly know," they still actually understood very little about black culture.[103] Weatherford went on to advocate for equal pay for black workers, as well as commensurable standards in housing, sanitation, and roads; professional training for some blacks; reform schools for black youth; "justice" in the courts; and the end of lynching.[104] Moreover, even though he did not agree with the tactics of W. E. B. Du Bois, he did recognize and sympathize with what he saw as Du Bois's bitterness. Specifically, Weatherford pointed out the lack of human compassion Du Bois received from whites at the death of his young child.[105] In this event, which Du Bois related in *The Souls of Black Folk* (1903), the young black professor is following the funeral procession through Atlanta and overhears whites flippantly referring to "Niggers" as he passes.[106] Weatherford believed in the sacredness of human personality and considered that blacks shared this quality with whites. Weatherford too had recently lost his own child and knew well the pain Du Bois felt.

Yet even though Weatherford acknowledged that African Americans had a "soul" and "a real human personality" and that Jim Crow laws were not "fairly administered," his book did not call on whites to treat blacks as full social equals or to push for political changes to end discrimination.[107] Like almost all southern whites at the time, he believed there should be no "social intermingling" (which included sexual relations) between African Americans and whites—and he also claimed this to be true for "the best class of negroes."[108] In reality, even if he had not found such intermingling objectionable, stating this view at the time would have made the majority of his readers consider him dangerously radical, which would lead them to discount his entire book. By taking such a stance he might even have been risking some physical harm. In any case, in this study Weatherford implicitly accepted that blacks and whites would live segregated lives. The innovation of his book was in its explicitly calling for the conditions of African Americans to be made equal to those of whites.

Despite the text's pioneering nature, Weatherford made numerous statements that showed a degree of racism on his part and his acceptance of many generally held assumptions about the "place" of African Americans in southern society. Specifically, Weatherford approved the system of segregated schools, the fact that most blacks should receive industrial training, and the idea that this race would always largely make up the laboring class, and he frequently exhibited a somewhat romantic view of slavery.[109] He also wrote several statements that displayed a mixture of progressive ideas and conservative ones. For example, while he correctly recognized the negative role white southern political demagogues played in creating "race antagonism," he also blamed "educated" African American "radicals" and the "Northern enthusiast" for problems in race relations.[110] He believed that without these three groups, "relations between the races would be cordial enough."[111] Among those radical blacks, Weatherford specifically singled out Du Bois, William Monroe Trotter, and William A. Sinclair, and in this process Weatherford revealed his support for Booker T. Washington, who he considered "believes in conciliation and constructive work."[112] Weatherford felt that figures like Du Bois were far too critical and pessimistic about the status of race relations and white Southerners' attitudes. For all intents and purposes, Weatherford's book tried to highlight southern life's optimistic side. It is little surprise that as a white man attempting to appeal to a white southern audience, Weatherford took this approach.

In *Negro Life in the South* Weatherford labored to gain his white readers' trust and maintain their confidence. Among the ways he built his argument and tried to capture their attention was through appealing to the idea of self-preservation and the interdependence of whites and blacks.[113] Weatherford insisted in several places that white students should be interested in the condition of African Americans because blacks' status essentially affected their own lives. To make this point, Weatherford wrote that "our health, our intellectual advancement, and our moral lives are hedged about and often limited by the disease, the ignorance, and the immorality of another race."[114] Weatherford also used southern tradition, including the ubiquitous reference so commonly made in this period to the revered figures of Stonewall Jackson and Robert E. Lee, as he entreated his readers to take up concern for blacks. At one point he asserted, "It is because we are born in a section immortalized by such spirits as Lee and Jackson, who gave their lives for its welfare, that we, in this hour of our Southland's greatest need, will not prove traitors, but will, with the hearts of true sons, bring to its aid the largest knowledge, the sanest judgment, the clearest thought which loyal sons can bring."[115] In Weatherford's way of thinking, courage—as best exemplified by Lee's and Jackson's defense of the South in the Civil War—remained one of this region's finest traditions. Weatherford hoped that the current generation of white southern college men would have similar fortitude to face the problem of race and do something about it.

Weatherford also made his argument by appealing to the protection of white womanhood. Here his approach was heavily influenced by his traditional middle-class assumptions (a view that actually pervaded the entire text) about respectability and the gender roles of white men and women. Indeed, at several points when he referred to white women he wrote, "our women."[116] Thus, his progressive stance on race for the time was mixed with a gendered view of southern society. On this same issue Weatherford also added, "If we expect the black man to respect our women—and he must—then we must force our white men to keep hands off the negro girl—whether she be pure or impure."[117] Here and in other places Weatherford is quite bold to acknowledge that white men often assaulted black women.[118] On this subject he wrote, "There has been no small talk about social equality. I do not believe in social intermingling, nor do the best class of negroes. But where a white man uses his larger power and influence to force a negro girl to give up her purity, there is no question of social equality involved; the man is so infinitely below the level of the girl that he does not deserve to be mentioned in the same breath."[119] While the first two sentences of this quote were fairly typical for a white Southerner to make, the remaining statements were a rarity in 1910.

One additional comment needs to be made regarding Weatherford's discussion of black women. When Weatherford referred to white females, he called them "women," whereas when he wrote about their African American counterparts, he always used the term "girl." Racism—perhaps unconscious—was involved in Weatherford's terminology. Specifically, he did not consider black women to have the same status as white women. To refer to a black woman as a "girl" would have been the equivalent of using the word "boy," which whites often applied to black males whatever their age. Even though Weatherford did not fall into this habit in referring to black men, the fact that he did when writing about African American women reveals a mixture of sexism and racism on his part. In the South, African American women were confronted by this double blow of discrimination in this era.

Though Weatherford never expressed fear about how blacks would react to his book, he clearly did worry about the way white Southerners would receive it. Indeed, even as he was writing the text, a few of his fellow YMCA secretaries advised him against taking up the issue, one insisting, "'Look here, don't go and play the fool. What do you want to throw your influence away for and begin to dabble in the Negro question?'"[120] Once he finished the manuscript he remained hesitant about making the study public. This was in the summer of 1910, and Weatherford decided to delay its publication until he could try out the ideas on those attending the YMCA Southern Student Conference being held at Montreat, North Carolina.[121] To his surprise, the seminar presenting this book's ideas proved to have good attendance and participation, and afterward Weatherford received invitations to visit colleges "to present this new and evidently, to them, most interesting subject."[122] The text went to press later that year, and by 1916 Weatherford reported that roughly 30,000 copies had been sold and studied by southern college students, male and female and black and white.[123] Some of these readers would remember its influence years later, as was the case with the North Carolina State College YMCA president who recalled in 1943 that he had "got a lot out of the study of this book at the time."[124] Another white man, Mason Crum—who became a Duke University professor of biblical literature and spent his own life working to improve race relations—credited Weatherford's book as being what "had first awakened [him] to the plight of the Negro because of slavery."[125] Overall, in spite of the many problematic aspects of *Negro Life in the South,* this study did enable some white Southerners to know more about blacks and to talk more intelligently about race issues.

Not surprisingly, some of Weatherford's white audience found his book less than satisfactory. According to Weatherford, a professor at Clemson College in South Carolina originally agreed to lead a study course on it, presumably for a YMCA college group, but after reading it declared he could not because the author "was surely paid by the Rockefellers."[126] The insinuation referred to the Rockefeller family's philanthropic work in southern race relations, primarily by John D. Rockefeller Sr. at this time. Many whites in the South found such efforts intrusive and meddling, threatening their conception of southern tradition. Therefore, this Clemson professor was basically voicing his view that the book was too liberal for him, since he equated the Rockefellers' programs with racial liberalism.

Negro Life in the South also received some criticism from African Americans. In a 1924 *Journal of Negro History* article examining YMCA activities among blacks, one of the participants in the original 1908 Atlanta conference leveled a critique of the study. Jesse Moorland noted that though all the gathering's members had helped "outline" the project, Weatherford had "developed the book in his own way and had it published without submitting the manuscript to the committee"; he added, "The book, therefore, contains some matter which otherwise would have been eliminated."[127] Weatherford never revealed why he took this step, but it is likely his busy schedule and his domineering personality, as well as some trepidation regarding how black committee members might react, all contributed to this decision. Weatherford wrote with the purpose of bringing results, and he was not someone with whom it was always easy to work. Thus, it seems consistent with his hard-driving style for him to have pressed on to finish the project, rather than slowing the publication to allow the other conference participants time to review it. After the enthusiasm he received for the study at the 1910 Southern Student Conference, getting the product out—rather than waiting to debate what he probably considered to be "minor" details—was his first priority.

Perhaps one further issue Moorland and the other African Americans from that conference found troubling in *Negro Life in the South* was that Weatherford had created a text primarily for southern white male students. Weatherford had clearly made this group his intended audience and had even dedicated the book in the following terms: "TO THE COLLEGE MEN OF THE SOUTH, IN WHOSE TOLERANT SPIRIT AND UNSELFISH INTEREST LIES THE HOPE OF THE NEGRO RACE."[128] Since Moorland and another black YMCA secretary had been on the committee, it is fair to assume they probably wanted a book that could be used among African American college students as well. Yet Weatherford could not remove himself from the mindset that whites had to do something *for* blacks, rather than *with* them. His closest contact was with white students, and he worked from the paternalistic perspective that they were the ones who would lead the change.

Despite all the book's shortcomings, it does appear that the study helped launch a new interest in the issue of race within the YMCA. Even Moorland in his 1924 critique recognized the text's widespread use in white southern colleges, adding, "This effort helped to make possible the interracial program of today."[129] According to Weatherford, after reading *Negro Life in the South* white college students at the University of South Carolina, University of North Carolina, University of Alabama, and other schools initiated specific projects for African Americans, particularly providing black youth and workers with meeting places for recreation or lectures. Perhaps more important, Weatherford reported that white students began visiting black colleges at this time, a small but significant step that allowed the former to meet educated African Americans and also created the opportunity for each to "know something of what the other group thought."[130] Contributing heavily to the larger effect this book made was the support Cleveland H. Dodge, a wealthy and influential industrialist and chairman of the student subcommittee of the YMCA's International Committee, provided after reading it.[131] Because of his enthusiasm for the study and its subject, Dodge helped establish the Race Relationship Fund within the YMCA, providing $10,000 for a period of five years for various activities.[132] This money led to the hiring of Arcadius McSwain (A. M.) Trawick of Nashville (Weatherford's brother-in-law) to do race-related work, presumably among white students, and also to the addition of Channing H. Tobias to the YMCA staff for similar duties among blacks.[133] Tobias would go on to become a key figure in the YMCA, later heading up its Colored Men's Department and, after leaving the Y, serving as the chair of the Phelps Stokes Fund (a northern philanthropic organization that financed black education).[134] Dodge's donation also made it possible for Weatherford to travel with Jackson Davis (rural supervisor of Negro schools in Virginia and later member of the General Education Board) to see and photograph African American living conditions in the South. In turn, Weatherford made these pictures into slides and presented this material to white student groups in his YMCA travels.

In addition to these other initiatives, the Race Relationship Fund provided financial support for the first region-wide student conference for African Americans in the South.[135] This initial gathering, styled after those at Northfield and Lake Geneva, took place in 1912 in Kings Mountain, North Carolina. It brought together representatives from twenty-eight African American colleges; a number of white YMCA leaders also attended, among them A. M. Trawick and Weatherford. Kings Mountain would remain the annual meeting place for African American college YMCA groups for more than twenty years.

Weatherford's first book led to another study on the conditions of African Americans, *Present Forces in Negro Progress*, published just two years later. Indeed, the preface to this new text noted that its purpose was to add further information on the subject as a result of student interest in *Negro Life in the South*. Weatherford's 1912 study was similar in tone to the earlier one but showed more depth and was based on a greater amount of research and statistical data. In the end, though, Weatherford essentially made the same argument as he had in his first book: white Southerners needed to recognize the conditions of African Americans and do something to improve them.

Weatherford continued to make appeals that were progressive for this time. He called for better living and sanitary conditions for black homes and schools, criticized white landlords who exploited their black tenant farmers, pushed for more African American farm demonstration agents, pointed out the need for playgrounds and public parks for blacks, and advocated for nurseries for black servant women's children in the homes of white women.[136] Providing child care for African American domestics was something few, if any, liberal white women were doing then. As Weatherford discussed the circumstances blacks endured, he wrote very forcefully and passionately about whites' responsibilities, noting, "We allow practices which no self-respecting community ought to allow, and all these things result in indifference, immorality, physical inability and death for the Negro—*and we are his murderers*."[137] Weatherford was also sensitive to terminology that described blacks. At one point in the text he admitted his disapproval of the term "old-time darky" when referring to African Americans during slavery.[138] Weatherford also took the unusual step of having the "N" in "Negro" capitalized in his book (something that had not been done in the previous text), a decision that he intended as a sign of respect for this group. His printer did not originally comply with Weatherford's style in the first page proofs but made the corrections only after Weatherford sent it back with the instructions "to reset the whole book *the way it had been written*."[139]

Another slight difference from the first book was the broadening of the intended audience. Weatherford still expected his basic readers to be white Southerners, but he also recognized (probably because *Negro Life in the South* had been studied by some African American YMCA college groups) that a few black students might read these pages; thus, at one point he acknowledged them.[140] The book also reached beyond college students. Because of Weatherford's emphasis on black farmers and his chapter on this subject, he secured the support of the U.S. secretary of agriculture and the financial aid of the Chicago philanthropist and Sears, Roebuck leader Julius Rosenwald to send the book out to all the southern farm demonstration agents.[141] Thus, this new text built on the earlier one and made a few shifts in a more progressive direction.

Yet the book was not without its faults, and they were numerous. Weatherford still accepted Jim Crow and was unable to free himself from a number of racial prejudices. His own racism was exhibited particularly in the section where he generalized about the "mental and moral traits of the Negro."[142] Weatherford believed, on the basis of a loose application of Darwinian theories, that these behavioral characteristics were the result of blacks' African heritage and environment and were also hereditary.[143] Just before listing what he considered these typical African American traits to be, he wrote, "It is to be noted, of course, that the white man possesses many or all of these characteristics in greater or less degree, for whites and blacks started with the same general nature; but the environment of Africa has accentuated certain characteristics for the negro, and the environment of Europe has accentuated others for the whites."[144] Weatherford went on to claim that blacks lacked "self-control"; tended to be lazy and indulge in sex, food, alcohol, and tobacco; were superstitious and "cruel" to animals and one another; often were "vain" and "conceited"; and had a "lack of initiative."[145] These were their negative attributes, but he also listed what he termed "Strong Points in Negro Character."[146] Nevertheless, in the process of pointing out this group's sense of loyalty, "gratitude," "generosity," kindness, humor, religiosity, and musical talent, he patronized them to some extent.[147] For example, as he mentioned African Americans' penchant for humor, he wrote: "There is no better amusement than to sit down near a railroad station where a dozen negroes are congregated and, unobserved, listen to their sallies. It is all so quaint, so naive, and withal so full of genuine humor that it furnishes real recreation."[148] While Weatherford intended this statement to be a compliment, his words diminished rather than raised respect for blacks. It was comments like these that probably led the historian Carter Woodson, a leading figure in the founding of the Association for the Study of Negro Life and History (1915), in 1932 to label *Present Forces in Negro Progress* a "scandalous and libelous work."[149] Overall, despite what appears to be a sincere and real concern for African American people, Weatherford could not step very far out of his time and place.

Weatherford's racism resulted from his basic assumptions regarding how environment influenced a person. Progressives, whose views Weatherford generally shared, emphasized that environmental factors were the key determinant in understanding people's actions and characteristics. Thus, change these conditions and change the person. Racists considered that there was something inherent in one's race (which could not be altered) that explained people's behavior. At this time Weatherford's perspective was basically a mixture of these two views, since he considered environment a critical factor in forming character, yet he also thought that these behavioral traits could be passed on biologically. For example, Weatherford stated that he believed the current status of African Americans was "not because of inherent racial disability, but because [their] environment ha[d] been unfavorable."[150] At another point, however, he insisted that blacks had begun to "acquire" more self-control over the past centuries since they had been in America, the point being that he thought this behavior was somehow passed on genetically.[151] Overall, it seems that Weatherford believed races could change over time, a fairly progressive stance in the early twentieth-century South. Yet he also held the view that environmental factors, which were crucial to determining behavioral characteristics, maintained an influence that extended over multiple generations.

To provide white college students with more information on African American culture, Weatherford also took one additional step along educational lines. He gathered together what he termed a "library" on this subject (in actuality, this ranged from seven to ten books) and "got rights to publish" them.[152] These texts were written by whites and blacks and ranged from "scholarly" studies and advocacy pieces on race to collections of African American literature and autobiography. Weatherford's plan was that this set could be bought by white students and could provide them with "knowledge of the Negro."[153] According to Weatherford, this project began shortly after the publication of *Negro Life in the South;* among the texts included were Booker T. Washington's *Up from Slavery* (1901), Lily Hardy Hammond's *In Black and White* (1914), one of Joel Chandler Harris's "Uncle Remus" books, and verse by the African American poet Paul Laurence Dunbar. In 1915 this compilation included Booker T. Washington's

Up from Slavery and *The Story of the Negro* (1909), Weatherford's *Negro Life in the South,* Edgar Gardner Murphy's *The Basis of Ascendency* (1909), Gilbert Thomas Stephenson's *Race Distinctions in American Law* (1910), and Albert Bushnell Hart's *The Southern South* (1910).[154] In general, this project continued Weatherford's basic approach to improving race relations at the time. He was trying to provide southern white college students with information about blacks, a subject on which they were basically ignorant. In some ways Weatherford's method was an understandable strategy for that time; yet in later years Weatherford would return to this approach when it was no longer appropriate.

Weatherford's race relations activities in this period also included involvement in a newly formed Progressive organization, the Southern Sociological Congress. Gathering together men and women, white and black, from a variety of religious and social service–oriented backgrounds, this group began meeting in 1912 and continued until 1920.[155] The organization, which usually met for three to five days each year, began in its first three conventions with speeches and discussions on a variety of issues, including child labor and welfare, public health, the justice system, race relations and current conditions of Africans Americans, education, family problems, and church and social services. As one historian has noted, participants in this group met "to scrutinize, publicize, and exorcise the ills and afflictions of the South."[156] The inaugural meeting took place in Nashville, and over seven hundred participated; in subsequent years the congress held conferences in Atlanta (1913), Memphis (1914), Houston (1915), New Orleans (1916), Blue Ridge (1917), Birmingham (1918), Knoxville (1919), and Washington, D.C. (1920).[157] After the Memphis gathering the congress narrowed its program, focusing on a single issue, such as public health at its 1915 Houston meeting and citizenship in 1919 in Knoxville.[158] Eventually, the organization moved its headquarters from Nashville to Washington, D.C., and became "less oriented to social welfare work in the South and more involved in national movements" as a result of developments surrounding World War I.[159] In 1920 it became the Southern Co-Operative League for Education and Social Service, and by 1925 it was the Home Betterment League.[160] Consequently, over time racial issues became less prominent in its agenda. After 1919 most Southerners interested in that subject shifted their attention to a new interracial venture, the Commission on Interracial Cooperation (CIC).

Yet the Southern Sociological Congress's early attention to race relations was noteworthy. Over the course of its existence, fifty-two speeches were given and published on the subject, and fourteen of these were provided by black men and women.[161] The proceedings and addresses of several of the overall gatherings were published in book form for wider circulation, and in 1914 the NAACP's *Crisis* reported favorably about the congress's activities. Commenting specifically on a collection of race-related speeches from the 1913 congress published as *The Human Way* (1913), the *Crisis* noted that this book "is in its way epochmaking; its message is tremendous. Here are men and young men, Southern whites, saying precisely what *The Crisis* has been trying to say."[162] The congress also spawned other race-related organizations and gatherings. Indeed, the initial meeting in Nashville led James Hardy Dillard (a director of the Anna T. Jeanes and John F. Slater foundations, which both provided financial support for African American education) to create the Commission of Southern Universities on the Race Question.[163] In 1917 another extension of the Southern Sociological Congress was the Law and Order Conference on lynching held at Blue Ridge.[164] This council, which apparently only white men and women attended, examined numerous justice questions but focused particularly on eradicating mob violence. Race, in short, proved to be a fundamental element of the congress's work between 1912 and 1917.

Weatherford was active in the Southern Sociological Congress from its inception. For the 1912 Nashville meeting Weatherford served on a committee on "Negro Problems" and also spoke, his topic being "The Negro and the New South."[165] Surveying the history of the South since the end of the Civil War, Weatherford insisted that the region was making progress both economically and intellectually, but he pointed out: "The test of an individual or a nation is not in the realm of possessions nor in the realm of knowledge, but in the realm of relationships. It is not what we have or what we know that makes us great, but our attitude toward humanity."[166] Working from his long-held premise that all persons had value and were sacred, Weatherford encouraged the members to "think of the negro as a human being."[167] Basically Weatherford was offering a speech to encourage a different perspective on African Americans—a chance to allow these men and women to have lives wherein they could pursue their hopes and dreams, just as white citizens could.

Weatherford's participation at the 1913 and 1914 Southern Sociological Congress meetings varied little from his approach at the first meeting. He gave formal addresses at both and continued to serve on committees regarding racial issues. His addresses, "How to Enlist the Welfare Agencies of the South for Improvement of Conditions among the Negroes" (1913) and "Religion the Common Basis of Co-operation" (1914), were fairly self-explanatory.[168] In the first, however, Weatherford took a more passionate tone than usual. As he noted which institutions in the South were working to aid African Americans, he called for greater attention. He insisted that these agencies focus not just on whites, asserting: "Remember that we are not working for 20,547,420 whites, but for twenty million whites plus 8,749,427 negroes. We must not forget that we have a population of 29,296,847 and that we have no right to omit a single one of these when we are laying our plans for social betterment."[169] The following year in Memphis Weatherford concentrated on how religion could serve as a foundation for improving race relations. He wrote: "I know not how much emphasis the remainder of the country may put on the bearing of religion in the bettering of social conditions, but this I do know: that here in the South, where our great social problem is a problem of attitude toward persons of a different race, a different color, and a different heritage, there is only one thing that is far-reaching enough, only one thing profound enough, only one thing dynamic enough to make us all into a common humanity, and that is religion. No superficial humanitarianism or philanthropy will do this."[170] Weatherford believed it was crucial to change how whites viewed blacks and then alter conditions to allow for equal treatment. At this time Weatherford did not consider legal measures to be the best route to bring about this outcome because there were limits to this approach. He pointed out that "no amount of legislation can ever make us value the individual; it can only prevent or deter us from harming that individual. Law can never change our essential attitude toward humanity."[171] For Weatherford only the church and Christian faith could bring about this outcome. Overall, Weatherford's speeches before the Southern Sociological Congress concentrated primarily on changing conditions for African Americans and encouraging whites to adjust their attitudes toward this group, treating them as human beings. As one looks back on this time, it is clear Weatherford was moving in the right direction, but his hesitancy to call for political changes limited his effectiveness. While changing attitudes is important, on occasion people must be compelled to treat other groups fairly. Appealing to reason and people's guilty conscience would not always suffice to effect necessary change. Given the prevailing racial tensions at this time and the strength of white supremacy, however, Weatherford's approach may have been about the best a white southern liberal could muster.

Weatherford's actions at the 1914 gathering in Memphis indicate he was willing to do more than just talk about what he considered to be equal treatment. In that year the Southern Sociological Congress (May 6–10) overlapped for two days with a gathering of the National Conference of Charities and Corrections (May 8–15), and the responsibility for the evening meetings of these two days rotated between the organizations.[172] Before May 8 African American members of the congress had been provided seating on the main floor of the Orpheum Theater (the meeting place) rather than in the balcony, but they were probably nevertheless seated in a segregated section. Placing blacks upstairs was a common custom in the Jim Crow South, and allowing African Americans separate space on the ground level was intended as a gesture of goodwill. Yet it is important to recognize that the congress was encouraging not integrated seating of whites and blacks on the floor level but, rather, only what whites considered "equal" access. On the next evening, when the National Conference of Charities and Corrections was in charge of the session, its members refused to allow even this concession, relegating African American members of the congress to the balcony. This group did not accept this assignment and promptly walked out. When the Southern Sociological Congress took control of the following night's meeting, Weatherford led an effort to have blacks once again allowed in the theater's lower section. By this point, however, the building's owner refused. Committed to the initial arrangement, Weatherford worked out a new venue for the gathering at the First Methodist Church, this one presumably allowing for the earlier "near-equal" seating.[173] Weatherford would go on to credit this event with being pivotal in his securing respect from these black participants, particularly that of Robert Russa Moton, who was then a leader of Hampton Institute and later became Booker T. Washington's successor at Tuskegee Institute.

This incident, as well as Weatherford's speeches at the Southern Sociological Congress, reveals that while Weatherford wanted blacks to have conditions equal to those of whites, the races should still remain segregated. In Weatherford's mind there could be equality even within Jim Crow. In the Memphis seating episode Weatherford did not want blacks to be required to sit in the theater's balcony because it was not the arrangement accorded to whites. Furthermore, this practice humiliated these African Americans. Weatherford wanted their respect and believed they deserved his own and that of the other congress members. But for him this meant not that blacks and whites should be randomly dispersed throughout the floor level but that there should be designated sections for each racial group, and participants would thereby have equal status on the same floor.

Weatherford felt similarly about the relationship between blacks and whites in southern society as a whole. He was essentially a proponent of "dual civilizations," the idea that blacks and whites should have distinct cultures while, as he described it, "living side by side, each helping the other and neither begrudging the other any real achievement."[174] Basically each race would maintain its own schools, churches, businesses, and, most important of all, relationships while existing peacefully together in the same region. This idea for "dual" or "parallel civilizations" was originally set forth by another white southern liberal of this period, Edgar Gardner Murphy.[175] Murphy, born a little before Weatherford, in 1869, was an Episcopalian clergyman and exemplar of the southern Progressive movement. His plan for separate white and African American "civilizations" also called for allowing the races to have "equal" opportunities to grow and develop on their own. Within the scheme of segregation, calling for truly "equal" at this point was the southern liberal reform approach; its achievement would have been an improvement over existing conditions.

Weatherford's race relations work between 1910 and 1914 began bringing him notice in the YMCA, both inside and outside the South. In 1914 he made an extensive tour abroad for more than seven months, traveling from Jerusalem to Asia.[176] In China Weatherford spoke at the Royal Customs College under the pretense that he "was an authority on race."[177] He also lectured on this subject, as well as student religious life, in Japan and Korea. Overall, Weatherford received an enthusiastic response to his racial talks, apparently a reaction he did not expect. Indeed, Weatherford wrote to some of his southern friends at the time that he "was riding to glory on the backs of colored men."[178] While Weatherford's words here have a patronizing ring, they also suggest that he was surprised that addressing this issue would advance him within the YMCA. For Weatherford and his white friends, it was ironic that his taking up the concern of a people held in such low esteem in the South would actually prove professionally beneficial. Whites in the South who questioned this aspect of southern tradition usually experienced just the opposite effect on their careers.

Perhaps because of the perceived success of this 1914 trip and Weatherford's other foreign travels, John R. Mott offered him the opportunity to lead the YMCA's secretarial training program in China and teach religion.[179] But Weatherford declined this post, choosing to remain as the southern secretary because he felt his "task was to do something for the South."[180] He would maintain this sentiment in later years when other attractive job options were offered in attempts to lure him out of his native region.

After Weatherford returned to the United States, he continued and extended his race relations work through the 1910s beyond the YMCA. He maintained his involvement in the Southern Sociological Congress until it eventually dissolved, and he also made the discussion of racial issues a significant part of his Blue Ridge conferences. Furthermore, he became a critical figure in the creation of the Commission on Interracial Cooperation in 1919, the first major interracial organization in the South.[181] The Southern Sociological Congress had included black members and had focused heavily on the issue of race relations in its early years, but this emphasis on race lessened over time. Moreover, the congress's activities were heavily centered on its annual meeting; it was not an active and ongoing organization with a strong grassroots component. As the congress lessened in importance, a new movement was needed. In reality, the conditions of the late 1910s necessitated something immediate.

Indeed, the driving impetus for the CIC was the end of World War I and fears of escalating racial tensions. In this conflict more than 400,000 African American soldiers had fought in the "war to save democracy." Yet these returning black servicemen, particularly those from the South, did not enjoy full access to freedoms in their own country, and there was now fear among whites that they would no longer be satisfied with the denial of their rights. Moreover, some racist whites were uncomfortable with what they believed to be the social acceptance French white women had extended to black troops stationed in that country, presuming this experience might disrupt traditional segregated social relations in the South.[182] In short, some whites believed blacks needed to be reminded of their "place." Concerned citizens, black and white, worried that postwar conditions would lead to violence. Indeed, these fears turned out to be warranted: over twenty-five race riots took place in 1919, a period the African American poet James Weldon Johnson termed "The Red Summer."[183] The CIC began in the early months of 1919 with the purpose of preventing some of this violence and aiding in the readjustment of black soldiers returning to America.[184] Weatherford was among the founding members of this group.[185]

In actuality, both the YMCA and Weatherford played important roles in the CIC's development. Weatherford's connection to the formation of the CIC went back to his involvement in training YMCA secretaries for work with soldiers during World War I.[186] In the midst of this world conflict, the YMCA's War Work Council had been formed to direct and fund the activities of Association leaders in American and foreign military camps.[187] At these sites Y representatives provided religious, educational, and recreational opportunities similar to those found in local city branches. During these years, amid his other responsibilities as a YMCA secretary, Weatherford operated an institute at Blue Ridge that prepared 1,200 men to serve in these positions.[188] Because of his role in southern race relations and his connections throughout the South, Weatherford undoubtedly was aware of the growing concerns about racial unrest.[189] As a result, on the day of the Armistice, in 1918, Weatherford, "fearing ill feeling and possible race riots," put together a plan to extend his training program.[190] This time he wanted "to assemble at Blue Ridge white and Colored leaders from every community in the South to consider ways and means, and above all the proper spirit of dealing with the returned soldier."[191] Weatherford secured $75,000 from the War Work Council to carry out this agenda, and while it "was contemplated" that this group would meet in integrated fashion at Blue Ridge, this part of the plan later changed.[192] Eventually, Weatherford led the white group (a total of 902) at Blue Ridge, and Will W. Alexander, then the personnel director of the Southeastern Division of War Work of the YMCA, supervised a similar program in Atlanta for 509 African American leaders.[193] According to Weatherford, these men—mainly lawyers, educators, businessmen, and clergy—soon recognized the "problems were even bigger and more pressing" than expected and that "further steps" should be taken.[194] This led to a meeting in New York, and soon thereafter one in Atlanta in March 1919, at which Weatherford was present and the CIC was formed.[195] Funds from the War Work Council provided financial backing for the organization in its first years.

The basic program of the CIC was to create interracial committees throughout the South to address specific racial concerns. The main office would be run out of Atlanta by Will Alexander, but most of the real work was intended to take place in local communities, where the "'best' white and black men could cooperate in improving interracial relations."[196] As the CIC's Educational Director Robert Burns Eleazer noted, the program was not meant to be a forum for discussing the abstract question of "'the race problem'" or for the "'the purpose of dealing with race prejudice'"; rather, it was about getting "'leaders of the two groups together around some concrete situation which need[ed] attention.'"[197] Critical to this organization's philosophy was a principle that had rarely existed in previous race relations groups—whites should work "*with* the blacks rather than *for* them."[198] From the start of the CIC, organizers of the movement intended local committees to work for the following concerns: "(1) Celebrations for returning soldiers, (2) Improvement in traveling accommodations, both street car and railways, (3) Better school provisions, (4) Better housing, and the improvement of unsanitary conditions of homes and streets, (5) Parks and playgrounds, (6) The development of public opinion among white people which requires higher moral standards for all Negroes, (7) Secure industrial fairness—equal wages for equal work, (8) Justice before the law—this is intended to include the abolition of lynching."[199] YMCA secretaries would play an important part in getting these committees set up across the South, essentially serving as the point people in their home areas.[200] In short, the CIC stood for fixing or ameliorating individual issues and local concerns and for dealing with problems of segregation rather than challenging that system. This program, as outlined in the organization's initial "concerns," was basically the same Weatherford had called for in *Negro Life in the South* and *Present Forces in Negro Progress*.

In the late 1910s Weatherford was also involved in two other projects relating to race relations. Specifically, he was leading two institutions, the Blue Ridge Association for Christian Conferences and Training and the newly formed Southern College of the YMCAs (1919). Weatherford essentially created each of these educational ventures, which grew out of his passion for the YMCA, training, religious education, and southern race relations. Subsequent chapters will examine these two organizations in closer detail.

Between 1901 and 1919 the YMCA remained an important force in the South, and Weatherford played a central part in this organization's influence. His most significant role was pushing the Y to present a rational basis for religious belief as well as engaging with the social issue of race, and over this period he changed a lot. From no involvement in race relations in 1901, he became by the early 1910s one of the foremost spokesmen on the subject among white liberals. As a result of his efforts and those of others, the YMCA and its female counterpart, the YWCA, proved to be critical centers for developing southern liberals of this period. John Egerton in his extensive study of southern race relations in the first half of twentieth century has acknowledged this fact as well:

> The YMCA and YWCA were among the first church-related agencies to address social concerns. Many of the Southerners who yearned to do something about race relations in the twentieth century—and almost all of the ones who had strong religious ties—could trace their awakening in some degree to the exposure they got at the Y. Student associations for men and women, black and white, were opened across the South by W. D. Weatherford and others in the first quarter of the century; in the second quarter, these young people became the leaders who moved the associations forward. Among other things, they did away with the racial barriers that the culture imposed and that paternalistic leaders like Weatherford enforced.[201]

Perhaps Egerton is a little too critical of Weatherford in the period after 1925. Nevertheless, it is clear in the earlier era that Weatherford was behind a number of the first steps taken to improve southern race relations. In many ways Weatherford pushed the YMCA to the extent that was possible in the South at this time. He did not challenge Jim Crow but, rather, worked for reform within this system, trying to educate white Southerners about the condition of blacks and challenge them to make changes. He did this through his textbooks, YMCA travels, and support and participation in race-related and interracial groups. In short, he had an important influence on the direction the southern YMCA took on race. Yet Weatherford obviously had his limits. His middle-class and traditional perspective, his emphasis on the individual aspects of religious faith, and his own racism sometimes diverted and limited his achievements. Still, it is important to recognize that Weatherford did not have to take up the issue of race. In the context of the South at this time it was a risk to his personal reputation as well as his professional career. In the early period of Blue Ridge, Weatherford would truly test what remained possible in the South, particularly with visits from an old friend he had made years before at a YMCA student conference.

3

Sowing the Seeds of Southern Liberalism

In late April 1926 George Washington Carver (then working as a horticulturalist at Tuskegee Institute) wrote to John W. Bergthold, student secretary of the National Council YMCA in the South. The scientist thought the secretary would "be interested to know" that he had "received 499 letters from the young men whom [he had] met summer before last at Blue Ridge."[1] He went on to say, "I hear from all of those who [were] in the cottage where I stopped, that is the Virginia Cottage. Three of these young men have already been to Tuskegee, and four or five have promised to come down this summer."[2] Carver had attended the Blue Ridge Association for Christian Conferences and Training in June 1924 to speak and provide a presentation of his work on peanuts.[3] Carver frequently traveled throughout the South presenting his scientific work, but this trip was unusual. This time he spoke and stayed at the YMCA conference center that ostensibly served only the white students of the region.[4]

Carver's experience at Blue Ridge was significant for what occurred during that visit as well as its aftermath. Having "slept among and dined" with the all-white Virginia YMCA delegates, Carver and these young men had broken the South's segregated custom.[5] In the context of the times, this was an extraordinary event. In 1901 President Theodore Roosevelt had invited Booker T. Washington to dine at the White House.[6] This simple act, which seemed to imply social equality between blacks and whites, "outraged" Southerners, eliciting their fury and a debate that lasted for months.[7] Challenging Jim Crow remained unusual and risky in the years that followed. Southern whites who faced up to segregation also experienced a severe backlash in this period. In 1926 (two years after Carver went to Blue Ridge), a prominent white proponent of improved race relations and the director of the Commission on Interracial Cooperation—Will Alexander—dared to voice his support for repealing Jim Crow laws while speaking in Birmingham, Alabama.[8] Southern newspapers quickly denounced his statements, and Alexander received phone calls threatening his life if he did not leave town. Thus, within this milieu, the visit and stay of an African American scientist at an all-white southern conference center in 1924 appears remarkable.

Carver's trip to Blue Ridge was also significant for the lasting relationships that resulted from it. The tremendous amount of correspondence from these young white men and their subsequent visits to Tuskegee show that Carver had a profound influence. By 1930, according to one of Carver's biographers, he had received almost a thousand letters from his "'dear Blue Ridge boys.'"[9] Carver's connection with some of these young men would continue until his death in 1943. The existence of Blue Ridge as a place committed to improving race relations had made this interaction possible. The extent to which the conference center achieved progress on this issue demonstrates the limits of what was possible for a southern institution at this time.

Without a doubt, Blue Ridge was an atypical meeting space in the early twentieth-century American South. Weatherford had created this institution primarily to serve as the permanent location for white YMCA and YWCA students of the South to meet, and its programs focused on developing Christian character and making its participants aware of their responsibilities as followers of Jesus. Furthermore, it served as a site for a variety of YMCA and YWCA conferences and leadership events. From the center's inception, Weatherford, as its president, sought to connect its programs to addressing societal problems, particularly the "race question," as it was called at that time. In a period when the races were largely segregated from one another, his Blue Ridge provided a space where white ministers, professors, educators, YMCA and YWCA leaders, and southern male and female college students could meet and discuss the subject of race. Furthermore, as a result of Weatherford's efforts, its programs and workshops on occasion provided contact with black leaders and African American college students. Reflecting on the significance of Blue Ridge later in life, Weatherford proudly wrote: "Blue Ridge has probably done more than any other single institution to make the white people of the South conscious of their responsibility to serve this largest minority group in America. . . . The spirit of cooperation developed there has sent thousands of the choicest college

George Washington Carver in the 1920s or 1930s. (Courtesy of Willis D. Weatherford Papers, Southern Historical Collection, Wilson Library, University of North Carolina at Chapel Hill)

students back to their respective colleges or out into the world as advocates of better racial understanding."[10] In essence, this conference center's philosophy, as guided by Weatherford, was that race relations would be improved by broadening bright young students' perspectives on race, and these students, in turn, would change the world through their future work.

Scholars have recognized Weatherford's work to improve race relations and have given passing attention to Blue Ridge's connections in this effort.[11] Although the conference center remained "officially" segregated until 1952, this was never strictly true, as African Americans attended as speakers and student delegates throughout its existence. Though their attendance was limited, in the context of the segregated and racially hostile South, even a small presence was significant. This chapter seeks to provide a close examination of Blue Ridge's influence from 1912 to 1952 and emphasizes the center's distinctiveness and limitations. This YMCA retreat was an important place for improving race relations in the period because it provided a site where the subject could be discussed and blacks and whites could communicate. Here Weatherford was able to sow the seeds of southern liberalism, influencing the work of future southern leaders who came to challenge segregation and racial inequality.

From 1912 to 1952 Blue Ridge was one of the very few southern places where the subject of race could be talked about in an open, tolerant, rational, and intelligent context. Indeed, in the South of the 1910s and 1920s there were no other similar arenas of the size and scale of Blue Ridge where such radical conversations were held. There really was no other *place* like it. It is true that the socialist labor school Commonwealth College—located in rural Arkansas—did begin its existence in 1922, but its student body and faculty never included African Americans.[12] Moreover, its enrollment was never greater than fifty-five.[13] In the 1930s more extreme options would spring up, yet these ventures too were reticent to attempt desegregation. The famous Highlander Folk School in Monteagle, Tennessee, which would later become an important training center for participants in the Civil Rights movement, began in 1932.[14] Still, in 1934 it decided against admitting black students, fearing the backlash from the local community.[15] The exceptionally progressive arts school Black Mountain College (which ironically had its campus at Blue Ridge between 1933 and 1941) also refused to integrate even in the early 1940s.[16] It too feared local opposition, considering the risks of "arson and violence."[17] Another radical undertaking, Clarence Jordan's Koinonia—an interracial farm community in Georgia—did not become organized until 1942.[18] Overall, radical organizations were virtually nonexistent in the South between 1910 and 1930.

Individual radicals who questioned segregation were also largely absent from the region until the early 1930s. Glenda Gilmore recognizes this fact in *Defying Dixie: The Radical Roots of Civil Rights, 1919–1950* (2008). Indeed, she focuses on "outside agitators"—particularly expatriates and communists who fought against the racial status quo of this period.[19] Other scholars, such as Anthony Dunbar, who have examined radicalism in this era find little activity before 1930.[20] In those years, if one was radical, one typically had to leave the South.

When Blue Ridge opened its doors in 1912, the South was truly a racially divided region. During the early twentieth century this section of the United States had become more entrenched in segregation and racism.[21] Jim Crow laws became more detailed, and hostility between blacks and whites intensified. Morton Sosna notes that the years between 1890 and 1920 "were in many ways the grimmest that blacks had faced since the end of slavery"; "violence, disenfranchisement, and tightening segregation characterized Southern race relations."[22] Throughout the South racial violence raged during these years. High numbers of lynchings took place—more than seven hundred occurred in the region between 1904 and 1913.[23] Race riots also erupted in major southern cities at the turn of the twentieth century, including Wilmington, North Carolina (1898), New Orleans (1900), and Atlanta (1906).[24] Segregation not only separated blacks and whites in public facilities, transportation, and schools but also pervaded the lives of these groups. African Americans and whites often lived in different areas of town and frequented their respective shops, doctors, and churches. In large part, the two races lived in separate worlds, and what little interaction did occur took place as whites employed black servants and farmworkers. In this polarized context Weatherford organized the Blue Ridge Association.

Though the center was a Christian institution, it went beyond simply training YMCA leaders in methods of evangelism. Weatherford's Blue Ridge program worked to build Christian leadership, teaching the application of faith principles to relationships in society. This effort occurred through a variety of summer conferences, programs, and activities that addressed these concerns to college students, YMCA leaders, educators, ministers, social workers, and business leaders. Among the center's objectives, according to Weatherford, was to try "constructively to find Jesus' attitude toward human life," and he hoped this attitude could be applied to people's "relation to others in business, in manufacturing—race relations and industrial problems."[25] In short, Weatherford argued that the "central aim of Blue Ridge" was "to help to bring Jesus' religion to bear on modern life, and to help to realize Jesus' dream for society."[26] Overall, as Blue Ridge addressed racial issues, it concentrated on changing the perspectives and attitudes of individuals who came in contact with its programs. It was not a place that argued for structural changes in the political or economic system. Rather, it sought to change how people interacted with one another in day-to-day life—particularly how whites perceived and treated African Americans. There are obvious limitations to this individualized approach, but Blue Ridge's effort to challenge the racial status quo in this period deserves analysis because no other place like it existed in the South.

Much of the conference center's attention was focused on white YMCA and YWCA college students. The main event for these young men and women was the annual Southern Student Conference.[27] Here students participated in various workshops and activities and heard presentations. In this setting, these young men and women were exposed to prominent southern and national politicians, educators, and religious leaders, including William Jennings Bryan, William Louis Poteat, and Harry Emerson Fosdick.[28] It was usually during these conferences that white students had interactions with African American speakers and YMCA delegates from black colleges.

Beyond those students who attended the Southern Student Conference, Blue Ridge had perhaps a more profound influence on the limited number of young men and women who served as the center's working staff. Each summer, roughly one hundred juniors, seniors, and graduate students from southern colleges came to Blue Ridge to care for the center's facilities and take classes offered by Weatherford and other professors.[29] Known affectionately as "PWs"—"Poor Working Girls" and "Poor Working Boys"—these students were supposed to have a B average or better and be involved in some "Christian enterprise on their respective campuses" to be considered.[30] As time went on, these students were even able to take classes for college credit while working there.[31] Following Weatherford's vision for education, scholarship and physical work were to go hand in hand.

Indeed, the manual labor these students performed not only was critical for the institution's functioning but served greater pedagogical purposes as well. Weatherford believed that "the experience of slavery had left a deep psychological scar on the South and its attitude toward work. He

YWCA Southern Student Conference. The banners represent the colleges these young women attended. (Courtesy of YMCA Blue Ridge Assembly)

YMCA Southern Student Conference, June 17, 1921. (Courtesy of YMCA Blue Ridge Assembly)

Blue Ridge staff, 1924. (Courtesy of YMCA Blue Ridge Assembly)

reasoned that the slave hated labor because it branded him as inferior, and the white man shunned labor because he thought it was the slave's province."[32] Weatherford wanted to change these attitudes and instill instead the idea "that any task which added richness to human existence was a sacred task."[33] Thus, he envisioned that the work they did was teaching them important lessons. As summer workers went about these responsibilities, Blue Ridge leadership held them to high standards in speech and behavior. Racist language in particular was not permitted among the staff. One anecdote from the first summer that Blue Ridge operated provides a good sense of the tone Weatherford tried to set there.[34] A young woman from a Virginia teacher's college lost her purse (which contained her money and train ticket) while traveling to the center.[35] To help with this dilemma Weatherford assigned her a spot in the dining hall as a waitress. Yet when Weatherford later checked in on her, he found she had left the job. Weatherford found her crying in her room, where she complained, "I can't serve a table. That is what niggers do in my home."[36] Weatherford responded "firmly" and "gently . . . that any labor which served a human being's needs was sacred and worthwhile" and that "the word 'Negro' was spelled with a capital 'N' and did not have two 'gg's' or an 'i' in it."[37]

Besides these young white student workers, the conference center employed black servants on its grounds.[38] Approximately fifteen male and female African Americans worked cleaning cottages, providing food ser-

Arriving at Lee Hall, 1919. (Courtesy of YMCA Blue Ridge Assembly)

vices, taking care of the laundry, and running the boiler house—the majority serving in the kitchen.[39] Some of these workers came in daily from Black Mountain, whereas others were housed in the segregated living quarters, Booker T. Washington Hall, at Blue Ridge.[40] Little information is known about these men and women, the circumstances of their work, and their perspectives on the environment there. In terms of sheer numbers, Weatherford's special collegiate labor force handled the vast majority of the Blue Ridge work: baggage services, laundry, cleaning, groundskeeping, and serving food.[41]

Weatherford estimated that between 1912 and 1944, 3,200 students worked as staff there.[42] While this number is not particularly large, it was Weatherford's aim that these men and women would contribute to the lives of many more. Because they were potential leaders, Weatherford hoped to transform their minds through this summer program of work and study and lead them to positively affect their schools and communities across the South.[43] According to Weatherford's records, about a quarter of these young men and women went on to "Christian or social" work, becoming ministers, missionaries, social workers, and YMCA/YWCA secretaries.[44]

Employed YMCA secretaries, in these years, often took advantage of undergraduate and graduate training that was available at Blue Ridge. Beginning in 1919, Weatherford organized the Southern College of the YMCA in Nashville to train YMCA leaders for the South.[45] In fact, the summer quarter of this program operated at Blue Ridge until 1936, when the school folded.[46] These students took several courses, which ran from the middle of June to the end of August, and had access to the speakers and programs associated with the various conferences that assembled on the grounds throughout the summer. Many of these graduate students were also part of the working staff, which enabled them to pay for their educational experience.

Overall, Blue Ridge had a relatively significant influence on a portion of white southern young men and women in this period. The conference center's activity grew steadily through the 1910s, bringing in 1,552 people in 1912; 1,771 in 1913; 2,000 in 1914; 2,100 in 1915; 1,650 in 1916 (apparently because of heavy rains and flooding in the area); 2,200 in 1917; 4,381 in 1918; and 4,258 in 1919.[47] While the program was growing in participants, it also was casting a wide net across the South, pulling in people from many places. The first issue of the *Blue Ridge Voice*—the center's official magazine—noted that the 1919 conference represented "practically every college, every Y.M.C.A., every Y.W.C.A., and many of the churches, clubs, etc. in the South."[48] In this period, with this type of reach, the assembly served as an important gathering place for southern college and graduate students.

Records from the Blue Ridge programs of the 1910s also indicate that the center's effect went beyond students. Church leaders, educators, and business professionals were also the beneficiaries of the assembly's opportunities.[49] Given the center's broad collection of current and future southern leaders, it was a key site where southern issues and problems could be discussed.

Blue Ridge was important not only for the constituency it served but also for the atmosphere it fostered. Specifically, it aspired to freedom of speech. In 1924 Weatherford penned an editorial in the *Blue Ridge Voice* entitled "The Constructive Message of Blue Ridge," which defended this policy.[50] While the exact issue is not clear, it seems there had recently been a controversy over the center's activities, particularly what some of the speakers had said. Weatherford responded to these complaints by insisting:

> We believe 99 per cent of the things said at Blue Ridge are sound and constructive, forward looking and helpful. The other 1 per cent is purely personal opinions, not the official utterances of Blue Ridge. To avoid this 1 per cent would mean to put a censorship on all expression. This would kill all progress and stifle truth at its birth. It would be a sad day when such a step was taken. We have confidence that the 99 per cent constructive truth will not in any sense be vitiated by the 1 per cent of negative teaching. It is simply the adventure of finding truth, and those who will not make the adventure surely will never know the truth.[51]

Thus, it is fair to say that Weatherford wanted Blue Ridge to be a place open to ideas, even some that might be controversial.

This openness was not always met with approval from the residents of the surrounding area. On occasion, Blue Ridge received anonymous threats when it became known African American speakers would be attending the center.[52] Indeed, one of these threats seems to have been followed up. In August 1919 a black YMCA secretary came to Blue Ridge and a "disgruntled white man in the neighborhood made his disapproval of this integration known." Several weeks later the laundry building near Lee Hall burned. Weatherford believed the fire was the work of this man.[53]

Beyond these physical threats, Blue Ridge also had to consider the reactions of its supporters and be careful not to alienate them. Particularly, funding issues placed limits on Blue Ridge's activities. Monetary support for the center in these years came largely from three areas: northern and southern philanthropic organizations and individuals, southern YMCAs, and conference fees.[54] Southern YMCAs, however, contributed only minimally, as funds were given on a voluntary basis. Philanthropic organizations and individuals, on the other hand, while proving helpful to larger infrastructural projects and special conferences, nevertheless could not be depended on to sustain all of Blue Ridge's budget costs. The fees that conference participants paid were essential in keeping the institution afloat. Thus, it was necessary to keep the program schedule full and well attended. Blue Ridge, as a result, had an important incentive not to be seen by southern leaders as too radical a place. If it was, then college and university presidents, as well as YMCA and YWCA leaders, would hesitate to send their students there, not wanting to expose them to "dangerous" ideas. If fewer students came, not only would funding be less, but also, and more important in Weatherford's way of thinking, the vision of Blue Ridge would not be realized. Overall, there was always this tension between pushing too hard against racial prejudice (and possibly losing both monetary and general support for Blue Ridge) and not pressing hard enough.

An exchange between Weatherford and a YWCA secretary chairing the Blue Ridge Committee for the Southern Student Conference of 1926 illustrates this continuing tension quite nicely. Ruth Scandrett, general secretary for the Florida State College for Women, wrote to Weatherford in early May 1926, requesting his sanction for inviting to Blue Ridge "colored speakers who will have the privileges that are extended to other guests in the use of rooms and in the use of the dining hall."[55] Until this time Blue Ridge policy was to place black guests in a private room separate from the main dining hall for their meals. Weatherford responded with a three-page letter that illustrates how he attempted to balance idealism with practicality. While he was sympathetic to Scandrett's request, he denied it and outlined the conference center's rationale. Weatherford pointed out the contributions the center had made to improving race relations in the South but maintained that the Blue Ridge board felt that "to put colored delegates in the main dining room was in their opinion to dogmatize on what the South should do as a whole," and that this act would be objected to by "scores of parents" and "thousands of our other friends."[56] Furthermore, Weatherford noted what consequences these objections might have on Blue Ridge's finances. Pointing out the monetary limits under which the center was already working, he insisted, "They would practically empty their buildings if it was noised abroad that we seated colored guests indiscriminately in our main dining hall."[57] In the end Weatherford urged that if Scandrett and the YWCA conference wanted to bring African American guests, they should seat them in the private dining room. If white conference participants wanted to sit with them there, that would be fine. This compromise, surmised Weatherford, allowed these black guests to come to Blue Ridge. It also avoided the public display of blacks and whites eating together that many southern whites would have found so offensive. Nevertheless, this was a concession Scandrett and the YWCA were unwilling to make.[58] It is noteworthy that Weatherford had no problem with whites choosing to eat with the black guests, as such an action was taboo at this time. It appears that for him personally this was not an issue; however, as the leader of the institution, he was very much concerned with how this public act might be perceived by many of Blue Ridge's white guests.

Reflecting later in life about his overall work in race relations, Weatherford recognized that his compromises on issues such as this one had often left people on both sides of the question unsatisfied. He commented: "This work has brought me into many very delicate and difficult positions. It has caused its full share of criticism and heartache. Some of my white friends have berated me for going too fast; some of my colored friends have called me names because I would not go faster."[59] Struggling with this dilemma and the limitations under which he worked in this period, Weatherford nevertheless supported freedom of expression at Blue Ridge, recognizing that to restrict it would weaken the center's influence.

Thus—despite Weatherford's and Blue Ridge's concessions—given the number and diversity of conferences and participants, the center remained a unique location where "the race problem" could be discussed in the 1910s and 1920s. One symbolic addition to the center in 1920 attests to Weatherford's efforts to make Blue Ridge a different kind of place and more comfortable for *all* its guests, black and white. In that year, it was decided to add to Blue Ridge's main meeting chamber, Robert E. Lee Hall, a portrait of Abraham Lincoln as a companion to the painting of the hall's namesake.[60] Weatherford's speech at the unveiling asserted that "Lincoln and Lee [were] not Northern and Southern, but American."[61] He went on to say, "We believe that these two great souls as they look out from their portraits across this room . . . will forever be a sign to those who enter our building that there is no North and there is no South, but we are one and inseparable."[62] Though plans were mentioned at this same event to "ultimately" include a Stonewall Jackson painting in the hall, the addition of Lincoln's portrait was emblematic of the center's openness to racial concerns.[63] Also part of this ceremony was the Fisk University Quartette's rendering of "O Freedom."[64] Perhaps the Lincoln painting made these African American singers feel a little more welcome at Blue Ridge and may have comforted future participants and speakers who came to the hall as well.

Given Weatherford's interest in racial matters, it is not surprising that Blue Ridge hosted southern Christian leaders, black and white, for conferences on race. One such meeting took place in 1917, when Blue Ridge was the site of a law and order conference. This meeting brought together forty-eight "educators, ministers, social workers, clubwomen, church workers, doctors, judges, public officials, and YMCA/YWCA personnel" who represented "nearly every state in the South . . . [and] included twelve women and several blacks."[65] The conference focused on the problem of lynching but also discussed the migration of southern blacks, legal measures to prevent mob violence, methods to change public perceptions of lynching, and "the role of religion in racial reform."[66] Interracial meetings like this were a rarity in the South at this time.

Blue Ridge was also the location for early efforts by the CIC. In August 1920 a three-day conference was held there that brought together religious leaders to discuss the "relationship of the church to race problems."[67] Including over seventy-five participants, it assembled a range of ministers and college presidents from across the South. These participants voiced their support for the CIC and local interracial organizations, denounced lynching, called for better schools and housing for blacks, and urged white Southerners to live up to the "equal" element of the "separate but equal" creed. Rather than challenging the South's segregation laws and customs, the group wanted to address the stark unfairness of that system as it was practiced. Fitting well with the philosophy of the CIC, the group's published declaration—"An Appeal to the Christian People of the South"— began by affirming loyalty to "the principle of racial integrity" and ended by noting an "unswerving and unalterable adherence to both the principle and the practice of race integrity."[68] This coded language indicated the group's members held to the South's segregated customs and specifically believed that the white and black races should remain distinct. Even more liberal Southerners often felt it necessary to reveal their faithfulness to this principle to ensure that they were being heard, and such statements also kept many white Southerners from writing this group off as too radical. Overall, the well-intentioned CIC group was working within Jim Crow to alleviate racial problems.

Though it is unclear if that gathering included African Americans, Blue Ridge increasingly did become a place where blacks could speak and attend as participants. Reflecting on his work on the subject of race later in life, Weatherford commented that "Blue Ridge was the first place in the South where outstanding colored leaders could come to present to the leadership of the white South in large numbers, the needs and problems of the Negro people and the ways of meeting the same."[69] According to Weatherford, the first instance when African Americans were present at Blue Ridge was sometime around 1915.[70] Such interracial interactions were rare and scattered in the 1910s, but in the years to come the presence of blacks became more regular. Before 1917, Blue Ridge records are very limited, so the reasoning behind the center's drive to bring in more African American par-

The railroad depot, Black Mountain, North Carolina (1919). Blue Ridge is approximately two miles out of town. (Courtesy of YMCA Blue Ridge Assembly)

ticipants is left to speculation. It is more than likely that this new energy resulted from Weatherford's concern over increased racism and violence following the return of black soldiers after World War I. With the growth of the CIC, "interracial cooperation" had become the byword of the times for white liberals, and Weatherford was keeping up with this trend at his own institution. This fact, along with his close association with other southern liberals and the relative seclusion of Blue Ridge in the mountains of North Carolina, made the center a fitting place to bring blacks and whites together. Indeed, the earliest African American speakers to come had close ties with the CIC.

Another contributing factor to an increased presence of African Americans at Blue Ridge was the institution's age. By 1919 Blue Ridge had been in existence for seven years and had become an established southern conference center. As noted earlier, Blue Ridge had grown from serving 1,552 people in 1912 to handling 4,381 participants in 1918. Considering this increase in attendance, Blue Ridge must not have been seen as too far out of the mainstream, or as a place too radical for college YMCAs and YWCAs and other conference groups to send people. With this type of stability and in the context of this racially charged period, it is likely Weatherford and Blue Ridge leadership saw it as their Christian responsibility to work to improve race relations through some limited inclusion of African Americans at the center's conferences and programs. In short, Blue Ridge's stable reputation and the circumstances of the times allowed for some risk to be taken toward more progressive initiatives.

African American observers of this period recognized black attendance at Blue Ridge as noteworthy. In late July 1920 Lester Walton—a writer for a national black weekly newspaper—reported the visit of Tuskegee Institute's Principal Robert Russa Moton to the assembly.[71] Moton, the successor to Booker T. Washington, came to address a gathering connected to the CIC and to provide an African American perspective on contemporary race relations. Walton, who traveled with Moton to Blue Ridge, had been skeptical of this new interracial organization. Noting his Missouri birthplace, Walton recognized he had the "'you've got to show me' trait."[72] Yet his remarks about the visit were positive, and he left the meeting quite optimistic about the possibilities of the nascent CIC. According to Walton, Moton spoke to a crowded audience on July 18 on the subjects of lynching, social equality, disenfranchisement, and Jim Crow transportation. The next morning Moton led a small discussion group of young men and women from Mississippi. Even after the success of the night before, Walton admitted he was still somewhat uncertain about how this smaller group would respond, particularly since they were "white Mississippians and Baptists!"[73] Yet he reported that during the session, "all questions and answers were respectfully given and without embarrassment or trace of ill feeling."[74] Overall, Walton described the atmosphere at Blue Ridge as open to and respectful of Moton's visit. The tone of Walton's article shows his surprise and pleasure at what he had witnessed. Absent from this report, however, is any mention of where Moton and Walton lodged for the one night of their stay. Considering the fact that Blue Ridge was in such an isolated place and the travel involved in getting there took some effort, it seems likely that the African American visitors—as was the case with all visitors—would have wanted to spend the night there. This information, nevertheless, remains unavailable.

Blue Ridge records indicate that Moton's association with the center continued in subsequent years. He seems to have returned in 1921 and 1922 for the YMCA Southern Student Conference.[75] The length of his visits, as well as his accommodations, remains unclear.[76] Weatherford and Moton stayed on friendly terms and in communication in later years. Indeed, Weatherford took student groups to visit Tuskegee several times in the 1920s.[77] Moton's presence at Blue Ridge in the early 1920s signaled a trend of black speakers coming regularly to the conference center.

In 1923 another member of Tuskegee's faculty—George Washington Carver—came to Blue Ridge.[78] It had been over twenty-five years since he and Weatherford had initially met, and by this time Carver was famous. Since the mid-1910s—with his invitation to the British Royal Society for the Arts, a supposed job offer from Thomas Edison, and his work with peanuts—Carver had been gaining status.[79] In 1921 he had met before the House Ways and Means Committee regarding the peanut tariff, an event essentially fixing him as "the peanut man."[80] Newspapers featured pieces on Carver, and in March 1923 the *Atlanta Journal* devoted a full page to him.[81] Between 1920 and 1922 Carver had even been invited to speak to a few southern white college audiences.[82] Therefore, it was with this background in mind, along with their previous acquaintance, that Weatherford invited Carver to Blue Ridge as a guest of the YMCA Southern Student Conference held in June of that year.[83]

Carver's visit to Blue Ridge was a huge success. Writing to a friend soon after the conference, Carver reported having given "a demonstration on the possibilities of the peanut" and remarked that his audience "seemed to have enjoyed it immensely."[84] At that event, the scientist had spoken before the entire gathering. Carver also brought an exhibit on agriculture that was displayed throughout the week. As a result of his experience at Blue Ridge, Carver struck up several relationships with students and began exchanging letters with them. Throughout his life he had a tendency to develop such friendships, and he mentored a large number of young men and corresponded with them.[85] Some of these youngsters even went to visit Carver at Tuskegee. His collected papers from Tuskegee are filled with letters he received and the carbon copies of those he sent. Carver's appearance at Blue Ridge in 1923 was the beginning of his connection with a number of white YMCA students.

The most significant friendship Carver developed from this visit was with Jim Hardwick, a student at Weatherford's YMCA Graduate School.[86] On July 2 Hardwick wrote to Carver, noting that he had already received a letter from Carver and going on to say, "Again professor let me tell you how Christ has used you to enable me to see more of this great love in this world of ours. I believe He is using you in a way that you cannot realize and like you said I guess you are better not to be able to realize it."[87] Hardwick remained in correspondence with Carver until 1937 and received nearly three hundred letters in that period.[88] Hardwick was from Blacksburg, Virginia, had attended Virginia Tech, and had been captain of its football team.[89] He was also the descendant of slave owners. Apparently the friendship they developed was so close that Carver later even visited Hardwick and his mother at their plantation.[90] In the ensuing years Hardwick and Carver made plans to meet at Blue Ridge for other conferences.[91]

Among the many intriguing aspects of this friendship is how the two met. According to Ethel Edwards's biography of Carver, the two chatted briefly the night of Carver's speech after Weatherford's introduction. Hardwick later followed up this initial encounter by going to Carver's room in Lee Hall to talk.[92] What is interesting about Edwards's account is that apparently Carver was placed not in segregated quarters but in the center's main lodgings. Furthermore, Edwards insists Carver ate with Weatherford in the dining hall.[93] If Carver was indeed not segregated on this trip, Blue Ridge was an extremely open place for its time. Even if Edwards's version is incorrect, however, Carver's visit to the conference still remains significant because it exposed these white college students to a professional African American scientist.[94] It is likely that most of these young men had never been in the presence of an accomplished black specialist before. His attendance there showed them that African Americans were capable of high achievement. Another future southern liberal, Katharine Du Pre Lumpkin, coming of age in this era, gives some sense of the effect seeing professional blacks had on white Southerners at this time. In her 1946 autobiography she wrote:

> It seems that now and then young men were listening to such a man as Dr. George Carver, who as a notable scientist even though a Negro, was known to pry open Southern minds by the sheer fact of his existence. It was so at least if he appeared before us. To our incredulous minds it took seeing to make us believe or even consider the possibility that Negroes might not *all* (we emphasized *all*) be as inferior as we Southerners supposed; that they could and did achieve—in some instances, we added; that to them also, or to some of them rather, might belong the full title and dignity of human being.[95]

Weatherford had intended Blue Ridge to be a place where YMCA students' exposure to and interaction with professional blacks could subtly change their attitudes and perspectives. Carver's visit surpassed even Weatherford's expectations, however, for in the case of Hardwick specifically, the visit went beyond simply a brief contact to the creation of a lasting relationship.

In 1924 Carver returned to Blue Ridge for the Southern Student Conference, arguably making an even greater effect. Writing to John W. Bergthold—then YMCA student secretary of the Southern Region—several weeks after that visit, Carver related his extraordinary experience at Blue Ridge. Carver had stayed as a "guest of the Virginia Delegation" during his time there.[96] This meant that on this visit he had not been segregated but had eaten and slept among the all-white group. Moreover, student interest in Carver had been immense. As soon as he arrived, people wanted to have "personal interview[s]" with him; thus, these had to be limited to fifteen minutes per person. Carver reported that these "would begin at four in the morning" and last until "twelve at night."[97] While at Blue Ridge, Carver was also asked by several state delegations to be their guest for the following year, and he was invited by Knoxville College, Berea College, Lynchburg College, Millsaps College, Georgia Tech, and Piedmont College to visit their schools in the coming year.[98] When Carver wrote to Bergthold in early August, he had already received forty-one letters from these young men as well as a "peck of the finest apples from one of the N.C. boys."[99] Carver brought his note to a close by declaring that at Blue Ridge, "the whole atmosphere seemed to be saturated with the Christ spirit of helpfulness. The dear boys seemed to take special delight in making me very happy. This was equally true of the Professors."[100] In 1961, nearly forty years after this conference, George H. Jones, then a member of the General Board of Evangelism of the Methodist Church, would still remember this event, writing to Weatherford about how much this meeting had influenced his life.[101] All in all, Carver's 1924 visit had been a sensation.

It appears other noteworthy events transpired at Blue Ridge on this occasion that Carver left out of his story. Howard Kester's unpublished "Radical Prophets: A History of the Fellowship of Southern Churchmen" provides background to explain Carver's stay with the Virginia group. Kester had been one of the students from Lynchburg College who hosted Carver. According to him, at a planning retreat in the spring of 1924 for the Southern Student Conference, John Bergthold informed Kester and the other participants that accommodations for Carver had not yet been found.[102]

Since the Lynchburg YMCA delegation was expecting more than twenty students to attend and had already rented a cottage, "Creggy View," Kester volunteered to let the scientist stay with them.[103] Kester noted, "Upon hearing what I had done, our students were delighted, and they made plans to see that he was comfortably lodged and that at least one of us would share his meals sent over from the dining hall each day."[104] Since Blue Ridge still segregated the dining of blacks and whites, Carver's stay, in effect, integrated Blue Ridge.

Kester's version also recounts the development of some controversy over Carver's presence at Blue Ridge. Specifically, the Florida and Louisiana students had "threatened to withdraw en masse" if he spoke.[105] As Carver prepared to take the podium, Will Alexander tried to calm the situation, "chid[ing] the assembled students for their rude and discourteous attitude toward Negroes."[106] Eventually Carver spoke on the subject of diversified agriculture and received hearty applause. Amazingly, Kester claims that the leader of the Florida group stood, explained what his faction had intended to do, and apologized. The Louisiana group also "behaved as Southern gentlemen should."[107] After Carver and Kester's interaction that week, the two struck up a close friendship that would last until Carver's death. Less than two weeks after the conference ended, the two had already exchanged letters; Kester wrote to Carver, "You will never, never know just what your friendship means to me."[108]

Carver's 1924 experience at Blue Ridge was recognized by other blacks as a significant step forward in race relations. His friend Martin Menafee, the treasurer of the Voorhees Normal and Industrial School in South Carolina, acknowledged his pride in Carver's successful trip and noted that his stay with the Lynchburg boys was "certainly a rare thing to happen among our people."[109] He went on to say, "Your trip will be an eye opener in that section as well as other sections where these boys live."[110] After Carver shared some of Kester's letters with Menafee, Menafee noted, "Many great things are happening."[111] It is also clear from Kester's later work that he had been deeply affected by meeting Carver. All this had been made possible by Weatherford and Blue Ridge.

An important detail regarding Carver's visit is that it was to the YMCA—rather than YWCA—Southern Student Conference. In this period in the South racism was often intimately tied with gender concerns. Exposing white college women to black men would have upset a large portion of Southerners at this time. This anger could be expressed in violence or—perhaps more likely in this case—by the withdrawal of support for Blue Ridge. Weatherford and the leaders of Blue Ridge were well aware of these risks. As a result, when Carver did come to Blue Ridge, it seems that it was to meet with white male Y students only.[112] Carver's presence or that of other black men would almost certainly have been unwelcome at the YWCA conference. These concerns also surely played a significant part in why Ruth Scandrett (of the Blue Ridge YWCA Southern Student Conference committee) requested female—rather than male—black guests for their 1926 program.[113]

While Carver's visit influenced primarily the white male students who gathered at Blue Ridge, it also had an effect on the black student delegates who attended. Before the conference, Bergthold had notified Carver that "a fraternal delegation of students from the Kings Mountain Student Conference" would also be there "during these two Good-will or Interracial Days."[114] During this period, Kings Mountain—the YMCA conference center for African Americans—and Blue Ridge exchanged a small number of delegates each year for their conferences. According to Benjamin Mays's autobiography, while the white students who went to Kings Mountain were fully integrated into that conference, this was not true for blacks who went to Blue Ridge.[115] African American students there were segregated in their accommodations and meals. Yet despite these circumstances, they still attended, and Carver's presence in 1924 had an influence on at least one of their number. A young man, George W. Watkins, from Virginia Union University, wrote to Carver in early December 1924, acknowledging how much he had been "impressed" with Carver and his work and inviting him to visit Richmond and the university.[116] It must have been a strange, and yet inspiring, experience for this young African American to have seen a fellow member of his race speaking at the white conference center of the South.

Black speakers continued to attend Blue Ridge from the mid-1920s onward. In 1925 the African American educator Mary McLeod Bethune came.[117] In the following years several presidents of African American institutions were invited to Blue Ridge—Mordecai Johnson of Howard University in 1926 and John Hope of Morehouse College in 1928.[118] While surviving records leave little information on Bethune's and Hope's experiences, it is clear Johnson's presence was not quickly forgotten. Indeed, on his visit the southern taboo against whites and blacks eating together was challenged. Arriving at Blue Ridge around the time of the evening meal, Johnson was "rushed" into the dining hall by John Bergthold to be seated with the other conference guests.[119] Johnson was light-skinned and "passed" without notice as he was served his meal. As a result, this southern dining custom, at least in a technical sense, had been broken.

While there, Johnson presented before the entire conference body a powerful speech entitled "Christianity in Race Relations."[120] Appealing to these white students who were the future leaders of the South, he encouraged them to have "reverence for the life of every living creature" because he believed "that kind of reverence w[ould] break down race antagonism in America and in the world."[121] Johnson was adamant that these students bring the love of Jesus to their relationships with African Americans. Instead of advocating structural and political change in this speech, he emphasized that change began with individuals and how they chose to interact with one another. Indeed, he insisted, "I don't advise you to start out putting your hand on this political measure, and putting your hand on this institution trying to change it around. This is not where you begin. You start out with John Jones when you meet him tomorrow morning—the individual toward the individual—acting radically upon the principles of creative love."[122] Johnson recognized that such actions would have a "cost," and that students should be willing to bear these if they were to be true to their faith.[123] Overall, Johnson's words were representative of Blue Ridge's approach in furthering race relations. Change would take place as individuals interacted in truly Christian ways with one another.

Blue Ridge did not directly encourage its participants to challenge the structure of Jim Crow, but it did have an effect on this issue. Exposure to ideas at the conference center contributed to some participants' questioning southern norms. A controversy involving the interrelated issues of race and gender that arose at Blue Ridge in 1928 illustrates this point.[124] V. L. Roy, president of the State Normal College in Natchitoches, Louisiana, noted that several white women from his school had complained that at Blue Ridge black delegates had been eating with whites and staying in the same dormitories.[125] He circulated this information to other southern college presidents, cautioning them about the dangers of Blue Ridge. Moreover, Roy argued, "These young women have, every one of them, returned to us as thoroughly and fully unsound on the question of social equality between the races as the most ardent negrophile could desire."[126] It seems as if experiences at Blue Ridge were affecting the perspectives these young women held. Roy was incensed by these radical views, and Weatherford had to defuse the situation. To assuage the college president, Weatherford noted the center's policy that blacks eat in private rooms at Blue Ridge.[127] Nevertheless, Weatherford moved on to defend the presence of blacks as speakers and guests at Blue Ridge.[128] In a letter to another Mississippi college president involving this same problem, Weatherford made similar appeals. While noting that Blue Ridge did not preach "a gospel of social intermingling," he insisted he was "glad to plead guilty to the conviction that we must treat the Negro as a human being and as Christians ought to treat him."[129] Overall, Weatherford believed the racial stances that he and Blue Ridge took at this time were as liberal as the conference center could take and still keep its doors open. To go further would have alienated a number of southern colleges and created controversy, and Weatherford did not want to risk losing Blue Ridge's support and students.[130] Eventually this issue subsided. Yet it demonstrates that despite Blue Ridge's unwillingness to officially integrate and challenge structural racism, it was chipping away at the system and affecting its participants' perspectives. In the eyes of conservative white Southerners like Roy, it was a place that was "unsafe" and dangerous to the southern racial status quo.

Experiences at Blue Ridge not only changed perspectives but also influenced how some of its participants responded to racism and chose to spend their lives. Kester claimed that the leader of the Louisiana delegation—one of the groups that had threatened to walk out on Carver's 1924 Blue Ridge speech—later tried to prevent a lynching in Louisiana.[131] Kester implies that Blue Ridge had been a pivotal experience in this man's life, thus explaining this bold action. While it is unclear how much Carver's visit affected that Louisianan, it is obvious that it made a deep impression on the life's work of Jim Hardwick and Howard Kester. Hardwick became a YMCA secretary and continued working in race relations. In the 1930s he and Carver traveled throughout the South as the latter spoke to white college groups.[132] Along the way Hardwick set up meetings and secured accommodations. After Carver's death in 1943, the historical record becomes silent on Hardwick's career. Howard Kester became even more active than Hardwick in the years after meeting Carver. Kester developed into a true radical on racial, religious, and economic matters.[133] In 1926, after spending several weeks with Carver at Tuskegee, he attempted to create the George Washington Carver Fellowship, whose purpose was "to unite all kindred spirits, whatever race, religion or nationality, who behold in the universe the most sublime expression of Love, Truth and Beauty, through which the Great Creator eternally speaks concerning the things that He has created."[134] That same year Kester would declare that Carver was "the man who has been and is to this day the greatest inspiration in my life."[135] Though the Carver Fellowship never materialized, Kester did embark on a career of service, participating in progressive racial and economic organizations such as the Fellowship of Reconciliation, the Committee on Economic and Racial Justice, the Southern Tenant Farmers' Union, and the Fellowship of Southern Churchmen. In 1937 Kester would write: "One of the significant moments in my life occurred when I met Dr. George Washington Carver. . . . I have spent hundreds of invaluable hours with this great but simple man who opened to me new vistas of a more abundant life here in the South."[136] Kester ended his career as a college professor teaching history and geography at Montreat-Anderson College.[137] He had traveled full circle, as the school was near the town of Black Mountain. Kester had spent his life actively working to create a more just society by challenging the structures of racism.

In the 1930s a subtle shift in how Blue Ridge dealt with accommodating African Americans began. Until this time, the two major issues had been where black guests would stay at the center and with whom they would eat. It was the dining question, however, that remained at the forefront. The public nature of eating—because it took place in the presence of large numbers of people and could cause controversy—made complying with the custom of segregation such a critical concern. Nevertheless, because of a number of changes occurring at Blue Ridge in the late 1920s and early 1930s, this issue would gradually diminish in importance by the end of the decade.

Finances proved to be one of the chief reasons for this change. Through the mid-1920s, Blue Ridge was a very well attended conference center, attracting many gatherings and large groups; more than 4,300 people visited the grounds in 1925, for example.[138] But this success would be partially responsible for the center's future financial troubles. Because Blue Ridge was such a popular retreat, the growing crowds had necessitated construction of more buildings and facilities to accommodate them. To cover these costs, Blue Ridge leaders began selling bonds (backed by the Blue Ridge property) in 1922.[139] The debts accumulated from these bonds and the building campaigns would eventually become an albatross around their necks as conference numbers declined.

Through the 1910s and 1920s Weatherford tried a number of ventures to publicize Blue Ridge and address the institution's financial issues. Earliest among these was the *Blue Ridge Voice,* which began running in 1919 and featured Blue Ridge events, pictures, and reprints of speeches made at the center. This magazine proved to cost more than it brought in, however. As a result, when cost-cutting measures were instituted in 1927, this publication was discontinued.[140] Another endeavor, the Southern College YMCA (SCY) Camp, created in 1923, was a boys' summer camp operated on the Blue Ridge grounds.[141] It too proved unsuccessful, running for less than a decade before being scrapped.[142] One of the major reasons Blue Ridge struggled financially throughout this period was that it was officially operated only in the summers. Thus, it depended on the income from these few months to provide for its year-round upkeep. For a conference center comprising numerous buildings, located in the mountains where pipes freezing in the winters was always a problem, maintenance was an expensive proposition. Finding a way to rent out the Blue Ridge facility in the fall, winter, and spring was a critical necessity. In the fall of 1926 Weatherford initiated a new undertaking to meet this challenge, opening the Lee School for Boys.[143] Primarily a boarding school, the institution was centered on a classical education and designed to emphasize character, citizenship, and religion. But it too did not work out. After three years of operation it had accumulated a debt of $41,668.56.[144] By 1929 disputes over the role of J. A. Peoples (the school's headmaster) had led to his being dismissed from the faculty, and relations between him and Weatherford became nasty.[145] With low morale among its faculty and continuing financial troubles, the school closed in the spring of 1931.[146] The failure of these projects, along with the center's mounting debt and the general economic climate of the country owing to the Great Depression, contributed to Blue Ridge's serious financial troubles.

Besides the strain of Blue Ridge, Weatherford himself had a number of other personal and professional pressures weighing on him at this time. Serving as the president of the YMCA Graduate School and being that school's chief development officer was no easy feat, as philanthropic bequests to that institution became more difficult to secure. Also taxing his physical and emotional well-being was the critical health of his second wife. After nearly seven years as a widower, Weatherford had married Julia Pearl McCrory on May 27, 1914.[147] The two met when McCrory—then a YWCA secretary at Winthrop College, in South Carolina—came to work at Blue Ridge in the summer of 1912.[148] Weatherford's new bride was fifteen years his junior, and by 1916 they had their first and only child, Willis Jr.[149] Sometime in 1925, however, she had developed a respiratory illness.

Eventually diagnosed with pleurisy, Julia left Nashville to go to a sanatorium in Colorado.[150] Her separation from Weatherford and their son made this a trying time. Her illness and health care expenses also placed a heavy weight on Weatherford's personal finances.[151]

All these pressures reached a peak when Weatherford offered his resignation as president of the Blue Ridge Board of Directors on the last day of 1929.[152] Noting his twenty-two years of continuous service, he wrote, "The time has come when someone else should take this load and serve the South through this institution."[153] Weatherford outlined several reasons for his decision, noting the growing demands on his time from the YMCA Graduate School and the dissatisfaction by some Blue Ridge supporters of the present leadership.[154] Apparently Weatherford's request was not granted, however, and he continued in his role at Blue Ridge until 1944.

The institution's financial resources remained strained in this period. In 1930, with the Great Depression setting in, the attendance at Blue Ridge dipped below 1,400.[155] Nevertheless, Blue Ridge's struggles mirrored a similar trend among other Association centers across the country.[156] Weatherford attributed their problems to the growth in denominational conference grounds (which took significant numbers of their former clientele), as well as trends in modern life. He highlighted particularly the roles the radio and the automobile were playing, the former making it easier to hear "outstanding speakers of the country without going to Conference Grounds," and the latter allowing people "to travel far and wide."[157] Though Weatherford perhaps did not recognize it, also contributing significantly to the center's troubles was the collegiate YMCA's decline as an organization in this period.[158] In short, this was a tough time for anyone trying to operate a Y meeting place.

By 1932 the situation at Blue Ridge was getting desperate. In January of that year the treasury had no funds, and creditors were demanding payment from the institution.[159] In this critical time, Weatherford even paid one bill out of his personal funds to keep the center afloat.[160] But the most pressing concern for the center was the $160,000 bond indebtedness it carried. As these bonds came due in 1933, Blue Ridge had no way of paying them. By August of that year, the bondholders had made moves to foreclose on the Blue Ridge property.[161] In light of Blue Ridge's impending failure, Weatherford worked with the YMCA Graduate School Board of Directors to purchase the property. In the end, through a complicated legal arrangement, the Y institution in Nashville acquired Blue Ridge for approximately $70,000 by paying the bondholders a portion of the bonds' worth.[162]

After the transaction had taken place at the end of 1933, the Blue Ridge Association for Christian Conferences and Training went out of existence and was replaced by a new institution. Several months earlier, Weatherford, H. W. Sanders, and J. J. Ray had received a charter for an organization—the Blue Ridge College, Incorporated.[163] They had made this move as part of the deal to transfer the Blue Ridge property to the YMCA Graduate School. The Blue Ridge College was in effect a separate organization from the YMCA Graduate School, but the latter's purchase of the Blue Ridge bonds made the existence of this new corporation possible. Basically, the former Blue Ridge Association was retired—along with its existing debts—and this new institution (Blue Ridge College) began with a clean slate. Through Weatherford and the Blue Ridge Association's skillful and somewhat questionable maneuvers, Blue Ridge had been saved.[164] The reason that these proceedings were "somewhat questionable" is that neither the YMCA Graduate School nor the new Blue Ridge College would be responsible for paying any outstanding debts, even though the leadership of the new Blue Ridge College was essentially the same as that of the old Blue Ridge Association. While this change had taken place through a legal sleight of hand, it nevertheless reveals the deep commitment Weatherford had to Blue Ridge's survival.

In the midst of this alteration, Weatherford had also found a solution to the previously vexing problem of securing revenue from Blue Ridge's off-season. In the summer of 1933 a new college was seeking suitable facilities for its nascent educational program and found Blue Ridge to be an appealing place. Black Mountain College, as this new institution would come to be known, carried on negotiations with Weatherford in that period and secured a lease of the Blue Ridge grounds for the fall 1933 and spring 1934 semesters.[165] Designed as an arts school, it proved to be an unusually innovative and progressive institution for the region and for the country. It would operate without a president or a credit system and also lack the usual designations for the four undergraduate years.

Black Mountain began its existence with some controversy, as it was started by several ex–faculty members from Rollins College in Winter Park, Florida.[166] Chief among the new school's organizers was John Andrew Rice—Rollins's classics professor. Rice had been dismissed from Rollins because it was claimed he had been "disruptive of peace and harmony" there.[167] These supposed disturbances had included his calling "a chisel one of the world's most beautiful objects, whisper[ing] in chapel," and putting "'obscene' pictures on the walls of his classroom."[168] Rice appealed his case to the American Association of University Professors (AAUP), and a Johns Hopkins University philosophy professor, Arthur O. Lovejoy, headed south to lead an inquiry into Rice's termination. By the time this investigation officially "vindicat[ed]" Rice, the classics professor had already moved on with his plans for Black Mountain College.[169] As talks between Blue Ridge and Black Mountain progressed in the summer of 1933, Rice's iconoclastic style, and the liberal perspective of the school's other faculty, raised some questions from Blue Ridge's Christian leadership. The two cultural perspectives of the institutions—one modern, the other Victorian—were at odds. While Blue Ridge certainly needed tenants and the revenue they could provide, it was also important that suitable renters—whose values did not offend the property's owners and visitors—be found. As a result, Weatherford felt it important when Lovejoy assured him "'that no complain[t]s on moral grounds have been sustained' against any of the former members of the Rollins College faculty now at Black Mountain."[170] With these assurances, Black Mountain College began its association with Blue Ridge, renting the facilities for $4,500 a year.[171]

Nevertheless, even with this new revenue, Blue Ridge continued to struggle financially through the 1930s and early 1940s. The Great Depression continued to lead to lower attendance rates, and as the United States became involved in World War II, rationing also adversely affected the conference center. Not surprisingly, over time the relationship between Black Mountain College and Blue Ridge began to sour. Disputes over the upkeep of Blue Ridge as well as debates about the property's rental cost developed. Moreover, there remained a philosophical division. Black Mountain College had no religious foundation underlying its mission, and this fact increasingly put the group in conflict with Blue Ridge. In 1938 Weatherford noted his opinion about the college, writing, "They are not at all a satisfactory tenant. Their ideals are not our ideals; they have no interest in religion and their conception of human values are certainly not our conception."[172] Black Mountain College's progressive and unorthodox teaching style even created further financial issues for Blue Ridge. As fund-raisers worked to gain money for the center, Black Mountain College's association with Blue Ridge was harmful at times. Some donors even became confused about the relationship between the two institutions as it became rumored "that the Blue Ridge property ha[d] been sold to a bunch of Atheists from Florida."[173] One prospective contributor thought Black Mountain College was "teaching paganism nine months and that Blue Ridge was teaching Christianity three," clearly finding the balance of this arrangement unsatisfactory.[174] Nevertheless, these troubles did not last long for Blue Ridge, as the connection between the institutions would cease in the spring of 1940. At that time Black Mountain would move into its new campus at nearby Lake Eden.

As Black Mountain College made plans to leave, Weatherford sought other options to gain revenue in these financially strapped times. This time he tried to create a young women's preparatory school—Cragmore School for Girls—yet this academy never got off the ground.[175] In 1941 Weatherford explored leasing out the facility to the government in this period of war, approaching Will Alexander, who was working for the federal government in Washington, D.C.[176] This plan also did not work out, however. The summer of 1942 proved to be "a very, very poor season," as business dropped considerably and the center ran a deficit of $4,000.[177] Gas and rubber rationing, in particular, was also affecting Blue Ridge as it became difficult for people to drive and take summer vacations. By January 1943 creditors were pressing Blue Ridge for overdue payments, and Weatherford was forced to begin cutting timber on the property.[178] At this time Blue Ridge was also carrying $60,000 in bonded indebtedness.[179] With all of these complications to consider, Weatherford was once again faced with the conundrum of saving Blue Ridge.

One of the alternatives available was to sell the property to the YMCAs of the Southern Region.[180] In the fall of 1943 this transfer occurred, and the YMCAs of the ten southeastern states chartered a new organization—the Blue Ridge Assembly.[181] This group was formed to raise money from the southern YMCAs to pay off Blue Ridge's debt.[182] In return, Weatherford and the Blue Ridge College board would turn over the property to this new body.[183] This move would also end Weatherford's official leadership of Blue Ridge. Thus, beginning in 1944 the Blue Ridge Assembly took over the management and control of the conference center and the burden of its debts.[184] By November 6, 1945, the Blue Ridge property was officially in the hands of the Blue Ridge Assembly with a board composed of thirty-nine laymen and YMCA secretaries from the ten southern states.[185] The burden of Blue Ridge had finally been lifted from Weatherford's shoulders.

Several years before Weatherford's breaking ties with Blue Ridge, an official from the national YMCA had been critical of his handling of racial issues at the center. At that time, though Blue Ridge was racially liberal in the context of the South, another YMCA conference center—Hollister—had begun instituting more progressive racial policies. This camp, located near Branson, Missouri, served as the meeting place for the YMCAs and YWCAs of the Southwest region.[186] In the summer of 1934, this official, Sherwood Eddy, wrote to Weatherford, noting that in his recent trip to Hollister that region had shown "more remarkable progress than any other that I know of in the Student Movement,—culturally, spiritually, and, most remarkable of all, in race relations. There every year where white and colored student delegations share the same tables and the same cabins, and there is at least one colored leader of groups, they seem to be solving the race problem better than in any area I know of in America or South Africa."[187] Eddy told Weatherford, "When I asked the colored students how things were at Blue Ridge, they said that they would never go to Blue Ridge until they were treated right."[188] Eddy, noting his long admiration of and friendship with Weatherford, and recognizing that he had "been one of the outstanding leaders in our country in the matter of race relations," went on to chide him for his racial policy at Blue Ridge. In the end Eddy stated that he thought Weatherford had the opportunity to "do more to advance race relations just now than any man in North America."[189]

Despite his friend's criticism, Weatherford continued to move cautiously on this issue, particularly in his concern to comply with North Carolina segregation laws.[190] Specifically, Jim Crow codes requiring separate bathrooms for blacks and whites proved to be a major obstacle Weatherford encountered in constructing Blue Ridge's racial policies. From the 1930s forward, Weatherford noted the existence of these statutes as an obstacle in having black guests. Indeed, he struggled to act in accordance with state laws while also not "embarrassing" African American visitors. The complexity of this issue was outlined when Weatherford wrote to a YWCA official who was considering holding an interracial conference at Blue Ridge in 1936. Weatherford noted:

> The North Carolina law requires that all public places shall furnish separate toilets and baths for white and colored people. This means that in order to meet the law, I must put at the disposal of your conference four separate toilets and baths. If it is an "open meeting" or so-called "public," my lawyer tells me we must put the sign "white

and colored" on the bath room doors. On the other hand, he informs me that if it is a "closed" or "private" group, we would not have to put these signs up but we must have a sufficient number of baths and toilets to meet the separate needs.[191]

In this case, Weatherford tried to follow the law while also not posting Jim Crow signs that would humiliate the center's black visitors. As noted before, he did not believe that challenging the law was the best approach to bringing change.

While one might argue that Weatherford was simply hiding behind the law to mask his own racist beliefs, the evidence does not bear this out. It seems clear that he thought it perfectly fine to have black guests and that they should not be discriminated against and made to feel unwelcome. In the summer of 1932, Abel Gregg of the National Council of the YMCA in New York wrote to Weatherford commending him and Blue Ridge for allowing "our Negro delegates in the company without any discrimination."[192] Gregg went on to say he had also experienced a "chuckle" over "the Negro and white man occupying the same room" and Weatherford's objection to it.[193] Weatherford responded that his concern had been that if this had been known in the South, it would have "very likely give[n] us very great difficulty."[194] Weatherford further noted, "While I believe in being fair, I do not believe in being foolish."[195] Weatherford clearly knew that providing fair treatment to blacks was right. Yet he was not willing to openly challenge the structures in society causing discrimination against blacks. While he probably recognized that this larger system lay at the root of the problem, it never was his way to concentrate on changing that foundation. He worked to make improvements through different channels—principally through changing the perspectives of young people and calling Christians to see their duty to respect all individuals, regardless of race.

As Weatherford encountered legal questions concerning segregation, he repeatedly sought advice from his lawyer regarding the exact requirements of the law. In January 1936 Weatherford contacted his counsel about the legality of "a young colored woman occupying the dormitories along with the white women" at an upcoming conference.[196] Robert Williams, his attorney, responded, "While I do not find any criminal law making you criminally responsible . . . I find so many constitutional and statutory provisions relating to other phases of the race question that I do not think it advisable for you to adopt such a policy."[197] Weatherford took this advice and made it the Blue Ridge policy to house African Americans in their own rooms with private baths to comply with the law. In later instances when African Americans came to the center, he would return to Williams's guidance to defend his handling of the issue.[198] Still, Weatherford's actions show his devotion and priority to Blue Ridge, since he checked with his lawyer to see what he could do successfully. This kind of action was not that of a racist who believed that all had to be segregated.

Nevertheless, Weatherford clearly recognized that Blue Ridge needed to maintain a full conference schedule with large groups to keep its balance sheet out of the red. This pressure caused him and the Blue Ridge leadership to gradually relax aspects of their racial policy in the mid-1930s and accept African Americans and subject them to less discrimination than in earlier periods. In the winter of 1936 Weatherford wrote to his lawyer about an upcoming conference studying "future social problems of the south" in which he wanted to include African American participants, adding, "They will not come if they cannot permit these speakers to sit down in the main dining room."[199] Weatherford requested Williams's legal advice, writing: "I will be glad to have you counsel me carefully about this—for as you see to give up these conferences would probably cost us several thousand dollars, and you know we cannot afford that loss. On the other hand we must of course obey the letter of the law." Ironically, whereas in Blue Ridge's earlier years Weatherford had been very timid on race because he feared controversy and the loss of white financial support, he now considered relaxing the center's rules because he realized too conservative an approach might cost it business.

By the late 1930s Blue Ridge's eating policy had visibly loosened. African Americans and whites could eat together—as long as this fact was posted in preconference bulletins and other printed materials—in the main dining hall, and this practice seems not to have raised the same level of controversy as it had in 1926 with Mordecai Johnson.[200] In 1938 a YMCA secretary from Providence, Rhode Island, Gren O. Pierrel, wrote to Weatherford inquiring about this issue, admitting that he understood its complexity.[201] Pierrel noted that he would understand if black delegates could not be accommodated because in his own association "we have not found it possible to mingle the white and the colored men together in our membership" or "for them to have full freedom of our dining room."[202] Weatherford responded, "We can handle this without any difficulty whatever."[203] He added, however, that one "precaution" needed to be taken.[204] Weatherford

Sowing the Seeds of Southern Liberalism   103

Regional conference, Fellowship of Reconciliation, Blue Ridge, North Carolina, July 8–10, 1939. (Courtesy of YMCA Blue Ridge Assembly)

American Christian Ashram, Blue Ridge, North Carolina, August 10–24, 1940. (Courtesy of YMCA Blue Ridge Assembly)

maintained, "A statement should be sent to the general secretaries of the South saying that the conference would have a few colored secretaries who would be treated as any other delegates."[205] This new policy shows a shift in how Blue Ridge and Weatherford dealt with the eating issue. Whereas in earlier times blacks had been kept away because their presence there might offend whites, now if potential white participants learned that black delegates would be treated as equals and could not deal with this plan, these whites would have to stay home. By 1939 the "regular policy" was to allow black delegates to sit with "the Conference to which they belong."[206] Gradually, an opening on the eating question had developed.

Despite the progress made on the dining issue, it is important to note that Blue Ridge's racial guidelines would relax only up to a point. While the conference center might flout some southern customs, it refused to challenge the law. In particular, it did not budge on allowing blacks and whites to share rooms at the conference center. From the perspective of Weatherford and the Blue Ridge leadership, their methods of handling racial issues were advanced for the time in the South. Also from their angle, there was no problem with skirting the North Carolina separate bathroom law for blacks and whites by putting all African Americans in rooms with private baths. Even though blacks were receiving different treatment from whites, Blue Ridge officials did not consider this to be discrimination. Thus, Weatherford and Blue Ridge became frustrated when other groups pressed them to go further in the mid-1930s.

This dissonance between the Blue Ridge leadership and some groups became very clear in 1936 as the leaders of the National Student Council of the YWCA were planning an interracial gathering and considering Blue Ridge as a possible site. After corresponding with Weatherford, they were under the assumption that African American participants at that upcoming seminar would not experience any discrimination, and that black and white secretaries could room together if they so chose.[207] After Helen Morton—one of the organizers of this conference—went to Blue Ridge and reviewed the arrangements, however, Weatherford told her that she was mistaken, "that there would be no variation from the single rooming clause."[208] In a letter in which Morton wrote to those involved in this event's planning, she outlined her meeting with Weatherford and clearly provided both perspectives on the issue: "As he sees it, there is no discrimination where everyone occupies a single room at double room rates. As we see it, wherever special arrangements have to be made because of the presence of Negro staff members, no matter how desirable these arrangements may be, discrimination does exist."[209] This YWCA group did not meet at Blue Ridge that year. Morton went on to comment that it had been "a serious mistake to have chosen North Carolina for a national meeting" and that she feared "we stand to lose whatever trust we may have built up over the years from our Negro and white constituency in maintaining a non-discriminatory standard for our national meetings."[210] Obviously, Weatherford and Morton were coming to this issue with two different concerns. Morton thought about this event in terms of maintaining the goodwill and faith between blacks and whites in the YWCA that had slowly and carefully been built over the past years. Weatherford was concerned with this as well, but his first interest lay in preserving his institution and making sure it was not put at risk because it broke North Carolina law.

Even though Morton's YWCA group did not find Blue Ridge's racial policy satisfactory, it is important to understand the context Weatherford was working in by recognizing that at this same time there were whites in the Deep South who viewed Blue Ridge as extreme. In the fall of 1937 a series of editorials ran in the *Mississippian*—the University of Mississippi's student newspaper—regarding the "radical" nature of Blue Ridge and Weatherford.[211] Dave Hamilton, an Ole Miss graduate student, berated the conference center for "advocating, if not practicing, the most dangerous doctrine of racial equality."[212] He found it especially abhorrent that students had served meals to African Americans there, noting, "For an Ole Miss man or woman to wait on the table of a negro seems most repulsive to me, whether the negro be a Ph.D. or a field hand."[213] Hamilton also went on to blast Blue Ridge for advocating pacifism. This piece in the *Mississippian* drew responses, and the newspaper ran an open forum to air out further perspectives, including a rejoinder by Hamilton. J. A. Parker, a recent Blue Ridge attendee, offered a thoughtful response arguing that Weatherford's actions—while perhaps radical by Mississippi standards—nevertheless were being true to the message of Jesus's teachings and the work of the YMCA.[214] Hamilton remained incensed by the goings-on at Blue Ridge, taking on a particularly irrational tone as he wrote, "When a Mississippi student waits on the table of a negro the state itself is offended. When a negro is presented as an equal and addresses the student by his or her name on first acquaintance the honor of the entire white population of the state is at stake."[215] These editorials showed that Weatherford's fears about Blue Ridge being seen as too radical a place were not too far misplaced. Weatherford had a good understanding of the thoughts and feelings of white southern college students, the result of his long career in student YMCA work. Moreover, he understood that articles like these had the potential to smear the Blue Ridge name and result in decreased student participation at the center. With these ideas in mind, he compromised on how far he would push the center's racial policies.

The Southern Student Conferences of the YMCA and YWCA had undergone many changes since the 1920s as the Y's student movement responded to racial concerns. In truth, this faction of the Y's constituency—particularly the YWCA—proved to be the most aggressive in pushing for change on the subject of race. Until 1928, there were two separate organizing councils for white and black college students in the South.[216] Blue Ridge operated as the site for the white college students, and Kings Mountain, North Carolina, served as the location for the African American students. As noted before, a limited number of African American students attended Blue Ridge as fraternal delegates under segregated conditions through the late 1920s.[217] In 1928, however, Kings Mountain stopped this policy of sending delegates to Blue Ridge until these visitors "could do so on the basis that other delegates attended."[218] This practice of not sending African American delegates to Blue Ridge continued through 1936, until a new relationship developed that merged the black and white councils, and for a few years the former practice of exchanging fraternal delegates resumed. Then, in 1938, Kings Mountain "voted themselves out of existence" and created an interracial student conference that met at the historically black Talladega College in Talladega, Alabama.[219] Thus, two student conferences (the YWCA and YMCA had merged into one conference sometime in the early 1930s)—one for white students at Blue Ridge and an interracial one at Talladega—ran concurrently until 1942.[220]

In 1943 a new site had to be found for the YMCA-YWCA interracial student conference because Talladega College would not be operating a summer session.[221] Conference organizers, including Howard Kester, considered several options as they searched for a new location. Weatherford weighed the pros and cons of bringing it to Blue Ridge, trying to position it in June before the white student conference.[222] By placing it early in the season, he would have avoided having many guests on the grounds and thus lessened the chance for controversy. Also at this point in the summer, he could have made the grounds "private"—thus circumventing some of the North Carolina segregation laws. Whether the other Blue Ridge leaders would ultimately have agreed to allow the interracial conference to meet there proved to be a moot point, because Blue Ridge did not operate in 1943 because of the exigencies of the Second World War.[223] Organizers of the interracial conference then approached Black Mountain College as a possibility to see if its Lake Eden campus might offer favorable accommodations.[224] Yet since this interracial conference wanted "to do away entirely with any kind of segregation," Black Mountain College faced the same North Carolina segregation laws that had complicated Blue Ridge's racial policies. Even this radical educational institution was hesitant to make such a move. W. R. Wunsch, rector of the college, wrote to the conference organizers, noting, "While I heartily disagree with segregation, I think it is the better part of wisdom to obey the law if it requires segregation, to get our freedom within the law. There is more progress to be made that way, it seems to me, than by disregarding the law."[225] In the end, the conference was held from June 10 to 15 at Berea College in Kentucky.[226]

The Blue Ridge conference for white students and the interracial conference continued to exist separately for several more years, and the latter moved to several different locations. In 1944 the interracial conference moved to Hampton Institute in Hampton, Virginia.[227] For the summers of 1945 and 1946 it was held at Camp Highland Lake, North Carolina, and in 1947 it again met at Berea.[228] In 1945 Blue Ridge had adopted a new policy outlining the procedures for entertaining African Americans at the center.[229] But by this time Weatherford had retired and the Blue Ridge Assembly leadership was managing the facility. This group laid down very specific guidelines that included the following provisions:

1) The aggregate number of such bona fide members, delegates and program participants shall not exceed five persons, or five per cent of the total number registered for such conference (whichever shall be the larger).
2) None of such members, delegates or program participants may bring to Blue Ridge any member of his or her family as a guest.
3) The laws of the State of North Carolina shall be faithfully complied with; and in order to accomplish this, any such conference shall engage in advance and pay for rooms with private baths and toilet facilities for all such negro members, delegates, and program participants.
4) Otherwise, there shall be no difference made or permitted as between white and negro delegates and participants in such conferences, as to accommodations and privileges provided for and extended to the members of such conferences.[230]

In essence, this new policy moved Blue Ridge in a more conservative direction than it had been headed in before. While the circumstances before this time may not have been much different from those that resulted from the new regulations, there had been more flexibility during Weatherford's leadership. Writing to a YMCA friend from the Midwest, Weatherford took some issue with the new administration at Blue Ridge, noting that its members "were not as progressive either religiously or socially as I would like to see," and he recognized but implicitly regretted the "rigid stand" they had taken "of only permitting certain numbers to be entertained at Blue Ridge."[231]

Nevertheless, these provisions proved applicable to the YMCA-YWCA Southern Student Conference only until 1948 because in that year there would no longer be two separate conferences, as an inclusive group met at Berea College.[232] The leadership of the Southern Region at this time chose to officially endorse only one conference, and it was to be interracial. By 1952 Blue Ridge would change its regulations and would finally host the one interracial YMCA-YWCA Southern Student Conference.[233] At this gathering Weatherford was invited to preach the Sunday sermon.

Despite Weatherford's invitation to speak at the 1952 student conference, he had not always placed his full support behind the move to make the student conference interracial. His reasoning, however, reveals a key emphasis he carried throughout his life. Weatherford always placed religion over any other particular issue. He felt that being faithful to his Christian beliefs included having a concern for social issues, specifically poverty, peace, and race and labor relations. But his faith also included a concern for personal morality and Christian living—particularly practicing honesty, sobriety, and sexual purity. As early as 1934 he believed that the Student Movement of the YMCA in North America was putting too much emphasis on the problems of "war, peace, and race relations," to the exclusion of "simple moral practices on our Campuses."[234] Weatherford noted that he was "tremendously interested" in all those worthy issues, but he believed that the student YMCA needed to maintain an interest in campus problems—particularly issues of personal morality such as cheating, dishonesty, and drunkenness.[235] By 1939 Weatherford sensed that the leadership of the southern student movement was pushing to make the student conference at Blue Ridge an interracial one.[236] Weatherford found that frustrating, not primarily because of race and his personal views on the issue, but rather because of the implications of such an act. In a letter to Arden French,

Louisiana State University YMCA secretary, he poured out his frustrations about the drive to create a single interracial student conference that would bring to Blue Ridge over a hundred African American students. Weatherford noted, "You know as well as I do that would mean that the white delegates would probably drop down to a hundred or a hundred and fifty and that we would cut the throat of Student work in the South."[237] In short, Weatherford was greatly concerned with how the emphasis on race would affect white Association participation.

These frustrations intensified in 1948 as the move to have only one inclusive YMCA-YWCA student conference in the South was finally completed. Weatherford and other YMCA leaders of his generation believed it important to have interracial meetings—but not at the cost of the whole movement.[238] They felt certain some white college students would stop participating if the only option for conferences was interracial. They believed it essential to continue the all-white gatherings for these students, as well as to provide conferences that were not focused exclusively on the issue of race. In February 1948, as debates continued within the student movement over these matters, Weatherford clearly expressed his views on the subject to his longtime friend and the North Carolina State University YMCA leader, Ed King.[239] "First let me put myself squarely behind the value of interracial meetings," Weatherford began his letter, adding, "I believe they are valuable as showing the way to better understanding, and giving representatives of both groups a chance to know each other first hand."[240] He felt that these meetings would not "solve the problem of Christian Student Leadership," however, because there would be too much emphasis on the subject of race at these gatherings. He believed at this time that a separate white conference, which would also give attention to matters of Christian leadership and campus problems, was still needed. Without it, he thought, "the Christian work for men in the South will suffer tremendously and in many colleges will die."

Weatherford's line of reasoning also reveals his deeper assumptions about interracialism. He thought about this work in terms of how it affected the perspectives of whites and blacks alike and improved their relationships. He did not argue from the position that it was simply fair and right for both groups to be able to meet together. Perhaps growing up in a world where Jim Crow had always been the norm made it difficult for Weatherford to think any other way.

For those who supported interracial student conferences, there were essentially two perspectives, gradualist and progressive. White YMCA leaders like Weatherford who mildly backed these meetings believed compromise was needed to keep making progress. One day the white South would be ready for interracial student conferences. Yet at that time they feared that moving too quickly would result in many white southern college students ceasing their participation in these conferences and perhaps even their Y involvement. The gradualists also felt race—while important—was becoming the primary issue in the student movement at the expense of attention to Christian leadership and personal morality. The other group—primarily African Americans and younger Y students and leaders—believed equality was the most pressing issue at the time. Compromise had moved things along too slowly. From their view, these gradualist policies had been going on for generations, and there were few results to show for all the work. They were ready for real change. The possibility that some students would be alienated from the Y movement because the progressives pressed ahead was not their major worry. In their minds, the principle of equality trumped practical concerns about numbers in the student movement. In the end, for those in Weatherford's group, gradualism proved much easier to rationalize because they were not black and did not experience discrimination.

In assessing Blue Ridge's interracial work, it is important to recognize both the center's limitations and its achievements. Blue Ridge never advocated complete integration or "social equality," but by providing a forum for discussing race relations, it opened itself up to a number of complexities. Indeed, once African Americans were allowed at the center, a host of "problems" arose. Specifically, accommodating and feeding these guests proved complex within the context of southern racial etiquette and North Carolina law. Weatherford and the leadership of Blue Ridge walked a fine line between holding to their goal of improving race relations and pushing too hard and alienating the support necessary for the institution's survival. In a 1925 letter Weatherford revealed this struggle. Writing about the "Negro problem," he expressed his frustration at "militant Negro leaders" who believed the "only way to get their rights [was] to fight for them."[241] Weatherford continued: "I confess I have some sympathy for those who feel this way, and yet I think they are probably in danger of defeating their own purposes. . . . Of course, a man like Du Bois hopes that by their militant tactics they may reach their goal earlier, but in my own judgment they may not reach it at all along this line."[242] Blue Ridge's gradualist approach to race relations always reflected Weatherford's attitude. And like most white liberals, Weatherford believed he knew the correct pace of change.[243]

Nevertheless, despite Blue Ridge's seemingly moderate approach, the institution did begin whittling away at the racist structure of southern society. In 1924 Carver briefly integrated the center, sharing meals and sleeping at Craggy Cottage with the white Lynchburg delegation. In 1925 a young white woman at Blue Ridge talked of the unthinkable: the possibility of blacks and whites intermarrying.[244] This was a truly radical idea for the time, as interracial marriage was a felony in North Carolina and against the law in most other southern states.[245] Weatherford spent a good deal of effort heading off the potentially explosive consequences of that comment. Other events happened in ways that could not be controlled by the Blue Ridge leadership. Mordecai Johnson's 1926 visit illustrates this point. John Bergthold was able to take Johnson into the main dining hall and have the university president served. This action showed the absurdity of the Jim Crow system. If Johnson was so light-skinned and could pass without notice, why did people so tenaciously cling to segregated customs? By the late 1930s blacks and whites were eating together at the center and occupying rooms in its main meeting hall.

Overall, the limitations of Blue Ridge are also obvious and apparent. From 1912 to 1952 it was mainly an all-white conference center. In those years it did not openly dispute segregation, argue explicitly for social equality between blacks and whites, or condone interracial relationships or marriage. Though black leaders and students faced less discrimination over time, Blue Ridge never became open to black guests who wanted to spend their vacations there as whites did. Blacks could come only by invitation or as members of conference groups. In truth, the number of black leaders, speakers, and students who went to Blue Ridge in these years probably never exceeded a few hundred. For the most part, these African Americans endured some form of segregated accommodations and dining.

Yet it is also important to recognize what Blue Ridge accomplished. It did serve as a place where whites and blacks could meet and discuss racial problems. It was also a space where some blacks could come to speak and offer their views. Moreover, the conference center exposed whites—particularly young college men and women—to middle-class and professional African American educators and leaders, a new and enlightening experience for many of them. Blue Ridge also fostered an environment in which blacks were not thought to be innately inferior human beings. African Americans were capable of improvement, and Christians should treat them as individuals with value. These views were far from the norm in southern society in this period.

Though perceptions cannot be quantified, it is clear that white students in particular were affected by what they saw, heard, and experienced at Blue Ridge. The relationships that some white youngsters developed with black speakers—like Carver—proved to be life changing. People like Kester went on to devote their lives to racial reconciliation and a radical understanding of the Christian faith. Of course, Kester was atypical, and it would be unfair to attribute his efforts completely to his experiences at Blue Ridge. Nevertheless, it is clear that the conference center played a pivotal part in his life and that of many others. Don West, Frank Porter Graham, Martin England, and Francis Pickens Miller all recognized the influence Weatherford and Blue Ridge had had on their lives. West and England had worked as Blue Ridge PWs in the summer of 1929.[246] West—who became a radical on economics and race—wrote to Weatherford in 1958, noting, "My early contact with your teachings did much to influence and direct my own life interests."[247] England, who also considered joining Weatherford's YMCA Graduate School in Nashville, commented that Weatherford had helped him to "a new understanding of what the Kingdom of God really is."[248] England went on to aid in founding Koinonia with Clarence Jordan, and as the two made plans for establishing the community, they visited Weatherford in 1942.[249] Miller—who became general secretary of the World Student Christian Fellowship and also challenged the conservative forces in Virginia politics in the late 1940s and early 1950s—credited Weatherford's role in his development.[250] At the time of Weatherford's ninety-first birthday, Miller wrote to him, asserting, "You were responsible for my beginning to think about our race problem and for starting me on the road to becoming a southern liberal."[251] Weatherford also had an influence on Frank Porter Graham in his early years as a student at the University of North Carolina and later, when Graham served as that school's YMCA student secretary.[252] The two remained friends over the years as Graham rose to prominence, and Graham—in the wake of the 1954 *Brown v. Board of Education* ruling—credited him "with preparing the minds of Southern youth of earlier decades for the historic Supreme Court segregation decision."[253] Overall, what is most significant about Weatherford's leadership of Blue Ridge is that he provided a space where race relations could be openly discussed. This had multiple and far-reaching consequences.

Between 1912 and 1952 Blue Ridge was a place where first steps could be taken to improve race relations between whites and blacks. Under Weatherford's leadership, this institution helped begin the process of changing individuals' perceptions about race. Its program was slow and gradual. Even so, it represents what was considered possible in the South at this time if one wanted to address race relations but also desired one's institution to survive. How hard to push against the racial status quo in this period remained the major struggle for Blue Ridge. Yet the efforts of this small YMCA conference center in the mountains of North Carolina helped initiate the change that would later move more rapidly.[254]

4

Professionalizing the Southern YMCA

In 1919 Weatherford received an offer to assume the presidency of Berea College in Kentucky.[1] The fact that he was extended such an opportunity speaks to his prominence in the South and his leadership abilities by this point. Indeed, it was a tempting proposition. Weatherford had been a member of Berea's Board of Trustees since 1915, and the school's religious heritage and its combination of learning and labor matched his interests. He turned it down, however. At this time Weatherford's commitment lay with the southern YMCA, particularly the Blue Ridge Association for Christian Conferences and Training and a newly formed institution, Southern College of the Young Men's Christian Associations. The story of the latter is critical to understanding the achievements and limitations of his reform activities in the 1920s and 1930s.

Southern College (renamed the YMCA Graduate School in 1927) was a unique institution with an ambitious vision.[2] Situated in Nashville, near Vanderbilt University, Scarritt College for Christian Workers, and George Peabody Teachers College, the school was created to provide professional training for YMCA workers.[3] These "secretaries" filled positions as leaders of college YMCAs, worked in local city branches, and served at state, regional, and national administrative levels. This new institution was intended for white southern men and concentrated not only on training them to provide health and exercise programs, but also on giving them broader knowledge through a liberal arts education that would fit them to minister to the social and spiritual needs of the community.

When it was founded in 1919, the school became the only one of its kind in the South. Two other YMCA training centers already existed in the United States to prepare Association leadership, Springfield College

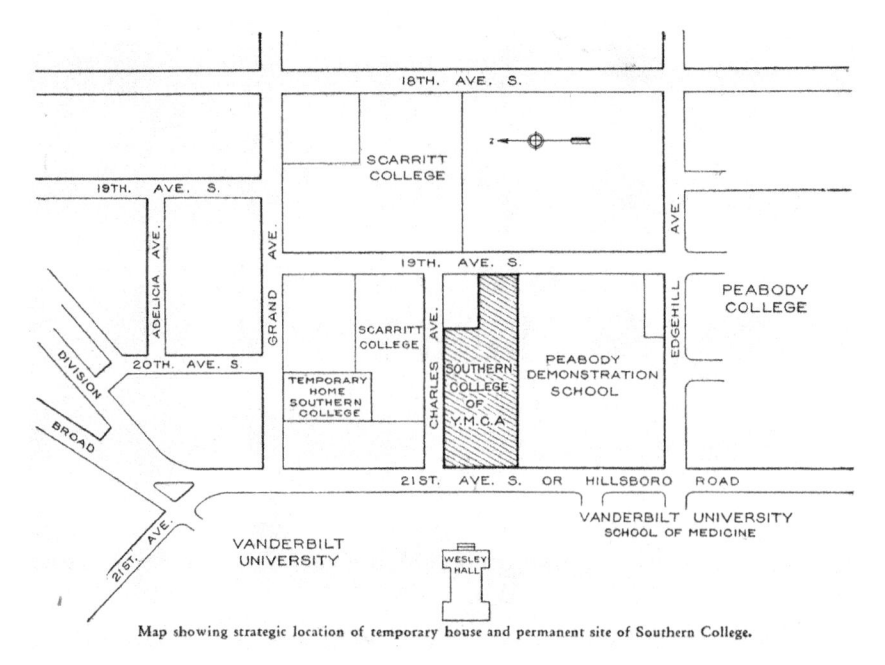

Map showing strategic location of temporary house and permanent site of Southern College.

Map showing the locations of Southern College of the Young Men's Christian Associations and numerous other educational institutions in Nashville. (Courtesy of Willis D. Weatherford Papers, Southern Historical Collection, Wilson Library, University of North Carolina at Chapel Hill)

in Springfield, Massachusetts, and George Williams College in Chicago.[4] These institutions had been started in the late 1800s, and though they served students from all regions of the country, only a "small number" of Southerners participated in their programs.[5] According to Weatherford, there were three reasons these two northern YMCA training schools were not attractive to future southern YMCA secretaries.[6] First, he believed that their programs were more fitted for service in urban areas, and the South at this time was still largely rural. Second, these colleges were located a considerable distance outside the region, which required significant travel and separation from home, which discouraged many Southerners. Finally, northern Associations paid graduates of these colleges higher salaries than their counterparts below the Mason-Dixon Line, thus making it unlikely that Southerners trained in Springfield and Chicago would return to their native region for their careers. Weatherford could have also added another factor. These northern colleges did not address the issue of race relations between blacks and whites—a significant concern any southern YMCA leader would undoubtedly face.[7] Training that included concentration on this subject was vitally needed to prepare Association secretaries for work in the South. Serving as the institution's only president from 1919 to 1936, Weatherford faced this issue, advocating a largely gradualist position that emphasized knowledge of African Americans and provided opportunities for interaction with them. Overall, through the YMCA Graduate School Weatherford sought to raise the standards and expand the mission of the southern YMCA. In these same years he remained active in the running of Blue Ridge; yet in this period the true focus and passion of his life was the YMCA Graduate School. For a number of reasons—principally the economic conditions of the Great Depression as well as the declining influence of the collegiate YMCAs across the nation—the school eventually closed, losing its educational facility in Nashville when it could not repay its $155,000 loan from Vanderbilt University. Weatherford never completely reconciled himself to this project's failure, remaining bitter about it in later years.

Several scholars have examined the importance of the YMCA Graduate School, but these writers have failed to emphasize the significance that its story has for understanding southern liberalism.[8] Indeed, a detailed picture of this institution reveals much about Weatherford's ideas on religion, race, and education in the years between 1919 and 1936. The ambitious vision of the school—particularly its attention to race relations and its program for providing interaction with African American institutions of higher education—deserves more attention. Through a close examination of the YMCA Graduate School's records as well as other documents unavailable to earlier writers, this chapter will expand on previous scholarship, exploring the quality and substance of the school's educational program and its contribution to the South and the YMCA at this time. In the end, though Weatherford sought to create a top-notch institution for preparing white southern YMCA secretaries, this vision was never truly realized. Like an examination of his administration of Blue Ridge, an analysis of his tenure at the YMCA Graduate School reveals the limits to his liberalism.

Before the organization of this new school, Weatherford had been making his home in Nashville, working as the YMCA international student secretary for the South and Southwest and spending his summers at Blue Ridge.[9] At the time of the founding of the YMCA Graduate School, Weatherford was arguably the most important figure in the collegiate southern Y.

His travels throughout the region and his running of Blue Ridge had particularly made him well known. Moreover, he had been the author of several race relations and religious texts used by YMCA study groups.[10] These factors also probably explain why he was considered for the Berea presidency. By 1919 Weatherford was in his mid-forties, had been covering this region for over fifteen years, and had a wife and young son to care for. The opportunities to be settled in Nashville with his family and to invest himself in the building of a school devoted to the professionalization of the YMCA secretariat were very appealing.

Nevertheless, Weatherford was hesitant at first to take the presidency of the nascent institution. Indeed, he initially refused the call, not accepting it until after considering it for six months.[11] Weatherford's reservations were due partly to his feelings that a divide existed between his liberal perspective and those of more conservative southern state YMCA secretaries. These persons in particular may well have found his progressive views on race and peace unsettling.[12] Weatherford wanted their clear support before stepping into the role of leader of this new school.

Administrative changes taking place in his work as the international student secretary for the South also contributed to his making this career shift. Specifically, a recent restructuring of his department had essentially taken away his staff, ultimately leaving him alone in carrying out his duties.[13] As Weatherford later explained his decision to lead this new school, he noted this issue and commented, "I was willing to withdraw to enter the College at the close of the War because I saw so very little hope ahead for doing a real piece of work in the South with only one man in the field."[14] Thus, a number of elements—both professional and personal—combined at this time to attract Weatherford to this new post. And once he made this shift, his commitment lay with making this school successful. With characteristic enthusiasm and drive, Weatherford threw himself into the task of building the college. Indeed, Weatherford would turn down another promising job in 1924—that of a full professorship at Yale University—to maintain his attention to this institution and his concern for his native region.[15]

The origin of the YMCA Graduate School had both immediate and long-term causes. The precise timing resulted from the perceived success of training programs the southern YMCAs had operated during and immediately following World War I, which had helped inspire the Commission on Interracial Cooperation. According to Weatherford, it was at this time, during these postwar sessions, that several international YMCA secretaries came to him wanting to "establish a School for the training of our regular workers."[16] Blue Ridge was considered as a site, but Weatherford concluded that its "educational facilities were not adequate."[17] A committee, of which Weatherford was a member, was organized to study the possibility of a school and a suitable location.[18] Eventually it was determined that Nashville, with its established higher educational structure, would prove a fitting location for a YMCA training college, and on May 2, 1919, the school was organized.

The longer-term reasoning behind the YMCA Graduate School's existence grew out of Weatherford's own experience as the international student secretary for the South and Southwest. For over fifteen years Weatherford moved throughout this region, visiting private and state institutions, speaking and working with college YMCA chapters and student bodies, encouraging them in Christian living and an awareness of social concerns. Weatherford believed his work had been successful because he was able to make an intelligent argument for Christianity and the relevance of the YMCA that appealed to students in this skeptical era. Yet Weatherford did not achieve this perceived success because he had attended the YMCA schools in Chicago or Springfield. Rather, he came to feel his broad educational background at Vanderbilt and his continued study since graduation had been key. After specializing in English literature for his graduate work and finishing his Ph.D. in that field, he continued to read widely.[19] Over time, Weatherford came to believe a rigorous liberal arts education with attention to sociology, history, religion, and theology—as well as specialized YMCA training in athletic leadership and Association history and methods—was vital for a YMCA secretary to be effective in the college setting.[20] Moreover, he believed this type of expansive training was also critical for preparing YMCA secretaries to be sound leaders of local Y organizations.

Essentially, Weatherford came to see the position of YMCA secretary as a profession that took real preparation, rather than a transient position that people could enter without any background save athletic experience. As one scholar of his school has noted, Weatherford's dream was not the reality at the time since "most salaried 'Y' workers during this period were untrained and they generally approached their work on a temporary basis."[21] Weatherford's vision for the newly formed school was that it would prepare leaders to be equipped to meet the spiritual as well as the physical needs of people. As he would later argue in one of his commencement addresses to the school's graduates, he strongly believed they needed to be "thinkers first and doers second."[22] Specifically, here he was asserting that being a YMCA secretary was not just about setting up athletic activities and other programs. This job required more depth and insight for these leaders to be effective at meeting all levels of people's needs. To sum up, the YMCA Graduate School merged Weatherford's two abiding passions, religion and education. Broad liberal arts training combined with practical skills would prepare YMCA secretaries to be valuable leaders in the South, increasing the effectiveness of that organization and helping transform the region and country. The YMCA Graduate School would reflect Weatherford's philosophy and vision.

Despite such grandiose intentions, the school began rather inauspiciously. At the institution's tenth anniversary, in 1929, Weatherford recalled those early days, noting, "We opened our school in rooms rented from the Vanderbilt School of Religion. We had a staff of five workers, two of whom were on half time, we had fifteen students, we had not a dollar in endowment or equipment."[23] The school not only began with this close connection to Vanderbilt but also remained intimately related to the university throughout its existence, particularly with the School of Religion.[24] Indeed, until 1927, the YMCA school used Vanderbilt's divinity school for its offices, classrooms, and boarding space for its students.[25] Also throughout this period a reciprocal credit system existed between the YMCA Graduate School and Vanderbilt. Students at the Y school could take up to half of their work at the other institution, which allowed for diversity of course offerings and flexibility.[26]

The Graduate School operated on the quarter system. Three terms (fall, winter, and spring) took place in Nashville, the fourth quarter being held at the Blue Ridge Association in Black Mountain, North Carolina.[27] In this summer program, the Graduate School's professors and students moved to Blue Ridge, the latter usually serving on the center's working staff, which provided them a way to earn their living and educational costs. As noted before, undergraduate students also made up this staff, and they were required to take at least one of the courses offered by the Graduate School in combination with their work activities. Employed YMCA secretaries also had the opportunity to take course work in these months. Though they could not graduate without spending time in Nashville, this work was intended to make them more effective leaders and give them credit if they later chose to matriculate at the YMCA Graduate School.[28]

This combination of undergraduate, graduate, and employed secretaries

Summer quarter group, 1926. (Courtesy of Willis D. Weatherford Papers, Southern Historical Collection, Wilson Library, University of North Carolina at Chapel Hill)

all as students in the same classes, however, had some drawbacks. Weatherford's vision for Blue Ridge was that it would be a place of work and scholarship. Since both undergraduates and graduate students on the working staff had to fulfill their labor duties as well as their course work, these responsibilities put added demands on students' study and class time, particularly at busy points, such as when conference groups checked in or out. This pressure almost certainly strained the academic program's intensity. Some of the undergraduates may also have not been as interested in their studies as they were in having the experience of being around other young people and spending a summer in the cool mountain climate. According to a critical survey of Blue Ridge by the National Council of the YMCA in 1925, "Classes were diluted by this unwilling or disinterested group and also by some that were not equally well prepared."[29] Overall, the academic rigor of the YMCA Graduate School's summer term had some real limitations.

When Southern College of the YMCAs opened in September 1919, it initially offered courses for white male undergraduate and graduate students. Three degrees, a bachelor of arts, master of arts, and doctorate in physical education (D.P.E.), were obtainable.[30] Nevertheless, Weatherford believed the professionalization of the YMCA secretary truly required graduate work. From the early years at the school he intended it to be a "professional school of graduate grade," essentially taking only students who had completed four years of college.[31] This setup, however, did not prove possible because many of the students he was able to recruit were not very well prepared. Indeed, two out of the school's first five graduates received only their B.A.[32] In 1927 the school officially dropped the bachelor's program and in theory admitted only college graduates; the institution's name was changed to YMCA Graduate School to reflect this move.[33] Yet even though the undergraduate program was dissolved, students continued to receive the B.A. until 1933.[34] The real heart of the school's program was the M.A., as roughly two-thirds of the school's graduates received this degree.[35] While a doctorate was available, few of these were ever conferred. Yet the institution was innovative in its offering, being one of the first three institutions in the United States (the others being Columbia University and New York University) to provide this program.[36] The D.P.E. was eventually superseded by a Ph.D. in that field, and a combined total of five men achieved this terminal degree in these years.[37] Over the course of the institution's seventeen-year history, there were approximately one hundred graduates from the school, and about one-third of them received a B.A.[38]

Throughout the school's existence a limited number of white women also attended. Most of them would have been Blue Ridge summer staff workers, but a small portion also matriculated in Nashville.[39] In the early years most of the women students at the school were spouses of the male students, but no women graduated in the period. In 1927, however, a woman, Mrs. Henry Hart, petitioned to be able to receive a degree if she finished her coursework.[40] Taking this request to the Graduate School's Board of Directors, Weatherford recommended "the faculty be given the privilege of offering degrees in such cases to women."[41] The board accepted, and in 1929 two women, Luan Traudt Carroll and Lucy Gillean, received their master's degrees.[42] Over the course of the Graduate School's life, six women earned degrees, all the M.A.

The opportunities offered to white women for education at the school were not extended to African Americans of either sex. But in 1927 a committee was appointed "to consider the possibility of working out training for Negro secretaries."[43] Writing to John H. McGrew, a secretary in the YMCA's Colored Work Department, Weatherford invited him to join this group, which included Will Alexander, R. H. King, and Weatherford, to study the idea.[44] Plans were made to meet that summer at Blue Ridge. The discussion of this issue at that gathering or in subsequent talks is not recorded, but African Americans were never officially accepted as students at the YMCA Graduate School. As a result, the black Associations were not willing to financially support the school and chose instead to send their money to the Chesapeake Summer School, a training center for African American secretaries run at the time in Bordentown, New Jersey.[45]

Nonetheless, it appears several black students did take courses unofficially at the YMCA Graduate School in the 1930s. Writing to Clarence Shedd, a Yale Divinity School professor who later inquired about this arrangement, Weatherford noted that it occurred for three consecutive years, but he went on to say, "They were not matriculated and they did not pay fees for that was not possible without violation of the law, but we could do as we did in Nashville quietly because of the fact that there was nobody to raise an issue about it and the students simply came in and set [sic] in on the classes."[46] As he had at Blue Ridge, Weatherford was facing segregation laws that made it illegal to educate white and black students together. And just as he handled it cautiously in North Carolina, he did so in Tennessee.

Very little is known of the African American students who went to the YMCA Graduate School. Yet documents show that one of these was a graduate of Nashville's state black university—Tennessee Agricultural and Industrial State Normal School (A and I).[47] In the spring of 1934 this man attended Weatherford's Applied Anthropology course, a race relations seminar that probably was the class that attracted other black students to the school. Weatherford spoke positively of this man, noting that he was "a very choice chap" who was "working with a group of colored boys here in the community."[48] The A and I graduate was serving at Bethlehem Center in the city. Run by the Methodist Church, this was one of Nashville's settlement homes that offered social outreach, including housekeeping skills, education, and recreational opportunities to the city's poor, particularly African American youth.[49] According to Don Doyle's history of Nashville since the 1920s, this institution brought together social work students from Fisk, Scarritt, and other colleges.[50] It is likely that the YMCA Graduate School would have contributed such workers, and it is probably through this association that this African American man took the initiative to go to Weatherford's class. While Weatherford's attitudes were no doubt seen as somewhat paternalistic, his sympathy and concern for African Americans, his attention to the issue of race relations, and his published work on the subject all would have made it appealing to study with him.

Another possibility explaining this black man's interest and that of the other "unofficial" African American students at the YMCA Graduate School is the connection between Weatherford and the eminent Fisk sociology professor at the time, Charles Spurgeon Johnson. In 1934 the two coauthored a book, *Race Relations: Adjustment of Whites and Negroes in the United States*.[51] Intended as a college textbook on the subject, it had nearly six hundred pages covering a broad range of topics from the origins of race to issues in the relationships between blacks and whites in the United States at the time. The book also had the curious feature of having each chapter in the table of contents initialed by the corresponding writer, so that each chapter's author would be clearly indicated. At this time such a coauthored book on this subject was unusual, and, according to its introduction, "no textbook in sociology ha[d] heretofore been undertaken by a white man and a Negro as joint authors."[52] In chapter 5, which discusses Weatherford's later work at Fisk, I will undertake a more thorough analysis of this book. But the important thing to remember at this point is that Weatherford's willingness to work with Johnson on such a project was atypical, revealed his prominent reputation in this realm, and, furthermore, signaled his continuing concern over racial conditions.

Since the school's inception in 1919 Weatherford had been teaching race relations courses. This inclusion was unusual among southern colleges at the time: only thirty-nine higher educational institutions included courses on "The Negro" by 1930.[53] Indeed, Weatherford offered a total of four under the listing "Applied Anthropology."[54] Describing these classes in 1935 to Fisk University's librarian, Carl White, Weatherford noted: "The first course is a general outline for physical anthropology meant to orient the student to the idea that it does take a long time to develop or change a race. The second is a study of race development. The third is a course in the creative expression of the American Negro. The fourth course is a course in problems of bi-racial civilization."[55] Weatherford taught these "anthropology" classes in Nashville—where the African American students had sat in—as well as at Blue Ridge, where white men and women college students had access.

Despite Weatherford's lingering racism, which is evident from these course descriptions, students did receive some benefits from taking them. In 1927, after Blue Ridge students completed one of these anthropology courses, Weatherford required them to reflect on its significance.[56] According to one student, Mary Heath, this particular class had covered a wide range of topics including "lynching, Negro newspapers, the legal status of the Negro, economic conditions, labor unions, migration movements, Negro crime, poetry, novels, and certain proposed solutions."[57] Such matters as these were often ignored by many white Southerners at this time, but the students' reactions showed the course had interested them and produced a profound effect on how they viewed these issues.[58] One pupil, Rachel Phillips, commented that she had developed "a deep appreciation for [African American] literature and especially his poetry" and also felt "ready and willing to work with the Negroes, that is in some social service work, a thing which I did not believe I would ever be able to do."[59] Another participant in the class, Jerome A. Conner, wrote very candidly about what this experience had meant to him:

> Upon entering this class, I was of the opinion that the negro was a "nigger," worthy of little consideration and practically no effort on the part of the white man. . . . However I have come to recognize that the negro is a human being and a soul covered by God with the black skin that caused me so readily to dislike him. I know that his present-day reactions are largely determined by his inheritance, his social environment and his physical environment of centuries past. His faults are logical and his short-comings are not due to his own efforts, or lack of effort, altogether.[60]

Weatherford's course emphasized the environmental factors that accounted for the status of African Americans at this time. The circumstances of slavery and discrimination since Emancipation, as well as their African past—which Weatherford tended to overdo—explained the perceived cultural inferiority of black Americans. Weatherford's argument was that this status was not fixed but changeable, although this might take a very long time. As these course reflections reveal, this view was not so apparent even to white Southerners attending college in the 1920s. Most of them held such racist views that even Weatherford's moderate progressivism here seemed astounding. Educating this group about African American history and culture was an important way for them to move beyond the negative stereotypes of blacks that they had previously been taught.

Despite Weatherford's attempt to offer a progressive message in this course, the class would go only so far, particularly in what programs it advocated for changing the inequality that existed between blacks and whites. While Weatherford insisted his school's "function" was not "to teach men what to think but to teach them how to think," the responses from these students and his course assignments indicate that Weatherford was essentially advocating a gradualist position.[61] Since Weatherford held this view himself, his instruction was slanted to encourage his students to accept it. He emphasized knowledge and appreciation for African American achievements—particularly in literature, poetry, and music—believing that as students became aware of these facts, their views on blacks would change. As perspectives broadened, he hoped these future leaders would work toward providing better education and opportunities for African Americans, and slowly over time—this might take generations—blacks would receive political and social equality. One student's evaluation of the course helps illustrate Weatherford's perspective. Lucile Watkins wrote, "After six weeks of Anthropology, I see more clearly than ever my part in racial adjustment doesn't consist in having heated arguments with this teacher or that girl—at least until I've acquired more facts than I've been able to get in these six weeks. The biggest thing I've gotten out of this course is a knowledge of the place I can get facts I want—books on the Negro, books of the Negro—and a growing idea that doing the 'next steps' accomplished more than the antagonism that results from too much radicalism."[62] In this case, it is clear that Weatherford's priority was in educating these students about African American life and culture, rather than pushing them toward any political involvement to change the nature of discrimination. In another evaluation, E. F. Martin noted his belief in this style of slow but steady progress. This young man commented that African Americans should not be held down by "hindering" their education and being kept in servile roles; it would be better to "gradually give the Negro a better educational system, and as he develops give him a voice in government and also to give him a better chance in the economic life of the country."[63] Efforts to end Jim Crow segregation were not advised, and few students seemed to have departed "Applied Anthropology" viewing such structural change as the best means to correct racial problems. Indeed, only one of the twenty-three students, Rachel Phillips, responded that there was a need to use political measures, noting that she "wished to see something done immediately about the injustice in courts and in politics" and that she was "highly enraged about lynching and mobs."[64]

Weatherford's assignments for this course reveal a mixture of progressive views and cautious moderation. The reading list for the 1934 class includes W. E. B. Du Bois's *The Souls of Black Folk,* poetry by Paul Laurence Dunbar and Claude McKay, plays by Alain Locke, Booker T. Washington's autobiography, *Up from Slavery,* and Robert R. Moton's *What the Negro Thinks.*[65] Having to read Du Bois at a white southern institution at this time would not have been as palatable to students as reading works by more conservative figures like Washington and Moton. Indeed, Weatherford's inclusion of Du Bois's work, as well as those from Harlem Renaissance writers, represents a forward step for this period. In his 1932 course, Weatherford also had his students read Du Bois's *Dark Princess* (1928), a novel examining race and radical politics, as well as Charles Waddell Chesnutt's *The House behind the Cedars* (1900), which explores the complexity of race in the South for light-skinned blacks and the phenomenon of "passing."[66] Yet despite exposing his students to African American radical and conservative views on race, Weatherford's course was clearly pushing them toward an acceptance of the latter approach. For example, on the anthropology exam of 1932, Weatherford required his students in one section to "criticize Dubois 'Dark Princess.'"[67] Of the eleven questions on this test, most asked to describe or compare various black writers and artists, yet this was the only one that explicitly asked students to "criticize." *Dark Princess* was a radical book for its time. Its protagonist, Matthew Towns, is an African American man who has a sexual relationship with an Asian princess and is involved in a plot to use violence against white Americans. It seems clear Weatherford wanted his students to be wary of violence and interracial relationships. He sought what he termed a "sane" and "constructive" approach, clearly not what he considered Du Bois's style to be.[68] In another series of questions for his 1934 course, Weatherford asked his students to describe Du Bois's, Washington's, and Moton's "philosophy of progress."[69] He obviously wanted them to know the different perspectives of each, but it seems overall that his students would have known to which he subscribed. Indeed, evaluations of Weatherford's teaching style reveal that several of his students found him to be less than completely open-minded, having a tendency to show some "dogmatic attitudes."[70]

One other exam question provides evidence of Weatherford's bias. For the 1933 anthropology test Weatherford laid out a scenario strikingly similar to one he had encountered several years earlier at Blue Ridge. In 1926 the YWCA secretary for Florida State College for Women had wanted to bring in a few black women to speak at a conference at the YMCA center, but only if there would be no discrimination against them. Weatherford sanctioned these women's visit yet would not grant them the right to sit in the main dining hall with the white guests and students. The YWCA did not accept Weatherford's ruling and did not invite African American women to that conference. Weatherford's 1933 exam hypothesized a very similar situation, changing the issue from having black women leaders come and eat in the main dining hall to one of having African American female fraternal delegates attend and dine there.[71] After Weatherford set up these circumstances, his assignment to these students was to "write my answer to her," which was followed by a question asking them to state "your workable program."[72] It seems obvious from how this question was written that his class had discussed this particular issue and that Weatherford had defended his handling of this situation. And at first glance he appears to be asking neither a biased nor a leading question, since he was encouraging his students to see his position and then recommend their own, essentially allowing them to think for themselves. The key word to focus on is "workable," however. Students could not propose a truly radical position because he would have argued it was not feasible in that context. For example, if they had answered by arguing that these black students must be admitted to the dining room on equal terms with whites, Weatherford would have countered this was not a practical plan because of the problems that would have arisen. In short, by requiring these students to outline a "workable program," Weatherford was pushing them to accept his moderate approach on race.

 The issue of African Americans dining with whites was not merely an academic one for the YMCA Graduate School. It, too, faced this concern when having black guests at its facility. In 1928, after a meeting of black and white YMCA leaders at the school, the Southern Regional Association of Boys' Work Secretaries registered "a protest against the discrimination against negroes as have been in evidence by the necessity of having a private luncheon because the colored men in our group could not go thru the dining room."[73] Just as Weatherford had rationalized this eating policy at Blue Ridge, he wrote back to this critic emphasizing the practical issues at stake. Weatherford noted: "Let me say that we still live in the world and not in Heaven, and as one responsible for a big institution, it is perfectly impossible for me to live faster than I can lead the community in which I live. Of course you know as well as I do, that if we took Negroes into our cafeteria, we would have an empty room from then on, and it is useless for any group to register a protest unless they have the cash to put up the deficit. It is a plain matter of business which we simply cannot overlook."[74] Thus, "business" trumped fair treatment on this occasion. Even though this complaint was leveled, however, another black observer from this same event had also written to Weatherford praising "the uniform courtesy and thoughtfulness on the part of the office staff."[75] This man, Channing Tobias, was the senior secretary of the YMCA's Colored Work Department at this time.[76] Tobias went on to congratulate Weatherford on his work at the school and his influence on students' racial attitudes. He concluded his letter stating, "My visit to your institution has made of me an enthusiastic rooter for it."[77] These African Americans' complaints and praises directed at the YMCA Graduate School indicate the complexity of the times and suggest Weatherford's rationale for the moderate course in which he directed the institution. At this point it was likely that Weatherford would not deviate from that course until people like Tobias pressured him as well.

Despite the limits to Weatherford's academic classes, he did allow the perspectives of others to be aired in his classroom. In 1930 he began inviting black professors from Fisk University to deliver lectures on their specialized fields, such as African American folklore, music, literature, drama, and art.[78] The reception of these invited professors to his "experiment" was enthusiastic; John M. Work, Lorenzo Turner, E. Franklin Frazier, and Lillian E. Cashin accepted.[79] Cashin made plans to present "Negro Drama," and Frazier would talk on the "Negro family," whereas Turner would offer three lectures on "Negro literature," and Work—who directed the Fisk Jubilee Singers—would deliver one on "Negro music."[80] This arrangement continued in later years; in 1932 James Weldon Johnson lectured on poetry, Millard Burwell on African American folk music, and Turner on his earlier topic.[81] In 1934 Johnson returned to give four lectures, and two other Fisk professors also provided lessons.[82] It is not clear why Weatherford began extending these invitations at this time, though he noted in his initial letter in 1930 that "sometime ago I talked with Dr. Thos. E. Jones [Fisk's president] about getting cooperation" on this idea.[83] An optimistic view of Weatherford's intentions would be that he had esteem and respect for black culture and wanted to expose his students to experts in these fields. Moreover, providing interaction for these future YMCA leaders with professional African Americans would have been something Weatherford recognized as beneficial.

The source material on this subject does not lend itself to doubting the genuineness of Weatherford's motives, but other factors also probably played a part. It appears these African American men and women were there to discuss not political issues but academic work in their particular fields. Thus, it is unlikely that they would challenge Weatherford's gradualist approach, and he had little to fear from their presence. Moreover, another consideration probably played an important part in Weatherford's decision to bring in these scholars. Throughout the Graduate School's existence, finances were an issue; the school eventually collapsed because of them. Weatherford appealed to numerous northern philanthropic organizations to lend aid to the institution. Several of these, the Julius Rosenwald Fund, Laura Spelman Rockefeller Memorial Fund, and Phelp-Stokes Fund, had provisions to offer aid for race-related work, and Weatherford was able to secure significant funding for his school because of this aspect of the curriculum.[84] Thus, inviting African American professors from Fisk University would have been a visible way to show how the YMCA Graduate School was cooperating with black colleges in the city. Weatherford was a shrewd politician when it came to gathering financial support for his institutions, and a relationship between Fisk and the Y school would have been an achievement worthy of note. Indeed, it is clear that the YMCA Graduate School kept records of such accomplishments.[85] Yet at the same time, such efforts that appealed to northern donors probably did not sit well with many white Southerners. Thus, Weatherford's labors were double-edged, probably bringing larger donations from the North than the South, but perhaps at the expense of southern financial and nonmonetary support.[86]

Overall, the Graduate School received extensive financial backing from northern philanthropic foundations. Like other southern educational leaders of this period, Weatherford courted these givers to help build his institution, and he was very successful in his endeavors. In 1924 he secured an annual gift of $25,000 for five years from the Laura Spelman Rockefeller Memorial Fund.[87] Later this agency granted the YMCA Graduate School an additional $250,000, which Weatherford and the school's board appropriated toward constructing its own educational building in Nashville. John D. Rockefeller then provided an additional $15,000 a year for five years, a bequest that ended in 1935.[88] In total, including smaller grants for buying race relations material for the school's library, the Rockefellers had given the YMCA Graduate School a total of $465,000 by 1935.[89] The school also received over $18,000 in combined gifts from the Phelp-

Stokes Fund and Julius Rosenwald Fund in 1929 for race relations work and library materials.[90] The Rosenwald Fund went on to provide $50,000 to the Graduate School over the period 1931–36 to aid in the "establishment of a race relations department."[91] Another gift of $50,000 came from the heirs of the McCormick reaper fortune to help with setting up this post.[92] Thus, the promising nature of the school and its ambitious vision were reflected in the nearly $600,000 in donations from northern groups.

Weatherford's friendly relationship with Fisk led to more interactions with that school in the 1930s. In 1933, while Charles Spurgeon Johnson and Weatherford were working together on their book, the former invited the latter to visit and speak on one of the following topics: "The Plantation, or the Old South or the Attitude of the Church toward slavery."[93] Weatherford's class also made visits to Fisk in these years.[94] In 1934, one of Weatherford's anthropology course's requirements was a trip to Fisk's spring festival.[95]

An exchange relationship between the two schools' libraries fostered further interaction. Since its early years, the YMCA Graduate School had been trying to develop in its library a special collection of documents related to African Americans, with particular attention to the Old South.[96] This concentration grew out of Weatherford's own interest in race relations as well as his published work in that field. His previous books, *Negro Life in the South* (1910), *Present Forces in Negro Progress* (1912), and *The Negro from Africa to America* (1924) had put Weatherford in touch with these sources, and it is likely he had already developed his own personal collection of these materials. For his fledgling institution he sought to build a strong collection of these items, particularly since he taught classes in this area and also wanted graduate work—which would have required research in primary sources—at the school. Another reason behind the desire to put together strong holdings in this field was Weatherford's belief that this was a way to attract young white Southerners' attention to the plight of blacks. Writing to Fisk's President Thomas Jones in 1929, Weatherford outlined the following reasoning: "The most ready approach to the interest of the present white youth is through the history of the old South. Herein there is less of prejudice, and all antagonisms are sublimated by the glory and halo of a romantic past. White students will approach the study of the economic, religious, health and social conditions of the Negro in pre–civil war days without the least prejudice, and through such a study they easily pass over into a genuine interest in the present status of the Negro."[97] With this rationale in mind, the Graduate School began acquiring written documents of all types on this subject. Weatherford's efforts proved successful in securing this material, and the library amassed 2,338 books, pamphlets, bound and unbound magazines, and newspapers on slavery in 1930, and more than 4,600 by 1932.[98] This special collection would prove to be one of the strongest elements of the institution, and when it closed in 1936, it was sold to Fisk University for $20,000.[99]

During the Graduate School's tenure, these materials were available to other academic communities in Nashville, including Peabody, Vanderbilt, Ward Belmont, Scarritt, Fisk, and A and I.[100] Indeed, making these resources accessible to African American students from Fisk and A and I was unusual at this time. In 1928 Weatherford insisted that "only one other library in the South" was open to black researchers, and according to Graduate School records in 1932, such an arrangement "did not occur at any of the other college[s] for white students in Nashville."[101] It is not clear exactly which year the YMCA Graduate School's library became open to black visitors, but this was certainly the case by 1928. By 1932 Fisk and Weatherford's institution had developed a formal cooperative agreement to use each other's research facilities and also work together to gather race-related material and works of African American history.[102] While the Y school would specialize in materials on "the Negro in America before 1865," Fisk would concentrate on "the Negro outside of America" for this same period.[103] This agreement was not simply one of words. Weatherford reported to the Spelman Rockefeller Fund in 1932 that "Dr. Chas. S. Johnson and others at Fisk University were occasional visitors," and in 1933 he noted, "There has scarcely been a day in the last two years that some colored student was not in our reading room."[104] The special collection there was also used by Professor Merl R. Eppse of A and I for his African American history course and by Alva Taylor, the prominent social activist and Vanderbilt School of Religion professor, for his class on racial problems.[105]

The YMCA Graduate School's interaction with historically black colleges took place both in Nashville and outside the city. In Nashville it cooperated with schools with liberal arts programs (Fisk) as well as vocational ones (A and I).[106] A and I, later to become Tennessee State University, had opened in 1912 as the land grant institution for blacks in Tennessee.[107] Away from Nashville and Tennessee, the YMCA Graduate School also maintained a long relationship with Tuskegee Institute in Alabama, as students and professors took an annual trip there. Weatherford had known Booker

Robert Russa Moton and Willis Weatherford. (Courtesy of Willis D. Weatherford Papers, Southern Historical Collection, Wilson Library, University of North Carolina at Chapel Hill)

YMCA Graduate School group visiting Tuskegee. Weatherford is fourth from the left. (Courtesy of Willis D. Weatherford Papers, Southern Historical Collection, Wilson Library, University of North Carolina at Chapel Hill)

T. Washington and been supportive of his accommodationist program. After Washington died, Weatherford became friends with and—in some ways—developed an even greater respect for his successor, Robert Russa Moton.[108] Indeed, Moton seems also to have valued this relationship with Weatherford, inviting him to give Tuskegee's 1930 baccalaureate address.[109]

Though it is not clear the exact year these trips started, sometime before 1925 Weatherford began taking his students to visit Tuskegee.[110] It appears that the group (not more than fifteen ordinarily) usually comprised members of his anthropology class and that they normally spent several days there in the spring.[111] Interestingly, this group often included both white men and white women in a time when exposing the latter to black men was a very touchy issue.[112] The groups often met with faculty there, visited George Washington Carver's lab, and spent time with Principal Moton; on occasion they gathered with groups "to ask questions about present Race Relations."[113] This trip was a requirement of Weatherford's anthropology course. Evidently students who would not have felt comfortable going to Tuskegee did not need to sign up for this class: in one Graduate School memorandum Weatherford noted that "all students should plan to take [this trip] if they want credit on the course."[114] Even after the end of Moton's term in 1935, Tuskegee's new leader, Frederick D. Patterson, welcomed Weatherford, noting, "The annual group from the Y.M.C.A. Graduate School of Nashville will be looked forward to each year with pleasure."[115]

Trips to Tuskegee also often included excursions to a major southern industrial plant, the American Cast Iron Pipe Company (ACIPCO) in Birmingham, Alabama. Weatherford had been on the Board of Directors of this company since 1927.[116] The company's founder and a southern liberal, John J. Eagan, had passed away by that point, but Weatherford and Eagan had known each other through their early work in the CIC. Indeed, Eagan had been the first president of that group in 1919. Because a large share of ACIPCO's employees were African American (roughly 1,100 of approximately 1,500 in 1925), issues of race relations at the plant were important.[117] Moreover, the company was supposedly run on humanitarian principles—the Eagan Plan. This scheme, which included profit sharing among the employees as well as "housing, recreational, and educational innovations for employees," was apparently "all far ahead of [its] time in industrial Birmingham."[118] Weatherford would have been very much interested in showing his students this application of faith principles to business. Thus, these trips to ACIPCO allowed his students to examine the interaction of race, industry, and religion—all key concerns of Weatherford's.

On the 1934 trip to Tuskegee and ACIPCO, the limits to Weatherford's racial liberalism once again became apparent. On this tour the A and I graduate who had sat in on Weatherford's anthropology course was traveling with the group. As Weatherford made plans to visit ACIPCO, he wrote to one of the company's executives, laying out "a little complication."[119] Since the group would be eating lunch at the plant, Weatherford wanted to work out preparations for this black man to eat separately from the white group. Weatherford noted that someone "will have to make arrangements with the colored secretary to take him to lunch. I do not think there would be any embarrassment about the situation."[120] In this case Weatherford bowed to custom when he could have stood up with few repercussions. At this time at Blue Ridge Weatherford was still working out this complex issue, fearing the serious financial loss and decrease in participation there if he pushed things too hard. It is likely that issues in the Deep South regarding blacks and whites eating together were even stricter than in North Carolina. Weatherford must have been worried about how things looked in this situation. An integrated lunch at ACIPCO—while not having the same risks that it might have had at Blue Ridge—nevertheless could have caused a stir at the factory. Moreover, perhaps Weatherford was fearful that it might upset his rapport with some of the ACIPCO executives, or he may even have been concerned reports might get back to Nashville. No matter what his reasoning, he refused to transgress southern custom here. Weatherford's actions reveal how even a progressive Southerner at this time operated in the Jim Crow South.

Despite Weatherford's unwillingness to challenge the southern norm on this occasion, these field trips to Fisk, A and I, Tuskegee, and ACIPCO were noteworthy at this time in the South and an important part of this anthropology course. As one of the Graduate School's records shows, these visits were made so that students could "better understand the ed. problems and progress of the Negro."[121] Weatherford used these outings to expose his white students to other black college students as well as educated and professional African Americans from the middle and upper classes, probably a new experience for most of them. Moreover, Weatherford tested his students on what they saw and heard on these excursions, analyzing the various methods of each institution's particular educational program. Questions for his 1934 anthropology course exam included recalling certain details from these trips as well as comparing and contrasting the respective schools.[122] For example, one question asked them to state what Moton had said about Du Bois's "attitude."[123] Another asked students to "summarize Pres. Hales' talk at A & I."[124] Overall, these trips would have provided these students with more contact with black collegiate life than most of their other white southern contemporaries had.

The interactions between Weatherford's YMCA Graduate School students and those at various African American institutions also breaks down the assumption that Weatherford simply favored vocational education for blacks in this period. At this time many Southerners and Northerners, and even liberals of Weatherford's mold, thought that training that provided manual labor skills was best for blacks. Indeed, historians have been critical of northern philanthropic organizations that aided only vocational schools like Hampton and Tuskegee rather than liberal arts schools like Fisk.[125] Yet it is clear from Weatherford's work with Fisk in these years, and his later role as professor there, that he valued liberal arts training for blacks.

The quality of the YMCA Graduate School's other faculty varied over the course of its history. Indeed, the high standards for which Weatherford aimed were never fully achieved, despite his efforts to build a high-grade teaching staff. In the early years of the school, Weatherford was the only one to hold a doctorate.[126] The first head of its Physical Education Department, T. P. Ballou, claimed he was a Harvard M.D. For nearly four years he served in this role before it became clear that he did not have a medical degree or even the B.S. from the U.S. Naval Academy.[127] O. E. Brown, dean of the Vanderbilt School of Religion, had recommended Ballou for the position after getting to know him when the two had been YMCA workers during World War I. Though it seems his teaching abilities had not raised ire, when Weatherford became aware of Ballou's fraudulent credentials, he dismissed him. The next man in that position, Fredrick B. Messing, came to the YMCA Graduate School with his bachelor's and master's degrees from Hiram College and Springfield College, respectively.[128] Messing went on to receive his doctorate at the Graduate School in 1926, and he served as director of physical education until 1929. He was followed in this role by A. B. Miles, who also received his D.P.E. at the school, leading the physical education work there until its closing in 1936. Thus, the academic qualifications of this department's staff never reached top-notch status, starting with a man without any college education and subsequently led by two men who finished their doctorates at the school in which they were working.

Outside the physical education work, the school for the most part depended heavily on professors from Vanderbilt's School of Religion, as well as other departments of that university, to provide instruction. For the summer quarter Weatherford also secured professors from other colleges—free from their duties at their home institutions—to take on some of the teaching load. Because of Weatherford's experience as YMCA secretary working with southern schools, he was well connected in this region's academic circles, particularly with those professors who maintained religious commitments. Weatherford deftly used his extensive contacts and networks in the South to bring prominent figures to Blue Ridge to teach courses. Among the professors who frequently came from Vanderbilt were O. E. Brown, the English professor Edwin Mims, and the religion professor John Louis Kesler.[129] Samuel Chiles Mitchell (father of the economist Broadus Mitchell), a history professor at the University of Richmond, was another frequent lecturer during the Blue Ridge term, spending over twenty summers there.[130] Mitchell had been president of both the University of South Carolina (1908–13) and Delaware College (1914–20) before moving to Richmond to teach history in 1920.[131] In many ways he was a southern liberal of Weatherford's mold, if more than ten years the latter's senior.[132] His courses often focused on economic history and world political problems.[133]

Though the faculty of the Graduate School in these early years was not particularly strong, over time Weatherford did bring in more qualified academics. In 1925 he secured Ray Erwin Baber and Willard E. Uphaus to teach sociology and religious education courses, respectively.[134] Both held Ph.D.'s, Baber having earned his at the University of Wisconsin and Uphaus at Yale. These were the type of professors Weatherford sought, men who would strengthen the school's level of scholarship and teaching and also raise the institution's status.

Uphaus was a proponent of a socially engaged Christianity. Don West, the future radical poet, preacher, and labor and political activist, noted Uphaus's influence on him when he had been studying at Vanderbilt under Alva Taylor.[135] Uphaus apparently taught courses for both the YMCA Graduate School and the Vanderbilt School of Religion, and West later recalled that he "took courses with Willard."[136] Nevertheless, Uphaus's time at the YMCA Graduate School appears to have been cut short by a "nervous breakdown" he suffered in the winter of 1928.[137] In the spring of 1929 he was at a sanatorium in New York recovering, and in 1930 he was teaching at Hastings College in Nebraska.[138] It is unclear if he ever returned to do any teaching at the Graduate School after his breakdown.[139] Nevertheless, he went on to make a name for himself through peace work and acts of conscience in later years. Baber would also stay at the school only until the end of the 1920s, leaving in the spring term of 1929 to accept a post at New York University.[140]

Baber's decision to depart from the Graduate School reveals much about the general atmosphere among the school's faculty members and their view of Weatherford. In 1928 and 1929 Baber wrote a series of letters to Weatherford that showed his deep loyalty to him as well as the school, but he also expressed some criticism.[141] In particular, Baber was stressed by the institution's financial situation at that time. In his October 1928 note he contended that the faculty was plagued by "a feeling of uncertainty and worry" because of these money pressures.[142] He felt that this reality was greatly due to the "lack of information" that Weatherford had provided the faculty on this subject, and Baber pleaded that a meeting among this group be held to discuss things.[143] The following summer, in the midst of his considering a position at NYU, Baber laid out several other critiques of the Graduate School. Finances again ranked first in his list, but he also mentioned that the staff was too small, there were "so few students," there was a "rapid turnover in staff," and the four quarters of teaching was too heavy a load.[144] The last complaint deserves further comment. As noted before, Weatherford required professors to teach in Nashville during the fall through spring quarters and then go to Blue Ridge for the summers. This put an intense pressure on faculty and provided them little time for their research and personal relaxation. Through the spring of 1929 there was no official faculty policy regarding sabbatical leave, but in that year the Board of Directors moved to allow every third summer free for its professors.[145] This heavy teaching load as well as additional responsibilities at the college did not make working at the school an easy job. Moreover, Baber listed another issue, something over which the YMCA Graduate School had no control, that of the lack of support—financial and otherwise—from the Y Associations in the South. All these elements, along with personal considerations of financial security for his family, pushed Baber to leave.

Baber's letter also brought up the pressure that Weatherford was under as he tried simultaneously to raise money, teach classes, and administer the school. Specifically, Baber acknowledged the "everlasting lack of money, which lack has drained your time and nervous energy too much already," and kept Weatherford confined largely to development work not only for the school's annual budget, but for its endowment as well.[146] Also adding to Weatherford's stress was his wife's battle with pleurisy. On a trip to New York to raise money, the weight of all these pressures showed when Weatherford wrote to a fellow staff member after a long day, "I'm lonesome as a dog tonight—too tired to go anywhere—Darn this traveling job. I'm sick of it."[147] Julia would recover from pleurisy, but her health would again fail in 1933, compounding the demands already on Weatherford. Around the Christmas holidays of 1932 the Weatherfords' family dog had been acting rather unusual, "snapping" and "jumping" at them.[148] The animal was soon put down, but after an examination of the dog's skull revealed signs of "hydrophobia," it was decided that Julia and Willis should be given the "Pasteur serum" series of shots.[149] It turned out that Julia was allergic to these treatments; she developed a serious reaction that eventually left her paralyzed from the waist down. Though she would live until 1957, she was homebound and became progressively less able to function in the coming years. Thus, this terrible personal disaster occurred in the midst of Weatherford's efforts to save Blue Ridge in 1933 and his work with the YMCA Graduate School. It was a very hard time for him.

With Baber's position vacant, Weatherford used his relationship with the University of North Carolina's distinguished sociologist and liberal

Howard Odum to secure a new professor.[150] The two had known each other through the CIC, and Odum had also taught at Blue Ridge during the 1928 summer term.[151] Writing to Odum, Weatherford noted his desire for a research professor in the "field of Social Science, who has specialized on racial problems."[152] Weatherford went on to request a "Southern" and "Christian" man.[153] He inquired into the possibility of Arthur Raper, who was in the process of finishing his Ph.D. with Odum and working with the CIC in Georgia. Weatherford knew Raper through his interracial activities and may also have known of his involvement in the YMCA while an undergraduate at Chapel Hill.[154] Both experiences would have been appealing to Weatherford. After meeting with Raper in Atlanta in April 1930, Weatherford wrote to Raper, requesting him to visit Nashville and the YMCA Graduate School.[155] But at this time Raper was just finishing his dissertation—a comparative study of farm life and migration in two black belt counties in Georgia—and believed the research could "be of value only in so far as its findings are used."[156] He turned down Weatherford's offer but concluded the letter, "Let me assure you that I appreciate the faith which you have in me and I trust throughout the years we may be able to work together in our common task of making life more abundant for men, of whatever color, in Southern communities and throughout the world."[157] Eventually, Weatherford would secure another Odum student, J. Paul McConnell, for the sociology post. According to Odum, McConnell probably was a more suitable choice than Raper, particularly because of his active religious life.[158]

Over time McConnell would bring some esteem to the school, leading a sociological study of Nashville's African American boys in 1931. This work, edited by Weatherford and with the collaboration of four other Graduate School professors and the aid of students there, was published in 1932 as *A Survey of the Negro Boy in Nashville, Tennessee.* The project covered the physical, economic, educational, social, religious, and emotional aspects of this segment of the black community. The findings revealed various difficulties African American male youths faced in terms of home life, education, economic opportunity, personal health, and justice, and at times the survey recommended steps for improvement. The book received a favorable review in the *Journal of Negro Education* from Henry J. McGuinn, a sociology professor at Virginia Union University, who applauded the study's "candor and the scientific spirit in which the task [was] approached."[159] He particularly liked that the book explained the current status of African American boys as a product of their environment rather than race, noting, "The socioeconomic factor as it relates to health is everywhere pointed out and one notes little tendency to regard health as a function of race."[160] Overall, this short study provided a good picture of the challenges Nashville's young African American males faced in the early 1930s, particularly their frustration at "existing conditions" that resulted from Jim Crow segregation.[161]

Some of the YMCA Graduate School students also pursued sociological studies of their own, examining Nashville's black population for their master's and bachelor's theses. As migration rates from southern rural areas to Nashville increased in the early twentieth century, this city proved a particularly good place to examine urban problems. According to the historian Don Doyle, Weatherford had been "Nashville's pioneer in sociological surveys," particularly with his early books on southern blacks and his participation in the 1912 Southern Sociological Congress that gathered in Nashville.[162] Weatherford passed his interest on to his students, and, as Doyle notes, these students completed "numerous" projects on the city's poor African American population and suggested "modern social welfare programs."[163] Indeed, by 1933 seven students at the school had completed their theses on this topic.[164] The quality of the school's academic program in this field is evidenced by the fact that it was granted a charter in 1933 by Pi Gamma Mu, the National Social Science Honor Society, to open a chapter.[165]

In building the Graduate School, Weatherford not only focused on the faculty but also sought to develop an intellectual community there. Over the course of the institution's history he brought in well-known figures for special lectures. One of the early visitors to the school was the general secretary of the National Council of the YMCA, John R. Mott.[166] Mott presented three lectures examining the YMCA's contributions to the physical and spiritual life of men as well as its offering to "World Christianity."[167] Weatherford also arranged for prominent theologians and preachers to visit the school in Nashville. Among these were Edwin McNeill Poteat Jr. (nephew of William Louis Poteat and minister at the progressive Pullen Memorial Baptist Church in Raleigh, North Carolina), Edgar Brightman (personalist theologian at Boston University), and Henry P. Van Dusen (professor of the philosophy of religion and systematic theology at Union Theological Seminary).[168] Poteat delivered lectures in Nashville in 1930, and these talks were later published as *Coming to Terms with the Universe: A Study in the Philosophy of Religion for the Semi-Sophisticated*.[169] These lectures posited that "man's conception of himself" and "his conception of God" had not "kept pace" with the amazing strides in the understanding of the physical universe.[170] In essence, Poteat argued that God remained relevant in this world and that people needed to expand how they thought about the divine. Brightman came for the fall lectures of 1931, and the Graduate School published these under the title *Is God a Person?*[171] Van Dusen, at the time the dean of students at Union, brought forth a series titled "Reflections on the Christian Message Today," which was later published as *God in These Times*.[172] In general, all these speakers were liberal, ecumenical Protestants who sought to connect the message of Christianity with changing intellectual, scientific, and social trends. They were trying to make an intelligent argument for continued faith and belief in God in this era of increasing skepticism. Weatherford's efforts to include such men in his educational program in Nashville exemplified his high vision for the YMCA Graduate School. It also showed that it was easier, and safer, to be a liberal on religious matters than on racial ones at the time.

Chapel services provided another venue for bringing in notable and prescient presenters. The proposed 1933 schedule for this weekly service included poetry by James Weldon Johnson, "Social Problems of Races" by Charles Spurgeon Johnson, and an update on "The Situation at Wilder" by Alva Taylor.[173] Taylor's topic was particularly noteworthy because of the labor conflict in Wilder, Tennessee, at the time. Since June 1932, the Fentriss Coal and Coke Company's mining town had been embroiled in a bitter dispute.[174] Strikes, shootings, and bombings had all taken place since then, and Alva Taylor, along with the southern radicals Myles Horton and Howard and Alice Kester, had been involved in helping workers. Taylor's opportunity to speak on this issue shows that the school was aware of such issues and was engaged in these social questions. Indeed, one of the YMCA Graduate School's professors, Dagnall F. Folger, later helped blacklisted Wilder employees find new homes when he transferred in 1934 to work for the Home Subsistence Department of the New Deal's Resettlement Administration near Crossville, Tennessee.[175]

The approach of the Graduate School was largely ecumenical and somewhat open to other faith traditions. Flowing out of the YMCA's non-denominational tradition, it was entirely Protestant in its student body and faculty. Herbert Kohn, the executive secretary of the Young Men's Hebrew Association in Nashville, however, apparently "took some training" at the school.[176] Moreover, the Board of Directors over time came to include a small number of Jews. In 1931 Weatherford recommended that the board accept Lee Loventhal and J. B. Weil. He recognized the support that Loventhal in particular had already given the college and also noted that Jews were a "large element of influence in Nashville and the South which we need behind us."[177] The support of these men and particularly the economic backing they could provide (Loventhal's family headed an insurance company in the city) would certainly have been helpful.[178] Indeed, Loventhal was soon using his own Jewish connections to solicit funds for the school. Writing to a potential contributor in New York in 1933, Loventhal argued that the YMCA Graduate School was sending out to the South and West "young men imbued with liberality of thought along religious lines, so as to break down anti-semitism that may spring up in any community."[179]

After the loss of Baber and Uphaus, the faculty made some slight progress toward diversifying and gaining well-qualified professors before financial pressures in the early 1930s really began the process of trimming down the institution's personnel. In this period the school added a male Yale Ph.D. as well as several white women to its staff, including Ruth Coble in the Physical Education Department and "Miss Brasfield" as the librarian.[180] Yet in 1934 Dagnall Folger, the Ivy League–trained professor, left to take work with the New Deal's Home Subsistence Department.[181] By May 1935 the combined faculty and staff had dwindled to eight people.[182] Times were tough, and the Graduate School had trouble paying its employees and instructors, instead providing some of the faculty "compensation" in the form of "free rent in an old tumble-down building" it owned and meals at the school's cafeteria.[183] Louise Young, a white woman working at Scarritt College, later recalled having a female friend who served as the physical education teacher at the YMCA Graduate School in this period and the hard times this woman experienced.[184] Eventually Young helped this woman by finding her a job with the Works Progress Administration. Others left over the coming year, and by June 1936 Weatherford and Herbert Sanders (the school's treasurer and business manager) were the "only ones left."[185]

In the fall of 1936 the financial troubles of the YMCA Graduate School finally peaked as the school lost its building on Nashville's Twenty-first Avenue South to Vanderbilt University. Ten years earlier, the YMCA Graduate School board had authorized the construction of this facility.[186] This move was made even though the school did not have all the funds in hand to pay for the project. Roughly $300,000 in subscriptions—from individuals as well as southern Associations—still remained uncollected. To help pay the building costs the YMCA Graduate School borrowed $350,000 from Vanderbilt, expecting that once the construction was under way, the pressure to complete the project would provide leverage in securing outstanding donations. As the Great Depression came and deepened, however, the Graduate School could not secure all this money or find other adequate sources. By 1935 it still had over $200,000 in "uncollected subscriptions"; approximately three-fifths was owed by local Associations in the South.[187] At the same time, though some progress had been made on the school's debt to Vanderbilt, $155,000 was still owing. The Graduate School could not pay this money, nor could it pay the interest on the principal. Negotiations for making the YMCA Graduate School officially part of Vanderbilt were undertaken but broke down in the spring of 1936. In the end, Vanderbilt took possession of the former's building, Weatherford and the YMCA Graduate School board sold their exceptional library to Fisk, the winter quarters of the school ceased to exist, and Weatherford retired from the YMCA.

Besides the obvious pressures of the Great Depression, which made fund-raising nearly impossible for Weatherford and the school, several other factors contributed to the institution's demise. Despite successfully getting money from individuals and philanthropic organizations, the school was never able to raise a very large endowment. Indeed, it is unclear if it ever really had an endowment. As late as 1935 Weatherford was complaining of how he was still working simply to raise money for the annual operating budget when he really needed the "freedom to undertake the larger task of the endowment."[188] If that mission had been accomplished, the interest from these funds could have helped with the school's annual expenses and given Weatherford more time to administrate and teach. Yet it was just too hard to get money in this period, even for someone as able at fund-raising as Weatherford.

Another problem for the school was the lack of support from Y Associations in the South, specifically state and city organizations. Weatherford was continually frustrated by their apathy toward the school and interest in training YMCA secretaries. In 1936, as the school was at the brink of collapse, these groups provided only $6,000 toward the cause.[189] As Weatherford later commented on the school's collapse, this lack of financial support "illustrates the fact that the Southern Association did not believe in advanced training for secretaries sufficiently to put themselves squarely behind it, when the going was hard in their own associations."[190] Weatherford concluded these groups did not share his zeal for an educated secretariat.[191] Local Association leaders without advanced training may also have feared for their own job security if this education became standard. In short, Weatherford thought his vision for educating and preparing secretaries was too advanced to gain the necessary support from his fellow YMCA employees. What Weatherford did not recognize was that he was fighting against trends larger than just reluctant southern Associations, as the YMCA as an institution was on the decline in this period.[192] The same problems that had led to Blue Ridge's earlier foreclosure were at work at his school. All the drive and energy Weatherford brought to making these ventures succeed could not overcome this greater drift.

There is also one other reason for the financial pressure on the Graduate School. In 1933 the YMCA Graduate School borrowed $60,000 from the Life and Casualty Insurance Company of Nashville.[193] As it turns out, this money was used to buy the Blue Ridge property when the Blue Ridge Association for Christian Conferences and Training went bankrupt.[194] Indeed, the Y school took on increased indebtedness in this already financially strained period to save the other institution. Though Blue Ridge and the Graduate School were closely connected and such a move did have benefits for the latter, this action only exacerbated its money troubles. Weatherford himself recognized this complication, observing to a Blue Ridge board member, "I do not know whether I made a wise move in burdening the Y.M.C.A. Graduate School with $60,000 of debt in order to save Blue Ridge or not."[195] Nevertheless, he chose to do it, and this decision further pressed the Graduate School's balance sheet.

While the loss of the building ended the YMCA Graduate School's program in Nashville, the school did not technically cease functioning in 1936. The summer quarter at Blue Ridge continued for some years, at least until 1944.[196] At the commencement address in August 1936, Weatherford noted that the school was not dead and it would "continue to devote" efforts to the task in "the summer study at Blue Ridge."[197]

Even more interesting is that Weatherford set up a relationship between Blue Ridge and Yale Divinity School in this period to continue "training religious workers."[198] As noted earlier, Weatherford had been offered a job by Yale in 1924 but had turned it down to stay with the Y school. Yet Weatherford maintained close ties with the northern school in the years that followed, and there existed something of a pipeline between the two, as

Weatherford funneled some of his most talented students there. For example, Dagnall Folger had taken courses for two years at the Y school while completing his master's at Vanderbilt in the 1920s, and he returned to teach at the YMCA Graduate School in 1930.[199] He finished his Ph.D. in religious education at Yale in 1931. An M.A. graduate (1922) of Weatherford's school, Karl Zerfoss, also went on to Yale to complete his doctorate in the same field before moving on to George Williams College in Chicago for a career as a professor.[200] Jim Hardwick, who connected with George Washington Carver while in the YMCA Graduate School's 1923 summer term, attended Yale Divinity School for further studies, spending a year there in 1926.[201] Thus, this link between the two schools led Weatherford to make the logical move to develop an arrangement with Yale after the Y School lost its building in Nashville. The deal stipulated that the YMCA Graduate School's summer quarter at Blue Ridge would now be recognized by Yale for credit.[202] In addition, some of these students would then go to Yale for the fall and spring semesters, and Yale would help provide scholarships for their education. In 1937 twelve students from Blue Ridge went to Yale. Among this group would be Weatherford's own son, Willis Jr., a recent graduate of Vanderbilt.[203] Another noteworthy aspect of this cohort was that it included white women. Agnes Highsmith, a graduate of Wesleyan College in Macon, Georgia, along with at least one other woman, also became part of the Blue Ridge group at Yale.[204] Highsmith finished at Yale, as did Willis Jr.[205] This relationship between Blue Ridge and Yale lasted until at least 1939, but after that records do not reveal any further connection.[206]

The story of the YMCA Graduate School provides another avenue into understanding the boundaries of southern liberalism in the 1920s and 1930s. Despite the fact that the school did not advocate sweeping changes to southern racial conditions in the course of its existence, it did begin to have an effect on the attitudes of southern white secretaries and aid in the professionalization of this group. This was particularly the case among those who went to work in the college setting. By 1934, though 21 percent of the South's overall YMCA workers had received training from the YMCA Graduate School, more than half of the student secretaries had gone there.[207] While they were far from being radicals, they were sympathetic to the troubles of southern blacks and interested in working to improve conditions. In certain settings, even such a moderate stance was significant.

The experience of one former student of the Graduate School who went to work at a local branch of the YMCA in Vicksburg, Mississippi, gives some sense of how awful things could be at this time. Edgar Torrence (1934 M.A. graduate) wrote to Weatherford in July 1934, beginning his letter, "Since I came to Mississippi I have contacted the most unreasoning prejudice against the Negro imaginable."[208] He went on to explain how he had been castigated for calling the black washerwoman "the Colored Laundry Lady," adding that "everybody jumped on me—they said 'no nigger could ever be a lady.'"[209] Torrence also related a chilling tale of how the older white man who worked in the YMCA's locker rooms had nonchalantly revealed to him "three hair-raising stories about three 'damn niggers' that he had helped hang," telling his tale "just as calmly as I would tell a bed-time story."[210] Torrence was aghast at the situation there and wanted Weatherford's advice on how to proceed. As he put it, "If I let it be known that I am sympathetic to the Negro, it will probably put me on the spot, and make me unpopular with the very people with whom I have to work and associate."[211] Weatherford decided not to provide any guidance in letter form but made plans to speak with Torrence when the latter came to Blue Ridge that summer.[212] Torrence's sympathetic but cautious approach to race relations seems typical of the graduates the YMCA Graduate School produced. Extreme instances like this probably would have reinforced Weatherford's cautious gradualism.

Weatherford's years as president of the school were particularly hard ones for him, and they had a profound influence on the rest of his professional and personal life. His wife was stricken twice by major illnesses, pleurisy in the mid-1920s and the severe reaction to a rabies serum in 1933 that left her an invalid for her remaining years. The closing of the YMCA Graduate School's home in Nashville was a devastating blow for Weatherford. His passion had been given to making the school succeed in these painful years. Perhaps this explains why Weatherford would hold such a grudge against Vanderbilt's Chancellor Kirkland.[213] After 1936 Weatherford increasingly threw his attention and focus to Blue Ridge and the summer working staff there. He came to see that that work would be his most lasting contribution. Weatherford also took on other employment in Nashville, going to Fisk University in 1936, where he stayed ten years teaching religion and raising funds for the school. But from 1919 to 1936 the YMCA Graduate School was where his soul lay. Here he taught his students to be engaged in society with their hearts, heads, and hands. Weatherford's dream for this failed school is summed up well in his last commencement speech, in 1936: "To this end I charge you that you must be real thinkers; you must be leaders of those who are intellectually blind. You must be seers in the real sense—of seeing into the mysteries of God and interpreting those truths to men. To this end the Y.M.C.A. Graduate School has been dedicated. It has not been much interested in the secretaries' tricks of trade; it has been profoundly interested in developing insight, understanding, conviction, religious dynamic."[214]

Like Weatherford's administration of Blue Ridge, his running of the YMCA Graduate School represents the limitations to his liberalism. Despite the progressive and ambitious vision for this school that would professionalize the southern YMCA and prepare trained leadership for its institutions, this dream was not fulfilled. For all the interest and work in the field of race relations through classes on the topic and interactions with African Americans and black higher educational institutions, Weatherford continued to move gradually on this issue and at that time refused to challenge the larger structural problem of racism: Jim Crow segregation.

5

A Liberal but Never an Activist

During a critical period of the Civil Rights movement in 1964, Weatherford wrote, "In the present race struggle what a victory the South could achieve if we just had judgment enough and courage enough to come clean and quit fighting a fair chance for the Negro."[1] Weatherford was nearly ninety years old at this time, and by this point had lived long enough to see Jim Crow's hold on this region begin to loosen. In the same year he also recorded another comment regarding his extensive involvement in race relations. He noted, "I am one of the few men who has worked intimately with the Race issue for 53 years and yet have never gotten to some bitter fight over the issue."[2] While both these statements reveal Weatherford's lengthy and continued concern with this subject, the second remark illuminates a striking truth. Weatherford was clearly very proud that his efforts had not brought him into "some bitter fight," but he missed the implication that he had never pushed the issue hard enough to invite serious conflict.

Despite a scale-back in his involvement in racial issues after 1946, Weatherford remained a part of the conversation and active in this work.[3] Indeed, a few of his contemporaries lauded his activities in the late 1950s and early 1960s. In 1957 Benjamin Mays favorably reviewed what would be Weatherford's last published work on race relations, *American Churches and the Negro,* concluding, "Most men become conservative with the years and do not take courageous positions—not so with W. D. Weatherford."[4] In this book Weatherford called for the churches to catch up with the federal government's *Brown* ruling and desegregate their congregations.[5] Mays's appraisal of Weatherford's continuing liberal voice carried weight, particularly since Mays had been a longtime civil rights activist as well as a mentor of Martin Luther King Jr. Wilma Dykeman made a similar argument in her biography of Weatherford at the time, noting that his "liberalism" had increased with his age and citing Mays's comment in support of her view.[6]

While there is some validity to these statements, one should not be misled into thinking Weatherford stood on the cutting edge of the Civil Rights movement of the 1950s and 1960s.[7] In these years Weatherford remained a racial liberal, as evidenced by his support of the *Brown* decision, efforts at desegregating schools in western North Carolina, and insistence on the churches' taking a leading role in the equality struggle. Nevertheless, Weatherford did not take an active part in the nonviolent and civil disobedience efforts (the marches, sit-ins, boycotts, arrests) that were so crucial in dismantling segregation and what King called "unjust laws."[8] Compared to the more influential black figures of the Civil Rights movement of the 1950s and 1960s, such as Ella Baker, Rosa Parks, Medgar Evers, and King, and white activists, such as Myles Horton, Will Campbell, Clarence Jordan, Virginia Durr, and Ed King, Weatherford never displayed any urgency in pushing for immediate changes.[9] Instead, Weatherford's strategy remained to work within the legal system, pursuing the same gradualist approach he had taken all his life, which focused on educating and persuading whites of their responsibility to African Americans. In short, Weatherford always remained a liberal but never became an activist.[10]

To get some sense of Weatherford's evolving racial liberalism, it is important to understand what his views were in the late 1920s and how they shifted over the coming decades. In this earlier time Weatherford still accepted southern society's segregated order, maintaining his belief that whites and blacks could live in "parallel civilizations." A 1927 survey on racial attitudes he completed provides a more specific understanding of where he stood on particular issues. For example, on the question of whether "the Jim Crow law should be abolished," he responded, "It would be unwise to do so for the sake of [the] Negro at present."[11] To another inquiry regarding sexual relations between blacks and whites, Weatherford affirmed his belief that the "integrity of all races [is] important."[12] Yet in responding to this same questionnaire he also displayed several progressive views for the time, remarking that "Negro women should be protected" (presumably from rape by white men) and that industrial jobs should be open to all persons regardless of color; supporting interracial gatherings; writing that it is "nonsense" to think that "the Negro is foreordained to be a servant to the white man"; disavowing the idea that "the mind of the Negro is essentially inferior to that of the white man"; and advancing the view that African Americans should be provided with both vocational and professional educational opportunities.[13] Nevertheless, in 1927 Weatherford had still not yet reached the point where he could rec-

Willis Weatherford, probably in the 1920s. (Courtesy of Weatherford Family Papers)

ognize that true social justice for African Americans could not be obtained until Jim Crow was overturned.

In the coming years Weatherford slowly began to broaden his perspective. In 1933 a man from Eastern Kentucky State Teachers College inquired into Weatherford's thoughts about African American adolescent delinquency and the segregated school structure. At this time Weatherford noted, "Under present conditions, separate schools for Negroes and whites seem to be necessary in all sections of America where there are large numbers of the two races living side by side"; however, he did admit, "Where there is a comparatively small number of either one of the groups, it is perhaps possible to have mixed schools."[14] The implication here is that

Weatherford was not a strict segregationist, conceiving of the prospect of desegregated schools in some situations, a pretty progressive view for the time. His support for a dual education program was pragmatic rather than based on any idea of African American inferiority. Segregated schools in his mind were needed because he worried how black and white students would get along together; he believed that if the numbers of the minority group (either black or white) were small, then tension was less likely. Weatherford's perspective was not completely out of step with the progressive mainstream at this point, as even the radical W. E. B. Du Bois in these years recognized segregated schools might sometimes be necessary until blacks in an integrated setting could receive treatment, respect, and educational opportunities equal to those of whites.[15] Still, Weatherford's concern was more with how whites might react to such schools, worrying that pushing things too much or too fast might "upset" the progress that had been made on race up to this time.

Up until the early 1930s Weatherford had had very limited experience with black students, and most of this contact was at the collegiate or graduate level. But this changed significantly in 1936, when he took a job at Fisk University in the wake of the YMCA Graduate School's closing that spring. Organized soon after the Civil War by the American Missionary Association (AMA), Fisk—by the time Weatherford gained employment there— had become a well-established, historically black college in the South.[16] The AMA, founded in 1846, had been one of the earliest and most significant of the missionary agencies that sponsored educational programs for southern African Americans. Besides its relationship to Fisk, this society had been responsible for creating Hampton Institute, Berea College, Atlanta University, and what later became Dillard University. Fisk itself was formed on a "broad Christian foundation" and was started primarily to prepare African Americans to be teachers in the South following the end of slavery.[17] Along with Atlanta University, Fisk would have been one of the best southern liberal arts schools for African Americans to attend at that point, having W. E. B. Du Bois (1888) among its distinguished alumni.

The choice of Weatherford, a white man, to work at a black university had some precedent in this period. Indeed, it had been fairly common for a number of white liberals—male and female—to serve in historically black schools and colleges before this time. In fact, the administration and teaching at these learning centers had often been done by whites from the era of their founding (most after the Civil War) through the first quarter of the twentieth century. Increasingly, however, the trend had been moving toward more African American faculty and administrative control of these institutions, and this was particularly so at Fisk. In 1936 black professors made up one-half of its faculty, and by 1945 they constituted two-thirds of it.[18] By 1946 the school also had appointed its first African American president, Charles Spurgeon Johnson.[19] Thus, though it was not unprecedented for a white man like Weatherford to take a position at Fisk, the hiring of white faculty by black schools was becoming less common in this period.

The fact that Weatherford was also a Southerner apparently made his place there even more unusual. According to his later recollections, when he "first went to Fisk [he] was the only southern white man on the faculty and many of the students resented [him] being called."[20] A recent Fisk graduate of this period and later a distinguished American historian, John Hope Franklin, provides some sense of the context of this time and what it meant for Weatherford to take a job there.[21] Franklin completed his undergraduate studies in 1935, and in the fall of 1936 returned to teach history while in the midst of his graduate work at Harvard University.[22] Franklin recalled of Weatherford's move to Fisk: "Weatherford came out to Fisk and taught, you see, when that place [YMCA Graduate School] folded up. . . . The town was very incensed. People were very upset that this man would come. You know, it goes to show his colors, he was never straight. He must not ever have been straight. One, to write a book on race relations, which was a similar kind of statement, and two, to come over there and teach."[23] Because of Weatherford's involvement with African American higher education and his work in race relations at this time, Franklin viewed him in positive terms as an exception to white Southerners in general. In 1966 Franklin would describe Weatherford as "one of the truly important Southerners of our time."[24]

Weatherford's decision to work at Fisk also reveals something very important about his view of African Americans. Specifically, he believed a liberal arts education was appropriate for this racial minority. At this time many southern whites considered educating blacks to be "dangerous" because they feared it radicalized them. At best the only preparation some whites favored for African Americans was a vocational program that would prepare them for manual labor and service work. Only a very limited number of the more liberal-oriented southern whites would have supported a place like Fisk, since it provided a classically styled education that included Latin, Greek, and higher mathematics.

Weatherford himself, since his entry into race relations in the early 1900s, had also largely been a proponent of industrial training for blacks, particularly lauding the work of the two most widely known schools of this nature, Hampton Institute and Tuskegee Institute. In 1910, in his discussion of African American education in *Negro Life in the South,* he had declared, "If we are to be fair to ourselves, fair to the section in which we live, and fair to the negro race, we must see that a common school education is provided for all, that an industrial training is given to the majority, and that a more thorough and complete training shall be given to the capable few who are to become the leaders of this race."[25] Despite his emphasis on vocational training for the "majority" in this earlier period, this statement also reveals that Weatherford—even at that point—did not completely reject liberal arts and professional educations for blacks.

Indeed, over time Weatherford came to actively support the classical educational approach for African Americans. Between 1925 and 1929 he served as a trustee for Atlanta University.[26] A few years later, in a 1933 article published in the *Journal of Negro Education,* he declared, "Every phase of life and activity demands of the Negro the same thorough training that is demanded of whites."[27] Within a segregated world Weatherford considered that just as whites needed education to prepare their doctors, teachers, lawyers, dentists, and ministers, so too did African Americans. Thus, Weatherford's taking employment at Fisk was significant because this action further exhibited his interest in the professional education of blacks. It also represented another important shift in his work along the lines of race. Whereas he had worked before *for* blacks, he was now working *with* them, and as a white man, Weatherford now found himself in the minority.

At Fisk, Weatherford put into practice his interest in black higher education. Later in his life Weatherford reflected on why he had taken the job at Fisk: "I had written [four] books on [the] Race Problem, had visited scores of Negro colleges, but I wanted to have long intimate contact with an exceptionally advanced group of Negroes to find out just how capable they were, and to see whether I could really help a group of such Negroes to achieve real leadership. It was a chance to teach Negroes both on the undergraduate and graduate level and in the field of Phil. and religion."[28] Weatherford's comment that he wanted "to find out just how capable they were" reveals he may have had lingering doubts about black students' academic ability. Yet Weatherford probably would had attributed environmental conditions—lack of educational opportunities and access to teaching materials

Willis Weatherford during his time at Fisk University. He is in the bottom row, third from the left. To the right of him is W. J. Faulkner, Fisk's dean of the chapel. (Courtesy of Weatherford Family Papers)

and ill-equipped instructors—as the explanation for this situation, rather than any innate inability to learn on their part. Weatherford's ten years at Fisk had a powerful effect on him. He would later declare, "My experience at Fisk gave me a new appreciation of the struggle on the part of Negroes who want to be real leaders of their people."[29] This close association with African American students and many black faculty helped him develop more empathy for this minority group and better understand the difficulties they experienced living in the South in those years.

Fisk's strong academic reputation as a school for African Americans was a major drawing point for Weatherford. Fisk had steadily been raising its standards throughout the early twentieth century, and in 1930 it became the first black college that the Southern Association of Colleges and Secondary Schools accredited with a class A status.[30] Thus, Fisk at this time was certainly one of the outstanding colleges in the South for African Americans, and Weatherford was always interested in first-class institutions and students.

Weatherford's decision to seek employment at Fisk was also fairly logical in light of his circumstances. In 1936 he was at a particularly low point in his life. His dreams for the YMCA Graduate School had been dashed. His second wife was an invalid. Writing to a friend in early August of that year, Weatherford noted that he had received "a very good offer" from Fisk that was appealing because "it opens the way for me to continue things I have been doing; it keeps me in Nashville where my home is and it gives me freedom for the entire summer for handling Blue Ridge."[31] In another letter, to William J. Hutchins, president of Berea College, he also acknowledged this option, adding that it was a "rather remarkable opening in educational work."[32] Therefore, going to Fisk allowed Weatherford to remain close to his wife and Nashville activities and gave him the flexibility of spending his summers at Blue Ridge. Weatherford's long relationship with Fisk during his leadership of the YMCA Graduate School also certainly played a part in the invitation and its acceptance, as did the school's Christian foundation. Started with this heritage, Fisk maintained a religious background through the early twentieth century, even preparing many of Nashville's black ministers.[33] Considering Weatherford's strong faith convictions, this emphasis would have weighed heavily in any employment decision he made.

The exact terms of Weatherford's hiring are not documented, but it can be assumed from his later tenure at Fisk that he was brought there to raise money for the school, strengthen and develop its Religion Department, and teach in that field.[34] Until around 1940 the vast majority of Weatherford's service to Fisk was in fund-raising, securing financial contributions to the university endowment as well as bringing in funds for its Religion Department. In particular, Weatherford spent the fall term of 1939 exclusively trying to help the college reach its $3,000,000 endowment goal, of which $450,000 would be designated to support Fisk's Religion Department.[35]

With his long experience in fund-raising, Weatherford was skillful at this task, and he employed many of the same tactics on Fisk's behalf that he had used on Blue Ridge's and the YMCA Graduate School's. Weatherford appealed to many of the same organizations that catered to race relations work, particularly the Rockefellers' General Education Board, and he also made trips to New York City to meet with key donors.[36] Moreover, in his efforts at Fisk—like his work for other institutions—he played up the need for religious training. From his perspective, African American students desperately needed this type of education; he observed to one potential contributor, "There is great danger that the Negro will turn away from religion" because many educated blacks found the "emotional gospel" they had been raised on increasingly unsatisfactory.[37] Moreover, Weatherford feared that "many of the more intelligent Negroes feel that Christianity has failed" because of the prejudiced—or at the very least, apathetic—attitude numerous so-called religious whites held toward blacks.[38] Thus, Weatherford hoped that religion could be presented to Fisk undergraduates in a more logical and rational manner, which would help these students build what he considered a mature faith. Writing to one benefactor in 1939, Weatherford pointed out, "It is therefore imperative that in our colleges which are training Negro youth, religion should be presented as ably and as sanely as science, or mathematics, or economics. The rising generation must be shown that religion is a vital part of life, and that even the crude emotional form which he has known are testimonials of man's eternal search for God."[39] In many ways, this was the same angle Weatherford had taken when he tried to offer an intellectually respectable faith to white youths while working with the college YMCA in the early 1900s.

Similar to Weatherford's insistence that Blue Ridge and the YMCA Graduate School were critical to improving the South and race relations in the region were Weatherford's pleas regarding Fisk. For example, Weatherford ended one of his letters to a prospective donor in 1940 with the following words: "Fisk is in the South; it is of the South. It is trying to fit students to become leaders of this great minority group in the South."[40] In another instance Weatherford appealed to the Tracy McGregor Fund of Detroit to help Fisk develop a program for training librarians for African American elementary and secondary schools.[41] He hoped that this organization, which had aided white education in the South already, would, "in another section of the South, do an equally unique and far-reaching service for the educational life of the Negro."[42] In Weatherford's way of thinking, the South, white and black, needed Fisk.

It is unclear exactly when Weatherford begin his teaching on the Fisk campus, but it is apparent that this task became a more important and time-consuming function over the course of his service there. The available evidence indicates his classroom duties began at least by 1938, but it may have been earlier.[43] In that year he was appointed a "Lecturer in Religion and the Humanities" and was expected to teach one introductory humanities course each semester as well as philosophy of religion in the fall and ethics in the spring.[44] Weatherford was paid $1,000 for this work, which implies that he was still probably doing a good amount of fund-raising for which he must have been compensated separately. This humanities course—two semesters long—became a staple of the Fisk curriculum during Weatherford's time and was required for all sophomores.[45] The class was a broadly based history of thought, culture, and religion, one that had "taken the place of the old required courses in religion."[46] As an instructor, Weatherford particularly highlighted the importance of religion in his classes, noting that he hoped to "show all students that religion is an organic part of all normal life."[47]

Gradually, Weatherford's teaching load and involvement in the Religion Department grew over the late 1930s and early 1940s. He went on to become the department head, worked to build a religion graduate program, and helped sponsor extension programs for local African American ministers. By 1940 he was lecturing for four classes, Monday, Wednesday, and Friday.[48] Amid his teaching the following year he was also in the process of searching to find another professor who could teach both undergraduate and graduate students—in fact, someone who could "take charge of the department," as Weatherford expected to retire in "three or four years."[49] In 1943 Fisk's Board of Trustees granted Weatherford tenure and appointed him "Professor of Religion" with a salary of $4,000.[50] Around this time Weatherford was also trying to recruit African American students to Fisk's master's program in religion, both men and women.[51] Indeed, he went on to encourage one young woman from Hampton Institute to consider it, an action that indicated Weatherford's confidence in the academic ability of black women and showed just how far he had moved since 1910, when he referred to all black women as "girls" in *Negro Life in the South*.[52]

In the same period Weatherford was reaching out to the local black community, particularly African American ministers, through workshops and visits to black churches. He helped coordinate both a clergy-training group that met weekly and a summer ministers' institute.[53] These activities reveal that he wanted these ministers to adopt a more "respectable" and learned religious tradition and practice. Through all these activities it is fair to say that Weatherford was trying to impart his conception of Christianity—a liberal, middle-class version—to students and ministers. Weatherford had come to believe this was the soundest form of faith, and, like most people who consider that something is true for themselves, he assumed this version to be best for others as well.

Documents from Weatherford's files at this time indicate that he took a real interest in his students, remaining supportive of them through their years at Fisk and as they moved on to further education and work. Weatherford wrote numerous recommendation letters for them and maintained an ongoing relationship with some even after he left the university in 1946. From the surviving records it appears Weatherford took most notice of those who pursued religious studies and Christian vocations. For example, in 1943 Weatherford wrote to Drew Theological Seminary in New Jersey and Yale Divinity School in Connecticut trying to get E. P. Williams, a Fisk religion graduate student and local pastor, into their programs.[54] A year later Weatherford again used his connections to Yale to recommend a black woman to its theological school.[55] Weatherford also knew another Fisk graduate and minister, Curtis Holland, whom he kept in contact with for nearly a decade and helped with educational and job opportunities.[56] Holland apparently had been one of Weatherford's students in the Religion Department and went on to graduate work at Boston University (the school of the personalists to which Weatherford had strong ties). Over the years Holland continued to ask for Weatherford's advice about work and scholarship, and Weatherford maintained this relationship through the late 1940s.[57]

It is also clear from the correspondence Weatherford kept from these years that many of his students were appreciative of his support and teaching. One woman, Mildred Armour, wrote to Weatherford in 1942 after transferring to Howard University how much she had "enjoy[ed] Humanities, and especially the method in which [he] taught it."[58] In 1944 Frances Clark sent Weatherford a note expressing her thanks to him for his "interest" in her and help with securing a scholarship.[59] She concluded her letter, "I wish to thank you for your kindness again and I'm looking forward to seeing you in the fall."[60] Clark was majoring in religion and was interested in completing her M.A. in that field at Fisk as well.[61] Another student, Mercedes Martin, who had to leave Fisk because of a "nervous break down," wrote to Weatherford to thank him for his "offer to help" and to update him on her decision not to return to Nashville.[62] Two other students also sent Weatherford letters after he left Fisk in the fall of 1946 to note their gratitude to him; one commented, "Fisk is quite a different place this year without you and though you may enjoy your stay there [Berea College] we miss you no end."[63]

Two other connections Weatherford developed at Fisk also attest to his devotion to his students there. First, Weatherford built a relationship with the daughter of W. J. Faulkner, the school's dean of the chapel. Josephine Faulkner, an undergraduate at Fisk, went on to earn her M.A. under Weatherford and later asked him to perform her wedding ceremony, which he did.[64] According to Weatherford, this was a notable invitation. He observed: "I don't know of many white men who have officiated at Negro weddings. I was glad to be asked to do it."[65]

Weatherford's connection to Josephine Faulkner was probably the result of his close relationship to Dean Faulkner. Undoubtedly contributing to their bond was Faulkner's previous YMCA background and career.[66] Faulkner had received part of his education at Springfield YMCA College in Massachusetts. Besides that institutional tie, they obviously also shared an overall religious outlook as well as similar social concerns. Faulkner, however, was a more progressive and active figure on racial and peace issues than Weatherford. In the mid-1940s he was a member of the Fellowship of Southern Churchmen and of the Southern Council of the Fellowship of Reconciliation, and president of the Nashville branch of the NAACP, groups that would have put him among southern life's radical edges.

Weatherford also developed a relationship with another Fisk faculty member's child. Patricia Johnson, the daughter of the sociologist Charles Spurgeon Johnson, took her humanities course under Weatherford and went on to serve as a "reader" for him for the 1943–44 school year.[67] Weatherford described her as "a first class student—absolutely straight—courageous and well behaved."[68] When Wilma Dykeman later interviewed Johnson for her biography of Weatherford, Johnson recalled that Weatherford had not necessarily been "an easy person to know" but that she had appreciated the "academic discipline" he had imparted as well as his traits of "kindness, sympathy, and understanding."[69] Johnson apparently also asked Weatherford to perform her wedding, but Weatherford had to decline because of a conflicting appointment.[70] Nevertheless, what is important to take away from Johnson, Faulkner, and these other students' connections to Weatherford is that he clearly believed in Fisk and its mission and treated these black students as he did his white students. Despite his lifelong support of Tuskegee and its vocational approach to education, it is incorrect to think he approved only that instructional style. His actions at Fisk indicate his faith in African American educational ability and achievement in a classical humanities curriculum.

Of course not all of Weatherford's students at Fisk were happy with him, and his middle-class notions at times caused him to be judgmental of them. Weatherford particularly imposed his conception of what he thought "culture" meant on his pupils and held them to very high standards of behavior and scholarship. Reflecting on the Fisk students of this time, he later wrote:

> I believe the student body as a whole ranked well with most student bodies in native ability—save in their background experience. Most of them had come from better than average homes as to income—but their cultural experience was very low. To illustrate 75% of every new class came to my class room chewing gum. They were very sensitive to cultural status—I always told them by the end of the first week that no cultured man or woman chewed gum in public places. That stopped most of them. I also had to struggle with boisterousness—loud talk etc. Their home environment just did not give them cultural standards.[71]

Weatherford's vision of "cultural standards" was heavily influenced by his Protestant, middle-class perspective, and he saw his role as a professor as not only including giving attention to academic excellence but also imparting his Victorian behavioral standards on those who passed through his lectures.

As a result of Weatherford's strictness, a few issues appear to have developed. In particular, some students had concerns about his grading. One of these, Betty Grayson, in late May 1943 wrote to Weatherford about her disappointment in receiving a D in the spring humanities course.[72] As Grayson put it, "My mid-semester grade was a B and from the knowledge I gained in Humanities I know that I do not merit a D."[73] Though records do not reveal how this dispute was handled, the following fall semester another grading issue developed into a major problem. In November of that year Cora Emerson, a student at Fisk, got married (taking the new last name Reese) while in the midst of completing Weatherford's humanities course. Apparently in that term portions of the class were taught by different professors. Reese had not passed the music section, and for Weatherford's segment of the course she never took the exam. The following year she made plans to graduate and approached Weatherford to see if she could write a paper to make up his section of the class and receive credit for this required course. Weatherford would not allow this option but offered instead to let her take the exam. Apparently she did not follow through on this opportunity, and in the spring of 1945 she again inquired into the possibility of writing a paper to receive credit for humanities. Weatherford held to his earlier position, but this time he went to her home (she was sick at the time) to administer the test. After Weatherford graded it, and even allowed another religion faculty member to evaluate it, Reese still did not pass. Thus, Weatherford handed in a failing mark for her, one that he knew would prevent her from graduating.[74]

Yet things did not go as Weatherford expected. On commencement day Reese still received her B.A. Weatherford was incensed. He quickly wrote to President Jones to complain and inquire how this had occurred. Jones responded to him that the dean of the college, Alrutheus Ambush Taylor, had contacted him shortly before graduation and had assured him that Reese had enough credits to graduate without needing to make up her humanities grade.[75] Apparently this explanation did not satisfy Weatherford because Jones again wrote to him several weeks later with a copy of a letter from Dean Taylor containing "information that was probably not available to you at Commencement time."[76] This note does not survive, but whatever its contents were, it still did not assuage Weatherford's frustrations. In early July Weatherford sent a letter to his friend Frank Porter Graham, president of the University of North Carolina at the time, about this incident.[77] Weatherford posed the following scenario to Graham: "If a full professor fails to give any senior a passing grade in a course required for graduation in an A grade institution, can the dean or any other officer arbitrarily pass that student and permit him to graduate?"[78] Graham's response is also unavailable; nevertheless, Weatherford continued to hold a grudge over this issue, retelling this story to Wilma Dykeman as she prepared to write his biography nearly twenty years later.[79]

Weatherford's dissatisfaction over this episode stemmed from several causes. For starters, he had very high standards and wanted Fisk to live up to these as well. In his original complaint to President Jones he had commented, "I have heard a great deal of talk at Fisk about maintaining standards and I have done my best to help in this matter. If this type of procedure is to be winked at, then I feel that professors might just as well hand in 'A' grades for all students and not bother about examinations."[80] Indeed, the evidence available suggests that Weatherford's perspective has merit, particularly since the student had not passed a required course and had still been granted her degree.

Yet personal issues, as they often do, also factored into Weatherford's strong reaction and lasting frustration. To begin with, Weatherford believed his authority had been challenged, something he did not ever take lightly. Moreover, as a full professor who had made multiple efforts to give Reese the chance to earn credit for the course, he felt someone had gone over his head to allow her this concession. Still, even more pertinent to Weatherford's discontent was his low opinion of Dean Taylor. Weatherford wrote the following of him nearly twenty years later:

> The academic Dean—a PhD from Harvard was a black Negro who had evidently *"eased through"*! He had low scholarship standards—spent most of his evenings playing cards or just visiting. The last year I was there he passed a girl I had *failed* in a required course and gave her the degree. Had I stayed on I would have reported it to the Sou. Association of Schools and Colleges which might have cost Fisk her membership in that organization. It's a fact we have to face with patience and some degree of tolerance—they are not yet mature in many cases.[81]

Weatherford's disdain for Taylor reveals both some lingering racism on his part and his desire to impose his Victorian, middle-class worldview on others. His use of the word "they" is clearly racist because he was singling out a racial group as having a certain trait, in this case what he perceived as a lack of maturity. The reference to maturity also had racist undertones because whites had often thought of African Americans as childlike. Weatherford's other comments display classism. He had a strong dose of the Protestant work ethic in him, and his expectations of others were very high, at times unrealistic. In this case he took issue with how Taylor spent his nights socially, thinking that this lifestyle did not make Taylor a serious scholar. But Weatherford was unfair to Taylor. Besides being dean, Taylor was a historian on the faculty. By this point in his career he had published three books on African Americans in the South during Reconstruction, one as recently as 1941.[82] Taylor had received his B.A. from the University of Michigan and his graduate education at Harvard.[83] Before completing his Ph.D., he had been mentored by Carter G. Woodson and served for three years with the Association for the Study of Negro Life and History. In the 1940s Taylor was also probably working on his massive history of Fisk, which totaled more than 865 pages by the time he completed it in 1952.[84] In short, Taylor appears to have been no intellectual slouch.

Taylor's connection to Woodson may also provide another reason for

Weatherford's contempt, as Weatherford had some history of bad relations with Woodson. In 1924 Woodson reviewed Weatherford's *The Negro from Africa to America* rather harshly, closing with the statement "One may call the work a book of ill-assorted quotations together with a number of unwarranted opinions and conclusions."[85] Woodson had also been critical of some of Weatherford's earlier books on race relations. Woodson, and the scholarship on black history that he supported, stood as a challenge to the Dunning School, a group of historians who had dominated white academics' writing of southern history of the Reconstruction era.[86] In general, Weatherford accepted a variant of the Dunning School's interpretation, considering that Reconstruction had been largely responsible for the "antagonisms" between whites and blacks in that period and afterward.[87] In a 1936 review of Woodson's *The Story of the Negro Retold,* Weatherford had taken issue with what he thought was Woodson's "bias against all white people," commenting that in this book Woodson had not given "any credit whatever" to any "modern whiteman."[88] He added, "A history that is written with so much bias can hardly be called history." It is clear from their respective assessments that each did not hold the other's scholarship in high regard. Thus, even though Weatherford never discussed Taylor's specific scholarly work, the type of history Taylor wrote and his relationship to Woodson undoubtedly played a part in Weatherford's critical view of Taylor.

A year after the Reese episode Weatherford retired from Fisk, ostensibly to serve Berea College as a fund-raiser and an assistant to its president.[89] This decision coincided with President Jones's own retirement and the naming of Fisk's first African American president, Charles Spurgeon Johnson, who would assume this position in the fall of 1946. At first glance one may wonder if Weatherford's leaving was due to this change in leadership and some discomfort in the fact that Johnson was taking over.[90]

In fact, such a suspicion is not unwarranted, as Johnson and Weatherford did see racial concerns differently. Perhaps the clearest example of their conflicting perspectives on this subject comes from the 1934 college textbook *Race Relations: Adjustments of Whites and Negroes in the United States,* in which the two collaborated. In this text they expressed divergent views on the possibility of maintaining—as well as whether there should be—separate black and white cultures and races in America. Weatherford articulated his view that racial integrity and distinct cultures were very important.[91] At the time he could not imagine that "amalgamation" of whites and blacks, or for that matter of any other racial groups, as being positive.⁹² Indeed, he went so far as to use "scientific" evidence to show that the "crossing of races" in South America of an "Indian and Negro" and of "white and Indian" had produced an offspring that was "inferior to both parent races."⁹³ But in truth, Weatherford was only an amateur anthropologist, lacking formal training in this field. Johnson, a true sociologist, on the other hand, viewed the issue from a much more realistic perspective, considering the idea of maintaining a separate black culture in the United States "an impossible dream."⁹⁴ For Johnson it was not a question of good or bad, as Weatherford had made it, but one of realism based on scholarly knowledge of cultural interaction and history. Johnson understood that mixture of the races and cultures was inevitable.

Still, while Johnson and Weatherford differed on this major point, they both could nevertheless be broadly described as gradualists on race relations. Even though Johnson did not want to wait indefinitely to see changes take place, he recognized they probably would not occur quickly. He ended his last chapter of *Race Relations* by acknowledging, "A race problem is scarcely ever settled within a generation. Despite the discomforts on the one side and the anxieties on the other, the mills of the gods grind exceedingly slow. Perhaps, no one living today will see the end of either the discomforts or the anxieties."⁹⁵ Weatherford's approach to this issue had long been slow and steady. In one of his sections of *Race Relations* he commented, "What ten thousand years may bring forth we do not know, but for the present, amalgamation does not seem to offer any satisfactory solution."⁹⁶ Clearly, Weatherford's gradualism was much slower in form than Johnson's. Thus, a divide existed between the two regarding the pace of change.⁹⁷

While the differences between Weatherford and Johnson's race relations philosophies are readily apparent, however, the available evidence does not support the view that Weatherford left Fisk because Johnson was to be the new president, or even because of his dissatisfaction over the Reese affair. It is clear that Weatherford had a good relationship with Johnson's daughter and that he also held Johnson in high regard. Weatherford later commented, "Charles Johnson who was later elected the first Negro to be President of Fisk, was a[s] open minded and fair as any man I ever knew."⁹⁸ Considering Weatherford's personality and style, we can be certain he would not have offered such a compliment if he had thought otherwise.

In truth, Weatherford had actually been making plans to leave Fisk many years before his eventual departure at the end of the 1946 spring term, and long before Johnson was ever named to the Fisk presidency. In

1935 Weatherford had begun building a retirement home on a mountain peak above the Blue Ridge conference property.[99] This decision indicates he intended to depart Nashville in the coming years and make North Carolina his permanent residence. In 1941, while attempting to recruit another member for the Fisk Religion Department, Weatherford had also noted to his friend Gordon Poteat of Crozer Theological Seminary that he hoped to "retire some three or four years from now."[100] A year later he was trying to secure a secretary for his work at Blue Ridge, noting, "I am planning to move my home to Blue Ridge after two more years."[101] In 1944 Weatherford would have turned sixty-nine years old, well into retirement age.

Weatherford chose to stay on at Fisk through the spring of 1946, however, largely because of his interest and investment in its Religion Department and his desire to find a suitable replacement.[102] In early January 1946 Weatherford sent his letter of resignation to President Jones, even though Fisk's chief administrator and Weatherford's fellow members of the Religion Department apparently were urging him to remain.[103] On insisting that "it would not be good for the cause of Fisk for [him] to continue here," Weatherford pointed out several reasons why, including his commitment to Berea and job offer there; that his remaining would set "a bad precedent for retirement" at Fisk; and that the department already had five professors and it would be better for this group to have a chair "who will plan to stay a number of years."[104] At this point Weatherford had before him two options, one with Berea College and another with Wake Forest College near Raleigh, North Carolina, presumably also in fund-raising.[105] In the end he left Fisk at the close of the spring term of 1946 to accept the position in Berea, where he would spend his remaining years.

During Weatherford's time at Fisk, his racial views had gradually and slowly begun to change. In the midst of this experience with African American higher education, he had begun supporting the need for some political efforts to improve race relations and the status of southern blacks. In 1938 he gave his approval to the federal antilynching bill because, as he noted to a friend, even though he felt there had been "a tremendous amount" done to "reduce" this activity, "as long as lynching goes on and there is no prosecution of lynchers, we need to take more drastic action than we have."[106] In 1942 Weatherford applauded the overturning of a Georgia peonage law by the U.S. Supreme Court, commenting to the lawyer who had argued the case, "I am highly pleased that this law that I have always considered to be unjust and unfair has been declared unconstitutional."[107] Weatherford also came to recognize that the tactics white Southerners used to disenfranchise black voters needed to end. In the early 1940s he endorsed a federal law to abolish the poll tax, even writing to Tennessee congressman Al Gore Sr. in 1943 to encourage him to vote for its repeal.[108] Weatherford supported this action because of his involvement in the Southern Conference for Human Welfare, a progressive group of southern liberals that had begun meeting in 1938 to address the South's economic and social issues.[109] Weatherford remained on the periphery of this organization, never taking an active role in its leadership, but his connection to it and his support of these other activities still placed him among this period's leading southern progressives.

Also attesting to Weatherford's prominent place among southern liberals of this era was his participation in the Carnegie-Myrdal study on race. In 1939 he, along with "a limited number of carefully selected individuals of prominence," received an invitation to submit to one of the project leaders their autobiographical accounts of how they came to enter race relations.[110] This study, eventually published in 1944 as *An American Dilemma: The Negro Problem and Modern Democracy,* was led by the Swedish social economist Gunnar Myrdal and financed by the New York Carnegie Corporation. The tome, made possible through the aid of dozens of researchers and assistants, totaled nearly 1,500 pages and took almost five years to complete. Along with the numerous facts on the history and conditions of African Americans and white attitudes toward this group, Myrdal insisted there was a "dilemma" that characterized American society.[111] On the one hand, Americans celebrated and held to an idealistic view of freedom and equality for all, a view that grew out of the country's founding documents and heritage. Yet at odds with this vision was the truth that many whites—southern and northern—thought they were superior to African American people. Myrdal, nevertheless, was optimistic that American higher ideals would eventually win out, and that the long-standing structures of racial discrimination would pass away.

Though Weatherford was requested to submit a summary of his race relations involvement and history, his contribution was insignificant, perhaps because he was almost overwhelmed with other work at the time. Weatherford sent in a ten-page sketch he titled "My Experience in Race Relations"—something he admitted to a friend was rather hastily written on a rainy day while he was traveling in Washington, D.C.[112] In this short paper Weatherford revealed a certain optimism and pride in his race relations work, highlighting particularly his activities at Blue Ridge and the YMCA Graduate School, as well as his written works on the subject.[113] *An American Dilemma* does not seem to have pulled anything directly from Weatherford's reflection piece, and, indeed, his other published works are cited only a handful of times; most citations are from his and Johnson's recent *Race Relations* textbook.[114] Nonetheless, his invitation to participate shows that he was viewed as a key player in this field at the time.

During the late 1930s and early 1940s Weatherford also remained active in the Commission on Interracial Cooperation, later becoming a charter member of its successor organization, the Southern Regional Council.[115] The Chapel Hill sociologist Howard Odum had been the driving force behind this new group, nearly getting it off the ground in 1938, before the Southern Conference on Human Welfare, New Deal programs, and World War II sidetracked his idea.[116] During Odum's initial planning stage, in 1938, he consulted with Weatherford, seeking his support and ideas, and invited him to take a place on the national committee of this emerging organization.[117] Weatherford was interested in the prospects of this new agency, which would expand the work of the CIC, adding a broader attention to economic and rural life to the CIC's emphasis on race relations. Odum believed this regionalist approach would address the interconnected problems of race and economics.

The Southern Regional Council, however, was not organized in the way Odum had expected. Indeed, it developed by a rather circuitous route that grew out of the efforts of Jessie Daniel Ames—director of Women's Work for the CIC and executive director of the Association of Southern Women for the Prevention of Lynching—to reinvigorate the CIC in this period.[118] Ames had partnered with Gordon Blain Hancock, the African American Virginia Union University sociologist, to aid in this process. Using this connection, Hancock had helped organize a group of fifty-seven southern black men in Durham, North Carolina, on October 20, 1942, that put out what became known as the "Durham Manifesto." This document acknowledged that these men were "fundamentally opposed to the principle and practice of compulsory segregation" but also conceded that it was "both sensible and timely" to focus then on specific problems of racial discrimination rather than trying to end Jim Crow.[119] In subsequent interracial meetings following this declaration, as white leaders of the race problem attempted to respond, Ames's plan to hold the CIC together was thwarted, as Odum's regionalist scheme seemed to fit the mood of the times. Thus, Odum's vision would finally take effect in the fall of 1943 and early winter of 1944. The new group would attempt to be more biracial than the previous CIC, yet at its inception it still would not call for an end to segregation, a fact that would hamper this organization in the coming years.[120]

The issue of segregation was a major dividing point among white southern liberals. Many were fearful that pushing too hard against this institution would disrupt the progress that had already been made. Yet for those who favored challenging this structure, Jim Crow was seen as the key impediment to further progress on race. They felt that equality could not exist within a segregated society, and this system had to be abolished.

Until this time Weatherford himself had been unwilling to publicly call for ending Jim Crow. Nevertheless, there is strong evidence in 1943 to suggest he began to entertain the notion more seriously. In June of that year he attended the First Annual Institute of Religion at Howard University's School of Religion.[121] This conference brought together sixty professors, ministers, and theologians from twelve states, fourteen colleges and universities, and nineteen churches to examine the topic "The Christian Imperative and Race Relations."[122] The participants primarily were African American, coming from historically black colleges and congregations. Weatherford, as the head of Fisk's Religion Department, was invited as that university's representative. He shared with the others in attendance a Christian emphasis and a recognition that his faith compelled him to address this critical social issue.

At the gathering, different groups met to hear and discuss particular papers during the day; the entire body convened in the evenings and on the last day for further conversation and debate. From this general assembly a statement was issued with several proposals. This declaration included the following words: "It is our judgment that race relations in America do not conform to the demand of the Christian ethic. The differentiation of peoples by the mere fact of race, however equal the treatment, falls below the demands of the Christian ethic. We, therefore, cannot give our endorsement to any proposals which seek merely to improve existing conditions while, at the same time perpetuating the pattern of subordination and superordination. The Christian ethic admits no pattern of behavior which denies the essential dignity of personality."[123] The resolutions adopted by the institute were wide-ranging but focused particularly on the role Christian leaders and the church had in improving racial issues. The conference body specifically called for "equality of membership and fellowship" among races in local congregations; it demanded "that the churches teach the truth about the myth of racism and remove from all their methods and materials whatever tends to inculcate this myth and to include the facts about the contributions of non-white peoples to culture and civilization." It went on to "propose the use of mass action by church groups . . . in protest against definite and concrete evils in the community."[124] Moreover, it encouraged churches to "employ legal action for the repeal" of racist laws and "the altering of such legal practices as block justice and prevent racial minorities from enjoying their rights"; urged "every minister . . . to exercise his rights as an American citizen, recognizing the risks involved and that he encourage others so to do"; and pressed churches to provide "encouragement" and financial support to those "leaders who unselfishly and courageously work for a fundamental change in the present state of race relations."[125] Finally, the conference statement addressed the American economic system, questioning "seriously whether" the Christian ethic can be practiced "in a true sense under competitive capitalism."[126] In effect, the institute's pronouncement challenged segregation and supported civil rights activism, calling for the church to lead the fight in ending this structure.

Weatherford's exact reaction to these declarations is unclear. Other than noting his presence in leading one of the morning's devotions, the "Proceedings" do not mention his name.[127] Yet the wording of the institute's concluding statement leads one to suspect that it represented the group's consensus.[128] Furthermore, since Weatherford's personality and vocal style did not lead him to remain quiet when he disagreed, it seems safe to presume he was in general accordance with the institute's pronouncements. Indeed, Weatherford's notes from this meeting indicate that he may have taken part in drafting some of these resolutions. On one page headed "What do we want to do?" he wrote,

> We desire to establish the principle that there be no forced segregation in society or any of its phases. The Christian ethic demands that every person should be required to accept this principle as a basis of membership in the church. It demands also that every candidate for the ministry shall be required to accept this bearing of the Christian ethics. That the church should teach the truth about the myth of race. That the church apply this principle of equality of races in running its institutions—educational, economic, etc. The church should use

its influence to remove all laws which violate the rights of minorities according to the Christian Ethic.[129]

These strong words look very similar to what the institute produced at the conference's end.

The subject of nonviolent resistance was also discussed at this gathering. In particular, on another page of Weatherford's notes, he jotted down a reference to the "March on Washington program of non-violent disobedience."[130] Beginning in 1941 A. Philip Randolph had formed the March on Washington Movement (MOWM) as an all-black nonviolent protest group that intended to gather in the nation's capital to press for civil rights.[131] The initial event in 1941 was canceled after Randolph secured an order from the Roosevelt administration preventing companies holding defense contracts from discriminating against African American workers. Nevertheless, Randolph's organization continued to remain active, and in the summer of 1943 it had made plans for another march. Weatherford's notes relate to this latter affair, and they imply a somewhat hesitant endorsement of this approach, pointing out that participants who break laws must be willing to face the consequences. He wrote, "We suggest therefore that any who[se] conscience forces them to obey a higher law of love, must do so with a full determination to submit to whatever the laws of society may impose, in the spirit of Jesus Christ, for in so doing we believe they will best demonstrate the truth of their position."[132] In the end, Weatherford and the institute's declarations did not result in any major achievements, but this gathering did represent a growing movement to end segregation. Though it remained uncertain how far Weatherford would go to make these resolutions a reality, he apparently was contemplating a world without Jim Crow.

Weatherford's increasing support of political solutions related to preventing racial discrimination in the 1930s, and his tentative consideration of ending segregation in the early 1940s, raises an important question: Why was this shift in his thinking occurring at this time? These things began just before 1940, when Weatherford would have been nearly sixty-five years of age. For over thirty years during which he had been a spokesman for better race relations, he had always accepted segregation and steered clear of political solutions to these problems. What could explain such a major change?

It appears that Weatherford, as a gradualist, was in a lot of ways staying with the progressive current of the times by taking these stances. A new wave of growing black protest had developed in the 1930s and was picking up steam by the early 1940s.[133] The 1930s had been a time of tremendous strain for the United States. The Great Depression had stretched the lives of many Americans, and for Southerners, black and white alike, the economic woes that already existed were exacerbated. President Roosevelt's New Deal approach to the Depression had raised new issues, particularly regarding how these programs and funds would be available to African Americans. Thus, new solutions and actions were being taken. In particular, the conditions during the Depression of southern agricultural workers briefly brought together blacks and whites in Arkansas in the Southern Tennant Farmer's Union (STFU) in the mid-1930s, when sharecroppers and tenant farmers were evicted from farms or denied funds from the Agricultural Adjustment Administration.[134] The STFU proved to be a short-lived enterprise, but it demonstrated how racial groups could coalesce around common labor concerns and signaled the new energy of this period. By the end of the 1930s the issues of the South would also be further highlighted as the region became identified as the "Nation's No. one economic problem."[135] In response to that assessment, the Southern Conference on Human Welfare had organized and convened in 1938 in Birmingham, Alabama. Of the mainstream reform efforts it would be the largest and, as the historian John Egerton notes, "was far and away the most significant attempt by Southerners, up to that time, to introduce a far-reaching agenda of change and improvement to their native land."[136]

During the mid-1930s another important aspect of black protest had also developed. In this period the NAACP took on new life. In particular, it increased its activities to address segregation, focusing on the inequalities existing in higher education at the graduate level. Howard University Law School's Dean Charles Hamilton Houston and his young protégé Thurgood Marshall were critical on this front.[137] Their strategy, as Egerton notes, "was to compel the states to equalize educational opportunity for blacks and whites in graduate and professional schools, either by establishing expensive new programs in the black colleges or by desegregating the white institutions."[138] The basic idea was to pressure southern states to create schools that were separate *and equal,* the thinking being that the states could not afford to do so and thus would have to integrate. This approach took Houston and Marshall into several cases in the 1930s and 1940s.

One of the most important early victories they achieved came in 1938 with *Gaines v. Missouri.* In this case Lloyd L. Gaines, an African American, had been denied entry into the University of Missouri's law school because of his race.[139] The case eventually reached the U.S. Supreme Court, which ruled that the "equal" provision of *Plessy v. Ferguson* had been violated and that Missouri must set up a separate but equal law school for blacks or admit them into their established one. Still, even this case would be slow to bring changes, and it would take other ones to follow to finally bring down segregation in public education in the 1950s.[140]

Changes in racial issues were also propelled by the coming of World War II. This proved true for a number of reasons. For starters, preparation for the war, along with enlistment in military service, led to hundreds of thousands of Southerners, white and black, leaving their homes and provincial ways of life.[141] They sought jobs in new places that created new interactions and perspectives, and they fought alongside one another in a common effort, even though the armed services was still segregated at this point. Many white soldiers would later attest to the transformative nature of this experience.[142]

An even more important element driving change may have been the federal government's investment in this region as a result of the war. The world conflict led the national government to spend over $10 billion in the South between 1940 and 1945.[143] This money transformed the area, bringing new industries, training camps, and people into the region. But at the time, many of these jobs were denied to African Americans. These citizens were particularly angered by the employment discrimination they faced, and as a result, these conditions pushed forward a new form of black protest, mass action.[144] As noted before, this had played out in 1941, when A. Philip Randolph had threatened a march on Washington before President Roosevelt had capitulated.

The very purpose of World War II also put into question the prevailing racial setup of segregation in the United States. The war against Hitler and the Nazis was portrayed as a just one, where democracy was threatened by fascism and Hitler's radical views of a master Aryan race caused great unease.[145] Clearly, many Americans believed, this extremism had to be contained for the good of the world, but all these objectives seemed inconsistent with the institutionalized racism in the South, where whites were the dominant race and blacks did not experience democracy and equality. African Americans did not miss this point, either. As the historian Jacquelyn Dowd Hall notes, "African Americans and their allies were among the first to grasp the enormity of the Nazi persecution of the Jews and to drive home the parallels between racism and anti-Semitism. In so doing, they used revulsion against the Holocaust to undermine racism at home and to 'turn world opinion against Jim Crow.'"[146]

Considering all these circumstances, African Americans of all stripes—conservative to radical—were now ready to call publicly for an end to segregation. This had not always been the case. Along with Randolph's proposed MOWM in 1941 and the Durham Manifesto of 1942, the gathering at Howard University that Weatherford attended in 1943 signaled this shift.

Another issue in 1943 made it even clearer that the times were changing. At the University of North Carolina Press that year a dispute developed between its editor, William T. Couch, and the African American editor of a book to be published there, Rayford Logan. Couch was over twenty-five years younger (born in 1901) than Weatherford, and since the late 1920s had been effectively running the University of North Carolina Press. There he had helped build the strong reputation of this publishing house by putting out books on labor and race issues, from both white and African American authors.[147] In 1943 he approached Logan, a black historian from Howard University, to edit a collection of essays entitled *What the Negro Wants,* hoping to provide a wide variety of perspectives from conservative, moderate, and radical African Americans on the subject.[148] As it turned out, Couch was surprised to find all the volume's contributors wanted an end to Jim Crow, something he had not expected and did not want himself; he feared this stance might cause problems for UNC Press if put in print. Couch tried to dissuade Logan from publishing, but when Logan would not relent and threatened legal action if their contract was violated, Couch acquiesced. Couch made the unusual decision to add a publisher's introduction to the piece, trying to distance himself and the UNC Press from Logan's collection. In this rather rambling essay Couch made it quite clear that he held certain racist views, did not believe in "amalgamation" between the races, and was not ready for the end of Jim Crow. Indeed, at one point he revealed, "I believe that if complete elimination of segregation could be accomplished overnight—as many of the authors of this volume assume it ought to be—the consequences would be disastrous for everyone and more so for the Negro than the white man."[149] The fact that Weatherford was going in an entirely different direction at this point shows how a southern white liberal like him was adjusting to the changing times, and others, like Couch, were not.

Overall, Weatherford's consideration of directly challenging Jim Crow in 1943 seems to be a result of a number of factors. First, Weatherford had been serving Fisk for seven years by this point and certainly would have been more attuned to African American attitudes. Second, in 1943 the United States was in the midst of World War II and just emerging from the Great Depression. This war, just as World War I had pushed along race relations in the late 1910s, had again brought the issue to the fore. Logan's edited volume, in fact, was in part a work to show how the conditions of the war had affected African American attitudes. Black protests against segregation had grown by this point, and Weatherford's new perspective showed he was moving with the times.

Just before Weatherford's participation in the Howard conference, he also seems to have been slightly connected to the NAACP and its racial justice work, which perhaps contributed to his new perspective. His fellow Fisk faculty member W. J. Faulkner was the president of the local chapter, and in April 1943 the branch sponsored a visit from A. Philip Randolph to speak in Nashville.[150] While it is clear Weatherford received an invitation to that event, his attendance is unconfirmed. Moreover, the extent of his association with this organization, and whether he was actually a member, is also unknown. It is likely that he was not involved; he may have feared being connected to what many white Southerners would have seen as a radical organization. Nevertheless, in later years he provided some limited support to the NAACP, standing behind its Legal Defense Fund, which sought to bring racial justice through judicial cases.[151] His backing of this group would have made logical sense since he would have viewed its law-based approach as a proper and "constructive" one to changing race relations.

Weatherford's loose tie to the NAACP and his participation in the 1943 Howard gathering may also explain two of his subsequent activities along these lines. In 1946 he wrote to Bishop Paul B. Kern of the Methodist Publishing House of an "urge" weighing on his "soul."[152] Weatherford began the letter by noting his long history in race relations, even making the bold proclamation that he had "studied the question more intensely . . . than almost any other white man in America." He went on to insist that he thought the "time [was] ripe" for the "Methodist Church [to] be the instrument to bring Christianity as a whole to a new and vital outlook on this whole question." What Weatherford wanted to do was to have the opportunity, over a five-year period, to "voice this message"—the exact program was never made explicit—in all the annual Methodist conferences and in this denomination's most prominent congregations. His approach was cautious and "constructive," he assured the bishop, one he hoped could "be done with courage and directness without arousing too much antagonism." Noting that he already was working with Berea at the time and not searching for new employment, he made the point that he felt that such an approach "might have some aspects of a Wesleyan Revival, or a Lutheran Reformation."[153] Though Weatherford's vision apparently never materialized, this setback did not dissuade him from believing that the church was the best place from which racial progress could proceed.

The church and race were also on Weatherford's mind at this time because of a book he was bringing to completion. Since 1932 Weatherford had been working on a project examining the attitudes held by and programs offered by various Christian denominations to African Americans during slavery.[154] This work was just one of a series of studies on race that were in progress at this time at the YMCA Graduate School. By 1936 Weatherford had finished this "source book" and was seeking to have it published.[155] The text apparently contained ten chapters, each looking at the attitudes of a specific major denomination or, in the case of the last chapter, of "smaller denominations."[156] His efforts to get this work into print came to no avail in the 1930s, however.

Sometime thereafter Weatherford resumed work on this project. By the summer of 1944 he had completed a new draft that included the addition of a "full introductory chapter on what the leading churches are now doing and a closing chapter on the spirit and program which the hour demands."[157] In this last section, as he told one friend, he "pleaded that every Christian Church open its doors to all seekers after God without discrimination as to race, color, or creed," which he described as "my conviction of our present Christian duty."[158] Essentially, Weatherford was calling on white churches to desegregate their congregations, a very progressive idea for the 1940s. How much the Howard conference and the other larger events of the 1940s affected this view and the additional chapters in his book is unclear, but the timing of these new sections indicates there was probably some connection.

Through the mid-1940s Weatherford continued searching for a publishing house that would accept his manuscript. He returned to Nolan Harmon Jr., then of the Methodist Abingdon-Cokesbury Press (Harmon had been with the Historical Publishing Company in 1936 when Weatherford originally sent it there), as well as to the University of North Carolina Press.[159] Weatherford must have thought that these firms would now consider accepting it because of the added material, but again each organization declined. In the coming years Weatherford's study was also turned down by Doubleday, Abingdon Press, and even his old standby publisher, Association Press of the YMCA.[160] Most of these publishing houses were fearful about the marketability of Weatherford's book, a concern that perhaps was warranted. This apprehension may have been a reaction to both the work's more radical nature and the style of writing. Aside from the introductory and final chapters, the study was rather dull: the majority of the book was a chore to read. Eventually, in 1956, Weatherford made an agreement with the Christopher Publishing House of Boston to publish his book, a deal that required him to front $1,950 of his own money for the project.[161] *American Churches and the Negro: An Historical Study from Early Slave Days to the Present* was published in 1957.

An event three years before also had an effect on this final edition. On May 17, 1954, the U.S. Supreme Court handed down its epochal decision in *Brown v. Board of Education,* declaring that segregated public schools were unconstitutional. Just over a year later the Court issued a follow-up ruling proclaiming that educational institutions should proceed to integrate "with all deliberate speed."[162] Of course, the actual integration of educational facilities was still a long time in coming, and the Court's decision soon thereafter unleashed a massive resistance by southern whites.[163] White Citizens' Councils began appearing across towns and cities in the South, and by 1956 nineteen southern U.S. senators and eighty-one congressmen had signed the Southern Manifesto, declaring their opposition to the Court's ruling. Weatherford, still in search of a publisher at the time, took the *Brown* decision into consideration as he again added material to bring his *American Churches and the Negro* up to date.

This book proved to be complex and somewhat disjointed because of the two revisions that took place after the creation of the original 1936 manuscript. The addition in the 1940s, which appears to include most of the last two chapters eventually published, highlighted the context of the United States in World War II, lauded democracy, and insisted that if America wanted to maintain its prominence in the world, it needed to address its race problem.[164] These pages also showed how the churches had to act in new ways because of the changing times. After the *Brown* decision, Weatherford adjusted his book to fit with this momentous decision and its challenge to segregation. The changes Weatherford made, while making the book more relevant to the times, did not add to its readability.

The book had several objectives. In its foreword Weatherford described his fourfold purpose: (1) determine how much white churches knew about blacks and how interested they were in evangelizing this group in the antebellum period; (2) find out to what extent southern planters "understood their Negroes better than the present-day church members do"; (3) list the accomplishments and programs that the major Christian denominations were then supporting that "express interest and concern for the religious life" of African Americans; and (4) provide a call for action.[165] Weatherford intended his audience to be largely white southern church people, but in the last chapter he expanded his message to include all Americans, including blacks.[166] Thus, the fact that he appealed not only to people of the South but also to those throughout the nation justified the use of the word *American* in his title.

Weatherford made two basic arguments in *American Churches and the Negro*. First was the original point he had been trying to make in 1936, that white southern church people had treated African Americans (free and enslaved) with more concern in the pre–Civil War era than they had since then. Weatherford showed that in the earlier period slaves and whites often belonged to the same churches and worshipped together where—despite segregated seating—they sang the same songs, heard the same sermons, and took communion together.[167] Southern denominations after 1865 had become highly segregated, so there was very little interaction between white and black Christians. Thus, the implication was, Weatherford noted to one prospective reader, that present-day white Southerners "are much more indifferent to the Negro than our antebellum ancestors."[168] Weatherford saw pointing out this past "southern tradition" as a strategy for making white Southerners rethink how their churches excluded African Americans at that time. He remarked, "It is my hope that this study will show that a larger exchange of religious fellowship is in keeping with the very best traditions of the Old South."[169] Weatherford looked somewhat nostalgically at the past, downplaying the negative aspects and effects of slavery and emphasizing the religious sincerity, honesty, and "well-intentioned" motives of slaveholders.[170] His approach was very much in keeping with the way he had handled things before.

The other argument that Weatherford made came as a result of the changes taking place in the South and the world of the 1940s and 1950s. Frank Porter Graham, writing the book's introduction, acknowledged that it was Weatherford's contention that the churches needed "not only to catch up" with the federal government's stance on civil rights but "to lead the way in the building of spiritual communities of equal freedom, dignity and opportunity in local congregations and in the world neighborhood of human brotherhood under the Fatherhood of one God."[171] After a laborious treatment of antebellum church attitudes and these denominations' efforts at that time, Weatherford asserted the churches in 1957 still had a long way to go to bring about racial justice. He argued: "We are at the parting of the ways. The Christian forces of America simply must see to it that the Negro is accorded a full status of a citizen and a man. This demands a new spirit, a new attitude, a new fellowship."[172] Weatherford believed this meant that white churches should desegregate their congregations, be willing to invite black ministers as guests in their pulpits, and lead racial justice work.[173] White Christians in general should also "want economic equality, equal pay for equal work, and no discrimination in employment on account of race or creed" as well as "equal justice before the law," "equality" in education, and "*equal respect and courtesy to all men, white and black.*"[174] In short, Weatherford called for an end to segregation within the white churches and endorsed the idea that these Christians should also help lead the fight to end this institution in American society.

In *American Churches and the Negro* Weatherford addressed segregation in the same way he had always approached the issue of race relations, from a religious perspective. He believed this foundation provided the moral and practical impetus for change. As he noted to one philanthropic organization's representative, from whom he was seeking funding to make this book available for wider circulation, "You cannot change modes of thought and social action by law or force alone. There is needed an agency that can change men's minds."[175] Weatherford went on to claim that the church had "two great advantages," namely, that "it can take the religious high ground of brotherhood, and second because it is indigenous to every section of America, it speaks to each section and cannot be accused of being an outside voice in any section."[176] In particular on his second point, as a longtime Southerner, Weatherford realized the risk of being labeled an outside agitator.

Beyond his belief that the church was the best agent of change, Weatherford also considered its place in society to be at stake if it forswore its responsibility to address racism. Weatherford felt that a new attitude toward race relations was critical to the "future of Christianity."[177] Indeed, he was very much concerned about the church's image and its status in the social order, perhaps more so than about what was actually being done for blacks. In 1956 he commented to one friend, "I am greatly concerned lest the churches should lag behind in the forward movements being made in interracial understanding. That, it seems to me, would be a calamity, which religion cannot afford to have come about."[178] Religion was always above any other single issue for Weatherford.

Weatherford wrote *American Churches and the Negro* in a style very similar to that of his other books. Once more he was trying to educate whites (but this time not only Southerners) about past and present conditions and call for action. Yet what made the book different from his previous works on race was that in it Weatherford recognized that segregation must be attacked in the churches and in society. Circumstances had changed—particularly with the effects World War II and *Brown* had wrought. Nevertheless, Weatherford offered no political program to dismantle Jim Crow, nor did he make any mention of opposing the Southern Manifesto.[179] He also remained focused on what whites could do for blacks, rather than on what the two groups could accomplish together. Whereas such an approach had been at the forefront of southern liberalism in 1910, when he published *Negro Life in the South*, this was no longer the case in 1957. As events would show in the coming days, Weatherford was falling behind the curve.

The book, nevertheless, was reviewed favorably in a number of newspapers and periodicals at the time. As stated earlier, Benjamin Mays lauded it. Yet in truth Weatherford had solicited this review from him to be published in the *Christian Century* and also to be used in a number of African American newspapers because Weatherford recognized Mays's "name . . . carr[ied] weight."[180] Mays agreed and in subsequent correspondence noted to Weatherford, "The book will do a lot of good and it should be widely read."[181] Another African American scholar and a personal friend, W. J. Faulkner from Fisk, also wrote an affirmative review of it for the *Chicago Defender*.[182] Several white liberals commented positively on the book as well, among them the UNC playwright Paul Green, UNC sociologist Guy B. Johnson, and Wake Forest College Christian ethics professor G. McLeod Bryan.[183]

Yet there was one critical review—by H. L. Puxley, a Canadian minister, writing in the *International Review of Missions*. In particular Puxley questioned Weatherford's assertion that antebellum white church people "were more Christian than present-day churchmen in their attitudes toward the Negroes."[184] Puxley thought Weatherford was so clearly trying to prove this point that he may have "predetermined" his argument, choosing only the evidence that fit his thesis. His review was also sharply critical of Weatherford's last two chapters on the Christian denominations' present programs and his "call to action," which Puxley described as "sketchy and disappointing to the extreme." In fact, he called Weatherford's closing chapter "pathetic," particularly because it offered "no specific programme" other than urging whites to recognize African American Christians as their brothers and sisters. Puxley thought, in the context of Canada, that this idea was hardly a new concept. Puxley even considered some of Weatherford's practical suggestions to be condescending. He concluded his three-page critique by exclaiming, "Can a Boston publishing house honestly mean its dust-cover claim that this book makes 'an important addition to race literature?'"[185] But despite Puxley's insightful remarks, the book was certainly progressive for its time in the South.

Even before it had been published, Weatherford had decided its topic necessitated wide readership among church members. As a result, he determined to get it into the hands of the leaders of "all the denominations in America—2229 of them."[186] He secured an arrangement with his publisher to sell his book at about half price (dropped from $3.50 to $2) if he could front $4,458 to pay for the volumes sent to church leaders. As he had in the past, Weatherford turned to several philanthropic foundations to fund this project, this time the Harwood Endowment Fund, Cleveland H. Dodge Foundation, and Phelps-Stokes Foundation.[187] The last group, headed by Frederick D. Patterson, helped Weatherford make his plan a reality.

Weatherford also tried to get *American Churches and the Negro* into the hands of college students to be used in study groups. In November 1958 he wrote to Patterson of the Phelps-Stokes Foundation about an idea he had.[188] Before revealing his scheme, Weatherford discussed the significance of his *Negro Life in the South* and the study sessions that had developed from it in the early 1910s. Declaring, "Almost every leader of racial advance in the South comes out of that study class of the earlier years," Weatherford argued, "we desperately need to do something like that again."[189] This time he wanted to make his book, as well as James McBride Dabbs's *The Southern Heritage* (1958), the focus of such attention.[190] Dabbs was a white Southerner born in 1895, a South Carolina plantation owner with deep familial connections to the Old South.[191] He was also an English professor and a man of substantive Christian faith. Like Weatherford, he was a southern liberal, in some ways more progressive than Weatherford, having been involved in the Southern Regional Council and serving as its president in 1957 and also being a member of the Fellowship of Southern Churchmen. A few years later, when Martin Luther King wrote his "Letter from Birmingham Jail" (1963), King included Dabbs in a short list of white Southerners who "had grasped the meaning of this social revolution and committed themselves to it."[192] In fact, Dabbs's book made an even stronger call to completely do away with segregation than was found in Weatherford's work. Dabbs wrote to white Southerners insisting that Jim Crow was not necessary to their way of life, and that they should not overreact to the political and social changes being made. Weatherford approved of Dabbs's views, and Weatherford's idea was to bind their works together so they could be bought inexpensively and studied at the same time. As Weatherford noted to Patterson of the Phelp-Stokes Foundation, "Mine would give the background that looks towards the future; his would give the present situation with implications of the past." He added, "The two would make a wonderful combination."[193] Weatherford hoped such a program might reach as many as twenty thousand college students.

Weatherford's plan also included getting someone in the field to organize these study sessions in the colleges. He wanted to secure a "first class worker who could command respect in the colleges and universities" and speak in these institutions.[194] Patterson was receptive to Weatherford's idea, and Weatherford went ahead to pursue George S. Mitchell.[195] Mitchell was an economist and a southern liberal; he was also the son of Weatherford's old friend and Blue Ridge teacher Samuel Chiles Mitchell.[196] The younger Mitchell, however, declined to participate, largely because he was in retirement, living in Scotland at the time. Weatherford's overall scheme to use his and Dabbs's books also apparently did not materialize. Nevertheless, Weatherford's efforts in this regard show that he was pursuing the same line of approach he had been using since 1910, when groups studied *Negro Life in the South*. Though his method remained progressive, it was an outmoded strategy by 1959. But this was the style in which he was most comfortable. As late as 1965 he would still be pushing his book—this time toward white churches—as a helpful guide to the dilemmas churches faced as a result of the Civil Rights movement.[197]

Weatherford also promoted another of his old standby strategies in the 1960s in an effort to resolve racial problems. In 1963 he aided in organizing a YMCA interracial gathering of two hundred college students in Miami, Florida.[198] Roughly a quarter of these students were African American, and according to Weatherford and one student participant, it proved to be a "significant" event.[199] Weatherford worked to raise money for a follow-up conference in 1964, one that would, he hoped, bring together four hundred students for a five-day meeting to "study . . . the problems that face students, with extra emphasis on the imperative urgency of our achieving racial equality and good will."[200] Not surprisingly, Weatherford viewed this approach as "the most constructive way to meet this [racial] situation in the South."[201] Overall, these interracial conferences and the projected study groups connected to his and Dabbs's books would be the closest thing to a program Weatherford ever developed in the 1950s and 1960s to improve the South's racial problems.

Through the 1960s Weatherford also pursued other means of helping the South come to terms with the Civil Rights movement. His most concrete effort was pushing for the integration of western North Carolina schools. In these years Weatherford was a member of the Asheville Area Council on Human Relations, a local offshoot of the Southern Regional Council. In 1962 schools in this region of the state were still segregated, which led to poor educational opportunities for the small minority of African American students there (6 percent of the population of these counties).[202] Because of the separate black and white school systems in these counties, many black students attended one-teacher schools or were forced to travel over one hundred miles each day for class. If black students could go to the local white schools, it would be much more convenient for them and would also be less expensive than supporting dual schools systems. Weatherford favored desegregating these white schools, considering this step to be very logical and reasonable; he even met with North Carolina's Governor Terry Sanford at the time on this subject.[203] Weatherford's participation in such an organization as the Asheville Area Council on Human Relations to implement desegregation shows he remained a pragmatic gradualist. He was working in one area to address an overwhelmingly logical concern.

As late as 1965 Weatherford continued to work for school desegregation, this time in the broader sense of the entire South. Writing to Paul Anthony of the Southern Regional Council that year, Weatherford commented:

> I am thoroughly and absolutely in accord with the demands of the courts with reference to desegregation but I have dealt with these problems long enough to know you cannot change a whole society, particularly when it pertains to their biases and prejudices. You cannot do it even in a year so I hope we won't be too impatient with the people in their local communities for we have all sorts of people to

deal with. I have deep sympathy for the school superintendent who is dealing with this problem of desegregation. Of course we know that is right and the people would be wise to live up to what the Government demands but it is mighty hard for some of them to see it. So, my counsel is to summon as much patience as we can and deal constructively with the non-conformists.[204]

Here Weatherford clearly indicated his support for school integration, yet he also evidenced his continuing gradualism. Moreover, he in essence showed he was more sympathetic to the whites dealing with the changes than blacks who were pushing for their rights.

Weatherford's approach to confronting racial inequality raises the question of how he viewed Martin Luther King Jr.'s activism in these years. While the historical record does not contain any of his direct comments regarding King, it can fairly be surmised that Weatherford would not have found his methods the most satisfactory.[205] The civil disobedience program of King—and others to the left of him—was never one with which Weatherford felt comfortable. He had spent his whole life—he was seventy-nine years old at the time of the *Brown* decision—pursuing a gradualist plan, being careful not to provoke backlash from southern whites. Changing by this point for him was difficult, if even possible.

Nevertheless, though he may not have approved of these methods, it appears Weatherford did respect King. Following King's winning of the Nobel Peace Prize in 1964, a dinner in Atlanta was held in his honor, which two of Weatherford's friends attended. Writing to Weatherford soon after this event, Rachel Schilling noted, "I'm sure you would have enjoyed being there," implying that he must have viewed King positively.[206] Moreover, Weatherford and King shared a common theological basis in personalism.[207] King had completed his doctorate at Boston University under the influence of this school of thought. Indeed, the language King used in his "Letter from Birmingham Jail" about the sacredness of personality was nearly identical to the words Weatherford often employed. Specifically, King discussed in that letter his hope that the South would one day be a place "where all men will respect the dignity and worth of human personality."[208] Overall, the major difference between King and Weatherford was not in their goals for racial equality but in their strategies and their desired pace of change.

Weatherford's last public comment on race came in a *Charlotte Observer* article published on December 2, 1966. Celebrating his ninety-first birthday at Emory University in Atlanta, Weatherford observed to a reporter, "Significant progress has been made in race relations in recent years."[209] He went on to note, "But we're going to have to go a lot further."[210] Thus, even after the federal legislative gains of 1964 and 1965, he still saw that work needed to be done. This observation was rather remarkable for a southern white man who was raised in the Jim Crow South and was in the tenth decade of his life.

In many ways Benjamin Mays's earlier comment was right: age had not made Weatherford more conservative on race. After the 1950s Weatherford simply looked less liberal in comparison to the leading figures involved in civil rights. Weatherford's outlook on race had clearly broadened throughout his life, even in the years after 1930. In 1932 he had been for a segregated order of society, yet about a decade later, in 1943, he began to have second thoughts about that stance. By the late 1940s he recognized that if the churches wanted to maintain their place and credibility in society, they had to combat segregation in their congregations. After the *Brown* decision, Weatherford put his support behind school desegregation and the overall goals of the Civil Rights movement. His method for ending Jim Crow always remained gradualist, focusing particularly on the use of books, educational programs, and conferences. After he left Fisk in 1946, *American Churches and the Negro* would be Weatherford's most visible contribution to race relations.

Still, there is one case in which Weatherford can fairly be criticized about his race relations work: the way in which he viewed his achievements. Weatherford was content with how he had always approached the subject. Indeed, he never, in all his writings, looked back and criticized himself for how he had handled racial issues. It does not appear that Weatherford ever considered that he should have done things differently. Moreover, he viewed positively the previous generation's race relations efforts (of which he had been a leader), focusing on the progress that had been made rather than emphasizing the instances in which liberals like himself could have pushed things further. He believed that the programs and approaches he had always used had been successful. Throughout his entire adult life Weatherford placed his faith in the power of education to bring about change. He believed that if white Americans were just better informed and educated about the past, as well as the ongoing conditions of African Americans, this new understanding would result in the end to racial problems. He did not see the need for something more radical to be done, nor did he ever endorse and place his support behind nonviolent resistance and civil disobedience. Perhaps such an outlook is a result of Weatherford's determined personality and tendency always to highlight the positive rather than the negative. Still, his views and responses to these issues differed markedly from those of the vast majority of African Americans and white activists at the time.

6

Bringing a Revival to the Mountains

In 1953 W. D. Weatherford wrote to the famed playwright Paul Green of the University of North Carolina at Chapel Hill about plans for an outdoor drama—ultimately entitled *Wilderness Road*—to be held at Berea College in Kentucky.[1] At the time, this institution was known for its unique blend of work and learning, its mission to Appalachian residents, and its tuition-free policy.[2] Berea was soon to celebrate its centennial, and Weatherford was leading the effort to have a play written and performed, to highlight and bring national attention to the college's educational program and history. In light of Weatherford's long involvement in race relations, however, it initially might seem surprising to read the following instructions he passed on to Green: "I am sure you should be free to use the dramatic incidents in the life of John G. Fee, our founder, and others; but I am equally sure we do not want a *Race Drama*. This is not Berea's chief concern. Our real concern is the Appalachian Mountain boys and girls. The race issue is just one illustration of our sense of the dignity of all persons. To that doctrine, and to do something about it, we are unalterably dedicated."[3] The "dignity of all persons"—Weatherford's basic religious conception—grew from his belief in personalism. Throughout Weatherford's life this theological grounding guided his social work, and after 1946 he would, while applying this philosophy, direct most of his activities to the concerns of Appalachia.

Despite Weatherford's instructions to Green, racial concerns had actually been a vital part of the Berea heritage. From the school's founding through 1904 it had included male and female African American and white students, there being at least as many black students as white before 1893.[4] Indeed, for nearly its first half century of existence, interracial education was central to Berea's mission, which made the college a very unusual place in this period of southern history. The college's motto, "God has made of one blood all peoples of the earth," also spoke to its founding principles. Yet in 1904, during the "nadir" of southern race relations, the Kentucky legislature passed the Day Law, which made it illegal to educate white and black students together. Berea, after losing its appeal to overturn this act, stopped admitting African Americans.[5] In the coming years, the university turned instead to a commitment to the white young men and women of the Appalachian region, intensifying a trend already under way since the early 1890s when it was begun by its president William Goodell Frost.[6] By the time Weatherford wrote to Green in 1953, Berea was just beginning to reintegrate, having started this process in 1950.[7] Nevertheless, the college's well-established mission to mountain students at that point had become its primary concern, and the school's integration moved slowly in the coming years. Weatherford's suggestion to Green only further illuminates how Berea's chief constituency at this point remained overwhelmingly white Appalachian students.

The college's shift in emphasis in the early 1900s parallels a similar one that took place in Weatherford's own life in the 1940s. Just as a concern for the Appalachian region came to overshadow Berea's commitment to African Americans, the same was true for Weatherford after 1946. Leaving Fisk University in that year, Weatherford put the greatest part of his energies into serving Berea and white Appalachia's needs. Yet, as his 1953 letter to Green reveals, what connected Weatherford to this new interest was his religious belief in "the dignity of all persons"—the very idea that had impressed on him the need to do something for African Americans in 1908. Overall, Weatherford's Christian convictions made him feel a responsibility to address Appalachia, and just as these beliefs—along with his middle-class values and faith in the power of education—had kept his race-related work and achievements within certain boundaries, the same proved to be the case in this field as well.

Indeed, there were many similarities between Weatherford's Appalachian work and his previous efforts in race relations. Weatherford saw Appalachians as members of a minority group too, ones who were underprivileged and exploited and who needed better opportunities. Just as it was difficult for him to recognize that African American social justice could not be obtained without ending the structures of racism, however, it was hard for him to see that addressing Appalachia's larger economic issues had to be tackled before the region's poverty and social problems could be more fully resolved. And in both cases his plans relied heavily on the dissemination of information about these constituencies to the wider public. Once these data were known, he assumed, change would follow.

In Appalachia, Weatherford believed the combined forces of education and religion could bring a revolution. In his view, the church—both within and outside the region—had a special role to play in improving this area. In particular, Weatherford wanted to revitalize mountain churches, making them more vibrant, efficient, and "respectable"—a vision comparable to his earlier efforts for religion in the first decades of the twentieth century when he worked for the collegiate YMCA. Weatherford also trusted that education would help these residents rise above their plight. Overall, he hoped that he could aid in bringing a renewed sense of worth to these people, and as a liberal in the classical sense, he was optimistic progress could be made.

Weatherford's interest in bringing pride to white Appalachians, however, represents a slightly different focus from that he had had with southern blacks in earlier times. In fact, Weatherford's race-related activities and books were seldom (particularly in the years before 1934) directed toward African Americans and building their self-esteem. Instead, he intended mainly to change southern whites' opinions and assumptions about blacks and their culture. Weatherford's advocacy for southern mountaineers, though, was targeted at those both within and outside the region.

Yet Weatherford's clear devotion and sincere concern for this region and its people were colored by a certain paternalistic attitude as well. Writing from his home, Far Horizons, in 1964 to Wilma Dykeman, Weatherford revealed the following thoughts and images:

> As I write this morning (Feb. 19, 1964) I look out from my mountain top through a picture window on a world glistening white with snow. Every mountain, every tree, every shrub speaks of beauty. But I cannot help seeing in my imagination thousands of little families of children huddled around small fires in dingy rooms all through these mountains—and I know they can hardly see the glory of the world through their darkened windows. When will the school and the church, and all the host of us who have had better opportunities wake up to the crying need of these boys and girls in the mountains—and do something to bring to them inspiration and the light of life. Or will this whole generation of boys and girls have to grow up in ignorance, poverty.[8]

Weatherford, nearly ninety years old by then, understood this region's challenges and believed he and other privileged individuals had a responsibility there. In 1946, at age seventy, when most people had retired, Weatherford dedicated his time and energy to Appalachia. In that year he became assistant to Berea College's President Francis S. Hutchins, initially serving primarily in fund-raising and student recruitment. Over the next twenty years Weatherford's involvement in this school and in the region expanded. Indeed, by 1960 one supporter of Weatherford's was referring to him as "the Albert Schweitzer of the mountains."[9] Weatherford's efforts in this section of the country would culminate in his leadership of a major scholarly survey of Appalachia (published in 1962) and his attempts to implement development programs as the region received national attention during the presidential administrations of John F. Kennedy and Lyndon B. Johnson.

In spite of his intense focus in the years after 1946, Weatherford and Appalachia had long been connected. In fact, Weatherford's parents were both natives of the southern highlands, a point he increasingly emphasized as he worked in this region and tried to connect himself with its people. Late in life he recalled the childhood stories his mother told him of her youth there and how these tales influenced his own interest.[10] During his collegiate years at Vanderbilt he studied Appalachian literature under William Baskervill and "occasionally took excursions" into the mountains.[11] In the midst of completing his dissertation, and while working for the YMCA, Weatherford and his first wife spent the summer of 1904 vacationing in western North Carolina, getting to know the residents on the North Fork of the Swannanoa River.[12] Weatherford was fascinated by his experience with these people and developed a certain attraction to the area. Indeed, his trip there played a significant part in his decision to build the South's YMCA conference center in Black Mountain, North Carolina, just a few years later. In 1914, the third summer Blue Ridge operated, Berea's President William Goodell Frost spent a week there, apparently finding Weatherford's setup rather appealing. According to Weatherford's recollections, Frost observed: "You are doing the same thing we are at Berea, namely combining work and study. But it seems to me you are even getting more out of it than we are. You must come on the Berea Board."[13] So Weatherford soon joined the college's Board of Trustees, remaining through 1963.[14]

Weatherford's involvement with Berea before 1946 would be steady but never intense. In 1919 Frost, who was retiring and helping find his own successor, recommended Weatherford for the presidency.[15] Weather-

Willis Weatherford with a group of children in 1959. (Courtesy of Willis D. Weatherford Papers, Southern Historical Collection, Wilson Library, University of North Carolina at Chapel Hill)

ford declined because he was committed to the YMCA at this time and its southern training school in Nashville. Still, Berea's religious, moral, and labor style continued to appeal greatly to him in the coming years. In 1939, as he gave a welcoming speech at the induction of Berea's new president, Francis S. Hutchins, Weatherford laid out his concern for the state of moral and religious instruction in U.S. colleges and universities. Speaking candidly, he said, "American education is making a determined effort to produce a generation of religious morons—and I must say I believe is succeeding well."[16] At Berea he noted, however, "We believe profoundly that education without moral and religious instruction is a misnomer."[17] Since 1930 Weatherford had been increasing his stake in Berea, becoming chair of the Board of Trustees in that year and of its Educational Policy Committee in 1935.[18] As retirement age came and went in the early 1940s, Weatherford felt that he owed Berea his undivided attention.

Weatherford's initial role at the college was largely in fund-raising.[19] In these years he teamed up with Bruce Barton, a fellow Berea trustee and a famous advertising figure of this generation, to gather support for the college.[20] Barton had made a name for himself at the school during the William J. Hutchins administration (1920–38) by writing a letter to twenty-four businessmen that apparently was 100 percent successful.[21] In this letter Barton played up the "pure blooded English" background of Berea's clientele and the possibilities for achievement of this "raw material," in "contrast to the imported stuff."[22] In matters of fund-raising Barton would refer to Weatherford as "a sort of combination of John the Baptist and Joan of Arc" because of his crusading efforts and zeal for Berea.[23] Weatherford, while not using xenophobic arguments on the college's behalf, nevertheless was always sentimental about Berea's mountain students and their backgrounds. Writing to a possible donor in 1950, Weatherford described the institution in the following terms: "Berea College was established almost one hundred years ago to help educate the boys and girls of the Appalachian Mountains. We choose 90% of our students from these mountains. These boys and girls are largely of Scotch ancestry, and are a hardy, upstanding group. All they need is education to make them a real asset to America."[24] Weatherford had a tendency to idealize these people and went on to do so in a book he published as part of Berea's hundred-year anniversary in 1955. In *Pioneers of Destiny: The Romance of the Appalachian People,* Weatherford gave a popular history of the Scotch-Irish who settled this region. For the most part, Weatherford accepted what the Appalachian historian Richard B. Drake has called the "Celtic Thesis," a view that Appalachia was peopled primarily by Scotch-Irish and other English "backcountry" immigrants who, by bringing their distinct ways of living there, defined the region's culture from that time forward.[25] By showing what Weatherford considered to be these people's exceptional characteristics, *Pioneers of Destiny* illustrated the constituency Berea served. Weatherford also used this emphasis in a very pragmatic manner, as a tactic to help raise funds for the school. Still, by this time, Weatherford seems to have forgotten the college's early mission to African Americans.

Nevertheless, Weatherford remained an excellent fund-raiser and "salesman" for Berea. One of the ways he accomplished this feat was by emphasizing his own personal connection to Appalachia in his correspondence, speeches, and books on the college and the region after 1946. Again and again he would note, "I'm a mountaineer," playing up his link to this section of the country because of his parents' birth there and his own experiences in the mountains while administering Blue Ridge.[26] For him, these "mountaineers" were his people, and this fact increased his investment in their lives and the region. Just as he had stressed his southern background in earlier years when trying to draw attention to race issues and gain credibility among white Southerners, now he reached out to gain support for Appalachian reform by touting his relationship to the region. Weatherford's romantic view of the mountain people of the nineteenth century also paralleled a similar view he had held of the Old South in earlier years.

Yet the Appalachian region that Weatherford encountered in the late 1940s was anything but idyllic. Though the Second World War had helped stimulate its economy briefly, this boom period did not last long. In these years the region faced a major outmigration of many of its residents, some leaving for military service during the war and others moving to northern and midwestern cities for better job opportunities.[27] Indeed, between 1940 and 1970 roughly 3 million people left Appalachia. Two major causes for this shift in population were the new, more advanced mining technologies and a lowered demand for coal. Over this time mechanization in the extractive industries increasingly displaced laborers, and a decreased need for coal after the war led to even greater cuts in the mining workforce.[28] According to the Appalachian historian Ronald D Eller, of the nearly 500,000 miners in 1945, fewer than half remained in 1960, and by 1970 this group had declined to 107,000. In the process, these industries left their mark on the environment, as unregulated mining techniques and activities "disfigured" mountains and polluted the region's streams and waterways.[29] These economic and ecological factors clearly pushed many residents from the mountains, but the possibility of better lives outside the region pulled them as well.

Yet for numerous emigrants the transition to these new places did not prove easy. Like southern African Americans who headed north during the Great Migration of the 1910s and afterward, mountaineers who journeyed to cities often struggled to adjust to the new ways of urban life, meeting discrimination from the established residents.[30] Mountain culture was typically at odds with the societies of these new places, and Appalachian migrants were at times derisively labeled "SAMs [southern Appalachian mountaineers], hillbillies, snakes, briar hoppers, and ridge runners."[31]

Those who remained at home clearly languished. Not only were mountain residents hurt by the changes occurring in the mining industries, but those who made their living through agriculture also suffered. Here also mechanization, along with increased costs of fertilizers and pesticides, made it more difficult for farmers to completely support themselves in this way of life.[32] Over the course of the 1950s, half of the farmers in the region went on to seek other employment; only roughly 6 percent of mountaineers held full-time work in agriculture by 1970.[33] Sadly, as Eller notes, "unemployment, poverty, and welfare dependence became a way of life in communities throughout the region."[34] By 1960 one in three Appalachian families lived below the poverty line, in contrast to one in five nationally.[35] All these problems led to a growing attention to the region in the 1950s and 1960s.

Even so, this section of the country had been a site of interest in the American imagination since the late nineteenth century. Beginning in the years after the Civil War, Protestant missionaries, "popular writers of the Local Color School," and business advocates illuminated the region through their works, allowing the rest of America to "discover" it.[36] Reformers like Berea's President Frost fit among the first of these groups, devoted to "saving" Appalachia through education and religious instruction.

Other missionaries to this region in the years that followed pursued similar goals of reform but also studied and provided information about it. Perhaps the most notable of these figures was John C. Campbell. Having grown up in Wisconsin, Campbell received seminary training at Andover Theological Seminary in Massachusetts between 1892 and 1895, and in this time became interested in the "Southern Highlands."[37] After educational service in Alabama, Tennessee, and Georgia, Campbell and his second wife, Olive Dame, led a major study of southern Appalachia. Financed by the Russell Sage Foundation of New York, the couple began their travels in 1908 for what became a three-year study.[38] After the final report was finished, Campbell expanded his interest to "encourag[e] new work and coordination and improvement of all efforts."[39] One of the products of Campbell's efforts was the Conference of Southern Mountain Workers in 1913 (later renamed Council of the Southern Mountains), which would become the major reform organization for this region in the coming years. Campbell died in 1919 while preparing his study, *The Southern Highlander and His Homeland,* and his wife Olive Dame Campbell in 1921 subsequently finished the project. In 1925 the Council of the Southern Mountains became stationed at Berea.[40]

Following publication of the Campbells' book, the region received sporadic attention through the 1950s. In 1935 the U.S. Department of Agriculture undertook an updated study that was published as *Economic and Social Problems and Conditions of the Southern Appalachians.*[41] In the 1950s the Council of the Southern Mountains, under the new leadership of Perley F. Ayer, brought renewed vigor to its work, supporting workshops for educators and social workers and pushing states for greater involvement in mountain concerns.[42] Many Appalachian reformers began to see that federal intervention and directed coordination would be necessary for solving the section's problems. It was within this milieu that Weatherford operated as he served Berea in the years after 1946, and his activities increasingly expanded beyond the college's interests into the broader region.

Indeed, it was in connection to Weatherford's sponsorship of *Wilderness Road* in 1955 that he was catapulted into his greatest advocacy work for Appalachia. Since the early 1950s Weatherford had been planning this event, considering it a large investment that would bring rewards to the college in the form of publicity, financial support, and respectability for mountain people.[43] In fact, when Weatherford secured Paul Green to write the play, Weatherford had already planned out all elements of the project, something that Green had never experienced before when approached for such work.[44] Over the coming years Green would develop a close friendship with and respect for Weatherford.[45] When the book form of the play was published, he would dedicate it to Weatherford.[46]

Yet the drama that Weatherford originally envisioned did not materialize in the way he had planned. Initially Weatherford wanted a "pioneer drama"—one that emphasized the "heroic" traits of these white mountaineers in the period leading up to Kentucky's statehood in 1792.[47] President Hutchins rejected this plan, however, because he felt it was too far removed from Berea's actual story.[48] Several women faculty members also objected to Weatherford's idea, one pointing out that Weatherford's version was too narrow.[49] Julia F. Allen, from Berea's Office of the Dean of Women, commented, "The Scotch-Irish heritage, the folk music, the folk arts and crafts, the early patterns of rural isolated living are all important; but the mining camps and textile mills, the T.V.A., the heterogeneous racial groups in the area—including the Indians and the Negroes, are important, too."[50] Weatherford was not really interested in such complexity but, rather, wanted primarily to highlight and bring respect to the region's white mountaineers and their supposed perseverance. The play that was finally produced focused on the period of Berea's early history.

Wilderness Road was set in the Civil War era, 1858–63. It begins as the main character, John Freeman (a white man), returns to his small Kentucky hometown after going to college in Ohio—presumably Oberlin—and tries with mixed results to run a school there. Freeman knows John G. Fee of Berea and receives support from him in the form of books and visits to his fledgling academy. Yet in the midst of debates over slavery and free speech, Freeman's school is forced to close. As the war comes, the town becomes divided between northern and southern allegiances. One of Freeman's students, Neill Sims, fights for the North because of his belief in the righteousness of its cause and rebukes Freeman for his pacifism. Yet after Neill gets hurt, Freeman ends up taking his place with the Union and dies in a battle facing his own brother, Davie. Overall, the story engages with the importance of education, religion, and freedom of expression, while also providing a view of mountain culture. Despite addressing the issue of slavery, this drama focuses almost exclusively on the perspective of white Kentuckians. As the Berea historian Shannon Wilson notes, African Americans—so vital in the early years of Berea's history—"were largely incidental in the play and were passive participants in their cause for freedom."[51]

Nevertheless, *Wilderness Road* was well received at the time, even garnering some national press attention. The *New York Times* reviewed the play's opening performance, commenting that Green's drama "boldly challenged the [southern] region tonight to view its race relations problem as part of the total democratic struggle to preserve free inquiry."[52] Placing the story in relation to the recent *Brown* decision, the reviewer saw in the drama the need for Southerners like Freeman to speak out against the prevailing conservative reaction. Weatherford wrote to Green a few days later to lend his support, noting, "I think you have a great play—not my play—but a great play."[53] For Weatherford the importance of *Wilderness Road* was to celebrate and draw attention to Berea, and so his goal had been achieved. The drama would run for three more summers, and over 160,000 attended; but after it lost a total of $25,000, the Board of Trustees stopped its production.[54] Weatherford was disappointed by this decision, yet he and Green would still try to rework and produce the play as late as 1967.[55]

At the time of *Wilderness Road*'s debut, Weatherford had larger dreams about how the play might also help with what he considered a religious "crisis" in the mountains. Writing to James Cannon, the dean of Duke University's School of Theology, in October 1954, he noted that an important point of the drama was "to set forward both education and religion."[56]

Weatherford went on to describe how the latter was currently at a low ebb, listing the following facts:

> First, thirty per cent of all mountain churches have an average of twenty-five or less members, and another twenty-five per cent of the churches have an average of fifty or less members. Second, there are more than fifty denominations and sects in these mountains. Third, sixty per cent of all mountain preachers have only high school or less education, with no theological education. Fourth, the great majority of mountain churches have no Sunday School, no women's society, no men's society, no youth organization. Fifth, the average church has one service a month or less. I need not comment on the results.[57]

In Weatherford's view these statistics constituted a major problem for Christianity in Appalachia.

Ever the planner, Weatherford went on to suggest a remedy to this situation. He wanted to enlist the cooperation of Cannon, who was Methodist, and gather other Christian leaders to stage religious assemblies each Sunday during *Wilderness Road*'s first summer with the theme "A Total Gospel for the Mountains."[58] Eight different Protestant denominations ended up participating over the course of that period, leading Weatherford to organize an interdenominational gathering the following year at Berea to "discuss ways of *cooperative action* in bettering the religious conditions of the region."[59] One of the issues Weatherford intended to tackle was helping mountain churches operate more efficiently. He hoped specifically that mountain congregations could find ways to share religious facilities, alternating over the course of a certain period, thereby making more effective use of resources. Weatherford's plans revealed his ecumenical outlook and faith in these religiously united efforts.

The interdenominational assembly met in June 1956 and generated activities in Appalachia that extended well beyond religious concerns.[60] Nearly one hundred Christian representatives attended, and at the end of the gathering they formed the Religious Workers' Conference for the Appalachian Mountains.[61] Evidently, however, early in the initial meeting many delegates determined that "adequate, accurate, and comparable data" about the region were needed for the group to effectively "plan a real forward movement" with mountain churches.[62] This statement sounded strikingly similar to Weatherford's rationale for writing his first book on race relations, *Negro Life in the South*, after the 1908 interracial meeting in Atlanta. Nearly fifty years later he still believed in the validity and usefulness of such an approach.

The last regional survey had been completed in 1935, and conditions had significantly changed because of migration patterns as well as economic developments. Participants in this 1956 gathering decided a new economic, educational, social, and religious study of southern Appalachia was necessary before effective regional religious planning and programs could be undertaken. Thus, as a result of this conference, a group was formed to carry out a new survey of southern Appalachia. Officially incorporated as the Southern Appalachian Studies (SAS) in 1958, the organization would be based at Berea and directed by Weatherford.[63]

Of course, such a substantial enterprise required money and skillful organization, and Weatherford went to work addressing these needs. Indeed, by 1958 Weatherford had gained the backing of the Ford Foundation with a $250,000 grant, along with an additional $60,000 in aid from universities and Christian groups.[64] Weatherford also began securing researchers and enlisting support from churches and state governments in the region, as well as from groups like the Council of the Southern Mountains. Prominent scholars from across Appalachia would conduct the study from 1958 to 1961, and in 1962 *The Southern Appalachian Region: A Survey* was published.[65]

It was an ambitious project. Under the leadership of Weatherford, Earl D. C. Brewer (Emory University professor of sociology and religion), Thomas R. Ford (University of Kentucky professor of sociology), and Rupert V. Vance (UNC professor of sociology), the study proceeded, along with the aid of eighteen other scholars.[66] There were several primary objectives. First, these researchers wanted to determine "what changes had taken place" in this section since the last survey, in 1935, and evaluate their effects on the region.[67] Next, they wanted to gather data about current conditions in regard to health, education, religion, and economics. The aim was to establish what Appalachian residents "really needed to bring them up to the American standards of living and culture"; the expectation was that the information they collected might "point to some practical solutions of the problems found."[68] In the end, these scholars determined the region was a "problem area" for the United States owing primarily to economic concerns rather than inherent issues with the people there.[69] As the noted Appalachian scholar Loyal Jones described the study, "The SAS saw the main

Willis Weatherford holding a copy of *The Southern Appalachian Region*, summer 1962. (Courtesy of Weatherford Family Papers)

problem as one of a failure of the American economic system to operate fully in the Appalachian region. The solution was assumed to be a method of bringing the fruits of this system to this backwater of American life."[70] *The Southern Appalachian Region* did essentially much the same thing as other books Weatherford had helped produce—survey an issue, put the information together, and then get the results out to trained people and the public to effect change. Weatherford believed knowledge would lead to action and improvement.

Weatherford himself contributed one chapter on twentieth-century Appalachian literature to this project. Evidently Weatherford assigned himself this task, but as it turned out, his initial draft was not well received by the other leaders of the SAS.[71] Thomas R. Ford, who was the editor of the volume, later recalled that Weatherford's paper, while being "solid," was "archaic in style."[72] Ford and Bruce F. Denbo, one of the editors of the University Press of Kentucky, recommended to Weatherford that he seek a collaborator for the chapter, a suggestion to which Weatherford acquiesced.[73] During this same time it appears Ford was also frustrated by another issue with Weatherford's section, specifically that he was "a little puzzled" by Weatherford's apparent goal of "'inspir[ing]' the mountain people" through this chapter; Ford asked, "What are they to be inspired to do?"[74] Ford hinted that Weatherford's inclination also was to applaud those writers who emphasized the positive traits of Appalachians, while dismissing those who "recorded undesirable characteristics."[75] Nevertheless, these issues seem to have been resolved when Wilma Dykeman coauthored with Weatherford a quick sketch of the region's most notable authors and their depiction of this culture.[76] The connection between Weatherford and Dykeman would grow over the coming years in their united concern for Appalachia, what the latter would come to refer to in 1964 as "our mutual gospel."[77]

The SAS program was part of an increasing national concern for the region taking place in the late 1950s. In these years, amid the cold war with the U.S.S.R., "Appalachia was an embarrassment to the nation," a section where capitalism and the market economy had failed.[78] After the successes of government intervention during the Great Depression and through the Marshall Plan in Europe, many American liberals now had immense confidence in the state's power to "alleviate want and mobilize for action."[79] At the same time, work in this section of the country, most notably by the Council of the Southern Mountains, was increasing. In particular, this organization put together tours of Appalachia for regional specialists and leaders that provided opportunities for viewing the area's poverty and other problems and chances to meet with local leaders and residents.[80]

Weatherford himself participated in several of these trips. In 1958, in connection with a conference on urban adjustment by the Council of the

Southern Mountains, Weatherford led a five-day trip through mountain counties in North Carolina, Kentucky, and Tennessee.[81] Most of the participants were from the cities of Cincinnati, Chicago, Cleveland, and Detroit, where the increased flow of Appalachian migrants was then settling. Weatherford introduced these visitors to a wide spectrum of mountain life in both rural and urban areas, including educational institutions, mining operations and towns, farms, churches, and industrial plants. The following year Weatherford, with the aid of James Brown, a rural sociologist from the University of Kentucky, guided another group of Northerners and Midwesterners, primarily educators, law enforcement officers, and city leaders, through parts of eastern Kentucky and Tennessee.[82] In the process he supplemented their firsthand experience with recent findings from the SAS project. Overall, Weatherford wanted these men and women to develop an understanding of and sympathy for Appalachian people, particularly when they returned to their communities and worked with them there. Weatherford was pleased when newspapers reported favorably on these tours, and he considered the articles an important instrument for changing public opinion in these northern and midwestern cities.[83]

It is difficult to assess the effectiveness of these trips, but the visit of a young man from Massachusetts in 1960 clearly influenced the trajectory reform took in this region in the coming years. That spring, the presidential candidate John F. Kennedy went to West Virginia to campaign for the upcoming May Democratic primary.[84] This state was just emerging from a particularly cold and hard winter, and Kennedy was touched by his experiences with the poverty he observed among the coal miners and rural residents.[85] Kennedy's nomination was far from assured at the time, and winning West Virginia would be an important indicator that his Catholic faith would not be an impediment to his presidential run. On the night before the primary vote, May 10, 1960, Kennedy pledged West Virginians, "If I'm nominated and elected president within sixty days of the start of my administration, I will introduce a program to the Congress for aid to West Virginia."[86] Kennedy won the state, and after being elected president he made strides to improve West Virginia and the greater Appalachian region through the Area Redevelopment Act in 1961 and the President's Appalachian Regional Commission in 1963.[87]

Also influencing Kennedy's interest and bringing Appalachia's plight into the American spotlight was the publication of a book on the region in 1963. In that year Harry Monroe Caudill's *Night Comes to the Cumberlands: A Biography of a Depressed Area* was released, becoming one of the most important works of the era on Appalachia. In this volume Caudill sketched the history of the Cumberland Plateau from frontier days, showing particularly how "greed, environmental abuse, and government neglect" had ravaged this area.[88] Caudill emphasized that most of these issues resulted from outside influences like absentee mine owners; yet he also pointed out problems within mountain culture such as "ignorance, clannishness, and an eagerness to accept public relief" that played a part in creating the region's conditions.[89] Caudill pleaded for government intervention on the scale of the Tennessee Valley Authority and the Marshall Plan to bring development, jobs, housing, and education to Appalachia. *Night Comes to the Cumberlands* was extensively read at the time, inspiring a number of journalists to report further on Appalachia.[90] Indeed, one of these pieces by the *New York Times* writer Homar Bigart made its way to President Kennedy in 1963. Sadly, Kennedy did not live long enough to enact changes in the region.

After Kennedy's assassination on November 22, 1963, Lyndon B. Johnson followed up on the former president's commitment there. As part of his War on Poverty, Johnson gave particular attention to improving Appalachian economic conditions. One important piece of legislation he pushed through was the Economic Opportunity Act in 1964, which established the Office of Economic Opportunity (OEC).[91] This department in turn created such programs as Head Start, VISTA (Volunteers in Service to America), Upward Bound (a high school dropout–deterrence program), and Job Corps (similar to the New Deal's Civilian Conservation Corps). Another accomplishment of Johnson's administration was the Appalachian Regional Commission (ARC), a joint federal-state organization, which came into existence in 1965. This agency defined the region broadly: Alabama, Georgia, Kentucky, Maryland, North Carolina, Pennsylvania, Tennessee, Virginia, West Virginia, South Carolina, New York, Mississippi, and Ohio all received representation.[92] While the OEC focused primarily on educational and youth programs, the ARC supported building infrastructure, particularly roads, schools, and healthcare facilities.[93]

In Weatherford's attention to Appalachia, he recognized that both federal and state governments would play an important part in improving the region. Writing to Wilma Dykeman in 1964, he acknowledged:

The economic need of the mountains is most pressing. The Governors of the Appalachian states are working at this faithfully. President Johnson has our Appalachian study report on his desk and is giving effective thought to it. We must find ways of cooperative efforts. We must open up the back valleys and coves with roads, we must get light manufacturing plants in, and we must help the little farmer get better pasturage, better breeds of stock, better markets and better knowledge, of how to make more out of his limited opportunities. It's a dark picture but I'm sure we can find ways out.[94]

In 1961 Weatherford made unsuccessful efforts to meet with Kennedy about these issues, and at this time he also worked with senators drafting legislation for the region.[95]

Still, Weatherford was not sure that economic measures would remedy all Appalachia's troubles. Preparing to speak at the second Appalachian Governors' Conference in 1961, he admitted that while new infrastructure and industry "were terribly important . . . they alone would not solve Appalachian problems."[96] Weatherford went on to argue that "no real man wanted to raise his children in a community where the school was poor, the church was weak, and medical facilities were non-existent."[97] Weatherford viewed these institutions as just as essential as jobs. Moreover, he felt the people of Appalachia needed a sense of self-worth and optimism about the future. Writing to Dykeman in 1964, Weatherford declared, "The elemental need is to give new hope and new appreciation for his own dignity and worth to the mountain person."[98] Overall, Weatherford envisioned a program for Appalachia that would bring new pride to its residents; churches would be at the forefront of reforming the region.

In 1962 another volume was published along with the overall study of southern Appalachia, this one highlighting religion's place in the region. Entitled *Life and Religion in Southern Appalachia: An Interpretation of Selected Data from the Southern Appalachian Studies,* it was coauthored by Weatherford and Earl D. C. Brewer. The study included information gained from interviews with over two thousand mountain households and 204 churches in seven states. The first part of the book focused on historical and ongoing cultural conditions there, and the remaining portion revealed statistics about the status of Christianity. The authors intended this volume to be a sort of study guide, to be used both within and outside the mountains by local congregations, denominations, women's groups, and social agencies.[99]

Weatherford hoped it would provide a benchmark, showing where things stood and what steps then could be taken for improvement.

Weatherford in these years viewed Appalachian churches on the whole as being highly "inefficient" and too conservative.[100] While he believed these congregations could be critical to improving the region, he did not think the state of religion there was satisfactory. For starters, he was concerned with the overall participation rates of mountaineers as well as their largely fundamentalist beliefs. Moreover, as Loyal Jones notes, Weatherford was often frustrated by those Appalachian congregations lacking business organization; Jones recalled Weatherford's exasperation when he complained, "Why can't these local churches have a budget?"[101] Weatherford was also alarmed that many mountain clergy had little formal education, believing this "lack of training" contributed to their being "ultra conservative," which in turn led them to divide the world into sacred and secular spheres. Overall, Weatherford thought such a combination kept these pastors focused exclusively on saving souls and resulted in their congregations having "little interest in and little or no share in public responsibility."[102] Writing to Dykeman in 1966, he maintained his opinion that ministers and their flocks were not sufficiently attuned to their "responsibility" to others.[103] He passionately stated, "The trouble is that so few churchmen see or even think about their responsibility to these needs. How few churches there are who even think of their having any responsibilities to the people surrounding them who are helpless in meeting these simple needs of their existence.... When will the church leaders wake up and make their church constituency wake up?"[104] Appalachian Christianity, in short, did not meet Weatherford's standards for a socially engaged faith.

Scholars writing about Appalachian religion in recent years have taken issue with some of the attitudes reformers like Weatherford had about mountain churches.[105] Often figures like him came from mainstream churches outside the region that sought to impose their conception of what "church" should be. Their more liberal view of Christianity in terms of theology and social involvement, together with certain middle-class cultural priorities, contrasted substantially with the style and practice of many Appalachian congregations. Loyal Jones notes that while these home missionaries were often well intentioned and produced many improvements in the region, they frequently had difficulty seeing mountain people's "culture and faith in their time and place" as "legitimate."[106] Moreover, these Christian reformers regularly treated their fellow believers with less than mutual respect, having a paternalistic attitude toward them. In Weatherford's case such a mind-set can be seen in his idea that Appalachian churches should share their facilities to reduce "wasting" resources by operating so many different buildings. Weatherford's proposal failed to consider how these members would feel about this arrangement. Commenting on a similar plan by another Appalachian reformer, Jones added that while "this is a fine ideal . . . it doesn't happen up the hollow any easier than it does on Main Street, U.S.A."[107] Weatherford also exhibited a certain amount of condescension toward mountain congregations when he spoke before a Catholic group in Raleigh, North Carolina, in the early 1960s. Here Weatherford proposed a plan to have Christians outside the region come into local communities and train ministers, while also providing supervision and financial support.[108] He seems to have taken it as a given that these local congregations would welcome such efforts. Nevertheless, it also should be noted that in these years Weatherford's view that Appalachian churches were not operating as they should be was just part of his greater overall critique of American Christianity. At this same time he was also admonishing mainline denominations for being "rich, lazy and satisfied."[109]

Weatherford's emphasis on the churches—both in the mountains and in the South generally—represents a shift in the major religious institution he supported. Before the 1950s Weatherford had been most heavily invested in the YMCA, believing that it would be the critical organization for religion and social action in the South. Yet by midcentury his faith in the Y had lessened, and from that period onward he placed his confidence in the church. Weatherford's move was probably a response to his failed effort with the YMCA Graduate School, his disconnection from the administration of Blue Ridge by this point, and the general secularizing and lessening importance of the YMCA as a Christian organization. After 1946 the Y did not figure into Weatherford's plans for Appalachia.

But Weatherford did have a special vision for the churches in the mountains. In particular, he saw these organizations as possible grassroots agencies in Appalachian communities. He hoped that they would be sites where local residents organized to address their particular neighborhood issues. For example, programs might develop out of these churches that deterred high school students from dropping out.[110] In the early to mid-1960s Weatherford also intended to enlist experts from religion and sociology to work in these areas and train indigenous leaders to confront their local problems. As Weatherford proposed such a "pilot project" in western

North Carolina in 1965—which might later be expanded to all of southern Appalachia—he went to the North Carolina Fund, a new poverty-fighting organization.[111] Though the Board of Directors apparently "had real interest" in his plan, it did not accept his proposal, considering it "more rightly the province of the churches than of the Fund."[112] Weatherford, while slowing down in the next few years, would continue to deliberate on ways to use these religious bodies to improve Appalachian life.

Beyond his attempt to energize the churches in the Appalachian cause, Weatherford's plans for the region also involved helping mountain residents maintain self-respect. In particular he addressed the complex issue of how government-support payments should be allocated. A 1964 meeting of the Council of the Southern Mountains appears to have pushed Weatherford to tackle this concern more publicly.[113] At that gathering, one of the speakers evidently proposed that the government should provide a living wage of $3,000 per year to qualified persons.[114] Weatherford challenged Robert Theobold, who made this suggestion, to flesh out how this money could be appropriated while still maintaining the receiver's "self respect," "individuality," and "dignity."[115] Theobold apparently did not present Weatherford with a satisfactory answer, and Weatherford left the meeting struggling to envision a way out of this Appalachian welfare dilemma. After deliberation, Weatherford arrived at an idea. He suggested these recipients be required—in exchange for relief money—to give something back to society, through a form of moral, spiritual, educational, or motivational service. How such a system actually would play out remains unclear, but Weatherford considered this extremely vital, insisting audaciously, "Anything less than this will destroy the self respect of the recipient, and it probably would be better for them to starve than lose their self respect."[116]

The following year Weatherford became a little more specific about his proposal. Asked by a reporter, Beverly Wolter of the *Winston-Salem Journal and Sentinel,* what could be done to resolve this problem, he maintained, "A dole is no answer."[117] Weatherford went on to roughly sketch his idea, which included giving a salary of three hundred dollars per month from government funds in payment for "service" that could be performed through such activities as working with schools and discouraging high school dropouts or helping sick and needy persons with domestic tasks. In response, Wolter commented that while this arrangement remained rather "nebulous," it also sounded a lot like "socialism," to which Weatherford replied, "What if it is?"[118] Although his plan was far from socialism, it certainly was very idealistic. Yet Weatherford went no further in explaining how his program would operate or how people would be held accountable.

Another project Weatherford worked on in these years was something he referred to as the "Appalachian Dozen." This undertaking included publishing a series of books, both fiction and nonfiction, to help bring a renewed sense of self-worth to Appalachian residents. These volumes were to be targeted primarily to inhabitants there, providing awareness of contemporary conditions and inspiring teachers, preachers, storekeepers, and Appalachian women to engage in the region's social concerns.[119] Weatherford also hoped this collection would "help Americans know who the Appalachian people are, what is their background, what their special contribution to American civilization has been and may yet be."[120] This set included *The Southern Appalachian Region* (1962), *Life and Religion in Southern Appalachia* (1962), Wilma Dykeman's *The French Broad* (1955) and *The Tall Woman* (1962), Garland Hendricks's *The Appalachian Shepherd* (1965), Jesse Stuart's *The Thread That Runs So True* (1958), James Stokely's "Bull-Session in a Mountain Country Store" (never published), and Weatherford's *Personal Elements in Religious Life* (1916), *Pioneers of Destiny* (1955), *Studies in Christian Experience* (1962), and "The Amazing Contribution of Appalachia to American Life" (never published). Weatherford's approach here was probably an outgrowth of his work on Appalachian literature in the 1962 survey, and he used money from the SAS budget to finance several of these pieces.[121] All in all, the Appalachian Dozen was very reminiscent of the "library" on race relations he put together in 1912 and 1915. The series also featured one other book by Dykeman, *The Prophet of Plenty*, a biography of Weatherford.

Weatherford and Dykeman had known each other since 1959. In that year she and her husband, James Stokely, were collaborating on a biography of Will W. Alexander, and in the process of verifying a story about Weatherford they sought him out at a conference he was attending in Tennessee.[122] After this initial meeting the two became close, particularly in their enthusiasm over Appalachian issues and as they collaborated on the literature chapter for the regional survey. Indeed, it might be fair to say that Weatherford had finally met his match in terms of passion for the South and Appalachia. Assessing the two, Loyal Jones later described Dykeman as "one of the most enthusiastic and indomitable women I knew," and Weatherford as "the indomitable old man that never gave up."[123] By the time Weatherford and Dykeman crossed paths, the latter was already an acclaimed writer whose works had confronted major issues in civil rights and Appalachia.[124]

Willis Weatherford with Jesse Stuart in 1960. The photo includes an inscription in the bottom right-hand corner that reads, "To Jesse Stuart and Dr. W. D. Weatherford from Billy Edd Wheeler, 7-12-60." (Courtesy of Willis D. Weatherford Papers, Southern Historical Collection, Wilson Library, University of North Carolina at Chapel Hill)

In her career she would go on to publish nearly twenty books, thereby earning numerous honors, including the 1985 North Carolina Award for literature. In 1969 she joined Berea's Board of Trustees.[125] As a result of their initial encounter, subsequent friendship, and common purpose, Weatherford commissioned Dykeman to write *The Tall Woman,* a fictional account of a mountain mother's influential role in local culture, to be part of his Appalachian Dozen.[126] Following this work, Weatherford planned for her to author one additional piece for the series, an imagined story of a man committed to the region, to be entitled *Apostle to Appalachia.*[127] Weatherford must have envisioned it to be a kind of companion to *The Tall Woman,* using this man's story as an inspiration to mountaineers to seek what he thought was a better life. Yet Dykeman encouraged Weatherford to shift the project, insisting on writing a biography of him instead because she believed this approach "would make it more real and more powerful."[128]

Bringing a Revival to the Mountains 209

Willis Weatherford's eighty-sixth birthday party (1961). *Left to right:* Francis Hutchins, unidentified man, Wilma Dykeman, and Weatherford. (Courtesy of Weatherford Family Papers)

Dykeman's book went through several title changes over the course of its development, revealing much about her and Weatherford's intended purpose for it. At various times it was called "A Prophet in the Mountains"; "An Apostle to Appalachia and Our Prophet of Plenty"; and "The Builder of a New Society (The Life Story of W. D. Weatherford)."[129] A short description of the first title read: "The story of a real leader dedicated to mountain people, meant to dignify mountain people in their own minds."[130] *Prophet of Plenty: The First Ninety Years of W. D. Weatherford,* the book's eventual title, was dedicated "to today's youth—tomorrow's leaders—to whom W. D. Weatherford pledged his talents, his energy, and the time of his life."[131] Even though Dykeman covered his whole life, as the title suggests, the essential function of her volume—as Weatherford and she had planned—was to bring attention to Appalachia and motivate its residents and those elsewhere.[132] It was a practical work of advocacy, one very much in the tradition of Weatherford's own books.[133]

The choice of the word *plenty* held a particularly significant meaning in the context of the times. In 1966 the United States was in the midst of the War on Poverty in Appalachia and throughout the country. Dykeman intended the book's focus on "plenty" to contrast with the term *poverty,* which was so much in American public discourse.[134] For her, being poor went beyond people's lack of access to material possessions and opportunities, which makes their lives difficult and painful. People can also be "poor in spirit," a fact that can affect the wealthy and underprivileged alike. Throughout her text Dykeman used variations of both "poverty" and "plenty" extensively, even writing on the first page, "This is the story of [Weatherford's] attack on poverty wherever he found it. It is also the record of his prophecy of the plenty which was, and is, available to a man or a nation."[135] The book was optimistic, upbeat, and hopeful—all characteristics of its subject.

In assessing *Prophet of Plenty,* it is important to remember that Weatherford commissioned Dykeman to write it and that he was directly involved in its production. While it was not originally his idea to have his life story put in print, he did pay her for the work and clearly helped as she gathered information on his life, speaking personally with her, providing written responses to her questions, and recommending people for her to interview. Dykeman and her husband together (at the time he was working on a tale about a mountain storekeeper for Weatherford that he never completed) were paid $12,000 ($1,000 a month for twelve months) to produce these works.[136] As Dykeman herself admitted, "This account of Weatherford's work is neither definitive biography nor formal scholarship," and though it was credible, the book for the most part portrayed Weatherford in a positive manner.[137] Indeed, Weatherford appears to have been quite pleased with the finished product: in the midst of his initial reading of it, he congratulated her for doing a "wonderful job."[138] Yet to what extent *Prophet of Plenty,* as well as the entire Appalachian Dozen project, had Weatherford and Dykeman's desired effect on Appalachian residents and other readers remains unclear. Indeed, as several works were not completed, the set never sold as a package. Overall, those books that were published probably had negligible effect; certainly they were much less influential than Caudill's *Night Comes to the Cumberlands* at the time.

Another activity Weatherford undertook for Appalachia in his years at Berea is more easily quantified. Beginning in 1949 and continuing through the mid-1960s, Weatherford actively recruited students from western North Carolina to attend this school, as well as college in general.[139] Taking time each year, usually in the month of January, he visited high schools in this region, going to as many as sixty in 1953.[140] Since the African American population was very small in this section of North Carolina, almost all his attention was directed toward white schools, but there is evidence he may have also traveled to black institutions as well.[141] His basic approach included speaking before the senior class—sometimes the entire student body—about the importance of education and then encouraging those with a B or better average to go on for a higher degree. He requested that those who could afford college find a suitable school other than Berea. Students lacking the necessary financial resources for collegiate education, however, should apply to Berea because of its tuition-free policy and commitment to serving underprivileged Appalachian youth.[142] First and foremost, Weatherford's desire was for these youngsters to get an education, whether this took place at Berea or somewhere else. Weatherford could be very persistent, at times visiting students' homes to talk with families and plead for their children's education.[143] His efforts would have an influence on the area, as forty-six students from Buncombe County alone enrolled at Berea in 1956.[144]

Several success stories resulting from his endeavors stand out. One young woman from Nantahala High School in North Carolina met Weatherford on one of his recruiting trips in 1954.[145] According to Weatherford, she apparently had an A average and was "more eager about the possibility of college than almost any person I ever met." The girl's family (there were seven total) lived on six hundred dollars a year. Berea ultimately accepted her, and in 1957 Weatherford encountered the young woman at the Conference of the Southern Mountains in Gatlinburg, Tennessee, which she was attending as a student delegate. She surprised him as he was eating breakfast, and in the process of their visit, credited him for her being at Berea.[146]

Another student, Billy Edd Wheeler, also was influenced by Weatherford to attend the college. Wheeler would become a distinguished songwriter, musician, and playwright in the 1960s and onward, writing such country hits as "Jackson" (for which June and Johnny Cash won a Grammy in 1967) and "The Coward of the County" (a song Kenny Rogers made famous in 1980).[147] Attending Warren Wilson College (then both a high school and junior college) in Swannanoa, North Carolina, in 1953, Wheeler met Weatherford (who was nearly eighty years old at the time) as the latter was apparently going door to door through the dorm, encouraging students to get a four-year degree at Berea.[148] Wheeler went on to the Kentucky college, graduating in 1955. He attended Yale Drama School in 1961, and Weatherford, who had maintained an interest in him, several times sent him money to help cover his tuition costs.[149] Ever the advocate of education

Willis Weatherford about 1955. (Courtesy of Weatherford Family Papers)

at high-quality schools, Weatherford was dismayed when he heard Wheeler might have to withdraw from Yale because he could not meet his expenses, so he gave Wheeler a "gift" of $250 to keep him there.[150] Wheeler later described Weatherford as being "like a hummingbird, always in motion and doing things."[151] It was a fitting image.

Weatherford engaged in several other ventures that benefited Berea as well as mountain residents. In 1964 he helped fund a program providing clothing and shoes for schoolchildren in Kentucky, West Virginia, and Tennessee; his idea was that making these necessities available would help keep students in the classroom.[152] In these years people also sought Weatherford's advice on specific issues in local communities regarding poverty and education. One situation related to a nineteen-year-old young man from Tennessee, recently orphaned, who was trying to attend the public schools while working full-time.[153] A teacher there, Mary Phillips Kirby-Smith, inquired of Weatherford if there was any "resource for further education for this boy in his particular circumstances?"[154] What became of this teenager is not known, but in light of Weatherford's commitment to such persons, it is likely he tried to do something. During this same time Weatherford also manifested his dedication to Berea through a gift of $15,000 to establish the Weatherford and Hammond Mountain Collection of books at the Berea library.[155] People and knowledge always remained his priorities.

Weatherford maintained his devotion to Appalachia until the end of his life, slowing only in the very last years. His secretary at Berea, Elizabeth Wyckoff, noted that in 1965, at the age of ninety, he was still spending "16 hours a day" on these concerns.[156] As he had earlier, when he focused on race relations, Weatherford continued trying to transform attitudes and perceptions by working primarily through religious organizations. Weatherford wanted people outside Appalachia to have a respect for these people, and he also desired for those within the region to develop a new pride in themselves. His vision was to create a brighter future for this area, a vital part of which included lessening the "individualism in the mountains" and instead inspiring a greater "sense of community responsibility."[157] At times his plans were unrealistic and hardly feasible. His methods could also be paternalistic, particularly in those cases in which he thought he knew a better way for congregations to worship and operate their churches. In the big scheme of Appalachian history, Weatherford stands in the long tradition of missionaries who made this region their cause. He failed to initiate any large structural changes, but it must be admitted that he did have a positive influence on the lives of many individuals there. Perhaps Weatherford's greatest achievement for Appalachia was in helping draw national awareness to this section of the country and its people's needs during a very difficult period.

Weatherford also made one final contribution to the Appalachian region, albeit indirectly, through his son, Willis Jr. In 1967 the younger Weatherford became president of Berea College, and he would remain in this role until 1984.[158] During his tenure he continued the school's devotion to the Appalachian region and economically disadvantaged students. He also helped as Berea worked through its own racial issues, as African American students returned in these years. Willis Weatherford Jr. would sustain many of his father's values, particularly in terms of his views on religion and education.

Conclusion

W. D. Weatherford's long life came to an end February 21, 1970, in Berea, Kentucky.[1] At the time he was living with his son (who by then had become the president of Berea) and his family. A memorial service was held near the college to honor Weatherford, and his funeral took place at the Methodist Church in Black Mountain, North Carolina. Afterward Weatherford was buried in a special plot alongside his wife Julia McRory (who had died in 1957) at the Blue Ridge Assembly. A massive boulder marks their graves, and the following was inscribed for Weatherford:

> WILLIS DUKE WEATHERFORD 1875–1970.
> FOUNDER, BUILDER, AND PRESIDENT OF BLUE RIDGE, 1906–1944,
> MAN OF GOD AND SERVANT OF MEN, LIFE LONG STUDENT,
> LOVER OF YOUTH AND FRIEND OF ALL RACES.
> MAN OF SOCIAL PASSION AND FAITH IN GOD WHO TAUGHT THE
> SACREDNESS OF PERSONS AND THE DIGNITY OF LABOR[2]

Like all people, Weatherford was a man shaped and limited by the times in which he lived. Yet he was also a man ahead of them for a good part of his life. In the context of the South in the early twentieth century, his liberal views on race and religion and his advocacy of education placed him out in front of many of his contemporaries. Over the course of his career Weatherford channeled his unusual energy and drive to take on projects in the YMCA, race relations, and the Appalachian region. He maintained an extraordinary faith in the power of education to bring about change, always focusing on training, study groups, conferences, and educational efforts. At times his plans were hardly feasible on a large scale, particularly in his call for mountain welfare recipients to perform community activities in exchange for relief payments. At other points, his proposals were perhaps too idealistic, as he often hoped that his books would inspire change. After being at the forefront of southern liberalism in the 1910s, he managed to keep pace through the early 1950s but fell behind after that period. From 1912 to 1945 he directed several institutions, and his struggles to push them in progressive directions were always tempered by his pragmatic efforts to ensure their survival. In the years following 1945, while continuing his engagement in the issues of race, religion, and the Appalachian region, his methods became increasingly outdated.

Those who involve themselves in reform always run the risk of being criticized. There is much Weatherford can be faulted for, but we should not work from the assumption that he had to undertake the activities that he did. Most white Southerners did not go against the status quo in these years. Weatherford's story is significant because it helps us understand why those white southern liberals who did act failed to go further in their critique of society in this period. While clearly elements of racism and class prejudice on their part played a factor in their actions, other concerns also accounted for their holding back.

In particular, Weatherford's life and actions show what was possible at this time in the South and reveal the importance of understanding someone within his or her context and circumstances. For Weatherford, particularly on the subject of race in the years before 1950, it was feasible for him to go only so far without endangering the institutions he led, perhaps losing the influence he had, and even putting himself and his family at some physical risk. Weatherford walked a fine line between trying to live up to his Christian ideals about the value of all persons and doing what was realistic. Nevertheless, the consequences he faced changed over time, and it became easier for him to do and say certain things. Weatherford can be judged more critically for not pushing harder as these options began opening up.

Weatherford and other white liberals were also limited by the fact that the South they hailed from had a weak tradition of reform and interest in social welfare; they had to keep the scope of their critiques within certain boundaries. This legacy made it difficult for Weatherford to criticize the structural issues that contributed to the region's problems of racism and poverty. Ironically, it seems that though personalism gave Weatherford a recognition of the plight of African Americans and those of the Appalachian region, this philosophy also probably inhibited his progressivism. This school of thought's heavy focus on the individual blurred his ability to see the importance of addressing Jim Crow and market capitalism's exploitive elements. As was true of many other white liberals of this period, Weatherford's Christian motivations were mixed with a sense of paternalism for those he tried to "help." Weatherford thought that middle-class values could, and should, be applied to all people, and this would bring about what he thought would be a better society. Weatherford trusted that humans were rational, and if men and women just had awareness—the result of education—then the problems of the day would work themselves out *gradually*. Particularly on the subject of African American civil rights, his gradualism was influenced by the fact that he personally did not suffer discrimination in his day-to-day life. He did not feel any urgent need to press harder.

Yet even within all the boundaries that Weatherford operated, he made notable achievements for his time, most clearly in his race relations work in the 1910s and 1920s. Weatherford also influenced generations of students who attended Blue Ridge through the 1940s as well as students at the YMCA Graduate School, Fisk University, and Berea College. Indeed, their exposure to Weatherford proved pivotal in pointing some of these youngsters in progressive directions, particularly in regard to racial issues. Although Weatherford attempted to be a scholar and would have liked to be one, his books and academic work never reached a highly analytical, rigorous level. Despite his interest in being an intellectual, his greatest talents lay not in the world of the mind. Weatherford's supreme abilities were in administration—inspiring creative and large projects and organizing and keeping them going. At times, however, he became so invested in his endeavors that he curtailed the very progressive social work that had brought him to create these projects.

Weatherford continued his engagement in social issues through his early nineties. Besides what appears to have been a sincere interest in the concerns of African Americans, people of the Appalachian region, and the state of Christianity, it seems that his activities and projects also provided a way to deal with the pain in his personal life. He was always a teetotaler, and work became his drug. In the years after the loss of his first wife and daughter, he threw himself into the YMCA, the building of Blue Ridge, and the issue of race relations. Indeed, Weatherford may even have first raised his voice on the plight of southern blacks because of the fact that he did not have to consider the repercussions of such work on his family. Weatherford's second wife went through two periods of illness, the second one slowly paralyzing and debilitating her.[3] Although he was clearly devoted to her, perhaps staying so busy helped him find some purpose in this life amid all the chaos he experienced. As a Christian man, how he reconciled these personal tragedies with his faith is unclear. It appears he simply continued, staying active and never coming to any definite conclusions on the spiritual questions.

Through all his life Weatherford was a liberal, optimistic about progress and maintaining the belief that education and inspiration would change people, who in turn would improve the world. Partly as recognition of his educational efforts for the South and Appalachia, both Berea College and the University of North Carolina at Chapel Hill bestowed honorary doctorates on Weatherford.[4] Indeed, as Rupert Vance recommended Weatherford to the UNC Committee on Honorary Degrees in 1961, he made an apt comment. He wrote, "It is difficult for me to think of a man of our region to whom a university education meant more or one who has been able to do more with his education over a long lifetime in many fields."[5] Weatherford's achievements were grounded in the opportunities his higher education and subsequent studies had made available to him. He expected that knowledge would also prove similarly helpful to others.

Acknowledgments

It is not easy to adequately express my appreciation to all those involved in helping me complete this project. Over a decade ago this work began when I visited Sam Hill in Black Mountain, North Carolina. On that late spring day I met Sam in town, and he drove me up to the YMCA Blue Ridge Assembly and then over to meet Anne Weatherford. She was the daughter-in-law of Willis Duke Weatherford and was then residing in his mountaintop home, Far Horizons. Sam believed that Weatherford's story was one worth pursuing, and he had encouraged me to make the trip there that day, noting that the experience would "enrich my life and work." He was right. Since that day the project has grown and blossomed and has continued to keep me interested and moving in directions I never would have anticipated.

I would like to thank the Rice History Department for its generous funding of my graduate education and the research for this project. I would also like to express my appreciation to the following people there who aided me: Thomas Haskell, Alex Byrd, Michael Emerson, Luke Harlow, Rusty Hawkins, Merritt McKinney, Blake Ellis, Greg Eow, Alyssa Honnette, Wes Phelps, Jim Wainwright, Allison Madar, Pat Burgess, Paula Platt, Rachel Zepeda, Lisa Tate, and Anita Smith. A special appreciation is due as well to Randal Hall, whose seemingly inexhaustible knowledge has been a constant resource throughout the years. Numerous visits to his office, countless phone conversations and e-mail exchanges, and his willingness to read portions of my work all helped me as I hit snags along the way. John Boles also deserves particular recognition. It was, without a doubt, one of my best decisions to attend graduate school at Rice and to be one of his students. His prompt replies to my questions and critiques of my written work and his encouragement, support, and commonsense advice all have been invaluable. Beyond his professionalism, he is above all a fine human being with whom it is a pleasure to work. I also appreciate his sense of understanding and his value of family. In particular, during a time in graduate school when I needed to be with my own family, he without hesitation supported my decision.

Other financial and research support was also critical to this project. I would like to thank the North Caroliniana Society for an Archie K. Davis Fellowship. This book would not have been possible without the help of the staff at numerous archives and institutions as well, specifically the Southern Historical Collection at the University of North Carolina at Chapel Hill, Berea College, Fisk University, Vanderbilt University, Appalachian State University, the YMCA Blue Ridge Assembly, the Kautz Family YMCA Archives at the University of Minnesota, the Amistad Collection at Tulane University, and the Weatherford Public Library in Weatherford, Texas. Thanks are extended to the following individuals: Laura Brown, Matt Turi, Becca Soloman, Lauren Hurley, Holly Smith, Biff Hollingsworth, Rachel Canada, Beth Howse, Melissa Logan, Jessica Popovitch, and Kurt Eckel. My colleagues at Averett University and around Danville have also lent support in various ways, among them John Laughlin, Robert Marsh, Jay Hayes, and the staff at Blount Library, who offered assistance with interlibrary loan materials.

Other scholars were important in helping me conceptualize my project and construct my arguments. Michele Gillespie has been a constant supporter since my undergraduate days. She has always been willing to read drafts of my project and offer thoughtful criticism, correspond via e-mail or phone, or meet to talk over various concerns. I truly appreciate her as both the fine scholar and person she is. Charles Israel shared his knowledge and interest in early twentieth-century southern religion, took time to talk in person and reply to my inquiries, and read portions of this work. Discussions along the way with Jim Barefield, Mac Bryan, and Donald Mathews also proved helpful. Finally, special thanks must go to Sam Hill. From that first trip to Black Mountain he has been an unfailing supporter and advocate. For his introduction to the Weatherford topic, as well as countless meals, conversations, tours throughout the Black Mountain area, and reading of the manuscript, I am ever grateful.

In the process of my research I had the good fortune to visit with several people who knew Weatherford personally. Thanks go out in particular to Loyal Jones and Billy Edd Wheeler. The Weatherford family (specifically Anne, Julia, Edie, Susan, and Will) have also been supportive of my research and given me both access to personal family documents and wonderful hospitality on several occasions. Anne Weatherford consistently made herself and Far Horizons available for my research. Her kindness and openness of mind made these interactions both fruitful and enjoyable. I also appreciate the generosity of Elizabeth Culbreth and John Vanderstar, who opened their beautiful mountain home to me for a research trip, providing me access to materials relating to Weatherford's first wife and her family. Nancy Kester Neale shared memories of Weatherford and made available documents relating to her father, Howard Kester, which aided in my research.

Finally, this project would not have been possible without the support I received from family and friends over the years. In particular I would like to thank Sam Walton, Gary Cagle, Jennifer Lanier, and Virginia Gay. I am also grateful for the constant encouragement I received from my parents, David and Jeanne Canady. It is hard for me to imagine better or more supportive ones.

Notes

Introduction

1. Linda O. McMurry, *George Washington Carver: Scientist and Symbol* (New York: Oxford University Press, 1981), 34.

2. Mark D. Hersey, *My Work Is That of Conservation: An Environmental Biography of George Washington Carver* (Athens: University of Georgia Press, 2011), 43.

3. W. D. Weatherford to Lucy Cherry Crisp, January 18, 1939, folder 2601, Willis Duke Weatherford Papers #3831, Southern Historical Collection, Wilson Library, University of North Carolina at Chapel Hill; and W. D. Weatherford to Lucy Cherry Crisp, January 18, 1939, box 3, folder F, Lucy Cherry Crisp Papers, collection no. 154, East Carolina Manuscript Collection, J. Y. Joyner Library, East Carolina University, Greenville, N.C.

4. The historian Morton Sosna, who has provided an excellent study of southern liberals, defines this group as "those white Southerners who perceived that there was a serious maladjustment of race relations in the South, who recognized that the existing system resulted in grave injustices for blacks, and who either actively endorsed or engaged in programs to aid Southern blacks in the fight against lynching, disenfranchisement, segregation, and blatant discrimination in such areas as education, employment, and law enforcement"; Morton Sosna, *In Search of the Silent South: Southern Liberals and the Race Issue* (New York: Columbia University Press, 1977), viii.

5. Weatherford usually went by his initials, W.D.

6. His 1962 honor was the result of a recommendation by his friend Rupert B. Vance, the distinguished UNC sociologist. The two had known each other over the years through YMCA-related activities; at the time of Vance's recommendation, Weatherford and he were involved in a survey of the Appalachian region. See Rupert B. Vance to "The Committee on Honorary Degrees," October 27, 1961, folder 3854, Weatherford Papers. For more on Vance see Daniel Joseph Singal, *The War Within: From Victorian to Modernist Thought in the South, 1919–1945* (Chapel Hill: University of North Carolina Press, 1982), 302–15.

7. For an insightful look into Weatherford's personality and style, see Cratis

Williams, "Dr. W. D. Weatherford, Sr.," box 108, folder 16, Cratis D. Williams Papers, W. L. Eury Appalachian Collection, Special Collections, Appalachian State University, Boone, N.C. Williams was a professor at Appalachian State and received the Weatherford Award at Berea College on May 12, 1980. In this twenty-page reminiscence he discusses his interactions with Weatherford from the late 1950s until the time of his death. For the dating of this award speech, see Cratis Williams to George Antone, October 22, 1984, box 108, folder 16, Williams Papers.

8. See David P. Setran, *The College "Y": Student Religion in the Era of Secularization* (New York: Palgrave Macmillan, 2007), 107–29; and Clifford Putney, *Muscular Christianity: Manhood and Sports in Protestant America, 1880–1920* (Cambridge: Harvard University Press, 2001).

9. After a stimulating small interracial gathering in Atlanta in 1908, Weatherford published *Negro Life in the South: Present Conditions and Needs* (New York: Association Press, 1910) and later *Present Forces in Negro Progress* (New York: Association Press, 1912). Weatherford continued to publish books and articles on the subject through the 1930s. See W. D. Weatherford, "Race Relationship in the South," *Annals of the American Academy of Political and Social Science* 49 (September 1913): 164–72; W. D. Weatherford, comp., *Interracial Cooperation: A Study of the Various Agencies Working in the Field of Social Welfare* (N.p.: Interracial Committee of the War Work Council of Y.M.C.A., [1920s]); W. D. Weatherford, *The Negro from Africa to America* (New York: George H. Doran, 1924); W. D. Weatherford, ed., *A Survey of the Negro Boy in Nashville, Tennessee* (New York: Association Press, 1932); W. D. Weatherford, "Changing Attitudes of Southern Students," *Journal of Negro Education* 2 (April 1933): 147–50; and W. D. Weatherford and Charles S. Johnson, *Race Relations: Adjustment of Whites and Negroes in the United States* (1934; repr., New York: Negro Universities Press, 1969).

10. Willis Duke Weatherford, ed., *Lawlessness or Civilization—Which? Report of Addresses and Discussions in the Law and Order Conference, Held at Blue Ridge, N.C., August 4th, 5th, and 6th, Nineteen Hundred and Seventeen* (Nashville: Williams Printing Co., 1917).

11. John Egerton has noted this tendency. He writes: "The YMCA and YWCA were among the first church-related agencies to address social concerns. Many of the Southerners who yearned to do something about race relations in the twentieth century—and almost all of the ones who had strong religious ties—could trace their awakening in some degree to the exposure they got at the Y"; John Egerton, *Speak Now against the Day: The Generation before the Civil Rights Movement in the South* (New York: Alfred A. Knopf, 1994), 426. Except for limited attention in greater studies of the YMCA, the history of the Y in the South remains basically untold. Though the full account of this institution's southern history cannot be related here, this study begins the process. For information on the southern Y, see Sherwood Eddy, *A Century with Youth: A History of the Y.M.C.A. from 1844 to 1944* (New York: Association Press, 1944); C. Howard Hopkins, *History of the*

Y.M.C.A. in North America (New York: Association Press, 1951); Nina Mjagkij, *Light in Darkness: African Americans and the YMCA, 1852–1946* (Lexington: University Press of Kentucky, 1994); and Setran, *The College "Y."*

12. See Robert F. Martin, *Howard Kester and the Struggle for Social Justice in the South, 1904–77* (Charlottesville: University Press of Virginia, 1991), 20–22; John M. Glen, *Highlander: No Ordinary School, 1932–1962* (Lexington: University Press of Kentucky, 1988), 17; Katharine Du Pre Lumpkin, *The Making of a Southerner* (1946; repr., Athens: University of Georgia Press, 1991), 178–80, 189–93, 197–239; Wilma Dykeman, *Prophet of Plenty: The First Ninety Years of W. D. Weatherford* (Knoxville: University of Tennessee Press, 1966), 49, 116–17; Charles J. Holden, *The New Southern University: Academic Freedom and Liberalism at UNC* (Lexington: University Press of Kentucky, 2012); and Tracey Elaine K'Meyer, *Interracialism and Christian Community in the Postwar South: The Story of Koinonia Farm* (Charlottesville: University Press of Virginia, 1997). Clarence Jordan was president of the University of Georgia YMCA in 1933 and was invited by Weatherford to Blue Ridge for the annual president's training school that year. See "list of college YMCA presidents," folder 1835, Weatherford Papers.

13. Shannon H. Wilson, *Berea College: An Illustrated History* (Lexington: University Press of Kentucky, 2006), 161.

14. Setran, *The College "Y,"* 155–56.

15. See Thomas R. Ford, ed., *The Southern Appalachian Region: A Survey* (Lexington: University of Kentucky Press, 1962); W. D. Weatherford, ed., *Educational Opportunities in the Appalachian Mountains* (Berea, Ky.: Berea College, 1955); W. D. Weatherford, ed., *Religion in the Appalachian Mountains: A Symposium* (Berea, Ky.: Berea College, 1955); W. D. Weatherford, *Pioneers of Destiny: The Romance of the Appalachian People* (Birmingham, Ala.: Vulcan Press, 1955); and W. D. Weatherford and Earl D. C. Brewer, *Life and Religion in Southern Appalachia: An Interpretation of Selected Data from the Southern Appalachian Studies* (New York: Friendship Press, 1962).

16. On the importance of religion as a motivating factor to many white southern liberals, see Sosna, *In Search of the Silent South*, 173–74.

17. W. D. Weatherford, *American Churches and the Negro: An Historical Study from Early Slave Days to the Present* (Boston: Christopher Publishing House, 1957). There is even some evidence he may have been moving in this direction as early as the early 1940s. See chapter 5 of this volume.

18. For other studies about southern liberalism, see Bruce Clayton, *The Savage Ideal: Intolerance and Intellectual Leadership in the South, 1890–1914* (Baltimore: Johns Hopkins University Press, 1972); Carl N. Degler, *The Other South: Southern Dissenters in the Nineteenth Century* (1974; repr., Boston: Northeastern University Press, 1982); Singal, *The War Within*; and Egerton, *Speak Now against the Day*.

19. Wilma Dykeman's *Prophet of Plenty* (1966) offered the first and remains the only full-scale treatment of Weatherford. To assess her biography, it is important to understand Dykeman's purpose for the book and the context in which it

was written. Dykeman was a novelist and amateur historian in this period and had produced several semi-scholarly works, including a biography of Will W. Alexander, a Commission on Interracial Cooperation (CIC) leader and New Deal figure. She and her husband, James Stokely, also wrote a journalistic report in the late 1950s after traveling throughout the South and interviewing people about race and the 1954 *Brown* decision. See Wilma Dykeman and James Stokely, *Seeds of Southern Change: The Life of Will Alexander* (New York: W. W. Norton, 1962); and Wilma Dykeman and James Stokely, *Neither Black nor White* (New York: Rinehart, 1957). In light of these works and common interests, Weatherford, when he had turned his attention to the Appalachian region in the early 1960s, commissioned her to write his own biography using funds from the Southern Appalachian Studies project he was leading at the time. See correspondence between Weatherford and Dykeman in folder 3573, Southern Appalachian Studies (1966): General Correspondence, N–W, Weatherford Papers. A close reading of her biography and the correspondence between the two reveals that she wrote with the purpose of advocating for the needs of Appalachia within the larger national War on Poverty campaign. Dykeman relied heavily on interviews with Weatherford and on answers that Weatherford wrote to questions she prepared. At the Weatherford family home, Far Horizons, there are several of Weatherford's personal notebooks where he apparently wrote answers to questions that Dykeman posed to him as she was researching his life. See unpaginated notebooks entitled "Notes by W. D. Weatherford, 3/21/64"; "College Life and Main Objectives of Work since College at Vanderbilt"; "Need for Study of Religion etc. in Appalachia"; "Growing Up in Weatherford, Texas"; "Fisk, Blue Ridge, Religious Discussions with Students and Professors"; all in Weatherford Family Papers, Far Horizons, Black Mountain, N.C. (now deposited and being processed at the Southern Historical Collection, Accession no. 101783). His responses and the markings in these notebooks suggest that Weatherford sent these to Dykeman when she was writing *Prophet of Plenty*, and she later returned them. At times she pulls directly from his written words for her book. Far Horizons is now occupied by Weatherford's daughter-in-law, Anne Weatherford, who made these documents available. Thus, *Prophet of Plenty* was written with the particular intention of bringing interest to Appalachia and inspiring people through the "exemplary" life of Weatherford. Dykeman argues that Weatherford's life was one spent addressing both physical and spiritual poverty, and she contends that Weatherford's philosophy of life and his way of living point to the potential for both physical and spiritual plenty. There have also been more scholarly treatments of Weatherford, those written by George Peter Antone Jr. and Sara Trowbridge Combs. See George Peter Antone Jr., "Willis Duke Weatherford: An Interpretation of His Work in Race Relations, 1906–1946" (Ph.D. diss., Vanderbilt University, 1969); and Sara Trowbridge Combs, "Race Reform in the Early Twentieth Century South: The Life and Work of Willis Duke Weatherford" (master's thesis, East Tennessee State University, 2004). Both works essentially focus on his efforts relating to race relations. Examining Weatherford's career until 1946, Antone's excellent dissertation argues that he was "a moderate and a paternalist," yet he also recognizes that Weatherford was a "pioneer" for his time (225). Nevertheless, his sources for the project were primarily documents Weatherford made available, interviews with the subject, and correspondence held at Vanderbilt's and Fisk's libraries. See George P. Antone to W. D. Weatherford, February 20, 1966, folder 3890; George P. Antone to W. D. Weatherford, [1967], folder 3901; and George P. Antone to W. D. Weatherford, May 20, 1967, folder 3901, all in Weatherford Papers. In connection with his analysis of Weatherford's race relations work, Antone also examined the importance and history of Weatherford's YMCA Graduate School. See Antone, "Willis Duke Weatherford," chap. 5, "Y.M.C.A. Graduate School," and George P. Antone, "The Y.M.C.A. Graduate School, Nashville, 1919–1936," *Tennessee Historical Quarterly* 32 (Spring 1973): 67–82. Following Weatherford's death in 1970, his papers were deposited at the Southern Historical Collection at the University of North Carolina at Chapel Hill. At the time he wrote his dissertation, in the late 1960s, Antone would not have had access to all these materials. Combs's recent master's thesis makes selected use of these papers and extends her treatment of Weatherford's involvement in race relations through the late 1950s. Her work complements, rather than challenges, Antone's assessment of Weatherford's race relations work, while placing Weatherford in the context of Progressivism. Besides these three focused works, Weatherford's activities have also received brief recognition by other scholars as part of their larger works. See George Brown Tindall, *The Emergence of the New South, 1913–1945* (Baton Rouge: Louisiana State University Press, 1967), 176–78; Sosna, *In Search of the Silent South*, 16–18, 20–22, 77; Anthony P. Dunbar, *Against the Grain: Southern Radicals and Prophets, 1929–1959* (Charlottesville: University Press of Virginia, 1981), 21–22; McMurry, *George Washington Carver*, 35, 201–2, 206; Martin, *Howard Kester*, 22, 25–26; David L. Chappell, *Inside Agitators: White Southerners in the Civil Rights Movement* (Baltimore: Johns Hopkins University Press, 1994), 35; Egerton, *Speak Now against the Day*, 44–48, 74, 77, 122–23, 130, 159, 175, 426; and Paul Harvey, *Freedom's Coming: Religious Culture and the Shaping of the South from the Civil War through the Civil Rights Era* (Chapel Hill: University of North Carolina Press, 2005), 66–67.

20. When Weatherford received the honorary UNC degree, one of the accomplishments the citation noted was that he had spent his life "teaching and practicing the social gospel"; A. C. Howell, "Citation for Willis Duke Weatherford on the Occasion of His Receiving the Degree of Doctor of Laws," June 4, 1962, folder 3760, Weatherford Papers. Vance's letter to the committee also mentions that Weatherford had "sought simply to apply the social gospel to regional development"; Rupert B. Vance to "Committee on Honorary Degrees," October 27, 1961, folder 3854, Weatherford Papers. For scholars who have described Weatherford as a "social gospeler," see Ronald C. White Jr. and C. Howard Hopkins, *The Social Gospel: Religion and Reform in Changing America* (Philadelphia: Temple University Press, 1976), 95; Ronald C. White Jr., *Liberty and Justice for All: Racial Reform*

and the Social Gospel (1877–1925) (1990; repr., Louisville: Westminster John Knox Press, 2002), 66; and Ralph E. Luker, *The Social Gospel in Black and White: American Racial Reform, 1885–1912* (Chapel Hill: University of North Carolina Press, 1991). Luker never explicitly calls Weatherford a social gospel spokesman, but his inclusion of Weatherford in the study implicitly makes this point.

21. Still, American religious historians have debated the exact meaning of the term *social gospel*. Indeed, the intellectual historian Paul K. Conkin has described this label as "one of the most imprecise in American history," noting further that "it has impeded the understanding of Church history more than any other simplistic concept"; Paul K. Conkin, *When All the Gods Trembled: Darwinism, Scopes, and American Intellectuals* (Lanham, Md.: Rowman and Littlefield, 1998), 63. In truth, the movement defies easy definition because of the variety of figures associated with it and their wide-ranging ideas and theologies; Christianity's long tradition of social concern and charity; and the fact that social gospel adherents never created an institution or denomination to forward its causes. The closest manifestation of an institution promoting the social gospel was the Federal Council of Churches (founded in 1908), but it was more fully connected to the broader ecumenical movement of the time. For more on the social gospel see Charles Howard Hopkins, *The Rise of the Social Gospel in American Protestantism, 1865–1915* (New Haven: Yale University Press, 1940); Henry F. May, *Protestant Churches and Industrial America* (New York: Harper & Brothers, 1949); Sydney E. Ahlstrom, *A Religious History of the American People* (New Haven: Yale University Press, 1972), 785–804; White and Hopkins, *The Social Gospel;* Luker, *The Social Gospel in Black and White;* White, *Liberty and Justice for All;* and Susan Curtis, *A Consuming Faith: The Social Gospel and Modern American Culture* (Baltimore: Johns Hopkins University Press, 1991).

22. See Walter Rauschenbusch, *Christianity and the Social Crisis* (New York: Macmillan, 1907), esp. chap. 5. Rauschenbusch further developed his thoughts on what the social gospel meant in Walter Rauschenbusch, *Christianizing the Social Order* (New York: Macmillan, 1912), and *A Theology for the Social Gospel* (New York: Macmillan, 1917). Quote from Ahlstrom, *A Religious History of the American People,* 785.

23. Rauschenbusch, *Christianity and the Social Crisis,* 421.

24. These views are generally laid out in Hopkins, *Rise of the Social Gospel in American Protestantism;* May, *Protestant Churches and Industrial America;* and Ahlstrom, *A Religious History of the American People,* 785–804. Also attesting to this dating is the death of key figures of the movement: Strong (1916), Rauschenbusch (1918), and Gladden (1918). Yet historians in more recent years have expanded this definition, causing more confusion in understanding a movement that was already rather nebulous. In 1976 C. Howard Hopkins and a younger scholar, Ronald White, collaborated on a reappraisal of this issue. Their new interpretation challenged Hopkins's own earlier analysis of the movement; the new study pushed "the boundaries of the definition of the Social Gospel in a variety of direc-

tions: women as well as men, South and North, rural as well as urban, Catholic and Jewish as well as Protestant"; White, *Liberty and Justice for All,* xii. See also White and Hopkins, *The Social Gospel,* xii. Moreover, the authors extended the timing of the movement, as they contended that "its impact continued long after its demise was forecast following World War I," and that it had reemerged in the Civil Rights movement of the 1960s; White and Hopkins, *The Social Gospel,* xi. Early twentieth-century racial reform efforts in the South also became classified as social gospel work. Previous scholars had excluded attention to race as an interest of the social gospel movement. Ahlstrom notes that with the exception of Francis Greenwood Peabody, there was a "prevailing lack of interest in Negro education and racial questions" among social gospel advocates; Ahlstrom, *A Religious History of the American People,* 795. Two more extended studies on the subject were published in the early 1990s, White, *Liberty and Justice for All;* and Luker, *The Social Gospel in Black and White.* Both books included an attention to African Americans practicing the social gospel as well. In the end, though the inclusivity of the new scholarship brought valuable attention to groups and issues previously neglected, the movement became so loosely defined that the distinction between the social gospel and the social application of Christian principles became very blurry.

25. Weatherford did read Rauschenbusch, however. See Weatherford's marked copy of Walter Rauschenbusch, *The Social Principles of Jesus* (New York: Association Press, 1916), Record Group no. 9, box 5, folder 8, W. D. Weatherford Sr. Collection, Berea College Special Collections and Archives, Berea, Ky.

26. Weatherford only mildly supported a few radical southern groups, specifically the Fellowship of Southern Churchmen, Koinonia Farm, and Highlander Folk School. In 1942 Weatherford described the Fellowship of Southern Churchmen's policy as "good" but did "not think they ha[d] ever done any remarkable things"; W. D. Weatherford to Ivan Lee Holt, February 6, 1942, folder 2923, Weatherford Papers. In 1958 Weatherford gave the group a ten-dollar donation; see receipt, December 26, 1958, folder 3729, Weatherford Papers. The extent to which Weatherford supported the interracial farm community Koinonia, near Americus, Georgia, is not known, but the cofounders of the group, Martin England (a former Blue Ridge summer worker) and Clarence Jordan (a college Y president), did make plans to visit Weatherford in the fall of 1942 to brief him about their newly organized project; see Martin England to W. D. Weatherford, October 12, 1942, folder 2871, Weatherford Papers. Weatherford also seems to have had little connection to Highlander Folk School. In 1959, in the midst of that organization's struggles to stay alive, Weatherford inquired of his longtime friend Robert Eleazer of Tennessee about the "'low-down'" on the school: "If they are really doing a first class job, I would not want to miss the chance to help them a little, but if, on the other hand, there are questionable things going on there, I would not want to risk my money on it. I do not know the facts and I am open-minded on it"; W. D. Weatherford to Robert Eleazer, September 8, 1959, folder 3828, Weatherford Papers. For examples of the limited radical tradition in southern religion, see

Dunbar, *Against the Grain;* Glen, *Highlander;* Martin, *Howard Kester;* K'Meyer, *Interracialism and Christian Community;* and David Stricklin, *A Genealogy of Dissent: Southern Baptist Protest in the Twentieth Century* (Lexington: University Press of Kentucky, 1999).

27. See Weatherford, "College Life and Main Objectives," Weatherford Family Papers.

28. Among southern religious historians there has been a lively debate over whether a social gospel tradition persisted in their studied region. Charles Howard Hopkins's original 1940 definition had seemingly left little room for a southern variant of this movement because the South had been largely a rural region in the late nineteenth and early twentieth centuries. Indeed, several historians of the American South have argued that the movement did not exist in the region. Chief among those holding this view has been Samuel S. Hill, who has argued that the "central theme" of southern religion has been the conversion of individuals rather than criticism of "social structures," the latter being what he considered the essence of the social gospel. In his influential book *Southern Churches in Crisis* (1966), written in the midst of the Civil Rights movement, Hill reproached white southern Protestant churches for their lack of social interest, particularly in regard to confronting segregation. Hill offered this description of the general attitudes of the region's white Christians in regard to race relations: "The white Christian's duty toward the Negro, as seen by the southern church, is to convert him and befriend him (in a paternal framework), not to consider altering the social traditions and arrangements which govern his (and everyone else's) life to so significant a degree"; see the revised edition, Samuel S. Hill, *Southern Churches in Crisis Revisited* (Tuscaloosa: University of Alabama Press, 1999), 73, 171, lxvi. The historian John B. Boles also agrees with Hill's assessment that southern religion has concentrated primarily on conversion rather than addressing societal concerns and criticizing the structures that lead to injustice; John B. Boles, "The Discovery of Southern Religious History," in *Interpreting Southern History: Historiographical Essays in Honor of Sanford W. Higginbotham,* ed. John B. Boles and Evelyn Thomas Nolen (Baton Rouge: Louisiana State University Press, 1987), 540, and John B. Boles, *The South through Time: A History of an American Region,* 3rd ed., 2 vols. (Upper Saddle River, N.J.: Pearson Prentice Hall, 2004), 2:448. In the discussion of southern Progressivism in the latter work, Boles notes, "Religious leaders dispensed charity to the destitute and battled such enemies of moral behavior as the whiskey distillers, though unlike northern Social Gospel ministers, they seldom constructed a theological critique of the social institutions that produced or allowed poverty and injustice" (2:448). Boles recognizes that a few "clerical radicals" have existed on the margins of southern religion, but he correctly notes that their influence has never been large and that this spirit certainly has not typified southern religious life; Boles, "Discovery of Southern Religious History," 540. He further adds that "occasionally" some "southern evangelicals protested some forms of economic and racial oppression" (543). Thus, while neither Boles nor Hill discounts that there

have been instances of social concern among southern evangelicals, their essential argument is that this has not been the overwhelming tendency of this region's religious impulse. Other southern scholars have produced studies illuminating southern religion's societal concern, sometimes referring to this work as a manifestation of the "social gospel" and at other points using the broader term "social Christianity." Wayne Flynt has perhaps been the most vocal proponent of this perspective, emphasizing the existence of social concern of urban ministers and congregations in Alabama; see Wayne Flynt, "One in the Spirit, Many in the Flesh: Southern Evangelicals," in *Varieties of Southern Evangelicalism*, ed. David Edwin Harrell Jr. (Macon, Ga.: Mercer University Press, 1981), 23–44; Wayne Flynt, *Alabama Baptists: Southern Baptists in the Heart of Dixie* (Tuscaloosa: University of Alabama Press, 1998), 251–398; and Wayne Flynt, "'Feeding the Hungry and Ministering to the Broken Hearted': The Presbyterian Church in the United States and the Social Gospel, 1900–1920," in *Religion in the South*, ed. Charles Reagan Wilson (Jackson: University Press of Mississippi, 1985), 83–137. John Patrick McDowell, Keith Harper, Paul Harvey, and Charles Israel have also provided analyses of other forms of socially engaged Christian work. See John Patrick McDowell, *The Social Gospel in the South: The Woman's Home Mission Movement in the Methodist Episcopal Church, South, 1886–1939* (Baton Rouge: Louisiana State University Press, 1982); Keith Harper, *The Quality of Mercy: Southern Baptists and Social Christianity, 1890–1920* (Tuscaloosa: University of Alabama Press, 1996); Paul Harvey, *Redeeming the South: Religious Cultures and Racial Identities among Southern Baptists, 1865–1925* (Chapel Hill: University of North Carolina Press, 1997); and Charles A. Israel, *Before Scopes: Evangelicalism, Education, and Evolution in Tennessee, 1870–1925* (Athens: University of Georgia Press, 2004). Harper also provides a helpful historiographical discussion of the debate about the existence of a southern social gospel; Harper, *The Quality of Mercy*, 1–14.

1. The Making of a Southern Liberal

1. "Notes by W. D. Weatherford, 3/21/64," Weatherford Family Papers.

2. Sosna, *In Search of the Silent South*, viii. See also Gunnar Myrdal, *An American Dilemma: The Negro Problem and Modern Democracy*, 2 vols. (New York: Harper & Brothers, 1944), 1:452–73; Bruce Clayton, *The Savage Ideal: Intolerance and Intellectual Leadership in the South, 1890–1914* (Baltimore: Johns Hopkins University Press, 1972); Singal, *The War Within;* and Egerton, *Speak Now against the Day.*

3. For information on Weatherford, Texas, see David Minor, "Weatherford, TX," in *The Handbook of Texas Online*, www.tshaonline.org/handbook/online/articles/hew3 (accessed April 18, 2016). There has been some confusion about whether this town was named for one of W. D. Weatherford's ancestors. Wilma Dykeman contends that it was named for W.D.'s uncle William Weatherford; Dykeman, *Prophet of Plenty*, 14. Minor's article on the town's history, however,

declares it was named for Jefferson Weatherford (1810–67), a Texas state senator who had helped write the bill establishing Parker County, of which Weatherford became the county seat when it was incorporated in 1858. According to an interview with W.D.'s father, Samuel Leonard Weatherford, for a local newspaper story in 1910, Jefferson Weatherford was his cousin. See R. K. Phillips, "Sketches from Life," *Weatherford Democrat,* February 18, 1910, photocopy of a clipping in Weatherford family vertical file, Weatherford Public Library, Weatherford, Tex.

4. See "Family Record," folder 3720, Weatherford Papers. Only seven of these children lived past childhood. The second child, Samuel Leonard Jr., born in 1861, died sometime in his first year as the result of burns. Margaret Weatherford lost three other children at birth, but these were unnamed.

5. Ibid., and untitled genealogy notes, folder 3720, Weatherford Papers. These notes probably were written by Flora Weatherford, W.D.'s older sister (born in 1867), with whom he maintained the closest contact among his siblings after leaving Texas. Her information conflicts somewhat with W.D.'s later memories of his parents' backgrounds, but this may be due slightly to some confusion on his part because of his age at the time. Weatherford noted that his father was born near Bristol, Tenn., which is near the Tennessee-Virginia border. See "Notes by W. D. Weatherford, 3/21/64," Weatherford Family Papers.

6. Untitled genealogy notes, folder 3720, Weatherford Papers. Weatherford noted she also lived in Yancey County, N.C., at some point, where she took the only six months of formal schooling she ever received. The exact location and dates of her residence in North Carolina are unknown, however. Weatherford also insisted both his parents were of Scotch-Irish descent, a point that he later emphasized in his involvement with Appalachian reform. See "Notes by W. D. Weatherford, 3/21/64," Weatherford Family Papers.

7. Flora Weatherford to W. D. Weatherford (n.d.), folder 3720, Weatherford Papers.

8. Untitled genealogy notes, 3, folder 3720, Weatherford Papers.

9. Ibid.

10. Ibid., 2+; and David Paul Smith, *Frontier Defense in the Civil War: Texas' Rangers and Rebels* (College Station: Texas A&M University Press, 1992), 151.

11. Untitled genealogy notes, 2+, folder 3720, Weatherford Papers. The writer is probably referring to the Battle of Dove Creek, January 8, 1865, which took place near San Angelo when Confederate soldiers and Texas state militiamen combined to attack Kickapoo Indians. Since W. D. Weatherford never made mention of his father being a Confederate, it is most likely Samuel Weatherford served in the state militia during the Civil War. See Elmer Kelton, "Battle of Dove Creek," in *The Handbook of Texas Online,* www.tshaonline.org/handbook/online/articles/btd01 (accessed April 18, 2016); and Smith, *Frontier Defense,* 151–55.

12. Flora to Weatherford, folder 3720, Weatherford Papers.

13. Ibid.

14. See untitled genealogy notes, 4; and "Family Record," both in folder 3720,

Weatherford Papers. According to Flora, a spark from the fireplace probably flew into the crib, setting it and the child aflame while his parents were out retrieving water for the home.

15. Flora to Weatherford, folder 3720, Weatherford Papers.

16. See ibid. and untitled genealogy notes, 4, folder 3720, Weatherford Papers.

17. Minor, "Weatherford, TX." At this time the town would have fit well with the historian Robert Wiebe's characterization of a provincial "island community" because of its local focus, isolation, size, and lack of transportation networks; see Robert H. Wiebe, *The Search for Order: 1877–1920* (New York: Hill and Wang, 1967), xiii.

18. Minor, "Weatherford, TX."

19. Jeri Echeverria, "Parker County," in *The Handbook of Texas Online*, www.tshaonline.org/handbook/online/articles/hcp03 (accessed April 18, 2016); and Deborah Liles, "Inventing the Past: How Historiography Contributes to Deceptions in Small Communities," paper presented to Parker County History and Heritage, Weatherford, Tex., January 19, 2010. Photocopy in possession of the author. Liles teaches history at the University of North Texas; this work was part of her dissertation.

20. Liles, "Inventing the Past," 5–6.

21. Echeverria, "Parker County."

22. The only mention of contact with African Americans during Weatherford's youth comes from his sister Virginia, who recalled listening to a black preacher near their home. See untitled genealogical notes, 4, folder 3720, Weatherford Papers.

23. See C. Vann Woodward, *Origins of the New South, 1877–1913* (Baton Rouge: Louisiana State University Press, 1951); and C. Vann Woodward, *The Strange Career of Jim Crow* (New York: Oxford University Press, 1955).

24. Boles, *The South through Time*, 2:467.

25. W. D. Weatherford, untitled handwritten essay (12 pp.) (1958–1961), 1, folder 3720, Weatherford Papers.

26. Weatherford, "Growing Up in Weatherford, Texas," Weatherford Family Papers.

27. See untitled genealogy notes, 5, folder 3720, Weatherford Papers; and Weatherford, "College Life and Main Objectives," Weatherford Family Papers.

28. Weatherford, "Growing Up in Weatherford, Texas," Weatherford Family Papers; and untitled genealogy notes, 4–5, folder 3720, Weatherford Papers.

29. See untitled genealogy notes, 4, folder 3720, Weatherford Papers. Wilma Dykeman portrays the family's financial situation in a more positive light, arguing that "the Weatherfords might have been poor by today's luxurious standards, but for their time and place they were solid middle-class citizens"; Dykeman, *Prophet of Plenty*, 15. This, however, is not the tone one gets from Weatherford's recollections in "Growing Up in Weatherford, Texas." Weatherford at one point, while comparing himself with a son of a prominent family in town, said he was "a very

poor boy." Also, in his discussion of his desire for a good education, he noted, "My home could not help me a cent financially."

30. Weatherford, "College Life and Main Objectives," Weatherford Family Papers.

31. "Notes by W. D. Weatherford, 3/21/64," Weatherford Family Papers; and Weatherford, "College Life and Main Objectives," Weatherford Family Papers.

32. See Anne Weatherford, interview by the author, September 11, 2009, Black Mountain, N.C. Anne Weatherford notes this information came through her husband's (Willis Jr.) first cousin Virginia. She was the daughter of W.D.'s older sister Flora Weatherford. Perhaps the closest Weatherford got to touching on the subject of his parents' marital problems was when he told a story of his mother's bravery while she was alone taking care of her young children on the frontier. Weatherford followed this story by noting, "To her dying day she had the nerve to defend both herself and her family. I owe to her and her determination my own determination to get an education." According to Anne Weatherford, Margaret Weatherford had asked her husband to leave the family, and perhaps this statement by W.D. is hinting at her fortitude. For quote see "Notes by W. D. Weatherford, 3/21/64," Weatherford Family Papers. Samuel Weatherford was living alone at the time of his death, though his wife was still alive; see "Death of S. L. Weatherford," *Weatherford (Tex.) Daily Herald,* January 18, 1913, 4, photocopy of a clipping in Weatherford family vertical file. One other document in Weatherford Public Library files on the Weatherford family indicates Samuel Leonard was living alone at the time of his death. See sheet with 1870, 1880, and 1900 U.S. Census reports for the Weatherford family.

33. See "Notes by W. D. Weatherford, 3/21/64," Weatherford Family Papers.

34. For examples of his support of Prohibition, see W. D. Weatherford to Donald Comer, November 12, 1928, folder 590; and W. D. Weatherford to John F. Baggett, April 19, 1939, folder 2583, both in Weatherford Papers.

35. See Weatherford, "Growing Up in Weatherford, Texas," Weatherford Family Papers. On this occasion Weatherford was working for the YMCA and was traveling in Texas visiting colleges. He and his father had dinner with a prominent family in town. Weatherford even missed his father's funeral in 1913. At that time he was out of the country on a YMCA trip. See "Death of S. L. Weatherford," *Weatherford (Tex.) Daily Herald,* January 18, 1913, 4, Weatherford family vertical file.

36. See "Notes by W. D. Weatherford, 3/21/64," Weatherford Family Papers.

37. Ibid.

38. Weatherford, "College Life and Main Objectives," Weatherford Family Papers.

39. David Minor, "Weatherford College," in *The Handbook of Texas Online,* www.tshaonline.org/handbook/online/articles/kbw07 (accessed April 18, 2016).

40. Ibid.; and John A. Lomax, *Adventures of a Ballad Hunter* (New York: Macmillan, 1947), 25.

41. Lomax, *Adventures of a Ballad Hunter,* 25–26; and Joe B. Witherspoon,

Weatherford College: Enlightening the Frontier, 1869–1986 ([Texas?]: n.p., 1986), 10.

42. Dykeman, *Prophet of Plenty*, 31; and "Notes by W. D. Weatherford, 3/21/64," Weatherford Family Papers.

43. "Notes by W. D. Weatherford, 3/21/64," Weatherford Family Papers; and Dykeman, *Prophet of Plenty*, 25–26.

44. "Notes by W. D. Weatherford, 3/21/64," Weatherford Family Papers.

45. Ibid.

46. Ibid.

47. Ibid. Dykeman, *Prophet of Plenty*, 32, states that Weatherford had been inflicted with typhoid in the spring of 1897, which caused his vision troubles. Weatherford, however, makes no mention of this illness affecting him as he relates this story in his personal notebook, blaming the trouble instead on his long hours of reading by poor lighting.

48. "Notes by W. D. Weatherford, 3/21/64," Weatherford Family Papers.

49. See Weatherford, "College Life and Main Objectives," Weatherford Family Papers.

50. Weatherford, "Growing Up in Weatherford, Texas," Weatherford Family Papers.

51. Ibid.

52. Ibid.

53. Ibid.

54. "Notes by W. D. Weatherford, 3/21/64," Weatherford Family Papers.

55. Setran, *The College "Y,"* 4.

56. See W. D. Weatherford to Fletcher S. Brockman, October 8, 1929; and R. H. King, memorandum, October 7, 1929, both in folder 3161, Weatherford Papers; Hopkins, *History of the Y.M.C.A. in North America*, 667; and Setran, *The College "Y,"* 265.

57. Weatherford to Brockman, October 8, 1929, folder 3161, Weatherford Papers.

58. McMurry, *George Washington Carver*, 34.

59. W. D. Weatherford to George Washington Carver, November 7, 1932, folder 3641, Weatherford Papers.

60. Hopkins, *History of the Y.M.C.A. in North America*, 667; and Setran, *The College "Y,"* 265.

61. Weatherford to Brockman, October 8, 1929, folder 3161, Weatherford Papers.

62. "Notes by W. D. Weatherford, 3/21/64," Weatherford Family Papers.

63. For Vanderbilt see Paul K. Conkin, *Gone with the Ivy: A Biography of Vanderbilt University* (Knoxville: University of Tennessee Press, 1985); and Israel, *Before Scopes*, 43–67.

64. "Notes by W. D. Weatherford, 3/21/64," Weatherford Family Papers.

65. Dykeman, *Prophet of Plenty*, 23.

66. Don H. Doyle, *Nashville in the New South, 1880–1930* (Knoxville: Uni-

versity of Tennessee Press, 1985), 235. For more information on the city's black population, see Bobby L. Lovett, *The African-American History of Nashville, Tennessee, 1780–1930* (Fayetteville: University of Arkansas Press, 1999).

67. Before the university's creation, Methodists did not have a top-notch school in league with Yale (Congregational), Brown (Baptist), or Princeton (Presbyterian); Randolph-Macon College in Virginia was the southern church's best institution. Tennessee Methodists began organizing in 1858 what would take shape as Vanderbilt in the 1860s and 1870s. Critical to the establishment of the school and its future success was a tremendous initial boost from Cornelius Vanderbilt, who provided gifts of roughly one million dollars. The Commodore, while not particularly religious, had been motivated to make this bequest because of family connections to Holland N. McTyeire (Vanderbilt board president) and owing to a desire to offer help to the South in the wake of the Civil War. See Israel, *Before Scopes*, 44; and Conkin, *Gone with the Ivy*, 7, 15, 17–19, 24, 31.

68. Conkin, *Gone with the Ivy*, 55, 102.

69. Ibid., 56.

70. Ibid., 129. It should be noted that Vanderbilt had few women students in this period (ten in 1892). Over its early history a small number had attended the school, these usually the daughters of faculty or members of the administration. Between 1892 and 1901, however, "women at Vanderbilt gained full legal equality"; ibid., 131–32.

71. Ibid., 129. The relationship between Vanderbilt and the Methodist Episcopal Church, South, became increasingly strained after 1900. In 1914 the two broke ties. See Doyle, *Nashville in the New South*, 201.

72. Conkin, *Gone with the Ivy*, 108.

73. Ibid., 110–11.

74. Ibid., 106–8. Conkin notes that chair-holding professors' total compensation (roughly $2,300 a year) in 1894 was actually less than that of their counterparts in 1875.

75. "Notes by W. D. Weatherford, 3/21/64," Weatherford Family Papers. Even though Weatherford never received seminary training, he still went on to become an ordained minister in the Methodist Church. He could perform baptisms, weddings, and funerals, but it is unclear if he could serve Communion. Anne Weatherford, interview by the author, September 11, 2009.

76. "Notes by W. D. Weatherford, 3/21/64," Weatherford Family Papers. Baskervill was one of several of Vanderbilt's early professors who earned their undergraduate degrees at Wofford College and later took the Ph.D. at the University of Leipzig in Germany. He was honored for both his teaching and his scholarship; he published a book on southern writers. See Conkin, *Gone with the Ivy*, 66–67, and Anja Becker, "Southern Academic Ambitions Meet German Scholarship: The Leipzig Networks of Vanderbilt University's James H. Kirkland in the Late Nineteenth Century," *Journal of Southern History* 74 (November 2008): 855–86.

77. See W. D. Weatherford academic transcript, Registrar's Office, Vanderbilt University, Nashville.

78. See "Notes by W. D. Weatherford, 3/21/64," Weatherford Family Papers. It should be noted that he received this honor sometime after he completed his B.A. in 1899. Vanderbilt was not granted this prestigious honor society until 1901. See Conkin, *Gone with the Ivy*, 133.

79. Conkin, *Gone with the Ivy*, 75; and Weatherford, "College Life and Main Objectives," Weatherford Family Papers.

80. Dykeman, *Prophet of Plenty*, 40.

81. Weatherford, "College Life and Main Objectives," Weatherford Family Papers. Vanderbilt's YMCA was organized in 1885. See Conkin, *Gone with the Ivy*, 79.

82. See Weatherford, "Growing Up in Weatherford, Texas" and "College Life and Main Objectives," both in Weatherford Family Papers; W. D. Weatherford pledge card, RG 935, Alumni Relations, box 2687, folder 100, Special Collections and University Archives, Vanderbilt University Library, Nashville; and Bill Traughber, "The History of Vanderbilt Athletics, part 1," August 27, 2008, http://vucommodores.cstv.com/genrel/082708aaa.html (accessed February 23, 2010).

83. Because Nashville was home to several institutions of higher learning for African Americans, including Fisk University, Roger Williams University, and Meharry Medical College, Weatherford might even have had some interaction with college-educated blacks. See Lovett, *African-American History of Nashville*, 144–72.

84. Conkin, *Gone with the Ivy*, 83.

85. Ibid., 83. Conkin does note one important instance in which Vanderbilt was the forum for more progressive views on race in this period. For the 1887 commencement ceremonies, George Washington Cable, a noted white southern liberal of the time and author of *The Silent South* (1885), spoke on racial issues.

86. Weatherford to Carver, November 7, 1932, folder 3641, Weatherford Papers.

87. Weatherford, "College Life and Main Objectives," Weatherford Family Papers; and Conkin, *Gone with the Ivy*, 76.

88. Weatherford, "College Life and Main Objectives," Weatherford Family Papers; and Conkin, *Gone with the Ivy*, 305.

89. Weatherford, "College Life and Main Objectives," Weatherford Family Papers.

90. Ibid.

91. Ibid.; and Conkin, *Gone with the Ivy*, 305.

92. Conkin, *Gone with the Ivy*, 103, 305.

93. Ibid., 305–6.

94. Weatherford, "College Life and Main Objectives," Weatherford Family Papers.

95. Ibid.

96. Conkin, *Gone with the Ivy,* 67.
97. "Notes by W. D. Weatherford, 3/21/64," Weatherford Family Papers.
98. Dykeman, *Prophet of Plenty,* 38.
99. Conkin, *Gone with the Ivy,* 107.
100. "Dr. Richard Jones Dies in Canada," *Vanderbilt Alumnus* 9, no. 1 (1923), Special Collections and University Archives, Vanderbilt University Library, Nashville.
101. Ibid.; and Herbert Z. Kip, "Tribute to Dr. Richard Jones," *Vanderbilt Alumnus* 9, no. 3 (1924), Special Collections and University Archives, Vanderbilt University Library.
102. "Notes by W. D. Weatherford, 3/21/64," Weatherford Family Papers.
103. Ibid.
104. Ibid.
105. Ibid.
106. Ibid.
107. Tagore was a Bengali writer whose published works earned him the Nobel Prize for Literature in 1913.
108. "Notes by W. D. Weatherford, 3/21/64," Weatherford Family Papers; and Weatherford, untitled handwritten essay, 5, folder 3720, Weatherford Papers. An analysis of Weatherford's master's thesis is not possible because no copies exist.
109. "Notes by W. D. Weatherford, 3/21/64," Weatherford Family Papers.
110. Conkin, *Gone with the Ivy,* 290.
111. Ibid., 89.
112. Peter Novick, *That Noble Dream: The "Objectivity Question" and the American Historical Profession* (New York: Cambridge University Press, 1988), 22.
113. Conkin, *Gone with the Ivy,* 89.
114. Weatherford academic transcript, Vanderbilt University; and Weatherford, untitled handwritten essay, 5, folder 3720, Weatherford Papers.
115. Weatherford, untitled handwritten essay, 5, folder 3720, Weatherford Papers.
116. Ibid., 6.
117. Ibid., 1.
118. Ibid., 3.
119. Ibid., 1.
120. Ibid., 2.
121. Ibid., 6.
122. Ibid.
123. Ibid.
124. Ibid., 7.
125. W. D. Weatherford, *Fundamental Religious Principles in Browning's Poetry* (Nashville: Smith and Lamar, 1907), 21.
126. Weatherford, untitled handwritten essay, 8, folder 3720, Weatherford Papers. Weatherford also made a similar argument on the same page of his essay,

noting, "Tennyson came to feel that it would be a cheat world which put into the soul of a man such deep longings for fuller life, and then made no provision for satisfying those longings."

127. Ibid., 10.

128. For his graduation dates see W. D. Weatherford's 1929 application for *Who's Who in American Education,* folder 923, Weatherford Papers. There has been some confusion about when Weatherford received his Ph.D., which is due mostly to Dykeman's assertion that "at the end of two undergraduate and three graduate years, Weatherford had won his three degrees at Vanderbilt," which implies that in 1902 he had completed his doctorate; Dykeman, *Prophet of Plenty,* 40. Dykeman almost certainly got this information from Weatherford's own written recollections, in which he noted, "When I finished 2 undergraduate and three graduate years at Vanderbilt I had gotten BA, MA, and Ph.D. degrees"; Weatherford, "College Life and Main Objectives," Weatherford Family Papers. Weatherford must have been confused in his older age or simply referring to finishing his coursework in 1902. The reason it took Weatherford so long to complete his dissertation is probably that he was working for the YMCA from 1902 onward, and it is likely he pushed to finish the project in 1907 because his first wife was expecting a child that year.

129. Weatherford, *Fundamental Religious Principles.*

130. Ibid., 6; and Conkin, *Gone with the Ivy,* 187.

131. Weatherford, *Fundamental Religious Principles,* 11.

132. Ibid., 89.

133. Ibid., 12.

134. Perhaps some of the blame for the lack of scholarly rigor found in Weatherford's dissertation must be shared by the professors who guided his studies and the caliber of work they expected under the structure of the Vanderbilt graduate program at the time. Though this curriculum represented an improvement over the one that existed before 1890, it still must have been lacking in many respects. Conkin notes that the number of Vanderbilt graduate students declined in the 1910s and that by 1920 the program had ceased. In 1927 Vanderbilt reorganized the graduate college into what would become "its modern graduate program," which continues in existence. Exactly how this new program of 1927 improved over the former is not specified. See Conkin, *Gone with the Ivy,* 290–91.

135. Weatherford, *Fundamental Religious Principles,* 17, 150.

136. Ibid., 89–90.

137. Ibid., 98.

138. Ibid., 123.

139. Ibid., 119.

140. The first instance comes from the foreword by Gross Alexander, who points out that the "result" of Weatherford's "interpretation" of Browning "is a fresh and breathing statement of the reality and personality of God" (ibid., 6). Furthermore, at several places in the text Weatherford emphasizes that Browning believed in

a personal God (36, 39, 152). At another point Weatherford illustrates another aspect of this philosophy in his study, showing how consciousness gives meaning to the world. He writes: "Nature without a thinking mind to interpret it is nothing. It is dead and useless. It is as music where no ear listens, or beauty where no eye sees. But when man steps upon the stage, every process of nature takes on a new significance" (41). Finally, in a footnote in which Weatherford discloses his acceptance of the ontological argument for God, there is a further comment that attests to personalism's bearing on his study. In this extended annotation Weatherford observes, "Then, if we mean that all conscious life is dependent on a universal self-consciousness, we arrive at a proof which is not easily refuted" (21n). Here he is referring to the relationship between human personality and the personality of God. Ralph Luker also recognizes the influence of personalism on Weatherford; see Luker, *The Social Gospel in Black and White,* 188.

141. In actuality the term *personalism* was not used to describe this philosophical system until 1905, when Borden Parker Bowne gave it this label. Before that time, though the essential ideas were there, he had referred to it as "objective idealism"; see Francis John McConnell, *Borden Parker Bowne: His Life and His Philosophy* (New York: Abingdon Press, 1929), 18, 131.

142. Edgar Sheffield Brightman, *Is God a Person?* (New York: Association Press, 1932), 4.

143. Borden Parker Bowne, *Personalism* (1908; repr., Norwood, Mass.: Plimpton Press, 1936), 266.

144. Brightman, *Is God a Person?* 5; and Bowne, *Personalism,* v.

145. Brightman, *Is God a Person?* 4.

146. Bowne, *Personalism,* vii.

147. Ibid., 11.

148. Ibid., 278.

149. Weatherford, "Need for Study of Religion etc. in Appalachia," Weatherford Family Papers; and Bowne, *Personalism,* 277–78.

150. Weatherford, "Need for Study of Religion, etc. in Appalachia," Weatherford Family Papers.

151. Conkin, *Gone with the Ivy,* 71; and Brightman, *Is God a Person?* 18. Tillett wrote a sympathetic review of Brightman's book; see Wilbur F. Tillett, "The Personality of God" (n.d.), folder 1529b, Weatherford Papers.

152. "Notes by W. D. Weatherford, 3/21/64," Weatherford Family Papers.

153. Some of the earliest southern white liberals came from religious backgrounds. One of the first was Atticus Greene Haygood, a Methodist minister and president of Emory College in Atlanta. Haygood laid out his concern for African Americans in 1881 in his book *Our Brother in Black: His Freedom and Future.* He believed that to be Christian required whites to treat African Americans differently. He was very outspoken about lynching, seeing mob violence as incompatible with faith. Yet he was not for social equality, and he did not stand up against the rising Jim Crow segregation laws taking root in this period. See Chappell, *Inside*

Agitators, 4. Another white man who spoke out in this period was Edgar Gardner Murphy. An Alabama Episcopalian, he started the Southern Conference of Race Relations in Montgomery in 1900 and wrote several books on this subject before his death in 1914. His views deviated little from those of Haygood. For scholarship on Murphy see Clayton, *The Savage Ideal;* and Ralph Luker, *A Southern Tradition in Theology and Social Criticism, 1830–1930: The Religious Liberalism and Social Conservatism of James Warley Miles, William Porcher Dubose, and Edgar Gardner Murphy* (New York: Edwin Mellen Press), 1984. Probably the most significant voice among white women in the early twentieth century was Lily Hardy Hammond (1859–1925). The wife of a Methodist minister, she was involved in various issues related to improving race relations within the structure of Jim Crow from 1903 through the next two decades. For more information on Hammond see Lily Hardy Hammond, *In Black and White: An Interpretation of the South,* ed. Elna C. Green (1914; repr., Athens: University of Georgia Press, 2008); and Anne Firor Scott, *The Southern Lady: From Pedestal to Politics, 1830–1930* (1970; repr., Charlottesville: University Press of Virginia, 1995), 195.

154. Conkin, *When All the Gods Trembled,* 54.

155. Ibid., 55.

156. For more information on Mathews and the differences between liberal and modernist Christians, see ibid., 111–39.

157. Ibid., 136.

158. On the subject of evolution, he basically supported the theory, noting in one of his later books that "humanity sprang from a common anthropoid stock"; Weatherford, *The Negro from Africa to America,* 28–29. See also Morgan Carter to W. D. Weatherford, October 28, 1927, folder 3622, Weatherford Papers; and Weatherford, *Present Forces in Negro Progress,* 13. In regard to matters of religious doctrine, though he remained somewhat orthodox and generally accepted the importance of the Crucifixion and "possibility" of miracles, there was some looseness in his beliefs that more conservative religious figures would have found unsettling at this time. Weatherford was no biblical literalist; and even when he proclaimed his faith in certain tenets, he did not declare them with the certainty some of his fellow Christians would have liked. For example, on an occasion when Weatherford was trying to defend his belief that Jesus was born of a virgin mother, his support proved less than solid. Weatherford wrote to his colleague: "I do not believe there is enough biblical material to prove the Virgin birth but certainly nobody is in position to deny it. I have personally said in my own class that I did not think it affected the case one way or another, because we had Jesus regardless of how he came, and that is the important matter for Christian experience." This was not a strong endorsement, and Weatherford's effort to shift the question to how this event was "important" for Christianity would have been a tendency among liberals of the time. In this same correspondence Weatherford moved on to discuss the Crucifixion of Jesus, noting that he believed it "was the most profound event in the history of civilization." Weatherford, however, steered clear of commenting

on the Resurrection and whether this event actually occurred. Liberal Christians increasingly found it difficult to maintain a belief in a literal bodily Resurrection of Jesus in this period. See W. D. Weatherford to L. B. Hindman, June 20, 1928, folder 753, Weatherford Papers. One final view that Weatherford held, on the issue of premillennialism, placed him in the liberal camp. This doctrine, based on a literal reading of sections of the New Testament, assumed Jesus would return to Earth to rule for a thousand years. Often held by conservative evangelical Christians, this outlook tended to lead to a pessimistic view on the possibility of change in this world. In this line of thought, Jesus would come back and set things right, and there was little humans could do before that time. Weatherford did not ascribe to this interpretation, noting on one occasion that "it seems to me that there is a false emphasis in the pre-millenarian doctrine." See W. D. Weatherford to R. H. King, February 24, 1930, folder 3186, Weatherford Papers. For a helpful discussion of premillennialism, see Conkin, *When All the Gods Trembled*, 60–63.

159. Weatherford's identification with personalism would also have placed him among liberals because followers of this philosophy were trying to accept and incorporate the new knowledge claims made by science in their faith while not allowing these advancements to explain away God and God's importance in the world.

160. Toward the end of his life he commented: "I may as well say it: My belief is that duty fulfilled brings more real joy than any seeking of passing pleasure ever brings. Perhaps that is a Spartan view but I still hold it's true"; Weatherford, "College Life and Main Objectives," Weatherford Family Papers.

161. While not a perfect fit, Weatherford's life does mesh closely with Daniel Singal's characterization of a southern "post-Victorian" at this time. Like Singal's examples of the historians Ulrich B. Phillips and Broadus Mitchell and the novelist Ellen Glasgow, Weatherford grew up in the late nineteenth century, and as he came of age he tried to "view the region's problems in the cold light of modern science." Perhaps he did not approach his task with the same degree of intellectual rigor as did these other Southerners, but it is clear that he, like them, could not "shake off the nineteenth century values [he] had been raised on" and escape his southern past and romantic image of the Old South. Despite the similarities to Singal's select group of "post-Victorians," Weatherford was never an intellectual on a par with them. For him, Victorian and, to an even greater extent, Christian values always held priority over the life of the mind. See Singal, *The War Within*, 36.

162. In Weatherford's preface to his 1910 book, *Negro Life in the South*, he writes, "It may be worth while to say that the author is a Southern man, a graduate of Vanderbilt University, and since leaving college, has been the Student Secretary of the International Committee of Young Men's Christian Associations of the South" (vi).

163. W. D. Weatherford, "A Significant Move" (1932), folder 1503, Weatherford Papers.

164. See William Malone Baskervill, *Southern Writers, Biographical and Critical*

Studies: Sidney Lanier (Nashville: Barbee & Smith, Agents, 1896). As a symbol of his esteem for Lanier, Weatherford later hung a life-size painting of the poet in his home. See "Notes by W. D. Weatherford, 3/21/64," Weatherford Family Papers.

165. Dykeman, *Prophet of Plenty*, 52.

166. Ibid., 40.

167. See Ada Trawick Culbreth, "Father," [4], Culbreth Family Papers, Waynesville, N.C.; and "Death Follows Brief Illness, Dr. A. M. Trawick, One of Nashville's Most Honored Citizens, Dead," *Nashville Banner*, May 9, 1911, clipping in Culbreth Family Papers. Ada—who wrote an informal history of her father—was the oldest sister of Lula Belle and later married James Marvin Culbreth. Documents from the Culbreth family are held at the Waynesville, N.C., home of Elizabeth Culbreth, the granddaughter of James Marvin Culbreth.

168. Anne Weatherford, telephone conversation with the author, March 16, 2010.

169. See "Willis Duke Weatherford Sr. and ancestors" photo album, Weatherford Family Papers; and Weatherford, "College Life and Main Objectives," Weatherford Family Papers. Lula Belle apparently died of "uremic poisoning"; see Dykeman, *Prophet of Plenty*, 61.

170. Weatherford, "College Life and Main Objectives," Weatherford Family Papers.

2. A Respectable Religious Message

1. "Notes by W. D. Weatherford, 3/21/64," Weatherford Family Papers.

2. Ibid.

3. Setran, *The College "Y,"* 17. At its inception the YMCA was essentially one of many humanitarian responses to the Industrial Revolution and urbanization. In the early 1840s George Williams, a newcomer to London and an apprentice in the drapery trade, along with some of his fellow workers, organized a prayer group in light of the supposed poor moral conditions in which they found themselves. Their club inspired similar gatherings among other businesses in London, and on June 6, 1844, this society was officially organized as the Young Men's Christian Association (YMCA). The intent of this organization, as one of the original founders noted at the time, was "to influence young men to spread the Redeemer's Kingdom amongst those by whom they are surrounded"; Hopkins, *History of the Y.M.C.A. in North America*, 5. The group comprised white-collar workers rather than industrial laborers, drawing most of its participants from the middle classes. In the context of this period, the Association proved to be a fitting scheme and setup, and by 1851 it had extended to sixteen cities in England, Ireland, and Scotland. American visitors to London, particularly those in the summer of 1851 to the Great Industrial Exhibition at the Crystal Palace, were exposed to this organization's structure and ideals, and they took back ideas to create their own Associations in their home cities. Within a few years, YMCAs had popped up in almost

every major city across the United States, as well as many smaller towns. See Hopkins, *History of the Y.M.C.A. in North America,* 4–6, 16–17; and Eddy, *A Century with Youth,* 129.

4. While the Y was clearly created to serve men, women were also involved in these early years, and some were even allowed membership. The YWCA (organized 1872) provided women with their own organization. See Hopkins, *History of the Y.M.C.A. in North America,* 39, 179–244, 292.

5. Ibid., 179.

6. Setran, *The College "Y,"* 4, 63.

7. Ibid.; Hopkins, *History of the Y.M.C.A. in North America,* 271–308, 625–56; Mjagkij, *Light in the Darkness;* Eddy, *A Century with Youth;* William H. Morgan, *Student Religion during Fifty Years: Programs and Policies of the Intercollegiate Y.M.C.A.* (New York: Association Press, 1935); and Clarence P. Shedd, *Two Centuries of Student Christian Movements: Their Origin and Intercollegiate Life* (New York: Association Press, 1934).

8. Shedd, *Two Centuries,* 94–97.

9. Ibid., 98; and W. D. Weatherford, "History of the Student Young Men's Christian Association in the South" (1949), 5, Biographical Records box 218, Kautz Family YMCA Archives, University of Minnesota, Minneapolis. There is also some debate whether Cumberland University in Lebanon, Tennessee, organized a YMCA in 1856. See Shedd, *Two Centuries,* 93–94; Hopkins, *History of the Y.M.C.A. in North America,* 37–38; Weatherford, "History of the Student Young Men's Christian Association in the South," 1–4, Kautz Family YMCA Archives; and Winstead Paine Bone, *A History of Cumberland University, 1842–1935* (Lebanon, Tenn.: Author, 1935), 95–96.

10. Setran, *The College "Y,"* 20.

11. Weatherford, "History of the Student Young Men's Christian Association in the South," 20, Kautz Family YMCA Archives.

12. Setran, *The College "Y,"* 27.

13. Hopkins, *History of the Y.M.C.A. in North America,* 276.

14. Ibid., 117; and Setran, *The College "Y,"* 3–4.

15. Hopkins, *History of the Y.M.C.A. in North America,* 120, 271, 276.

16. Setran, *The College "Y,"* 24–25; and Hopkins, *History of the Y.M.C.A. in North America,* 120–22.

17. Hopkins, *History of the Y.M.C.A. in North America,* 278; and Weatherford, "History of the Student Young Men's Christian Association in the South," 9, Kautz Family YMCA Archives. It is unclear if these twenty-six included ones in Canada.

18. Hopkins, *History of the Y.M.C.A. in North America,* 278.

19. Ibid., 280–81.

20. Ibid., 282.

21. Weatherford, "History of the Student Young Men's Christian Association in the South," 9, Kautz Family YMCA Archives.

22. Hopkins, *History of the Y.M.C.A. in North America*, 132.
23. Ibid., 85.
24. Ibid., 94.
25. Ibid., 111.
26. Ibid., 132–33.
27. Weatherford, "History of the Student Young Men's Christian Association in the South," 11, Kautz Family YMCA Archives.
28. Setran, *The College "Y,"* 3–4.
29. Hopkins, *History of the Y.M.C.A. in North America*, 294.
30. Ibid., 295, 300.
31. Ibid., 296.
32. Ibid., 300.
33. Shedd, *Two Centuries*, 309; and Hopkins, *History of the Y.M.C.A. in North America*, 637.
34. Shedd, *Two Centuries*, 309–11; Hopkins, *History of the Y.M.C.A. in North America*, 637; and Weatherford, "History of the Student Young Men's Christian Association in the South," 13, Kautz Family YMCA Archives. Though African American students apparently did not attend this or any of the early southern conferences, there is no evidence indicating that this region's YMCA leaders created this gathering primarily because of the issue of race.
35. Weatherford, "History of the Student Young Men's Christian Association in the South," 13, Kautz Family YMCA Archives; and W. D. Weatherford, "Facts about the Student Movement in the South" (1927), 1, folder 487a, Weatherford Papers.
36. Shedd, *Two Centuries*, 311.
37. Weatherford, "History of the Student Young Men's Christian Association in the South," 14, Kautz Family YMCA Archives.
38. It should be noted that African American students or participants were not welcome at these conferences. Not until 1912 did southern blacks have a summer gathering to attend. At this point Kings Mountain, N.C., became the site for black male students. See Hopkins, *History of the Y.M.C.A. in North America*, 638; and Willis D. Weatherford, "The Colored Young Men's Christian Association, the Interracial Committee and Related Subjects" (1949), 24, Biographical Records box 218, Kautz Family YMCA Archives. According to William Hunton, the first African American YMCA secretary, financial issues also played a part in blacks not being able to have their own assemblies until 1912. Specific reasons included the cost of travel as well as the need for African American students to work during their summer breaks. See Setran, *The College "Y,"* 78.
39. Dykeman, *Prophet of Plenty*, 56.
40. Ibid., 56–62.
41. Ibid., 52.
42. C. A. Rowland to W. D. Weatherford, July 21, 1952, folder 3807, Weatherford Papers.

43. Dykeman, *Prophet of Plenty*, 59, 61.

44. Weatherford, "College Life and Main Objectives," Weatherford Family Papers.

45. "W. D. Weatherford," in "YMCA Graduate School (1930) forms," folder 1048, Weatherford Papers; "Some Facts about W. D. Weatherford—Written at the Request of H. P. Anderson" (1902), Biographical Records box 218, Kautz Family YMCA Archives; and "Notes by W. D. Weatherford, 3/21/64," Weatherford Family Papers.

46. Hopkins, *History of the Y.M.C.A. in North America*, 283, 302–3; and Setran, *The College "Y,"* 62–63.

47. Setran, *The College "Y,"* 5, 63.

48. Ibid., 79.

49. Ibid., 80.

50. Exactly when Weatherford was ordained is unclear, but at least one document suggests this event occurred before he moved to Tennessee in 1897. This source notes that after he finished Weatherford College, "with eyes on the pulpit, he was ordained a Methodist Minister, but other service claimed him"; P. Whitwell Wilson, "The Projectile from the South," *Association Men* (October 1925): 59, Biographical Records box 218, Kautz Family YMCA Archives. One other letter attests to his ordination but does not indicate when this occurred. See "Office Secretary" of Blue Ridge Association to P. F. Jerome, May 28, 1914, Biographical Records box 218, Kautz Family YMCA Archives.

51. Weatherford, "College Life and Main Objectives," Weatherford Family Papers; and Dykeman, *Prophet of Plenty*, 41.

52. Weatherford, "College Life and Main Objectives," Weatherford Family Papers.

53. Ibid.

54. Setran, *The College "Y,"* 74.

55. Ibid., 75.

56. Ibid., 4

57. Dykeman, *Prophet of Plenty*, 41.

58. Ibid., 45; and Weatherford, "College Life and Main Objectives," Weatherford Family Papers.

59. See W. D. Weatherford's personal notebook titled "Fisk, Blue Ridge, Religious Discussions with Students and Professors," Weatherford Family Papers.

60. Weatherford visited the historically black Hampton Institute on September 10, 1911, along with Jackson Davis (superintendent of Negro Rural Schools in Virginia), and spoke to students on "clean life." See "At Home and Afield: Hampton Incidents, Addresses," *Southern Workman* 40 (October 1911): 590. He also visited Piney Woods School near Jackson, Miss. (date unknown). See Weatherford, "Fisk, Blue Ridge, Religious Discussions," Weatherford Family Papers.

61. Setran, *The College "Y,"* 78. This would remain the case until 1933, when African American college YMCA work was integrated at the national level (though

it took until 1937 in the southeast region). The Colored Work Department, however, remained in existence until 1946. See Hopkins, *History of the Y.M.C.A. in North America,* 648; Weatherford, "History of the Student Young Men's Christian Association in the South," 46–47, Kautz Family YMCA Archives; and Mjagkij, *Light in the Darkness,* 116, 127.

62. Dykeman, *Prophet of Plenty,* 45–47.

63. Weatherford, "College Life and Main Objectives," Weatherford Family Papers.

64. See Setran, *The College "Y,"* 140.

65. See Weatherford, "Fisk, Blue Ridge, Religious Discussions," Weatherford Family Papers.

66. Ibid.

67. "Notes by W. D. Weatherford, 3/21/64," Weatherford Family Papers.

68. Dykeman, *Prophet of Plenty,* 50.

69. Weatherford had the habit of recording the books he was reading at the end of his yearly datebooks. For example, in his 1948 book he recorded reading Alan Paton's *Cry, the Beloved Country* (New York: C. Scribner's Sons, 1948); in 1956 he included C. Vann Woodward's *Strange Career of Jim Crow* (1955); and in 1967, William Styron's *Confessions of Nat Turner* (New York: Random House, 1967). See 1948, 1956, and 1967 datebooks in possession of the author.

70. Weatherford, "Fisk, Blue Ridge, Religious Discussions," Weatherford Family Papers.

71. Ibid.

72. Ibid.

73. Ibid. For a slightly different version of this story, see W. D. Weatherford, *Introducing Men to Christ: Fundamental Studies* (New York: Association Press, 1911), 136–37.

74. Weatherford, "Fisk, Blue Ridge, Religious Discussions," Weatherford Family Papers.

75. Ibid.

76. In 1955 a man who attended the University of Texas between 1911 and 1915 wrote to Weatherford referring to him as "'Mr. Student YMCA'—at least for the South" of that time. See Jesse R. Wilson to W. D. Weatherford, December 21, 1955, folder 3812, Weatherford Papers. In 1969 a former student YMCA president of the University of Georgia noted Weatherford's influence on him when Weatherford went to speak in Athens in 1910. See E. P. Hall to W. D. Weatherford, January 14, 1969, Weatherford Papers. See also French W. Thompson to W. D. Weatherford, April 4, 1944, folder 3306; and Robert L. Kincaid to W. D. Weatherford, February 2, 1945, folder 3313, both in Weatherford Papers.

77. See Weatherford, *Introducing Men to Christ,* 11–12, 31–44, 47–60; and W. D. Weatherford, *Christian Life, a Normal Experience: A Study in the Reality and Growth of Christian Experience* (Nashville: Smith and Lamar, 1916), 43–57, 59–73, 75–89.

78. Weatherford, *Christian Life*, 5.

79. The line went "Weatherford is always here." See "Conference Song, 1913," in W. D. Weatherford, *Songs of Southern Colleges and Old Southern Melodies* (Nashville: Southern Student Secretaries of YMCA, 1913), 78.

80. See Anne Weatherford, interview by the author, September 11, 2009. Interview transcript is in possession of the author.

81. Dykeman, *Prophet of Plenty*, 1, 43; Wilson, "The Projectile from the South," Kautz Family YMCA Archives; and Robert B. Eleazer, "My First Eighty Years: A Brief Account of My Life for Those Who Come After," September 21, 1957, box 1, folder 24–26, 8, Robert Burns Eleazer Papers, Special Collections and University Archives, Vanderbilt University Library, Nashville.

82. Quoted in Dykeman, *Prophet of Plenty*, 49–50.

83. Putney, *Muscular Christianity*, 2, 7.

84. Ibid., 56–57.

85. Ibid., 6.

86. See Dykeman, *Prophet of Plenty*, 46; and Setran, *The College "Y,"* 113–14. Neither of these sources notes that he went to Emory. This information was deduced, however, by reading Weatherford's personal copy of Dykeman's book, which includes his comments, underlinings, and notes. This book is in the library at Far Horizons, Black Mountain, N.C.

87. Dykeman, *Prophet of Plenty*, 46.

88. Ibid., 46.

89. "Notes by W. D. Weatherford, 3/21/64," Weatherford Family Papers.

90. Weatherford, "College Life and Main Objectives," Weatherford Family Papers.

91. Ibid.

92. On Progressivism see William A. Link, *The Paradox of Southern Progressivism, 1880–1930* (Chapel Hill: University of North Carolina Press, 1992); Daniel T. Rodgers, *Atlantic Crossings: Social Politics in a Progressive Age* (Cambridge: Belknap Press of Harvard University Press, 1998); and Michael McGerr, *A Fierce Discontent: The Rise and Fall of the Progressive Movement in America, 1870–1920* (New York: Oxford University Press, 2003).

93. Wiebe, *The Search for Order*, 111.

94. Link, *Paradox of Southern Progressivism*, xi.

95. Boles, *The South through Time*, 2:445.

96. See Culbreth, "The Culbreth Family Story," 44–45, 48–49, 64, Culbreth Family Papers.

97. Ibid., 48–49. James Marvin originally married Bess Trawick, but she died early in their marriage. He later married Ada Trawick.

98. For more information on the Atlanta Race Riot, see Dominic J. Capeci Jr. and Jack C. Knight, "Reckoning with Violence: W. E. B. Du Bois and the 1906 Atlanta Race Riot," *Journal of Southern History* 62 (November 1996): 727–66; Mark Bauerlein, *Negrophobia: A Race Riot in Atlanta, 1906* (San Francisco:

Encounter Books, 2001); Allison Dorsey, *To Build Our Lives Together: Community Formation in Black Atlanta, 1875–1906* (Athens: University of Georgia Press, 2004), 147–66; David Fort Godshalk, *Veiled Visions: The 1906 Race Riot and the Reshaping of American Race Relations* (Chapel Hill: University of North Carolina Press, 2005); and Gregory Mixon, *The Atlanta Riot: Race, Class, and Violence in a New South City* (Gainesville: University Press of Florida, 2005).

99. Weatherford, *Negro Life in the South*, v; and Weatherford, "College Life and Main Objectives," Weatherford Family Papers. The specific YMCA building in which they met is unknown.

100. These black participants were John Hope, John Wesley Gilbert (professor), William A. Hunton, and Jesse E. Moorland (both YMCA secretaries). Besides Weatherford, the white men involved were W. R. Lambuth (missionary secretary of the Methodist Episcopal Church, South) and Stewart R. Roberts (physiology professor at the Atlanta School of Physicians and Surgeons). See Weatherford, *Negro Life in the South*, v.

101. For more information on Hope, see Ridgely Torrence, *The Story of John Hope* (New York: Macmillan, 1948).

102. Weatherford, *Negro Life in the South*, 4.

103. Ibid.

104. Ibid., 56, 82, 106, 165, 172, 169.

105. Ibid., 153.

106. W. E. B. Du Bois, *The Souls of Black Folk* (Chicago: A. C. McClurg, 1903), 212; and Weatherford, *Negro Life in the South*, 153.

107. Weatherford, *Negro Life in the South*, 152, 173.

108. Ibid., 167.

109. Ibid., 95–96, 105–7, 139, 30, 39, 62.

110. Ibid., 10–14.

111. Ibid., 14.

112. Ibid., 12–17.

113. Ibid., 7.

114. Ibid., 3.

115. Ibid., 25. See also 162 for another reference to Lee and Jackson.

116. Ibid., 168.

117. Ibid.

118. Ibid., 166–68.

119. Ibid., 167.

120. W. D. Weatherford, "The Cross in World Reconstruction," *Blue Ridge Voice*, June 1922, 9.

121. Weatherford, "The Colored Young Men's Christian Association," 19, Biographical Records box 218, Kautz Family YMCA Archives.

122. Ibid., 20.

123. Ibid.; and Weatherford, "History of the Student Young Men's Christian Association in the South," 26, Kautz Family YMCA Archives.

124. George R. Ross to W. D. Weatherford, October 28, 1943, folder 3785, Weatherford Papers. Ross also recollected that Wake Forest College's President William Louis Poteat had taught this book at that college among its student YMCA. See also Randal L. Hall, *William Louis Poteat: A Leader of the Progressive-Era South* (Lexington: University Press of Kentucky, 2000), 91.

125. Clare Taylor, "Mason Crum: Life Devoted to Bettering Race Relations," *Asheville Citizen,* July 7, 1969, clipping in folder 3678b, Weatherford Papers.

126. Weatherford, "History of the Student Young Men's Christian Association in the South," 26, Kautz Family YMCA Archives; and Weatherford, "Fisk, Blue Ridge, Religious Discussions," Weatherford Family Papers.

127. Jesse Edward Moorland, "The Young Men's Christian Association among Negroes," *Journal of Negro History* 9 (April 1924): 136. It should be noted that though Weatherford did mention the study's background and development, he did not claim to have the committee's endorsement of the published work. See Weatherford, *Negro Life in the South,* v–vi.

128. Weatherford, *Negro Life in the South,* [iii].

129. Moorland, "YMCA among Negroes," 136.

130. Weatherford, "The Colored Young Men's Christian Association," 23, Biographical Records box 218, Kautz Family YMCA Archives.

131. Ibid., 20.

132. Moorland, "YMCA among Negroes," 136.

133. Weatherford, "The Colored Young Men's Christian Association," 21–23, Biographical Records box 218, Kautz Family YMCA Archives. Money from this fund also probably supported a conference in 1914 for African American Christian students, in which Weatherford, Trawick, and Tobias all participated. See A. M. Trawick, ed., *The New Voice in Race Adjustments: Addresses and Reports Presented at the Negro Christian Student Conference, Atlanta, Georgia, May 14–18, 1914* (New York: Student Volunteer Movement, 1914).

134. Weatherford, *Interracial Cooperation,* 13–14.

135. Weatherford, "The Colored Young Men's Christian Association," 24–25, Biographical Records box 218, Kautz Family YMCA Archives.

136. Weatherford, *Present Forces in Negro Progress,* 74, 121, 122, 101, 111, 125–26, 178, 69.

137. Ibid., 74; emphasis in original.

138. Ibid., 26.

139. Dykeman, *Prophet of Plenty,* 78; emphasis in original. While "Negro" is capitalized throughout most of the text, there are still several instances where it is lowercased. It is unclear why this is inconsistent. For examples, see 32, 111, and 121.

140. Weatherford, *Present Forces in Negro Progress,* 32.

141. Dykeman, *Prophet of Plenty,* 79–80.

142. Weatherford, *Present Forces in Negro Progress,* 16. The historian Bruce Clayton's dissertation also made this point in the section where he discussed Weath-

erford's early race relations career and analyzed *Present Forces in Negro Progress;* see Bruce Clayton, "Southern Critics of the New South, 1890–1914" (Ph.D. diss., Duke University, 1966), 272–74. This study was later published as Clayton, *The Savage Ideal: Intolerance and Intellectual Leadership in the South, 1890–1914.* In this form, however, the section on Weatherford was omitted. In the midst of Clayton's research for his dissertation, he wrote to Weatherford, asking for his cooperation in the project. In this same letter Clayton commented that he had just finished reading Wilma Dykeman and James Stokely's biography of Will Alexander, *Seeds of Southern Change* (1962). Clayton also noted his interest in possibly pursuing a biography of Weatherford as a future project, adding, "I have a feeling that your contribution to southern race relations should be as well know[n] as Will Alexander's"; Bruce L. Clayton to W. D. Weatherford, February 22, 1965, folder 3878, Weatherford Papers.

143. Weatherford, *Present Forces in Negro Progress,* 13–16.

144. Ibid., 16.

145. Ibid., 19–24.

146. Ibid., 25.

147. Ibid., 26–31.

148. Ibid., 30.

149. Carter G. Woodson, "A Rejoinder to Dr. Tobias," *Chicago Defender,* July 30, 1932. Woodson also noted in this newspaper article that Channing Tobias and Jesse Moorland had "co-operated with" Weatherford and "approved" the publication of this book. Yet these men later went to Woodson, asking him to write a book "in answer to Weatherford." Woodson went on to write "The Case of the Negro," but, according to its author, it was never published because Tobias and Moorland thought he was "rather hard on preachers of a certain type." For more information on Woodson, see Jacqueline Goggin, *Carter G. Woodson: A Life in Black History* (Baton Rouge: Louisiana State University Press, 1993); and W. Fitzhugh Brundage, *The Southern Past: A Clash of Race and Memory* (Cambridge: Belknap Press of Harvard University Press, 2005), 151–57.

150. Weatherford, *Present Forces in Negro Progress,* 75.

151. Ibid., 20.

152. Weatherford, "Fisk, Blue Ridge, Religious Discussions"; and Weatherford, "College Life and Main Objectives," both in Weatherford Family Papers. Weatherford probably used the YMCA's publishing arm, the Association Press, to issue these books. This YMCA department began in 1907, and Weatherford published numerous of his own works through this organization. For more information on the Association Press, see Hopkins, *History of the Y.M.C.A. in North America,* 482–83.

153. Weatherford, "Fisk, Blue Ridge, Religious Discussions," Weatherford Family Papers. In 1912 this set apparently sold for five dollars. For the price see Weatherford, "College Life and Main Objectives," Weatherford Family Papers; and "Race Relationships in the South," advertisement in Weatherford, *Negro Life in the South,* rev. ed., 1915, [182].

154. "Race Relationships in the South," advertisement.

155. John Joel Culley, "Muted Trumpets: Four Efforts to Better Southern Race Relations, 1900–1919" (Ph.D. diss., University of Virginia, 1967), 114; and E. Charles Chatfield, "The Southern Sociological Congress: Organization of Uplift," *Tennessee Historical Quarterly* 19 (December 1960): 328–47.

156. Culley, "Muted Trumpets," 141.

157. See Chatfield, "Southern Sociological Congress"; Hall, *William Louis Poteat,* 81–82; and Egerton, *Speak Now against the Day,* 45–46.

158. Chatfield, "Southern Sociological Congress," 338, 344–45.

159. Ibid., 329.

160. Ibid.

161. Culley, "Muted Trumpets," 141–42.

162. "Some Frank Facts," *Crisis,* May 1914, 41.

163. Chatfield, "Southern Sociological Congress," 336.

164. Ibid., 346–47; and Weatherford, *Lawlessness or Civilization—Which?*

165. James E. McCulloch, ed., *The Call of the New South: Addresses Delivered at the Southern Sociological Congress, Nashville, Tennessee, May 7 to 10, 1912* (Nashville: Brandau-Craig-Dickerson Co., 1912), 220–25, 361.

166. W. D. Weatherford, "The Negro and the New South," in McCulloch, *The Call of the New South,* 221.

167. Ibid., 225, 223.

168. See James E. McCulloch, ed., *The South Mobilizing for Social Service: Addresses Delivered at the Southern Sociological Congress, Atlanta, Georgia, April 25–29, 1913* (Nashville: Brandau-Craig-Dickerson Co., 1913), 350–60; James E. McCulloch, ed., *The Human Way: Addresses on Race Problems at the Southern Sociological Congress, Atlanta, Georgia, April 25–29, 1913* (Nashville: Brandau-Craig-Dickerson Co., 1913), 8–18; and James E. McCulloch, ed., *Battling for Social Betterment: Southern Sociological Congress, Memphis, Tennessee, May 6–10, 1914* (Nashville: Benson Printing Co., 1914), 178–88.

169. McCulloch, *The Human Way,* 17.

170. McCulloch, *Battling for Social Betterment,* 187–88.

171. McCulloch, *The Human Way,* 9.

172. Culley, "Muted Trumpets," 126–29.

173. Ibid., 127, 128. For other information on this event, see Dykeman, *Prophet of Plenty,* 75–77; and Weatherford, "Fisk, Blue Ridge, Religious Discussions," Weatherford Family Papers. Dykeman's version, presumably based on Weatherford's statements in "Fisk, Blue Ridge, Religious Discussions," gives the impression that blacks were not segregated at all, but Culley's explanation seems more plausible.

174. Weatherford, *The Negro from Africa to America,* 431.

175. Ibid.; Weatherford and Johnson, *Race Relations,* 529–30; and Culley, "Muted Trumpets," 131, 136, 228, 232. For more information on Murphy see Clayton, *The Savage Ideal,* 12, 195–204; and Sosna, *In Search of the Silent South,* 12, 14–15, 22, 93.

176. Weatherford, "Fisk, Blue Ridge, Religious Discussions," Weatherford Family Papers. Weatherford had fairly extensive experience abroad even before this 1914 trip. In 1912 he helped lead a group of ten YMCA secretaries on a two-month trip to Jerusalem, Lebanon, Egypt, Italy, France, and England. See E. P. Hall to W. D. Weatherford, January 14, 1969, folder 3914, Weatherford Papers; Willis D. Weatherford, "The Training Program of the Southern Y.M.C.A.'s," 5, Biographical Records box 218, Kautz Family YMCA Archives; and Culbreth, "The Culbreth Family Story," 50, Culbreth Family Papers. Weatherford also noted in his 1914 speech before the Southern Sociological Congress that "some two years ago" he had toured seventeen different countries, including Turkey and parts of southeast Europe, "in many of which racial problems were most acute." Whether this trip was the earlier 1912 trip with the YMCA secretaries or another visit is unclear. See McCulloch, *Battling for Social Betterment,* 186. In 1913 Weatherford also was out of the country and so missed his father's funeral; see "Death of S. L. Weatherford," January 18, 1913, *Daily Herald,* Weatherford family vertical file.

177. Weatherford, "Fisk, Blue Ridge, Religious Discussions," Weatherford Family Papers.

178. Ibid.

179. Weatherford, "College Life and Main Objectives," Weatherford Family Papers. He does not give the exact date.

180. Ibid. The fact that China was politically unstable at this point (following a revolution in 1911) may also have played a part in his decision.

181. See Julia Anne McDonough, "Men and Women of Good Will: History of the Commission of Interracial Cooperation and the Southern Regional Council, 1919–1954" (Ph.D. diss., University of Virginia, 1993); Charles Kirk Pilkington, "The Trials of Brotherhood: The Founding of the Commission on Interracial Cooperation," *Georgia Historical Quarterly* 69 (Spring 1985): 55–80; Edward Flud Barrows, "The Commission on Interracial Cooperation, 1919–1944: A Case Study in the History of Interracial Movement in the South" (Ph.D. diss., University of Wisconsin, 1954); and Ann Wells Ellis, "The Commission on Interracial Cooperation, 1919–1944: Its Activities and Results" (Ph.D. diss., Georgia State University, 1975). For an informative study about the life and work of the early CIC director Will Alexander, see Wilma Dykeman and James Stokely, *Seeds of Southern Change: The Life of Will Alexander* (New York: W. W. Norton, 1962).

182. Ellis, "Commission on Interracial Cooperation," 7.

183. Tindall, *Emergence of the New South,* 152.

184. See Jacquelyn Dowd Hall, *Revolt against Chivalry: Jessie Daniel Ames and the Women's Campaign against Lynching* (New York: Columbia University Press, 1979), 62; Sosna, *In Search of the Silent South,* 22; Tindall, *Emergence of the New South,* 178; and Myrdal, *An American Dilemma,* 2:842–50.

185. See Dykeman and Stokely, *Seeds of Southern Change,* 58–59; and Egerton, *Speak Now against the Day,* 47. See also W. D. Weatherford, "John Joseph Eagan," 10–11, folder 3726; Paul N. Probst to W. D. Weatherford, June 20, 1933, folder

3645; and W. D. Weatherford to Paul N. Probst, July 13, 1933, folder 3645, all in Weatherford Papers. Probst wrote to Weatherford inquiring about his early involvement in the formation of the CIC because Probst was completing a history of this organization for his bachelor of divinity degree at Emory University at the time.

186. Weatherford, "The Training Program of the Southern Y.M.C.A.'s," 18, Biographical Records box 218, Kautz Family YMCA Archives; W. D. Weatherford to Judson G. Rosebush, December 31, 1932, folder 1531, Weatherford Papers; Hopkins, *History of the Y.M.C.A. in North America,* 577; and Weatherford, *The Negro from Africa to America,* 450–51.

187. Weatherford, "The Colored Young Men's Christian Association," 31–33, Biographical Records box 218, Kautz Family YMCA Archives.

188. Weatherford, "The Training Program of the Southern Y.M.C.A.'s," 18, Biographical Records box 218, Kautz Family YMCA Archives.

189. Weatherford later commented that "Negroes who had been in white homes in France and Germany would not be willing to live as they had before the war and should not"; "Notes by W. D. Weatherford, 3/21/64," Weatherford Family Papers.

190. Weatherford, "The Colored Young Men's Christian Association," 33–34, Biographical Records box 218, Kautz Family YMCA Archives.

191. Ibid., 34.

192. Ibid.

193. Ibid., 35–36.

194. Ibid., 35.

195. Ellis, "Commission on Interracial Cooperation," 11–12; and Weatherford, "The Colored Young Men's Christian Association," 35, Biographical Records box 218, Kautz Family YMCA Archives. According to Weatherford, the following people met at the Georgian Terrace Hotel in Atlanta for the founding meeting: John J. Eagan (businessman and YMCA supporter), M. Ashby Jones (pastor of Atlanta's Ponce de Leon Baptist Church), Plato Durham (Emory professor); Robert Russa Moton (Tuskegee Institute principal); as well as YMCA secretaries Richard H. King, S. A. Ackley, Will W. Alexander, and Wallace Buttrick. In her excellent dissertation, Ann Wells Ellis contends that though Weatherford and the YMCA played a prominent part in the CIC's creation, Moton and Thomas Jesse Jones (educational director of the Phelps-Stokes Fund) were the real "motivators in creating and financing the interracial movement." In December 1918 (following the Armistice) President Woodrow Wilson sent Moton and Jones to France to meet and discuss with African American soldiers "what their return home would mean." Ellis argues that these men were the ones who thought of the idea of creating local interracial committees to address race relations, and that Moton and Jones collaborated with the parallel efforts of the YMCA to start the CIC. See Ellis, "Commission on Interracial Cooperation," 7–16 (quotes on 15, 7).

196. Ellis, "Commission on Interracial Cooperation," 16.

197. Quoted in ibid., 22.

198. Ibid.; emphasis in original.
199. Quoted in ibid., 16.
200. Ibid., 16–18.
201. Egerton, *Speak Now against the Day*, 426.

3. Sowing the Seeds of Southern Liberalism

1. George Washington Carver to John W. Bergthold, April 21, 1926, George Washington Carver Papers in the Tuskegee Institute Archives, microfilm ed. (Tuskegee, Ala.: Carver Research Foundation, 1975), reel 9, frame 900 (hereinafter cited as Carver Papers).

2. Ibid.

3. McMurry, *George Washington Carver*, 202.

4. According to Benjamin Mays's autobiography, "Blue Ridge was the segregated conference ground for white students" and Kings Mountain, N.C., was the segregated site for black YMCA students of the Southeast; Benjamin E. Mays, *Born to Rebel: An Autobiography* (New York: Charles Scribner's Sons, 1971), 126. For more information regarding the locations and programs of other YMCA conference centers, see Hopkins, *History of the Y.M.C.A. in North America*, 614–18, 637–38.

5. Quoted in Martin, *Howard Kester*, 26. This action may also have broken the law. Howard Kester's unpublished "Radical Prophets: A History of the Fellowship of Southern Churchmen" also records Carver's stay with the Lynchburg delegates at Blue Ridge and notes the legal implications of the act. He writes, "It should be noted that every Southern state held it to be illegal for Negroes to either room or eat in white hotels or dining rooms. To violate the law was to run the risk of having your license to operate revoked"; Howard A. Kester, "Radical Prophets: A History of the Fellowship of Southern Churchmen," 1974 (photocopy in possession of the author; original in possession of Nancy Kester Neale, Asheville, N.C.), 23.

6. John Hope Franklin and Alfred A. Moss Jr., *From Slavery to Freedom: A History of Negro Americans*, 6th ed. (New York: McGraw-Hill, 1988), 278.

7. Ibid.

8. Dykeman and Stokely, *Seeds of Southern Change*, 273–75.

9. Ethel Edwards, *Carver of Tuskegee* (Cincinnati: Psyche Press, 1971), 149.

10. W. D. Weatherford, "My Experience in Race Relations," 10, folder 3678c, Weatherford Papers.

11. See Dykeman and Stokely, *Seeds of Southern Change*, 66; Tindall, *Emergence of the New South*, 176–78; Sosna, *In Search of the Silent South*, 22; Dunbar, *Against the Grain*, 21–22; McMurry, *George Washington Carver*, 201–4, 206–7, 210–11, 285, 298; Martin, *Howard Kester*, 22, 25–27; and Egerton, *Speak Now against the Day*, 44–48, 122, 159, 426. A short, popular history of Blue Ridge has also been produced by the institution; see *Eureka! A Century of YMCA Blue Ridge*

Assembly ([Black Mountain, N.C.]: [YMCA Blue Ridge Assembly], 2005). For extended studies of Weatherford, see Dykeman, *Prophet of Plenty;* Antone, "Willis Duke Weatherford"; and Combs, "Race Reform." Among these works, Dykeman and Combs give the most attention to Blue Ridge. Dykeman's biography of Weatherford provides helpful information on Blue Ridge and the limitations it worked under, whereas Combs's thesis provides the most scholarly examination of the Blue Ridge Assembly. For concentrated attention to Blue Ridge in Combs's work, see chaps. 4 and 5.

12. William H. Cobb, *Radical Education in the Rural South: Commonwealth College, 1922–1940* (Detroit: Wayne State University Press, 2000), 113. Indeed, Cobb notes that a black lecturer declined an invitation to visit the school in the 1930s because of the hostility toward African Americans in that area.

13. Ibid.

14. See Glen, *Highlander.* Interestingly enough, the founders of Highlander—Don West and Miles Horton—hatched the school's idea after meeting at Blue Ridge in 1932 (17). See also interview with Don West, January 22, 1975, Interview E-0016, Southern Oral History Program Collection #4007, University of North Carolina, Chapel Hill.

15. Glen, *Highlander,* 30.

16. Martin Duberman, *Black Mountain: An Exploration in Community* (New York: Dutton, 1972), 179.

17. Ibid.

18. See K'Meyer, *Interracialism and Christian Community.*

19. Glenda Elizabeth Gilmore, *Defying Dixie: The Radical Roots of Civil Rights, 1919–1950* (New York: W. W. Norton, 2008), 5.

20. Anthony Dunbar's study of southern radicals takes 1929 as its starting date. See Dunbar, *Against the Grain.*

21. See Woodward, *Origins of the New South,* and *The Strange Career of Jim Crow.*

22. Sosna, *In Search of the Silent South,* 11.

23. Antone, "Willis Duke Weatherford," 96. Antone draws these statistics from the National Association for the Advancement of Colored People, *Thirty Years of Lynching in the United States, 1889–1918* (New York: N.A.A.C.P., 1919), 29.

24. Egerton, *Speak Now against the Day,* 39. For the Wilmington riot see David S. Cecelski and Timothy B. Tyson, eds., *Democracy Betrayed: The Wilmington Race Riot of 1898 and Its Legacy* (Chapel Hill: University of North Carolina Press, 1998), and Glenda Elizabeth Gilmore, *Gender and Jim Crow: Women and the Politics of White Supremacy in North Carolina, 1896–1920* (Chapel Hill: University of North Carolina Press, 1996), 92–117. For New Orleans see William Ivy Hair, *Carnival of Fury: Robert Charles and the New Orleans Race Riot of 1900* (Baton Rouge: Louisiana State University Press, 1976). For Atlanta see Capeci and Knight, "Reckoning with Violence"; Bauerlein, *Negrophobia;* Dorsey, *To Build Our Lives Together,* 147–66; Godshalk, *Veiled Visions;* and Mixon, *The Atlanta Riot.*

25. W. D. Weatherford, "The Constructive Message of Blue Ridge," *Blue Ridge Voice*, October 1924, 1.

26. Ibid., 13.

27. Until the late 1920s, the YWCA and YMCA conferences were held separately yet took place in consecutive weeks at the start of June each summer. See "1921 Blue Ridge Conferences," *Blue Ridge Voice*, April 1921, 1.

28. Dykeman, *Prophet of Plenty*, 111–12. Poteat was a key progressive liberal of the early twentieth century and longtime president of Wake Forest College (1905–27); see Hall, *William Louis Poteat*. Fosdick was one of the most prominent liberal Baptist ministers and writers of the twentieth century. Adding to his renown was his role as the first pastor of New York's Riverside Church—an institution funded largely by John D. Rockefeller Jr. See Robert Moats Miller, *Harry Emerson Fosdick: Preacher, Pastor, Prophet* (New York: Oxford University Press, 1985). A number of other prominent religious and educational leaders came to Blue Ridge in these years, including Frank Porter Graham, H. Richard Niebuhr, Reinhold Niebuhr, Howard Odum, Rupert Vance, Arthur Raper, Liston Pope, and Samuel Chiles Mitchell.

29. Dykeman, *Prophet of Plenty*, 85–86; and Forrest D. Brown, "Blue Ridge Summer Staff," *Blue Ridge Voice*, November 1923, 10.

30. Dykeman, *Prophet of Plenty*, 87–88; Hopkins, *History of the Y.M.C.A. in North America*, 617.

31. These students were able to take classes offered by the Southern College's summer quarter after 1919. Dykeman, *Prophet of Plenty*, 86, notes that Weatherford also often taught a course on the philosophy of religion.

32. Ibid., 84.

33. Ibid.

34. For the dating of this event, see Weatherford, "Fisk, Blue Ridge, Religious Discussions," Weatherford Family Papers.

35. Dykeman, *Prophet of Plenty*, 87.

36. Ibid.

37. Ibid.

38. "Building Program at Blue Ridge," *Blue Ridge Voice*, January 1920, 1, notes a "special dining room for colored servants" being added to the main dining area that year.

39. See "Number of Delegates and Leaders at Each Conference of 1928," folder 745; and "Colored Help 1928," folder 823, both in Weatherford Papers.

40. "Schedule of Property Owned by the Blue Ridge Association," folder 747; and Weatherford to M. T. Workman, July 10, 1929, folder 879, both in Weatherford Papers.

41. See J. J. King to Weatherford, February 20, 1926, folder 346, Weatherford Papers; Brown, "Blue Ridge Summer Staff," *Blue Ridge Voice*, November 1923, 10; B. F. Vincent, "Blue Ridge Working Staff, Summer of 1926," *Blue Ridge Voice*, February 1927, 11–15; and "Number of Delegates and Leaders at Each Conference of 1928," folder 745, Weatherford Papers.

42. Dykeman, *Prophet of Plenty*, 93.

43. Ibid., 84.

44. Weatherford, "The Training Program of the Southern Y.M.C.A.'s," 17, Biographical Records box 218, Kautz Family YMCA Archives. See also Hopkins, *History of the Y.M.C.A. in North America*, 617.

45. Antone, "Willis Duke Weatherford," 129. Southern College of the YMCA changed its name in the late 1920s to the YMCA Graduate School in order to focus exclusively on graduate education. See also Antone, "The Y.M.C.A. Graduate School."

46. Antone, "Willis Duke Weatherford," 171; O. E. Brown, "The Fortieth International Convention of the Young Men's Christian Association, Detroit, Mich., Nov. 19–23, 1919," *Blue Ridge Voice*, December 1919, 1; and advertisement for "Southern College of Young Men's Christian Associations," *Blue Ridge Voice*, April 1921, 18.

47. "Building Program at Blue Ridge," *Blue Ridge Voice*, January 1920, 1.

48. "Debutante," *Blue Ridge Voice*, November 1919, 1.

49. Blue Ridge's breadth of exposure can be seen from the 1924 summer schedule that included the following conferences: Employed Officers' Conference; Southern Student Conference, YWCA; Southern Student Conference, YMCA; Missionary Education Conference; Home Demonstration Agents' Conference; Community Conference, YWCA; Southern Summer School, YMCA; Southern Industrial Conference; Southern Summer School of Social Service and Christian Workers; Southern College of YMCA, summer quarter; SCY Camp for Boys; Travelers' Aid Conference; and Regional Conference on Industrial Education. See "Blue Ridge Conferences, 1924," *Blue Ridge Voice*, June 1924, 1.

50. Weatherford, "The Constructive Message of Blue Ridge," *Blue Ridge Voice*, October 1924, 1, 13.

51. Ibid., 1.

52. Dykeman, *Prophet of Plenty*, 98.

53. Quoted in ibid., 98. The date is based on a reference to a new laundry building being built in "Building Program at Blue Ridge," *Blue Ridge Voice*, January 1920, 1. This article notes, "The laundry building which burned August 1, 1919, is already replaced."

54. C. Roger Hibbard, telephone conversation with the author, May 1, 2008. Hibbard is the current executive director of the Blue Ridge Assembly and aided in the publication of the center's centennial history, *Eureka! A Century of YMCA Blue Ridge Assembly*. According to Hibbard, Blue Ridge also sold some of its mountain property in the years before 1944 in order to keep the institution in operation.

55. Ruth Scandrett to W. D. Weatherford, May 10, 1926, folder 302, Weatherford Papers.

56. W. D. Weatherford to Ruth Scandrett, May 20, 1926, folder 302, Weatherford Papers.

57. Ibid.

58. Scandrett to Weatherford, May 29, 1926, folder 361, Weatherford Papers. The YWCA tended to be more socially progressive than the YMCA at this time. See Nancy Marie Robertson, *Christian Sisterhood, Race Relations, and the YWCA, 1906–46* (Urbana: University of Illinois Press, 2007), 106.

59. Weatherford, "My Experience in Race Relations," 11, folder 3678c, Weatherford Papers.

60. "The New Lincoln Portrait in Lee Hall," *Blue Ridge Voice,* June 1920, 1.

61. W. D. Weatherford, "Why We Wanted a Lincoln Portrait in Lee Hall," *Blue Ridge Voice,* June 1920, 1.

62. Ibid.

63. Ibid. David Blight has recognized the importance Lincoln's image held for African Americans in the early twentieth century. He notes that Lincoln's likeness could be found in black homes and churches, and particularly at events celebrating African American freedom. Blight writes, "Strategically, and with genuine sentiment . . . blacks honored Lincoln in season and out, but especially on the days when they remembered their freedom as a national matter"; David W. Blight, *Race and Reunion: The Civil War in American Memory* (Cambridge: Belknap Press of Harvard University Press, 2001), 369–70. Speaking more broadly on the importance of Lincoln's contribution to African Americans' freedom at this time, Robert Russa Moton acknowledged the president's significance in "The Negro's Debt to Lincoln," *Southern Workman* 51 (1922): 329–34.

64. Weatherford, "Why We Wanted a Lincoln Portrait in Lee Hall," *Blue Ridge Voice,* June 1920.

65. Combs, "Race Reform," 107. The proceedings of this conference were published in Weatherford, *Lawlessness or Civilization—Which?*

66. Combs, "Race Reform," 107–8.

67. "An Appeal to the Christian People of the South," *Blue Ridge Voice,* January 1921, 12–13.

68. Ibid.

69. Weatherford, "My Experience in Race Relations," 9, folder 3678c, Weatherford Papers.

70. W. D. Weatherford to A. D. Beittel, December 16, 1941, folder 2908, Weatherford Papers.

71. Lester A. Walton, "Interracial Commission on Southern Conditions," *New York Age,* July 31, 1920.

72. Ibid.

73. Ibid.

74. Ibid.

75. The *Blue Ridge Voice* announced the planned speakers for the summers in its April editions of 1921 and 1922. Both issues list "R. R. Moton, President of Tuskegee Institute" as part of the summer program. See *Blue Ridge Voice,* April 1921, April 1922, 4.

76. One questionable source may provide light on Moton's visits to Blue Ridge. Edwards, *Carver of Tuskegee,* 114, claims that Moton had been a guest speaker in

1919 at the conference center and had been placed in a separate cottage, his meals brought to him there. She insists that Weatherford was "apologetic" to Moton for these arrangements and that Weatherford noted that since Blue Ridge "was just establishing itself in the South," it was "trying to avoid friction." Since no other sources show Moton to have visited Blue Ridge in 1919, however, her assertion remains dubious. This story may refer to the accommodations that existed for Moton during 1921 or 1922. Edwards's biography of George Washington Carver was completed in 1948, but a publisher could not be found. In 1971 she privately published the volume in a limited edition of two hundred copies. Her book was written with the assistance of interviews with W. D. Weatherford and Jim Hardwick. Hardwick had met Carver at Blue Ridge in 1923 and maintained a close relationship with him until the latter's death. Edwards's book is a questionable source because several dates she gives for events do not match with the primary source record. The book is without footnotes, and thus her sources cannot be traced. It seems likely that the book's material relating to Blue Ridge is built largely on her interviews with Weatherford in the 1940s; see "Foreword" ([vi]) and "An Explanation" ([viii–ix]). Linda O. McMurry's excellent biography of Carver notes that Moton had been to Blue Ridge in 1920. She claims he was there for the "Southern regional conference" and that he "was housed and fed separately." How she arrived at this information is unclear, however, as she cites only Lester Walton's *New York Age* article, which makes no mention of this. See McMurry, *George Washington Carver,* 201, 344n8.

77. Carver to Weatherford, April 20, 1925, folder 3615; R. R. Moton to Weatherford, May 25, 1925, folder 3615; and Weatherford to Moton, February 5, 1930, folder 703, all in Weatherford Papers. Interestingly, Weatherford took both his male and female students to Tuskegee; see picture file P-3831, folder 17 of 20, Weatherford Papers.

78. See "Speakers and Leaders," *Blue Ridge Voice,* May 1923, 8; and J. E. Johnson to Carver, May 12, 1923, Carver Papers, reel 7, frame 380.

79. McMurry, *George Washington Carver,* 178. Edison's job offer to Carver remains undocumented. Though Carver often referred to it in speeches, he was never able to produce a copy of the telegram that made the offer, nor could the Edison Laboratory confirm it. For a discussion of this issue, see ibid., 177–78.

80. Barry Mackintosh, "George Washington Carver: The Making of a Myth," *Journal of Southern History* 42 (November 1976): 509.

81. Ibid., 517.

82. McMurry, *George Washington Carver,* 201.

83. Weatherford to Carver, April 19, 1923, Carver Papers, reel 7, frame 312.

84. Carver to Lyman Ward, July 6, 1923, Carver Papers, reel 7, frame 558.

85. According to Edwards, *Carver of Tuskegee,* 149, Carver wrote thousands of letters to whites during his life. Often in longhand, "they ranged from concise replies to factual questions to heartfelt outpourings of his philosophy of life."

86. Ibid., 119.

87. Jim Hardwick to Carver, July 2, 1923, Carver Papers, reel 7, frame 539.

88. Edwards, *Carver of Tuskegee,* [vi].

89. Ibid., 157. Hardwick in many ways embodied the remnants of the YMCA's focus on muscular Christianity.

90. Ibid., 157, 182–83.

91. Hardwick to Carver, February 1924, Carver Papers, reel 7, frame 863. In this letter Hardwick wrote: "I would rather be with you at Blue Ridge than anywhere. I look forward to this and pray Christ to give you a great message for the boys there."

92. Edwards, *Carver of Tuskegee,* 121.

93. Ibid., 119. There is some question about the accuracy of Edwards's story. First, she incorrectly dates their meeting to 1922 (ibid.). The letters between Carver and Hardwick show that they met in 1923. Second, she also claims that Carver had been to Blue Ridge in 1920. She asserts he was a guest speaker and was segregated during his visit, staying in the "Moton Cottage"—the one Moton had been in the previous year. There is no evidence to verify these facts; however, the letters between Carver and those setting up the 1923 trip seem to indicate that Carver had never been to Blue Ridge before. In one letter he asks, "Kindly let me know just how I can reach Blue Ridge"; Carver to J. E. Johnson, May 22, 1923, Carver Papers, reel 7, frame 406. Nevertheless, as Edwards's book was based on interviews with Weatherford and Hardwick, it seems likely that there is some truth to what she says occurred in 1923. The best scholarly biography of Carver is written by Linda McMurry. In her telling of the Hardwick-Carver meeting, however, she confuses this even more, repeating information from the alleged 1920 visit of Carver to Blue Ridge and his segregated accommodations. See McMurry, *George Washington Carver,* 202 and 344n8, 344n10. The exact details of this historical event remain unclear.

94. Carver's status as a credible scientist has been called into question in recent years. See Mackintosh, "George Washington Carver," 507–28, and McMurry, *George Washington Carver.*

95. Lumpkin, *The Making of a Southerner,* 198.

96. Carver to Bergthold, August 6, 1924, Carver Papers, reel 8, frame 137.

97. Ibid.

98. Ibid., frame 138

99. Ibid., frames 138–39.

100. Ibid., frame 139.

101. See George H. Jones to W. D. Weatherford, November 30, 1961, folder 3850, Weatherford Papers.

102. Kester, "Radical Prophets," 23.

103. Ibid. The cottage was actually called Craggy View. Blue Ridge Conference records show the speakers, their expenses, and accommodations. One document reveals that Carver stayed from June 19 until June 22. See "Conference Roster—Southern YMCA Student Conference, Blue Ridge-N.C., June 17–27, 1924," folder

50a, Weatherford Papers. Interestingly, another speaker—W. C. Craver—is also listed as staying at Craggy from June 19 to 21. It seems likely that this was William Craver, one of the black leaders of the YMCA. There is no other mention of him or why he stayed there, however. See Mays, *Born to Rebel,* 125.

104. Kester, "Radical Prophets," 23.

105. Ibid. Kester also places the black female educator Mary McLeod Bethune at this gathering. But Kester's memory on this point appears incorrect. Bethune would come the following year to Blue Ridge, and a letter to her from Carver seems to indicate she had never attended Blue Ridge before. See Carver to Mary McLeod Bethune, March 17, 1925, Carver Papers, reel 8, frame 1004.

106. Kester, "Radical Prophets," 24.

107. Ibid. It is not clear what Kester meant by this statement, particularly whether Carver ever discovered their plans to walk out.

108. Howard Kester to Carver, July 4, 1924, Carver Papers, reel 8, frame 9.

109. Martin A. Menafee to Carver, July 12, 1924, Carver Papers, reel 8, frame 60.

110. Ibid.

111. Menafee to Carver, July 19, 1924, Carver Papers, reel 8, frame 88.

112. It should be noted that some of the female working staff may also have had exposure to Carver during this visit. Yet the extent of this contact remains unclear, as there are no records of correspondence between Carver and "Blue Ridge girls" from this visit. Carver himself would have understood the dangers of such relationships. Perhaps this explains why the Carver Papers include only a few scattered letters between him and the young women he met at speaking events, in comparison to scores of letters to and from young men with whom he corresponded throughout his life.

113. See Scandrett to Weatherford, May 10, 1926, folder 302, Weatherford Papers. In this letter Scandrett requests specifically, "We should like to have two Negro women for the last three days of our conference."

114. Bergthold to Carver, June 9, 1924, Carver Papers, reel 7, frame 1240.

115. Mays, *Born to Rebel,* 127.

116. George W. Watkins to Carver, December 8, 1924, Carver Papers, reel 8, frame 515.

117. See Bethune planner, June 23, 1925, Mary McLeod Bethune Papers: The Bethune Foundation Collection, microfilm ed. (Bethesda, Md.: University Publications of America, 1996), reel 3, frame 829. Carver also wrote a letter encouraging her to attend. He recommended that she go instead of himself, insisting that "you will bring an entirely different and helpful [message] of the race problem before these young white students"; Carver to Bethune, March 17, 1925, Carver Papers, reel 8, frame 1004.

118. For the presence of John Hope see C. B. Loomis to W. D. Weatherford and J. J. King, May 17, 1928, folder 730; and Southern Student Conference 1928 pamphlet, folder 731, both in Weatherford Papers.

119. Martin, *Howard Kester*, 26.

120. Mordecai Johnson, "Christianity in Race Relations," *Blue Ridge Voice*, March 1927, 7–14.

121. Ibid., 11.

122. Ibid., 13.

123. Ibid.

124. Combs, "Race Reform," 93–99.

125. Ibid., 93.

126. Quoted in ibid., 93. According to Combs, Roy thought that "YWCA programs at Blue Ridge and two other conference centers had corrupted the views of State Normal college students with regard to race issues."

127. Ibid., 96.

128. Ibid., 95.

129. W. D. Weatherford to Joe Cook, May 25, 1928, folder 937, Weatherford Papers.

130. Indeed, at this time a number of Louisiana colleges (which had been attending Hollister—another Y summer conference retreat, in Missouri) had already chosen to end their association with that center because "colored delegates . . . were housed in the same dormitories as the white delegates"; D. B. Raulins to W. D. Weatherford, January 6, 1928, folder 781, Weatherford Papers.

131. Kester, "Radical Prophets," 24.

132. Edwards, *Carver of Tuskegee*, 173–86.

133. For an in-depth analysis of Kester, see John Egerton, *A Mind to Stay Here: Profiles from the South* (New York: Macmillan, 1970), 70–91; John Stark Bellamy, "If Christ Came to Dixie: The Southern Prophetic Vision of Howard Anderson Kester, 1904–1941" (Ph.D. diss., University of Virginia, 1977); Robert F. Martin, "A Prophet's Pilgrimage: The Religious Radicalism of Howard Anderson Kester, 1921–1941," *Journal of Southern History* 48 (November 1982): 511–30; and Martin, *Howard Kester*. For an overview of Kester's career, and his personal reflections on it, see Kester, "Radical Prophets."

134. Quoted in Martin, *Howard Kester*, 170.

135. Quoted in ibid.

136. Howard Kester, "Early Life of Howard Kester," 4, folder 235, Howard Anderson Kester Papers #3834, Southern Historical Collection, UNC.

137. Martin, *Howard Kester*, 153.

138. Robert B. Eleazer, "Blue Ridge, 1925," *Blue Ridge Voice*, October 1925, 1.

139. See advertisement, "A High-Grade Seven Per Cent Investment Offered by the Blue Ridge Association, $80,000 First Mortgage Bonds," *Blue Ridge Voice*, February 1922, 18. More important, Blue Ridge secured another $160,000 in bonds in 1928 from the Nashville Trust Company and Walter H. Gill, Trustees, against the property. It seems that Blue Ridge must have consolidated the earlier $80,000 bond issue into this 1928 agreement. See Robert R. Williams (Asheville, N.C., attorney representing Blue Ridge) to W. D. Weatherford, November 6, 1933, folder 1767, Weatherford Papers.

140. Weatherford to F. C. Abbott, August 17, 1927, folder 513, Weatherford Papers.

141. "The Boy and His Summer," *Blue Ridge Voice,* April 1923, 11.

142. The camp operated until 1932. After that there are no records of its existence. For the last record of the SCY Camp, see "Blue Ridge Association, 1932: SCY Camp," folder 1648, Weatherford Papers.

143. W. D. Weatherford, "The Lee School for Boys," *Blue Ridge Voice,* November 1925, 1, 10.

144. See "Report of the Fact Finding and Agenda Committee," 5, folder 1149, Weatherford Papers.

145. J. A. Peoples to Weatherford, November 19, 1929, folder 961, Weatherford Papers. In this letter Peoples wrote, "I wish to say to you that I feel that this whole transaction reflects less discredit on me than on you," and he noted Weatherford's "domineering egotism."

146. "Report of W. D. Weatherford to the Executive Committee of the Blue Ridge Association, Lee Hall, September 7, 1931," folder 1347, Weatherford Papers.

147. Dykeman, *Prophet of Plenty,* 91.

148. Ibid., 88–89.

149. McCrory was born in 1890. See Photo Album, "An Album of Julia Pearl McCrory Weatherford," Weatherford Family Papers.

150. Dykeman, *Prophet of Plenty,* 156. The exact dates and for how long she stayed in Colorado are not known. She was there for periods in 1926 and 1927. See R. H. King, memorandum to "each local Assn. in Southern Region including Student except Colored," March 10, 1927, folder 3113, Weatherford Papers.

151. It appears Weatherford had to ask for loans from some of his friends to help him pay for the costs of his wife's care. One of these gifts ($1,000) apparently came from his friend the YMCA leader John R. Mott. See R. H. King to Weatherford, June 14, 1926, folder 3095, Weatherford Papers.

152. Weatherford to P. S. Gilchrist, December 31, 1929, folder 950, Weatherford Papers.

153. Ibid.

154. Ibid.

155. "Approximate Numbers of Blue Ridge Conferences, Summer 1930," folder 1148, Weatherford Papers. It appears other YMCA conference centers were experiencing similar declines in this period. Between 1925 and 1929, the number of paying guest days at the YMCA camp at Silver Bay, New York, had dropped from 44,000 to 29,000, while at Lake Geneva, Wisconsin, they had dropped from 42,000 to 32,000. In this period Blue Ridge had dropped from 32,000 to 22,000 paying guest days. See Weatherford to P. S. Gilchrist, December 31, 1929, folder 950, Weatherford Papers.

156. W. D. Weatherford to E. J. Fuller, November 7, 1929, folder 948, Weatherford Papers.

157. Ibid.

158. Setran, *The College "Y,"* 4–5.

159. W. D. Weatherford to Phillips-Buttorff Mfg. Co., January 5, 1932, folder 1614, Weatherford Papers; see other examples of debts in the same folder under "Creditors."

160. Weatherford to Phillips-Buttorff Mfg. Co., January 5, 1932, folder 1614, Weatherford Papers.

161. W. D. Weatherford to "The YMCA Graduate School Board Members," August 21, 1933, folder 1693, Weatherford Papers.

162. W. D. Weatherford to R. R. Williams, December 26, 1933, folder 1767, Weatherford Papers. In this letter Weatherford notes he paid $47,500 to the bondholders. Therefore, the YMCA Graduate School must have paid only a percentage of the actual value of these bonds. Since the bondholders probably felt this was the best way to recoup any of their investment in the midst of the Depression, they took this offer. See also W. D. Weatherford letter, January 6, 1934, folder 1694, Weatherford Papers. In this mass letter Weatherford notes the property would cost exactly $69,749.75, and "there will probably be an additional expense of $300 for transfer of titles and other items we cannot now foresee." It is not clear exactly what the additional cost was that brought the price from $47,500—which was paid to the bondholders—up to the final figure of $69,749.75.

163. See *Raleigh News and Observer,* August 17, 1933, clipping in folder 1771, Weatherford Papers.

164. Weatherford was fully aware that this legal transaction would not result in the new corporation having any responsibility for the Blue Ridge Association's previous debts since he had consulted his lawyer about the liabilities of the YMCA Graduate School in making this move. See Robert R. Williams to W. D. Weatherford, November 6, 1933, folder 1767, Weatherford Papers. Though the ethics of this action may have been questionable, it appears Weatherford stayed within the law.

165. W. D. Weatherford to F. R. Georgia, July 7, 1933, folder 1791, Weatherford Papers. See also "Coeducation in a New College," *New York Times,* undated clipping in folder 1789, Weatherford Papers.

166. "Coeducation in a New College," *New York Times,* undated clipping in folder 1789, Weatherford Papers. See also Duberman, *Black Mountain.*

167. Quoted in Duberman, *Black Mountain,* 19.

168. Ibid.

169. Ibid., 19, 27.

170. Arthur O. Lovejoy to W. D. Weatherford, October 29, 1933, folder 3235, Weatherford Papers.

171. Duberman, *Black Mountain,* 31.

172. W. D. Weatherford to E. G. Wilson, October 12, 1938, folder 2466, Weatherford Papers.

173. C. J. Jackson to R. C. Bell, October 7, 1939, folder 2586, Weatherford Papers.

174. C. J. Jackson to W. D. Weatherford, December 9, 1940, folder 2794, Weatherford Papers.

175. W. D. Weatherford to Will Alexander, April 8, 1941, folder 2818, Weatherford Papers. See also folders 2835–2842, Weatherford Papers, for the Cragmore planning efforts.

176. Weatherford to Alexander, April 8, 1941, folder 2818, Weatherford Papers.

177. W. D. Weatherford to Southern Bell Telephone Co., October 12, 1942, folder 2894; and W. D. Weatherford to Mary Smiley, February 23, 1943, folder 2980, both in Weatherford Papers.

178. W. D. Weatherford to F. C. Abbott, January 7, 1943, folder 2892, Weatherford Papers. Weatherford noted, "We haven't cut any timber off the Blue Ridge grounds for thirty-five years."

179. W. D. Weatherford to E. S. Lotspeich, May 24, 1943, folder 2973, Weatherford Papers.

180. Ibid.

181. T. Walker Lewis to W. D. Weatherford, December 6, 1943, folder 2989, Weatherford Papers. These states were Alabama, Florida, Georgia, Kentucky, Louisiana, Mississippi, North Carolina, South Carolina, Tennessee, and Virginia.

182. See the following issues of "*Blue Ridge Voice:* Progress of Campaign to Secure $150,000 to Purchase, Remodel, and Begin Operating Blue Ridge," December 29, 1943; February 17, 1944; and June 30, 1944; folder 3790, Weatherford Papers.

183. W. D. Weatherford to Morristown Bank, January 22, 1944, folder 3788, Weatherford Papers.

184. See W. D. Weatherford to Member of the Board of Directors of Blue Ridge College, Inc., June 28, 1944, folder 3790; and W. D. Weatherford to A. J. Elliott, September 19, 1945, folder 3791, Weatherford Papers.

185. "YMCA's Purchase Blue Ridge Property," November 6, 1945, folder 3792, Weatherford Papers.

186. Begun in 1910, Hollister was located just south of Branson, Missouri. See Aaron K. Ketchell, *Holy Hills of the Ozarks: Religion and Tourism in Branson, Missouri* (Baltimore: Johns Hopkins University Press, 2007), 23.

187. Sherwood Eddy to W. D. Weatherford, June 10, 1934, folder 1880, Weatherford Papers.

188. Ibid.

189. Ibid.

190. When exactly these segregation laws went into effect is unclear, but before 1936 Weatherford did not mention them in his correspondence.

191. W. D. Weatherford to Mary Jane Willett, March 31, 1936, folder 2238, Weatherford Papers.

192. Abel Gregg to W. D. Weatherford, June 18, 1932, folder 1624a, Weatherford Papers. The reason that Blue Ridge had been allowed to be so open to black guests on this occasion is probably that the grounds had been largely empty at this time, and there was no one else in the building in which the conference guests

stayed. Thus, there was no one outside the conference to see that southern racial norms had been broken and to raise a complaint. See W. D. Weatherford to Abel Gregg, June 21, 1932, folder 1624a, Weatherford Papers.

193. Gregg to Weatherford, June 18, 1932, folder 1624a, Weatherford Papers.

194. Weatherford to Gregg, June 21, 1932, folder 1624a, Weatherford Papers.

195. Ibid.

196. R. R. Williams to W. D. Weatherford, February 4, 1936, folder 2261, Weatherford Papers.

197. Ibid.

198. For examples see W. D. Weatherford to Ed S. King, Harry F. Comer, and Mary Jane Willett, March 18, 1936, folder 2217; W. D. Weatherford to Gren O. Pierrel, February 18, 1938, folder 2517; and W. D. Weatherford to W. Norman Cook, March 1, 1940, folder 2743, all in Weatherford Papers. In 1939 Weatherford also sought the advice of Frank Porter Graham—president of the University of North Carolina at Chapel Hill—when he was considering allowing black students to participate in a training conference for the presidents of college YMCAs. Weatherford noted, "He tells me that the State constitution has a provision that white and colored students must be educated in separate institutions so we have a very decidedly difficult situation there"; W. D. Weatherford to Student Secretaries in South, December 5, 1939, folder 2660, Weatherford Papers.

199. W. D. Weatherford to R. R. Williams (n.d., but in folder dated 1936), folder 2261, Weatherford Papers.

200. In 1936 a committee of the Southern YMCA and YWCA regional councils had been set up to examine the history of the Blue Ridge–Kings Mountain "race history." Responding to the request of one of the committee members (on the bottom of this request letter in his own handwriting), Weatherford noted that for "some years" African Americans ate in the main dining room "on the condition that conference printed material has carried the simple statement 'there will be fraternal Negro delegates entertained as others guests.'" See W. W. McKee to W. D. Weatherford, October 5, 1936, folder 2351, Weatherford Papers.

201. Gren O. Pierrel to W. D. Weatherford, February 10, 1938, folder 2517, Weatherford Papers.

202. Ibid.

203. W. D. Weatherford to Gren O. Pierrel, February 18, 1938, folder 2517, Weatherford Papers.

204. Ibid.

205. Ibid.

206. W. D. Weatherford to Jesse F. Bader, August 18, 1939, folder 2744, Weatherford Papers. While black guests could sit with white guests of their conference, it remained an issue that attendees from other conferences might object to this practice. Therefore, on at least one occasion Weatherford arranged to have screens placed in the main dining hall to separate different conferences so that there

would be no complaints. See W. D. Weatherford to Herbert Sanders, April 29, 1941, folder 2849, Weatherford Papers.

207. Helen Morton to "Those of you who have been asking about the interracial arrangement at the Student Staff Seminar at Blue Ridge," June 23, 1936, folder 2219, Weatherford Papers.

208. Ibid.

209. Ibid.

210. Ibid.

211. See newspaper clippings, folder 2802, Weatherford Papers.

212. Dave Hamilton, "Inter-racial Equality Preached at Blue Ridge, Hamilton Writes," *Mississippian,* undated clipping in folder 2802, Weatherford Papers.

213. Ibid.

214. J. A. Parker, "Open Forum: 'Yours Received and Contents Noted'" (n.d.), folder 2802, Weatherford Papers.

215. Dave Hamilton, "Open Forum: 'Yours Received and Contents Noted,'" November 10, 1937, folder 2802, Weatherford Papers.

216. See Anne Queen's 1948 unpublished Yale Divinity School seminar paper, "A Study of the Development of the Interracial Conference in the South," 8, folder 357, Anne Queen Papers #5214, Southern Historical Collection, UNC. Queen wrote this paper for her class "Religion in Higher Education" under Professor Clarence Shedd.

217. Ibid., 7. See also Mjagkij, *Light in Darkness,* 112, where Mjagkij notes, "African Americans visiting Blue Ridge were 'segregated and humiliated.'" She pulls this comment from Mays, *Born to Rebel,* 127. She actually misconstrues it somewhat. In reference to Kings Mountain's 1928 policy, Mays wrote: "We could not control what Blue Ridge did, but we could control what we did. We agreed, further, that fraternal delegates from Blue Ridge would still be welcome at Kings Mountain, and that they would never be humiliated or segregated."

218. Queen, "A Study of the Development of the Interracial Conference in the South," 8, Queen Papers.

219. Ibid., 8–9.

220. For an example of the poster announcing the 1940 separate conferences, see "Two Southern Student Christian Conferences," oversized folder, Op-3831, Weatherford Papers. This poster lists both the Blue Ridge and Talladega conferences. It notes that Blue Ridge was "open to men and women students and faculty from white colleges in the ten southern states," while Talladega was "open to men and women students and faculty from any college—Negro or white—in the ten southern states."

221. Queen, "A Study of the Development of the Interracial Conference in the South," 15, Queen Papers.

222. W. D. Weatherford to Henry Ware, February 25, 1943, folder 2979, Weatherford Papers.

223. W. D. Weatherford to Mrs. Aultman Sanders, April 26, 1943, folder 2964, Weatherford Papers.

224. W. R. Wunsch to W. D. Weatherford, March 3, 1943, folder 2901, Weatherford Papers.

225. Ibid. Wunsch was appealing for Weatherford's advice on these matters and shared a portion of what he had written to the organizers of the interracial conference. Weatherford responded that he "heartily" agreed with this statement. See W. D. Weatherford to W. R. Wunsch, March 4, 1943, folder 2901, Weatherford Papers.

226. Queen, "A Study of the Development of the Interracial Conference in the South," 16, Queen Papers.

227. Ibid., 17.

228. Ibid., 26.

229. Ibid., 24.

230. "Resolution adopted by the Board of Directors of Blue Ridge Assembly, Inc. at the Annual Meeting in Atlanta, Georgia on February 17th, 1945," folder 357, Queen Papers. See also Queen, "A Study of the Development of the Interracial Conference in the South," 24–25, Queen Papers.

231. W. D. Weatherford to A. J. Elliott, September 19, 1945, folder 3791, Weatherford Papers.

232. Queen, "A Study of the Development of the Interracial Conference in the South," 1, 28–29, Queen Papers. Though there was only one "official" conference sponsored by the southern student YMCA-YWCA region, an unofficial one for whites continued in 1948 and 1949. This meeting, held at Blue Ridge, was organized primarily by students from North Carolina and South Carolina and had support from various southern states. See W. D. Weatherford, "History of the Student Young Men's Christian Association in the South," 49, Biographical Records box 218, Kautz Family YMCA Archives.

233. Rosalie Oakes to W. D. Weatherford, January 22, 1952, folder 3807, Weatherford Papers.

234. W. D. Weatherford to Samuel McCrea Cavert, June 21, 1934, folder 1867, Weatherford Papers.

235. Ibid.

236. W. D. Weatherford to Arden O. French, July 12, 1939, folder 2659, Weatherford Papers.

237. Ibid.

238. For examples, see Robert G. Bell to W. D. Weatherford, February 11, 1948; and J. Roy Cooper to W. D. Weatherford, February 23, 1948, both in folder 3799, Weatherford Papers. Bell and Cooper were YMCA secretaries at the University of South Carolina and Clemson College, respectively. In Weatherford's "History of the Student Young Men's Christian Association in the South," 48, he pointed out that the white female students who were members of the Interracial Student Council of the South particularly supported the interracial move. In the process he revealed his sexist belief that the white men were much more reasonable and pragmatic about the whole situation, noting, "The women have always taken a more absolutist position than the men on all social issues."

239. W. D. Weatherford to Ed King, February 3, 1948, folder 3800, Weatherford Papers.

240. Ibid.

241. W. D. Weatherford to George J. Fisher, February 6, 1925, folder 3617, Weatherford Papers.

242. Ibid.

243. Weatherford's approach to handling segregation in many ways parallels the way private southern college presidents went about desegregating their institutions after World War II. They too felt they understood and knew how to go about resolving this issue. See Melissa Kean, *Desegregating Private Higher Education in the South: Duke, Emory, Rice, Tulane, and Vanderbilt* (Baton Rouge: Louisiana State University Press, 2008).

244. W. D. Weatherford to William Heyburne, September 4, 1925, folder 148, Weatherford Papers.

245. Laws forbidding interracial marriage were not overturned until 1967, with the Supreme Court's ruling on *Loving v. Virginia*.

246. See Donald L. West to W. D. Weatherford, October 27, 1958, folder 3825; "Presidents of Student YMCA's on Working Staff at Blue Ridge," folder 3162; and J. Martin England to W. D. Weatherford, April 26, 1930, folder 1326, all in Weatherford Papers.

247. West to Weatherford, October 27, 1958, folder 3825, Weatherford Papers. For more information on West's life, see James J. Lorence, *A Hard Journey: The Life of Don West* (Urbana: University of Illinois Press, 2007).

248. Martin England to W. D. Weatherford, October 2, 1932, folder 1461; and W. D. Weatherford to J. Martin England, August 29, 1929, folder 918, both in Weatherford Papers.

249. Martin England to W. D. Weatherford, October 13, 1942, folder 2871, Weatherford Papers. For information about England's role in the creation of Koinonia, see K'Meyer, *Interracialism and Christian Community*, 35–41.

250. White, *Liberty and Justice for All,* 192.

251. Francis Pickens Miller, telegram to W. D. Weatherford, November 30, 1966, folder 3895, Weatherford Papers. See also Francis Pickens Miller, *Man from the Valley: Memoirs of a 20th-Century Virginian* (Chapel Hill: University of North Carolina Press, 1971), 19.

252. Dykeman, *Prophet of Plenty,* 49, 119.

253. Bill Lindau, "Graham Pays Tribute to Educator," *Asheville Citizen,* June 25, 1956, clipping in folder 3747, Weatherford Papers. For information on the friendship between Weatherford and Graham, see "Oral History Interview with Charles M. Jones," November 8, 1976, Interview B-0041, Southern Oral History Program Collection #4007, UNC.

254. Blue Ridge continues to exist. It is now officially known as YMCA Blue Ridge Assembly and is owned and operated by the YMCAs of the southern states.

4. Professionalizing the Southern YMCA

1. Wilson, *Berea College,* 116.

2. The name change reflected a desire to make the school a strictly graduate institution, offering only master's degrees and doctorates. See "Minutes of the Meeting of the Board of Directors of Southern College of Young Men's Christian Associations, Nashville, Tenn., May 21, 1927," 2, folder 418; and W. D. Weatherford to John Adams, October 7, 1927, folder 372a, both in Weatherford Papers. The issue of the length of the school's name, as well as the existence of other "Southern Colleges" in the South, also played a part in this decision. See "Report of W. D. Weatherford to the Board of Directors of Southern College, May 21, 1927," 10–11, folder 418, Weatherford Papers. For the sake of simplicity, the school will be referred to as the YMCA Graduate School throughout the rest of the text.

3. Willis D. Weatherford, "The Training Program of the Southern Y.M.C.A.'s," 20–21, Biographical Records box 218, Kautz Family YMCA Archives. See also Southern College Catalog and Announcements, 1922–1923, 3, folder 2, Weatherford Papers.

4. Hopkins, *History of the Y.M.C.A. in North America,* 175–77.

5. Ibid., 612.

6. Weatherford, "The Training Program of the Southern Y.M.C.A.'s," 19, Biographical Records box 218, Kautz Family YMCA Archives. Hopkins, *History of the Y.M.C.A. in North America,* 612–13, echoes this reasoning, apparently pulling directly from Weatherford's brief account of the training program of the southern YMCAs.

7. As late as 1935 Weatherford still insisted that these YMCA schools did not have "courses on Race Problems"; W. D. Weatherford to Carl M. White, December 11, 1935, folder 2059b, Weatherford Papers.

8. In her popular biography of Weatherford, Wilma Dykeman examines this institution, but she fails to treat it in a critical way. Based largely on interviews with and the personal writings of Weatherford, her work generally accepts his recollections of how the school was operated. From this source material she argues that it was a high-quality institution. Moreover, she agrees with Weatherford that Vanderbilt and Chancellor James H. Kirkland had essentially mistreated the YMCA Graduate School by foreclosing on the institution's property. See Dykeman, *Prophet of Plenty,* 131–60, 175–78. Another study comes from J. Edmund Welch, a professor of physical education, but his work focuses narrowly on the history of the doctor of physical education degree program there. See J. Edmund Welch, "The Y.M.C.A. Graduate School of Nashville," *Forum* (March 1969): 13–16. For a rough draft of this article see J. Edmund Welch, "The Y.M.C.A. Graduate School of Nashville: An Untold Story of One Early Doctoral Program in Physical Education," folder 3776b, Weatherford Papers. The best and most scholarly appraisal comes from the historian George Peter Antone in his dissertation on Weatherford's race relations career ("Willis Duke Weatherford") as well as in

an article exclusively on the Graduate School's history, "The Y.M.C.A. Graduate School, Nashville, 1919–1936," published in the *Tennessee Historical Quarterly*. In the latter, Antone provides a basic outline of the institution's history and educational program; the real heart of his work examines the fiscal decline and fall of the school. He disputes Dykeman's interpretation that Kirkland had unfairly treated Weatherford and the Graduate School and had hastily moved to foreclose on the property. He also questions Dykeman's assumption about the institution's quality. In essence I agree with Antone's argument regarding the relationship between Vanderbilt and the YMCA Graduate School, his interpretation of the economic collapse of the institution, and his criticism of Weatherford in this process. However, the YMCA Graduate School's academic program was stronger than Antone asserts.

9. See YMCA Graduate School staff, 1930, folder 1048, Weatherford Papers.

10. See all the following texts by W. D. Weatherford: *College Problems*, 3 vols. (Nashville: Publishing House of the M. E. Church, South, 1907–9); *Negro Life in the South; Introducing Men to Christ; Present Forces in Negro Progress; Personal Elements in Religious Life* (Nashville: Publishing House of the M. E. Church, South, 1916); and *Christian Life, a Normal Experience*.

11. W. D. Weatherford to Cecil Gamble, January 18, 1933, folder 3224, Weatherford Papers; and Dykeman, *Prophet of Plenty*, 147–48.

12. For examples of Weatherford's pacifism, see W. D. Weatherford to Herbert Hoover, December 3, 1931, folder 1257; and W. D. Weatherford, "Friends of the Radio Audience," March 1936, 8, folder 2140, both in Weatherford Papers.

13. W. D. Weatherford to W. H. Morgan, March 6, 1930, folder 1084, Weatherford Papers.

14. Ibid.

15. "'Y' College Head Declines Yale Call: Dr. W. D. Weatherford Prefers to Serve Southern Institution Here," clipping from unidentified newspaper, June 8, 1924, RG 935, Alumni Relations, box 2687, folder 100, Special Collections and University Archives, Vanderbilt University, Nashville. Weatherford was offered the chairmanship of Christian methods and would have been responsible for Yale's program for training YMCA leaders. The former holder of this position, Henry B. Wright, had recently died.

16. W. D. Weatherford to Judson G. Rosebush, December 31, 1932, folder 1531, Weatherford Papers.

17. Ibid.

18. According to Weatherford, the most "influential persons in the organization of the College were C. K. Ober, P. C. Dix, B. G. Alexander, R. H. King, and W. W. Alexander"; ibid.

19. See "Notes by W. D. Weatherford, 3/21/64," Weatherford Family Papers.

20. Indeed, Weatherford believed such broad training was essential for all "social and religious worker[s]" and they should specifically complete "advanced studies in Sociology, Economics, Psychology, Religious Education and kindred

subjects"; W. D. Weatherford, "Training of Social and Religious Workers," *Journal of Social Forces* 2 (January 1924): 211.

21. Antone, "Y.M.C.A. Graduate School," 68.

22. W. D. Weatherford, "What Kind of Workers Do Our Communities Need?" August 1934, folder 1851b, Weatherford Papers.

23. "Report of W. D. Weatherford to the Board of Directors of Y.M.C.A. Graduate School, Nashville, April 19, 1929," 1, folder 857, Weatherford Papers.

24. See Antone, "Y.M.C.A. Graduate School," 70; Conkin, *Gone with the Ivy*, 264; and "Report of W. D. Weatherford to the Board of Directors of Y.M.C.A. Graduate School, Nashville, April 19, 1929," 1, folder 857, Weatherford Papers.

25. Southern College, 1922–1923 Catalog and Announcements, 17, folder 2, Weatherford Papers.

26. Ibid., 16. This arrangement also existed with Peabody.

27. Ibid., 4.

28. The 1922–1923 school catalog notes that three hours of project work, along with a seminar, in the city of Nashville were required of each student; ibid., 18. Antone points out that "students were encouraged to be in residence throughout the year, that is three quarters in Nashville and the summer quarter at Blue Ridge. The requirements made this virtually mandatory"; Antone, "Y.M.C.A. Graduate School," 71.

29. J. W. McCandless, "A Survey of the Operations of the Blue Ridge Association and Accompanying Recommendations," 1925, 2, folder 768, Weatherford Papers.

30. Southern College, 1922–1923 Catalog and Announcements, 14, folder 2, Weatherford Papers.

31. Ibid., 13.

32. See "Graduates," folder 465; and "List of YMCA Graduate School Graduates, August 1935," folder 2133, both in Weatherford Papers.

33. "Minutes of the Meeting of the Board of Directors of Southern College of Young Men's Christian Associations, Nashville, Tenn., May 21, 1927," 2, folder 418; and W. D. Weatherford to John Adams, October 7, 1927, folder 372a, both in Weatherford Papers.

34. "List of YMCA Graduate School Graduates, August 1935," folder 2133, Weatherford Papers.

35. Antone, "Y.M.C.A. Graduate School," 71; and "List of YMCA Graduate School Graduates, August 1935," folder 2133, Weatherford Papers.

36. Welch, "Y.M.C.A. Graduate School," 13.

37. Ibid., 15. From 1919 to 1931 the D.P.E. was the doctorate offered. In 1932, however, the school began offering only the Ph.D. in physical education. See "List of YMCA Graduate School Graduates, August 1935," folder 2133, Weatherford Papers.

38. In the August 1935 records, an additional ten students seem to have been close to finishing, either lacking their thesis or "some little of academic work to be

completed." See "List of YMCA Graduate School Graduates, August 1935," folder 2133, Weatherford Papers.

39. See "Report of W. D. Weatherford to the Board of Directors of Southern College, May 21, 1927," 8, folder 418, Weatherford Papers.

40. Ibid.

41. Ibid.

42. See "Minutes of the Meeting of the Board of Directors Held at the Y.M.C.A. Graduate School, Nashville, Tennessee, April 19, 1929," 3, folder 618; and "List of YMCA Graduate School Graduates, August 1935," folder 2133, both in Weatherford Papers.

43. W. D. Weatherford to J. H. McGrew, July 1, 1927, folder 475, Weatherford Papers.

44. Ibid.; and Mjagkij, *Light in Darkness*, 39.

45. W. B. Mitchell Jr. to C. C. Shedd, September 26, 1930, folder 1239a, Weatherford Papers.

46. W. D. Weatherford to Clarence P. Shedd, May 17, 1937, folder 2365, Weatherford Papers.

47. See W. D. Weatherford to G. Lake Imes, April 16, 1934, folder 1912, Weatherford Papers.

48. W. D. Weatherford to C. D. Barr, May 8, 1934, folder 1967, Weatherford Papers.

49. See Don H. Doyle, *Nashville since the 1920s* (Knoxville: University of Tennessee Press, 1985), 52–53; and W. D. Weatherford, ed., *A Survey of the Negro Boy in Nashville, Tennessee* (New York: Association Press, 1932), 103. The Bethlehem Center also served as a meeting place for conferences. A "Conference for Colored Women" met there September 17–24, 1927, and Weatherford was on the program as presenting a session on interracial work. See "Conference for Colored Women" program, folder 486, Weatherford Papers.

50. Doyle, *Nashville since the 1920s*, 53.

51. See Weatherford and Johnson, *Race Relations*.

52. Ibid., viii.

53. Mark Ellis, *Race Harmony and Black Progress: Jack Woofter and the Interracial Cooperation Movement* (Bloomington: Indiana University Press, 2013), 159.

54. W. D. Weatherford to Carl M. White, December 11, 1935, folder 2059b, Weatherford Papers.

55. Ibid.

56. See "YMCA Graduate School (1927): Anthropology [course evaluations]," folder 373, Weatherford Papers. The content of these reactions suggests that this course may have been an accelerated form of Weatherford's race relations classes, encompassing aspects of all four courses in one. This probably would have been the case because the Blue Ridge summer working staff might have had only one opportunity to study race relations, whereas students matriculated in Nashville could take all four courses during their years of study.

57. "Reactions to the Term's Work. Mary Heath," folder 373, Weatherford Papers.

58. One caveat is necessary before further analyzing these students' comments. All the students attached their names to their statements. Thus, these students may have felt pressured to impress Weatherford with their "enlightenment" on the subject, and there may have been fear that their statements might affect their grades.

59. "Reaction to the Term's Course. Rachel Phillips," folder 373, Weatherford Papers.

60. "Reactions to the Term's Work. Jerome A. Connor," folder 373, Weatherford Papers.

61. Dykeman, *Prophet of Plenty*, 150.

62. "Reaction to this Term's Work. Lucile Watkins," folder 373, Weatherford Papers.

63. "Reaction to the Term's Work. E. F. Martin," folder 373, Weatherford Papers.

64. "Reaction to the Term's Course. Rachel Phillips," folder 373, Weatherford Papers.

65. "Anthropology Required Readings," 1934, folder 1873, Weatherford Papers. The 1933 anthropology class also read *The Souls of Black Folk*. See "Class in Anthropology," 1933, folder 1695, Weatherford Papers.

66. "To Class in Anthropology," 1932, folder 1439, Weatherford Papers.

67. "Anthropology Examination, Spring Quarter 1932," folder 1439, Weatherford Papers.

68. Weatherford continually used these two words in this period, which shows his moderate approach to race relations. For example, when Moton was appointed to fill Washington's place at Tuskegee, Weatherford praised the former as "one of the sanest and strongest representatives of the negro race"; see "Moton Appointed to Head Tuskegee," *New York Times*, December 21, 1915, 4.

69. "Anthropology," 1934, 3, folder 1873, Weatherford Papers.

70. See "Senior Student's [*sic*] Opinion Records for Faculty Members," 1932, folder 1470a, Weatherford Papers. This file includes six evaluations, and all but one of them indicate some level of rigidity on Weatherford's part.

71. "Anthropology Exam, 1933," folder 1695, Weatherford Papers.

72. Ibid.

73. L. T. Knotter to W. D. Weatherford, February 10, 1928, folder 652, Weatherford Papers.

74. W. D. Weatherford to L. T. Knotter, February 14, 1928, folder 652, Weatherford Papers.

75. Channing H. Tobias to W. D. Weatherford, February 6, 1928, folder 3627, Weatherford Papers.

76. See Tobias's biography in the finding aid for Channing Tobias Papers, Kautz Family YMCA Archives. For more information about Tobias, see Egerton, *Speak Now against the Day*, 125, 239, 287, 414.

77. Tobias to Weatherford, February 6, 1928, folder 3627, Weatherford Papers.

78. W. D. Weatherford to A. P. Watson and E. Franklin Frazier, February 13, 1930, folder 1047, Weatherford Papers.

79. See John M. Work to W. D. Weatherford, February 24, 1930, folder 1047b; Lorenzo D. Turner to W. D. Weatherford, February 17, 1930; E. Franklin Frazier to W. D. Weatherford, February 27, 1930; and L. E. Cashin to W. D. Weatherford, February 17, 1930, all in folder 1047b, Weatherford Papers. Cashin's letter refers to Weatherford's idea as an "experiment," indicating this probably was the first time that this arrangement had occurred between the schools. For a listing of these Fisk professors and other faculty at the time, see the school yearbook, *The Lighthouse, 1930*, vol. 1 (Nashville: Fisk University, 1930), 19–23, Franklin Library, Special Collections, Fisk University.

80. See Cashin to Weatherford, February 17, 1930; Frazier to Weatherford, February 27, 1930; Turner to Weatherford, February 17, 1930; and Work to Weatherford, February 24, 1930, all in folder 1047b, Weatherford Papers.

81. W. D. Weatherford, memorandum to "Students in Anthropology," March 15, 1932, folder 1439, Weatherford Papers.

82. W. D. Weatherford, memorandum "To All Y.M.C.A. Graduate School Students," March 13, 1934, folder 1873, Weatherford Papers.

83. Weatherford to Watson and Frazier, February 13, 1930, folder 1047b, Weatherford Papers.

84. Antone, "Y.M.C.A. Graduate School," 75.

85. See Tula B. Pellettieri to W. D. Weatherford, August 3, 1932, folder 1506, Weatherford Papers. For a listing of the uses of the YMCA Graduate School's special collection of race relations materials, particularly by other higher education institutions' faculty—including Fisk and A and I Normal—tabulated for the Spelman Fund, see W. D. Weatherford to Anna Blauvelt, August 5, 1932, folder 1536, Weatherford Papers.

86. Antone notes that Weatherford's decision to "press the issue" of race relations probably resulted in "significant" loss of financial support for the institution. Antone, "Y.M.C.A. Graduate School," 72.

87. W. D. Moore, memorandum, March 7, 1935, folder 2049, Weatherford Papers.

88. W. D. Weatherford to George O. Stoll, March 18, 1935, folder 2049, Weatherford Papers. It is unclear whether this gift came from the Laura Spelman Rockefeller Memorial Fund. The Spelman Memorial Fund dissolved on January 3, 1929, and merged with the Rockefeller Foundation. See description of Laura Spelman Rockefeller Memorial Fund on the Rockefeller Center Archive website: www.rockarch.org/collections/rockorgs/lsrmadd.php. In describing this $15,000 gift for five years, Weatherford notes only that Rockefeller's secretary, Arthur Packard, visited the college sometime in 1928. Yet the bequest was for five years and ended in 1935. Thus, it may have been a gift from the Rockefeller Foundation, since it began in 1930.

89. Moore, memorandum, March 7, 1935, folder 2049, Weatherford Papers.
90. Antone, "Y.M.C.A. Graduate School," 75.
91. Ibid.
92. W. D. Weatherford to Clyde Stillwell, October 27, 1928, folder 669, Weatherford Papers. This money actually came from Virginia McCormick, daughter of Cyrus McCormick. It appears, however, that this donation was arranged by Anita McCormick Blaine (Virginia's sister), who acted in Virginia's stead because of her mental health issues. For information on Blaine see Gilbert Harrison, *A Timeless Affair: The Life of Anita McCormick Blaine* (Chicago: University of Chicago Press, 1979). Weatherford courted Blaine for donations throughout the 1920s and 1930s. See "1925 YMCA Graduate School: Blaine, Mrs. Emmons," folder 64; "1926 YMCA Graduate School: Blaine, Mrs. Emmons (donor)," folder 198; "1927 YMCA Graduate School: Blaine, Mrs. Emmons (donor)," folder 379; "1929 YMCA Graduate School: Blaine, Mrs. Emmons (donor)," folder 836; and "1931 YMCA Graduate School: Blaine, Mrs. Emmons (donor)," folder 1326, all in Weatherford Papers.
93. Charles S. Johnson to W. D. Weatherford, April 10, 1933, folder 3644b, Weatherford Papers.
94. Pellettieri to Weatherford, August 3, 1932, folder 1506, Weatherford Papers. This document notes, "Each year classes from the Grad. School visit Tuskegee and Fisk University in order to better understand the educational problems and progress of the Negro."
95. Weatherford, memorandum "To All Y.M.C.A. Graduate School Students," March 13, 1934, folder 1873, Weatherford Papers.
96. "Lend a Hand in Developing a Unique Library in the South," *Blue Ridge Voice,* January 1926, 14.
97. W. D. Weatherford to Thomas E. Jones, February 22, 1929, folder 887, Weatherford Papers. Weatherford makes the same argument in his article "Changing Attitudes of Southern Students," *Journal of Negro Education* 2 (April 1933): 148–49.
98. "Slavery Items in the Y.M.C.A. Graduate School Library," folder 1505, Weatherford Papers. One important journal series that Weatherford worked to complete over the course of the institution's history was a run of *De Bow's Review,* a journal of economic and social life that ran from 1846 to 1880. Weatherford eventually gathered this series. Also, one of his graduate students, Don L. Moore, worked on an analytical index of this publication during his years at the school. Weatherford later finished this volume and in 1948 published it with his own funds. Weatherford also wrote a short history of the journal's namesake, James Dunwoody B. De Bow. See W. D. Weatherford, *Analytical Index of De Bow's Review* (Santa Barbara: Privately published, 1952); and W. D. Weatherford, *James Dunwoody Brownson De Bow* (Charlottesville: Historical Publishing Co., 1935).
99. "Reporting the Meeting of the Board of Directors of the YMCA Graduate

School Held in Nashville, Tennessee at the Hermitage Hotel at Four o'Clock, June 24, 1936," 4, folder 2119, Weatherford Papers.

100. Pellettieri to Weatherford, August 3, 1932, folder 1506, Weatherford Papers.

101. Ibid.; and W. D. Weatherford to Clyde Stillwell, October 27, 1928, folder 669, Weatherford Papers.

102. See "Working Principles for Cooperation between the Fisk University Library and the Library of the Y.M.C.A. Graduate School with Special Reference to Material on the Negro," 1932, folder 1504, Weatherford Papers.

103. Ibid.

104. W. D. Weatherford to Anna Blauvelt, August 5, 1932, folder 1536, Weatherford Papers; and Weatherford, "Changing Attitudes of Southern Students," 149.

105. Weatherford to Blauvelt, August 5, 1932, folder 1536, Weatherford Papers.

106. "Anthropology," 1934, 3, folder 1873, Weatherford Papers.

107. Doyle, *Nashville in the New South*, 113, 208–9.

108. In one of Weatherford's personal notebooks he wrote, "The two outstanding Negroes whom I knew better than any other were Dr. Booker T. Washington and Principal R. R. Moton who succeeded Washington. The lat[t]er seemed to me the more able." See "Fisk, Blue Ridge, Religious Discussions," Weatherford Family Papers.

109. R. R. Moton to W. D. Weatherford, April 14, 1930, folder 1037, Weatherford Papers.

110. See George Washington Carver to W. D. Weatherford, April 20, 1925; and R. R. Moton to W. D. Weatherford, May 25, 1925, both in folder 3615, Weatherford Papers. It is clear that Weatherford's group had been there before. Carver noted, "We are always delighted to have you come down to see us." Moton wrote, "I can say in turn that no group you have ever brought here has made quite so favorable impression upon our students and teachers alike."

111. See W. D. Weatherford to Prof. Taylor, April 18, 1928, folder 3626; R. R. Moton to W. D. Weatherford, April 14, 1930, folder 1037; W. D. Weatherford memorandum to "Students in Anthropology," March 13, 1932, folder 1439; W. D. Weatherford to R. R. Moton, May 4, 1932, folder 1543; J. J. Ray, memorandum to YMCA Graduate students, April 7, 1933, folder 1728; W. D. Weatherford memorandum "To All Y.M.C.A. Graduate School Students," March 13, 1934, folder 1873; and F. D. Patterson to W. D. Weatherford, November 1, 1935, folder 3659, all in Weatherford Papers. Weatherford also took pictures of his students, professors, and buildings during one of these Tuskegee trips. See picture file, P-3831, folder 17 of 20, Weatherford Papers.

112. In 1925 one woman went, in 1928 four, in 1932 one, in 1933 three, and in 1934 four. Also in 1934, the A and I graduate sitting in on Weatherford's course traveled with this group. See W. D. Weatherford to Albon L. Holsey, March 18, 1925, folder 114; Weatherford to Taylor, April 18, 1928, folder 3626; Weatherford to Moton, May 4, 1932, folder 1543; Ray, memorandum to YMCA Graduate stu-

dents, April 7, 1933, folder 1728; and W. D. Weatherford to G. Lake Imes, April 16, 1934, folder 1912, all in Weatherford Papers.

113. W. D. Weatherford to R. R. Moton, March 31, 1933, folder 1733; and Carver to Weatherford, April 20, 1925, folder 3614, both in Weatherford Papers.

114. Weatherford, memorandum to "Students in Anthropology," March 13, 1932, folder 1439, Weatherford Papers.

115. Patterson to Weatherford, November 1, 1935, folder 3659, Weatherford Papers.

116. Dykeman, *Prophet of Plenty*, 167–69.

117. See James Myers to W. D. Moore and C. D. Barr, January 24, 1927; and James Myers, "The Cooperative Plan of the American Cast Iron Pipe Company, History," 8, both in folder 472, Weatherford Papers. Employees apparently worked together in integrated fashion in the factory. See Ellis, *Race Harmony and Black Progress*, 177.

118. Dykeman, *Prophet of Plenty*, 168.

119. W. D. Weatherford to C. D. Barr, May 8, 1934, folder 1967, Weatherford Papers.

120. Ibid.

121. Pellettieri to Weatherford, August 3, 1932, folder 1506, Weatherford Papers.

122. "Anthropology," 1934, 3, folder 1873, Weatherford Papers.

123. Ibid.

124. Ibid. William J. Hale was the African American president of A and I at the time.

125. See James D. Anderson, *The Education of Blacks in the South, 1860–1935* (Chapel Hill: University of North Carolina Press, 1988).

126. Southern College, 1922–1923 Catalog and Announcements, 9, folder 2, Weatherford Papers.

127. Welch, "Y.M.C.A. Graduate School," 15.

128. Ibid., 16.

129. Dykeman, *Prophet of Plenty*, 108. See also Southern College, 1922–1923 Catalog and Announcements, 9–10, folder 2, Weatherford Papers. Mims had his Ph.D., whereas Brown had only an A.M. and B.D. and Kesler an A.B.

130. See "Years of Service at Blue Ridge," folder 2219, Weatherford Papers.

131. See the finding aid for Samuel Chiles Mitchell Papers, #1003, Southern Historical Collection, UNC.

132. Singal, *The War Within*, 59–60.

133. For example, see his courses for the 1924 summer term: "The Economic Development of the United States" and "Studies in Social Reconstruction"; Summer Quarter Courses, 1924, folder 16, Weatherford Papers.

134. "Strengthening the Staff at Southern College," *Blue Ridge Voice*, April 1925, 12.

135. See interview with Don West, January 22, 1975; Lorence, *A Hard Journey*,

20; and Connie West, Willard Uphaus illustration and caption, *Appalachian Heritage* 36 (Fall 2008): 5, 50.

136. W. D. Weatherford to G. Sarah Uphaus, March 5, 1928, folder 718, Weatherford Papers. For quote see interview with Don West, January 22, 1975.

137. Sarah Uphaus to W. D. Weatherford, February 27, 1928, folder 718, Weatherford Papers.

138. Willard Uphaus to W. D. Weatherford, April 16, 1929, folder 922, Weatherford Papers; and Josh Barbanel, "Dr. Willard Uphaus, Leader of Pacifist Causes in the 50's," *New York Times,* October 11, 1983, D31.

139. Weatherford noted that he was kept on the payroll until January 1, 1929. See W. D. Weatherford to J. V. Clarke, January 23, 1929, folder 840, Weatherford Papers. It also is not clear how West would have taken courses with Uphaus. The former entered the Vanderbilt School of Religion in fall 1929. Perhaps when West worked as a Blue Ridge PW in the summer of 1929, Uphaus taught a course then. See Donald L. West to W. D. Weatherford, October 27, 1958, folder 3825; and "Presidents of Student YMCA's on Working Staff at Blue Ridge," folder 3162, both in Weatherford Papers.

140. Ray Baber to W. D. Weatherford, June 19, 1929, folder 933, Weatherford Papers.

141. Ray Baber to W. D. Weatherford, October 27, 1928, folder 1094; Baber to Weatherford, June 19, 1929, folder 933; and Baber to Weatherford, June 29, 1929, folder 933, all in Weatherford Papers.

142. Baber to Weatherford, October 27, 1928, folder 1094, Weatherford Papers.

143. Ibid.

144. Baber to Weatherford, June 19, 1929, folder 933, Weatherford Papers.

145. See "Report of W. D. Weatherford to the Board of Directors of Y.M.C.A. Graduate School, Nashville, April 19, 1929," 8, folder 857; and Baber to Weatherford, June 29, 1929, folder 933, both in Weatherford Papers.

146. Baber to Weatherford, June 19, 1929, folder 933, Weatherford Papers.

147. W. D. Weatherford to Herbert Sanders, November 22, 1928, folder 705, Weatherford Papers.

148. Cecile Clark to Edgar Lotspeich, March 4, 1933, folder 1725; and Cecile Clark to Merrill Brown, March 1, 1933, folder 1661, both in Weatherford Papers.

149. Clark to Lotspeich, March 4, 1933, folder 1725, and Clark to Brown, March 1, 1933, folder 1661, both in Weatherford Papers.

150. W. D. Weatherford to Howard Odum, February 28, 1930, folder 1044, Weatherford Papers.

151. See Conference Roster for Southern Summer School, July 17–31, 1928, folder 734, Weatherford Papers; "Sixteenth Year of the Southern Summer School of Young Men's Christian Associations," *Blue Ridge Voice,* June 1927, 11; and Singal, *The War Within,* 151. Weatherford had also published a short article in Odum's sociology journal at UNC in 1924. See Weatherford, "Training of Social and Religious Workers."

152. Weatherford to Odum, February 28, 1930, folder 1044, Weatherford Papers.

153. Ibid.

154. For more information about Arthur Raper and his involvement in the YMCA at Chapel Hill, see Singal, *The War Within*, 328–38; and Louis Mazzari, *Southern Modernist: Arthur Raper from the New Deal to the Cold War* (Baton Rouge: Louisiana State University Press, 2006).

155. W. D. Weatherford to Arthur Raper, April 22, 1930, folder 1046, Weatherford Papers.

156. Arthur Raper to W. D. Weatherford, April 28, 1930, folder 3637, Weatherford Papers. His dissertation would be published as *Preface to Peasantry* in 1936. See Singal, *The War Within*, 333–35.

157. Raper to Weatherford, April 28, 1930, folder 3637, Weatherford Papers.

158. Howard Odum to W. D. Weatherford, March 17, 1930, folder 1044, Weatherford Papers.

159. Henry J. McGuinn, review of *A Survey of the Negro Boy in Nashville, Tennessee*, in *Journal of Negro Education* 2 (April 1933): 217.

160. Ibid.

161. Weatherford, *Survey of the Negro Boy in Nashville*, 118.

162. Doyle, *Nashville since the 1920s*, 32.

163. Ibid., 33.

164. "Theses in the YMCA Graduate School Library, October 19, 1933," folder 1729, Weatherford Papers. These were R. H. Athearn, "The Origin of Racial Attitudes in the Adolescent Boy" (1926); W. N. Cashion, "The Need for Playground Facilities for the Negro Children in Nashville" (1924); M. P. Chapman, "Leisure Time and Recreational Activities of the Negro High School Girl in Nashville, Tenn." (1932); E. P. Deacon, "The Physical Status of Negro Boys in the Junior High Schools of Nashville, Tenn." (1931); J. T. Hardwick, "The Economic Condition of the Negro in Nashville" (1922); A. S. Hurst, "Play of the Nashville Negro Boy" (n.d.); and D. G. McLaurin, "The Leisure Time and Recreational Life of the Negro Boys in Nashville" (1932).

165. Leroy Allen to W. D. Weatherford, July 15, 1933, folder 1924, Weatherford Papers.

166. E. S. Lotspeich, "John R. Mott Visits Southern Y College," *Blue Ridge Voice*, April 1925, 13–14.

167. Ibid., 14.

168. For Van Dusen see Henry P. Van Dusen to W. D. Weatherford, October 31, 1933, folder 1763, Weatherford Papers; and "Protestant Architect," *Time*, April 19, 1954, 62–66. For Poteat see "Edwin McNeill Poteat, Jr.," in *Dictionary of North Carolina Biography*, ed. William S. Powell (Chapel Hill: University of North Carolina Press, 1994), 129.

169. Edwin McNeill Poteat Jr., *Coming to Terms with the Universe: A Study in the Philosophy of Religion for the Semi-Sophisticated* (New York: Association Press,

1931). According to Weatherford's introduction to this volume (x), these lectures were also given at the 1930 YMCA Southern Student Conference at Blue Ridge.

170. Weatherford, introduction to Poteat, *Coming to Terms,* ix.

171. W. D. Weatherford, memorandum to YMCA Graduate School alumni, December 5, 1931, folder 1195, Weatherford Papers.

172. Van Dusen to Weatherford, October 31, 1933, folder 1763, Weatherford Papers. See Henry P. Van Dusen, *God in These Times* (New York: C. Scribner's Sons, 1935).

173. See "Suggestions for Chapels," 1933, folder 1706, Weatherford Papers.

174. Dunbar, *Against the Grain,* 1–15.

175. Ibid., 14.

176. Lee Loventhal to Felix Warburg, May 6, 1933, folder 1765, Weatherford Papers.

177. "Report of W. D. Weatherford to the Board of Directors of the Y.M.C.A. Graduate School at the Annual Meeting, May 2, 1931," folder 1232, Weatherford Papers.

178. See Lee Loventhal to W. D. Weatherford, August 9, 1938, folder 2498, Weatherford Papers.

179. Loventhal to Warburg, May 6, 1933, folder 1765, Weatherford Papers.

180. For a list of the YMCA Graduate School staff in 1930, see folder 1048, Weatherford Papers.

181. W. D. Weatherford to Personnel Division, June 10, 1935, folder 3262, Weatherford Papers.

182. See "National YMCA: Personnel Division, February–July, 1935," folder 3262, Weatherford Papers.

183. See interview with Louise Young, February 14, 1972, Interview G-0066, Southern Oral History Program Collection #4007, UNC. Faculty teaching the 1935 summer term at Blue Ridge were also not paid. See W. D. Weatherford, memoranda "To list of General Secretaries in Southern Region" and "To list of Graduates of YMCA Graduate School," September 25, 1935, folder 2051, Weatherford Papers.

184. For more information on Young, see Harvey, *Freedom's Coming,* 85.

185. W. D. Weatherford to R. P. Kaighn, June 9, 1936, folder 3270, Weatherford Papers.

186. "Reporting the Meeting of the Board of Directors of the YMCA Graduate School Held in Nashville, Tennessee at the Hermitage Hotel at Four o'Clock," June 24, 1936, folder 2119, Weatherford Papers.

187. Ibid.

188. W. D. Weatherford to George O. Stoll, March 18, 1935, folder 2049, Weatherford Papers.

189. Weatherford, "The Training Program of the Southern Y.M.C.A.'s," 23, Biographical Records box 218, Kautz Family YMCA Archives.

190. Ibid.

191. Ibid., 12.

192. Setran, *The College "Y."*

193. "Minutes of Called Meeting of the Y.M.C.A. Graduate School Board of Directors Held at the Chamber of Commerce, Nashville, Tennessee, Monday, December 11, 1933 at 11:45 a.m.," folder 1694, Weatherford Papers.

194. See Antone, "YMCA Graduate School," 80.

195. W. D. Weatherford to F. C. Abbott, December 29, 1933, folder 1772, Weatherford Papers.

196. W. D. Weatherford to Katherine George, October 18, 1944, folder 3787, Weatherford Papers.

197. W. D. Weatherford, "Commencement Address—Y.M.C.A. Graduate School—August 28, 1936," folder 2099b, Weatherford Papers.

198. W. D. Weatherford, memorandum "To Gen. Secretaries in Southern States and Texas, Okla., and Ark.," January 18, 1937, folder 2338, Weatherford Papers.

199. See YMCA Graduate Staff, 1930, folder 1048; and Dag Folger to W. D. Weatherford, August 12, 1929, folder 864, both in Weatherford Papers. Folger finished his dissertation in 1931, after teaching at Yale that year. See Dagnall Frank Folger, "A Comparison of Two Methods for Training Secretaries of the Young Men's Christian Association" (Ph.D. diss., Yale University, 1931).

200. See Dag Folger to W. D. Weatherford, February 11, 1929, folder 863; and "List of YMCA Graduate School Graduates," August 1935, folder 2133, both in Weatherford Papers.

201. David R. Porter, memorandum "To the Southern Field Council and Friends of the Student Association Movement," September 9, 1930, folder 3193, Weatherford Papers.

202. Weatherford, memorandum "To Gen. Secretaries in Southern States," January 18, 1937, folder 2338, Weatherford Papers.

203. "Yale Divinity School Scholarships—1937," folder 2346, Weatherford Papers.

204. See W. D. Weatherford to Agnes Highsmith, August 19, 1937, folder 2344; and "Yale Divinity School Scholarship—1937," folder 2346, both in Weatherford Papers.

205. Dykeman, *Prophet of Plenty,* 120, 188.

206. See "Y.M.C.A. Graduate School, Graduate Summer Quarter, Blue Ridge, N.C.," 1938, folder 2515; and "Minutes of the Y.M.C.A. Graduate School Board Meeting Held at Blue Ridge, N.C. in the Office of W. D. Weatherford," July 24, 1939, folder 2659, both in Weatherford Papers. This relationship may have ended in the early 1940s as Blue Ridge again faced financial troubles as well as the exigencies of World War II. Another explanation is that black students from Yale were not able to attend Blue Ridge. This concern came up in the spring of 1937, when there was the possibility of an African American male student from Yale (Edward Carroll) attending the Blue Ridge summer quarter. Weatherford corresponded with Clarence Shedd, a professor at Yale Divinity, on this question and insisted

that North Carolina segregation laws did not make this possible at the time. Shedd responded that he understood the difficulty of this situation, but he went on to add, "I must, however, say quite frankly that this is one of the problems we will need to work through very carefully if we are to find a basis of cooperative work between Yale and Blue Ridge"; Clarence Prouty Shedd to W. D. Weatherford, May 11, 1937, folder 2365, Weatherford Papers.

207. See "Y.M.C.A. Graduate School Bulletin," September 1934, folder 1925, Weatherford Papers.

208. Edgar Torrence to W. D. Weatherford, July 25, 1934, folder 2044; and "List of YMCA Graduate School Graduates," August 1935, folder 2133, both in Weatherford Papers.

209. Torrence to Weatherford, July 25, 1934, folder 2044, Weatherford Papers.

210. Ibid.

211. Ibid.

212. W. D. Weatherford to Edgar Torrence, August 21, 1934, folder 2044, Weatherford Papers.

213. Weatherford showed his animosity toward Kirkland and Vanderbilt in several of his letters from this period. In one letter he wrote, "The Chancellor has finally managed to rob us of our building"; W. D. Weatherford to J. J. Gray, Jr., June 20, 1936, folder 2126, Weatherford Papers. In another he wrote that Kirkland "took from us a $503,000 building to satisfy a $155,000 note plus $9,000 of interest"; W. D. Weatherford to Jackson Davis, July 9, 1936, folder 2109, Weatherford Papers. He also complained of this treatment in a memorandum to southern YMCA secretaries: "Well, Vanderbilt did us a dirty trick in taking our building costing $503,000 for their debt of $155,000 plus a year's interest"; Weatherford, memorandum "To Gen. Secretaries in Southern States," January 18, 1937, folder 2338, Weatherford Papers.

214. Weatherford, "Commencement Address—Y.M.C.A. Graduate School—August 28, 1936," folder 2099b, Weatherford Papers.

5. A Liberal but Never an Activist

1. Weatherford, "Fisk, Blue Ridge, Religious Discussions," Weatherford Family Papers. Recent scholarship, most notably from Jacquelyn Dowd Hall, has argued that the Civil Rights movement has a long history that precedes and extends beyond the "classical" period, which is usually designated from the 1954 *Brown* decision to the Voting Rights Act of 1965. Weatherford was certainly one of those persons whose work before 1954 can be placed within that scheme. See Jacquelyn Dowd Hall, "The Long Civil Rights Movement and the Political Uses of the Past," *Journal of American History* 91 (March 2005): 1233–64.

2. "Notes by W. D. Weatherford, 3/21/64," Weatherford Family Papers.

3. In a collection of personal reflections Weatherford made near the end of his life, he divided his career into "three definite phases," the periods of (1) his

student work with the YMCA, (2) his interest in race, and (3) his interest in the Appalachian people. Concerning this second phase, he went on to add, "My work on the Negro has never ceased but major attention was given to it from 1910 to 1940"; "Notes by W. D. Weatherford, 3/21/64," Weatherford Family Papers. One might find Weatherford's "withdrawal" from race relations somewhat surprising at this time in light of the fact that it was after the 1940s that the Civil Rights movement quickened in tempo and many of its greatest achievements were made. Clearly part of the reason he became less involved in race was because of his new work with Berea College and his interest in and intense focus on the Appalachian region. But certainly another explanation can be found in the fact that a more active and aggressive approach to achieving racial equality took hold in these later years. Weatherford and many other white liberals were often uncomfortable with these methods.

4. Benjamin E. Mays, "Dr. Weatherford Has Done It Again," *Christian Century* (n.d.), folder 3671, Weatherford Papers.

5. See Weatherford, *American Churches and the Negro*.

6. Dykeman, *Prophet of Plenty*, 234.

7. George Peter Antone insists Weatherford's "liberalism seems to have been bypassed by events, and was out of place" by the mid-1940s. See Antone, "Willis Duke Weatherford," 199.

8. See Martin Luther King Jr., "Letter from Birmingham Jail," April 16, 1963, http://abacus.bates.edu/admin/offices/dos/mlk/letter.html.

9. For brief sketches of these and other white civil rights activists of this period, see G. McLeod Bryan, *These Few Also Paid a Price: Southern Whites Who Fought for Civil Rights* (Macon, Ga.: Mercer University Press, 2001).

10. I am indebted to G. McLeod Bryan for helping make the distinction between an activist and a liberal in this period. Beginning in the 1950s, Bryan worked as a Christian ethics professor at Wake Forest College and involved himself in civil rights activism. In my interview with Bryan he noted how white southern liberals of the generation before him often did not become activists. Bryan also knew Weatherford. Bryan, interview by the author, July 14, 2010, Winston-Salem, N.C.

11. See "How Did Your Attitude toward the Negro Change?" folder 471, Weatherford Papers. For the context of the survey, see William H. Morgan to W. D. Weatherford, April 14, 1927, folder 471, Weatherford Papers.

12. "How Did Your Attitude Toward the Negro Change?" folder 471, Weatherford Papers. In 1936 Weatherford made another comment about relationships between whites and blacks. Writing to a friend in the YMCA, he observed, "Whatever we may think of it [intermarriage], this is not likely to come about in the next hundred years and it seems to me there is no particular value in pushing it when it interferes with other things." This indicates that Weatherford recognized the explosiveness of this issue and may have had fewer qualms about it personally than he was willing to state more publicly. See W. D. Weatherford to A. R. Elliott, January 15, 1936, folder 3273, Weatherford Papers.

13. "How Did Your Attitude Toward the Negro Change?" folder 471, Weatherford Papers.

14. W. D. Weatherford to Ellwood F. Hansen, May 16, 1933, folder 3645, Weatherford Papers. For Hansen's questions see Ellwood F. Hansen to W. D. Weatherford (n.d.), folder 3645, Weatherford Papers.

15. See W. E. Burghardt Du Bois, "Does the Negro Need Separate Schools?" *Journal of Negro Education* 4 (July 1935): 328–35.

16. Joe M. Richardson, *A History of Fisk University, 1865–1946* (1980; repr., Tuscaloosa: University of Alabama Press, 2006), 2–3, 9.

17. Ibid., 4.

18. Ibid., 114.

19. Ibid., 135.

20. Weatherford, "College Life and Main Objectives," Weatherford Family Papers.

21. See interview with John Hope Franklin, July 27, 1990, Interview A-0339, Southern Oral History Program Collection #4007, UNC. The writer John Egerton interviewed Franklin, focusing most closely on his early life, particularly Franklin's memories of his undergraduate years at Fisk University.

22. John Hope Franklin, *Mirror to America: The Autobiography of John Hope Franklin* (New York: Farrar, Straus and Giroux, 2005), 57, 67.

23. Interview with John Hope Franklin, Southern Oral History Program.

24. See advertisement for *Prophet of Plenty* in Weatherford Family Papers.

25. Weatherford, *Negro Life in the South*, 113.

26. See A. H. Yancey to Willis D. Weatherford, October 10, 1925, folder 3611, Weatherford Papers; and W. D. Weatherford to M. W. Adams, March 29, 1929, folder 3630, Weatherford Papers.

27. Weatherford, "Changing Attitudes of Southern Students," 147.

28. Weatherford, "Fisk, Blue Ridge, Religious Discussions," Weatherford Family Papers.

29. Ibid.

30. Richardson, *History of Fisk,* 118–19.

31. W. D. Weatherford to A. O. French, August 5, 1936, folder 2120, Weatherford Papers.

32. W. D. Weatherford to William J. Hutchins, July 8, 1936, folder 3354, Weatherford Papers.

33. Richardson, *History of Fisk,* 69–70.

34. In Antone's 1969 dissertation on Weatherford, he disputed Wilma Dykeman's claim that Weatherford's role at Fisk was primarily teaching. In a well-documented argument Antone clearly shows that Weatherford's early years were spent raising funds for the school and that his teaching function became more prominent in the 1940s. Yet in the process of making this point, Antone neglects to fully explore the teaching that Weatherford did do and to what extent this revealed his support for African American higher education. See Antone, "Willis Duke Weatherford," 183–90; and Dykeman, *Prophet of Plenty,* 182.

35. W. D. Weatherford to C. C. Converse, December 21, 1939, folder 3289; and A. A. Taylor to Thomas E. Jones, June 9, 1939, folder 3291, both in Weatherford Papers.

36. W. D. Weatherford to Thomas Jones, October 4, 1937, box 43, folder 8, Thomas Jones Collection, Franklin Library Special Collections and Archives, Fisk University, Nashville.

37. Weatherford to Converse, December 21, 1939, folder 3289, Weatherford Papers.

38. Ibid.

39. Ibid.

40. W. D. Weatherford to Charles Bransford, February 6, 1940, folder 3292, Weatherford Papers.

41. W. D. Weatherford to Judge Henry S. Hulbert, March 6, 1939, folder 3291, Weatherford Papers.

42. Ibid.

43. Weatherford noted in 1945 that "seven years ago" (1938) he had begun teaching a humanities course, which later became a required course for all Fisk students. See W. D. Weatherford to Thomas E. Jones, October 30, 1945, folder 3312, Weatherford Papers.

44. Thomas E. Jones to W. D. Weatherford, April 20, 1938, box 43, folder 9, Jones Collection.

45. W. D. Weatherford to Thomas E. Jones, October 30, 1945, folder 3312, Weatherford Papers.

46. W. D. Weatherford to Thomas E. Jones, January 10, 1946, box 43, folder 7, Jones Collection.

47. Weatherford to Jones, October 30, 1945, folder 3312, Weatherford Papers. In another letter Weatherford commented that the purpose of the class was to set "forth the place of religion in life"; W. D. Weatherford to Gordon Poteat, May 7, 1941, folder 2943, Weatherford Papers. See also "Humanities 150 Assignment" (n.d.), box 43, folder 10, Jones Collection.

48. W. D. Weatherford to Lloyd Killam, October 22, 1940, folder 2794, Weatherford Papers.

49. Weatherford to Poteat, May 7, 1941, folder 2943, Weatherford Papers.

50. Thomas E. Jones to W. D. Weatherford, February 27, 1943, folder 3298, Weatherford Papers; and Thomas E. Jones to W. D. Weatherford, March 20, 1943, box 20, folder 18, Jones Collection.

51. C. A. Chazeaud to W. D. Weatherford, March 27, 1943, folder 3296; and Benjamin E. Mays to W. D. Weatherford, March 26, 1943, folder 3299, both in Weatherford Papers. See also Samuel L. Gandy to W. D. Weatherford, January 4, 1944, folder 3303, Weatherford Papers.

52. W. D. Weatherford to Mildred LaVerne Streat (n.d.), folder 3296, Weatherford Papers; and Weatherford, *Negro Life in the South*, 167–68.

53. Weatherford to Jones, October 30, 1945, folder 3312, Weatherford Papers.

54. W. D. Weatherford to Lynn Harold Hough, February 24, 1943, folder 3297; and W. D. Weatherford to Luther A. Weigle, May 15, 1943, folder 3300, both in Weatherford Papers.

55. Luther A. Weigle to W. D. Weatherford, March 15, 1944, folder 3306, Weatherford Papers.

56. W. D. Weatherford to Curtis Holland, July 15, 1942, folder 3295; Curtis Holland to W. D. Weatherford, November 20, 1944, folder 3787; W. D. Weatherford to Curtis Holland, November 25, 1944, folder 3787; Curtis Holland to W. D. Weatherford, June 10, 1948, folder 3799; and Curtis Holland to W. D. Weatherford, July 28, 1949, folder 3801, all in Weatherford Papers.

57. Charles S. Johnson to W. D. Weatherford, June 26, 1948, folder 3800, Weatherford Papers.

58. Mildred Armour to W. D. Weatherford, July 18, 1942, folder 3295, Weatherford Papers.

59. Frances Clark to W. D. Weatherford, August 13, 1944, folder 3302, Weatherford Papers.

60. Ibid.

61. "Recommendations of the Department of Religion for Scholarship Awards for the Years 1945 and 1946," folder 3333, Weatherford Papers.

62. Mercedes Martin to W. D. Weatherford, September 4, 1945; and W. D. Weatherford to Mercedes Martin, September 20, 1945, both in folder 3313, Weatherford Papers.

63. Morris Brooks Jr. to W. D. Weatherford, October 18, 1946, folder 3316; and Daisy Lee Gaffney, December 16, 1946, folder 3318, both in Weatherford Papers.

64. Weatherford, "College Life and Main Objectives," Weatherford Family Papers.

65. Ibid.

66. See "Biographical Notes, Concerning W. J. Faulkner," 1945, folder 3310, Weatherford Papers.

67. Dykeman, *Prophet of Plenty*, 181–82; and Patricia M. Johnson to W. D. Weatherford, May 17, 1943, folder 3298, Weatherford Papers.

68. Weatherford, "Fisk, Blue Ridge, Religious Discussions," Weatherford Family Papers.

69. Dykeman, *Prophet of Plenty*, 182. It should be noted that these are not Johnson's own words but must be a paraphrase from Dykeman's interview with her. See also Dykeman, *Prophet of Plenty*, 241.

70. Weatherford, "Fisk, Blue Ridge, Religious Discussions"; and Weatherford, "College Life and Main Objectives," both in Weatherford Family Papers.

71. Weatherford, "Fisk, Blue Ridge, Religious Discussions," Weatherford Family Papers.

72. Betty Grayson to W. D. Weatherford, May 27, 1943, folder 3297, Weatherford Papers.

73. Ibid.

74. W. D. Weatherford to Thomas E. Jones, May 29, 1945, box 43, folder 17, Jones Collection.

75. Thomas E. Jones to W. D. Weatherford, June 2, 1945, box 43, folder 17, Jones Collection.

76. Thomas E. Jones to W. D. Weatherford, June 26, 1945, box 43, folder 17, Jones Collection.

77. W. D. Weatherford to Frank Porter Graham, July 11, 1945, folder 3311, Weatherford Papers.

78. Ibid.

79. Weatherford, "Fisk, Blue Ridge, Religious Discussions," Weatherford Family Papers.

80. Weatherford to Jones, May 29, 1945, box 43, folder 17, Jones Collection.

81. Weatherford, "Fisk, Blue Ridge, Religious Discussions," Weatherford Family Papers. Emphases in original.

82. See Alrutheus Ambush Taylor, *The Negro in South Carolina during Reconstruction* (Washington, D.C.: Association for the Study of Negro Life and History, 1924); Alrutheus Ambush Taylor, *The Negro in the Reconstruction of Virginia* (Washington, D.C.: Association for the Study of Negro Life and History, 1926); and Alrutheus Ambush Taylor, *The Negro in Tennessee, 1865–1880* (Washington, D.C.: Associated Publishers, 1941). For more information on Taylor see Brundage, *The Southern Past*, 156.

83. Richardson, *History of Fisk*, 113.

84. See Taylor's unpublished history of Fisk University, 1866–1951, "A Constructive Influence in American Life" (1952); and "Alrutheus A. Taylor, Tribute by C. S. Johnson," June 1954, Alrutheus Ambush Taylor Papers, Amistad Research Center, Tulane University, New Orleans.

85. Carter G. Woodson, review of *The Negro from Africa to America*, in *Journal of Negro History* 9 (October 1924): 577.

86. William A. Dunning was a historian at Columbia University, teaching there in the late nineteenth and early twentieth centuries. For more on Dunning see Peter Novick, *That Noble Dream: The "Objectivity Question" and the American Historical Profession* (New York: Cambridge University Press, 1988), 75, 77–80.

87. Weatherford, *The Negro from Africa to America*, 20.

88. See W. D. Weatherford to Mary Stahlman Douglas, January 30, 1936, folder 3723b, Weatherford Papers. The review was to be published in the *Nashville Banner*.

89. Weatherford to Jones, January 10, 1946, box 43, folder 7, Jones Collection.

90. Indeed, in Antone's dissertation on Weatherford, he argues that Weatherford's choice was tied to this fact and certain conflicting racial views between Weatherford and Johnson. See Antone, "Willis Duke Weatherford," 180–200. For more information on Johnson, see Richard Robbins, *Sidelines Activist: Charles S. Johnson and the Struggle for Civil Rights* (Jackson: University Press of Mississippi, 1996); and Patrick J. Gilpin and Marybeth Gasman, *Charles S. Johnson: Leader-*

ship beyond the Veil in the Age of Jim Crow (Albany: State University of New York Press, 2003).

91. Weatherford and Johnson, *Race Relations*, 527–30.

92. Ibid., 527–28.

93. Ibid., 528.

94. Ibid., 553–54.

95. Ibid., 554.

96. Ibid., 528.

97. Antone asserts that over the course of the 1930s and 1940s, economic and political changes in America (particularly those wrought by the Great Depression and World War II) heightened the differences between Johnson and Weatherford. He goes on to contend that while Johnson had moved with the times, coming to the stance of "refus[ing] to tolerate segregation," Weatherford had "undergone no marked change in attitude." Nevertheless, Antone does not provide evidence to substantiate this bold claim. See Antone, "Willis Duke Weatherford," 198–99.

98. See Weatherford, "Fisk, Blue Ridge, Religious Discussions," Weatherford Family Papers.

99. "Notes by W. D. Weatherford, 3/21/64," Weatherford Family Papers.

100. W. D. Weatherford to Gordon Poteat, May 7, 1941, folder 2943, Weatherford Papers.

101. W. D. Weatherford to Elizabeth Parker, February 27, 1942, folder 2943, Weatherford Papers. Weatherford also corresponded with another possible administrative assistant. See W. D. Weatherford to Coralie Witherspoon, March 6, 1942, folder 2961, Weatherford Papers.

102. W. D. Weatherford to F. Q. Blanchard, November 1, 1945; and Fred L. Brownlee to W. D. Weatherford, December 7, 1945, both in folder 3307, Weatherford Papers.

103. Weatherford to Jones, January 10, 1946, box 43, folder 7, Jones Collection. It should be noted that the same letter is in Weatherford's own papers at the Southern Historical Collection. This letter, however, is dated 1945 instead of 1946. Indeed, the letter in the Fisk Special Collections was originally dated 1945, but the "5" is marked through and a "6" written above it. The letter's contents indicate that the letter was actually written in 1946. For comparison, see W. D. Weatherford to Thomas E. Jones, January 10, 1945 [1946], folder 3312, Weatherford Papers.

104. Weatherford to Jones, January 10, 1945 [1946], folder 3312, Weatherford Papers.

105. Ibid. See also C. J. Jackson to W. D. Weatherford, November 6, 1945, folder 3312; and W. D. Weatherford to Luther Weigle, April 3, 1946, folder 3320, both in Weatherford Papers.

106. W. D. Weatherford to Sarah Louis, February 4, 1938, folder 2498, Weatherford Papers.

107. W. D. Weatherford to Leonard Haas, January 23, 1942, folder 2938,

Weatherford Papers. See also Emily H. Clay, memorandum "To the Members of the Commission on Interracial Cooperation," January 21, 1942, folder 2938, Weatherford Papers.

108. W. D. Weatherford to Albert Gore, May 3, 1943, folder 3783, Weatherford Papers. It is important to note that while Weatherford recognized the unfairness of poll taxes, he did not believe in the complete enfranchisement of all citizens. In a discussion of this issue at Blue Ridge in 1941 he noted he "would favor an educational qualification for all voters, black and white, to lift the level of our voting public." See "Politics and Negro Discussed," clipping from unidentified newspaper (1941), folder 2861, Weatherford Papers.

109. James A. Dombrowski, memorandum, May 1, 1943, folder 3782, Weatherford Papers. For information on the Southern Conference for Human Welfare, see Thomas A. Krueger, *And Promises to Keep: The Southern Conference for Human Welfare, 1938–1948* (Nashville: Vanderbilt University Press, 1967).

110. Ralph J. Bunche to W. D. Weatherford, October 23, 1939, folder 2601, Weatherford Papers.

111. See David W. Southern, "*An American Dilemma* Revisited: Myrdalism and White Southern Liberals," *South Atlantic Quarterly* 75 (Spring 1976): 182–97, esp. 182.

112. W. D. Weatherford to "Miss Clark" (n.d.), folder 2601, Weatherford Papers.

113. W. D. Weatherford, "My Experience in Race Relations" (1939), folder 3678c, Weatherford Papers.

114. Myrdal, *An American Dilemma*, 563, 564, 1215, 1230.

115. Charles S. Johnson and Howard W. Odum to W. D. Weatherford, February 1, 1944, folder 3667; and Inez B. Tillison to W. D. Weatherford, March 12, 1947, folder 3798, both in Weatherford Papers.

116. Egerton, *Speak Now against the Day*, 302.

117. Howard W. Odum to W. D. Weatherford, May 25, 1938; Howard W. Odum to W. D. Weatherford, June 4, 1938; and W. D. Weatherford to Howard W. Odum, December 19, 1938, all in folder 2508, Weatherford Papers.

118. Egerton, *Speak Now against the Day*, 302–12. See also Hall, *Revolt against Chivalry*.

119. Quoted in Egerton, *Speak Now against the Day*, 306.

120. Ibid., 311–16.

121. See "Proceeding of the First Annual Institute of Religion," June 7–12, 1943, folder 3330, Weatherford Papers. Several papers from this conference were published in the *Journal of Religious Thought* 2 (Autumn–Winter 1945): 1–59.

122. "Proceedings of the First Annual Institute of Religion," 2, folder 3330, Weatherford Papers.

123. Ibid., 15. The last three words of this paragraph were words Weatherford often used; they imply a reference to personalism.

124. Ibid., 16–18.

125. Ibid., 17.

126. Ibid., 18.

127. Ibid., 1.

128. Just before listing the resolutions, the "Proceedings" included the following statement: "The proposals listed below as adopted by the Institute represent for the most part recommendations made by combined Groups III and IV," of which Weatherford was a part; ibid., 15.

129. W. D. Weatherford, "What do we want to do?" folder 3331, Weatherford Papers.

130. Untitled notes by W. D. Weatherford (1943), folder 3331, Weatherford Papers.

131. See Egerton, *Speak Now against the Day*, 213–16; and August Meier and Elliott Rudwick, *CORE: A Study in the Civil Rights Movement, 1942–1968* (1973; repr., Urbana: University of Illinois Press, 1975), 11, 15, 21.

132. Untitled notes by Weatherford (1943), folder 3331, Weatherford Papers.

133. In her influential article on the "long civil rights movement," the historian Jacquelyn Dowd Hall argues that this struggle "took root in the liberal and radical milieu of the late 1930s" as labor and race interests merged. See Hall, "The Long Civil Rights Movement," 1235, 1245–46.

134. Egerton, *Speak Now against the Day*, 154–57; and Dunbar, *Against the Grain*, 88–89.

135. See Egerton, *Speak Now against the Day*, 180.

136. Ibid., 197.

137. Ibid., 151–53.

138. Ibid., 152.

139. Boles, *The South through Time*, 474; and Egerton, *Speak Now against the Day*, 152–53.

140. An example of this slow change can be seen in Frank Porter Graham's handling of Pauli Murray's application to graduate school at UNC Chapel Hill in 1938. Murray, an African American woman, was not admitted and ended up attending Howard Law School instead. UNC did not allow black students to matriculate until 1950. See Holden, *The New Southern University*, 108–12; and Egerton, *Speak Now against the Day*, 232–33.

141. Egerton, *Speak Now against the Day*, 201.

142. Ibid., 327.

143. Ibid., 207. For more on the importance of federal spending in the South in the mid-twentieth century, see Bruce J. Schulman, *From Cotton Belt to Sunbelt: Federal Policy, Economic Development, and the Transformation of the South, 1938–1980* (Durham: Duke University Press, 1994).

144. Egerton, *Speak Now against the Day*, 213.

145. Ibid., 254.

146. Hall, "The Long Civil Rights Movement," 1247.

147. The press published, for example, history books by John Hope Franklin, journalistic pieces by Virginius Dabney, and sociological works on lynching by Arthur Raper. For more on Couch see Singal, *The War Within*, 265–301.

148. For more on the controversy that ensued, see Rayford W. Logan, *What the Negro Wants* (With a New Introduction and Bibliography by Kenneth Robert Janken) (1944; repr., Notre Dame: University of Notre Dame Press, 2001); and Singal, *The War Within*, 299–301.

149. Logan, *What the Negro Wants*, xx.

150. See NAACP invitation postcard to W. D. Weatherford, April 20, 1943, folder 3666, Weatherford Papers.

151. The "Committee of 100" in support of the N.A.A.C.P. Legal Defense and Education Fund, Inc., memorandum, March 15, 1965, folder 3878, Weatherford Papers. This form letter begins "Dear Friend" and is a request for monetary support for this organization's legal work in Alabama at the time. It seems likely that Weatherford had some connection to this group if he received this letter, perhaps having even donated funds at some earlier point.

152. W. D. Weatherford to Paul B. Kern, ca. 1946, folder 3318, Weatherford Papers.

153. Ibid.

154. See "Y.M.C.A. Graduate School Studies in Social and Religious Engineering," book list, 1932, folder 1529d; and "Research in the Attitudes of the Southern Churches toward the Negro, Particularly during the Slave Period," January 28, 1932, folder 3209, both Weatherford Papers. Weatherford would also cite this manuscript in Weatherford and Johnson, *Race Relations*, 215.

155. W. D. Weatherford to G. L. Worthington, April 1, 1936, folder 3661, Weatherford Papers. Worthington worked with the Historical Publishing Company in Charlottesville, Va. Weatherford also submitted the manuscript to the eminent University of North Carolina Press. See W. T. Couch to W. D. Weatherford, April 4, 1936; W. D. Weatherford to W. T. Couch, April 9, 1936; and W. T. Couch to W. D. Weatherford, April 16, 1936, all in folder 3661, Weatherford Papers.

156. Weatherford to Worthington, April 1, 1936, folder 3661, Weatherford Papers.

157. W. D. Weatherford to Nolan Harmon Jr., November 13, 1944, folder 3303, Weatherford Papers. See also W. D. Weatherford to Thomas Jones, July 28, 1944, box 43, folder 17, Jones Collection.

158. W. D. Weatherford to Ed King, February 3, 1948, folder 3800, Weatherford Papers.

159. W. D. Weatherford to Nolan B. Harmon Jr., December 12, 1944, folder 3303; W. D. Weatherford to Alice T. Paine, December 4, 1945, folder 3313; and W. D. Weatherford to Alice T. Paine, January 17, 1946, folder 3319, all in Weatherford Papers.

160. Clarkson N. Potter to W. D. Weatherford, June 20, 1951, folder 3804; Emory Stevens Bucke to W. D. Weatherford, September 10, 1956, folder 3813; and L. K. Hall to W. D. Weatherford, January 10, 1947, folder 3797, all in Weatherford Papers.

161. Arthur J. Christopher to W. D. Weatherford, September 18, 1956, folder 3667, Weatherford Papers.

162. Clive Webb, ed., *Massive Resistance: Southern Opposition to the Second Reconstruction* (New York: Oxford University Press, 2005), xi.

163. See George Lewis, *Massive Resistance: The White Response to the Civil Rights Movement* (London: Hodder Arnold, 2006); Numan V. Bartley, *The New South, 1945–1980* (Baton Rouge: Louisiana State University Press, 1995), 187–222; and Numan V. Bartley, *The Rise of Massive Resistance: Race and Politics in the South during the 1950s* (Baton Rouge: Louisiana State University Press, 1969).

164. Weatherford, *American Churches and the Negro,* 283, 288–90. For example, Weatherford noted that beyond Christianity, "our ideals of democracy force us to give a fuller and more meaningful status to the Negro," and he went on to point out the fears of "Nazism," "Fascism," and "Hitlerism" if the United States failed to do so.

165. Ibid., 17–21.

166. An example of Weatherford's focus on Southerners is found in his foreword: "Since most southern people have a high reverence for the great leaders of the Old South, and since most of us have a nostalgic appreciation of the finer elements in that old southern civilization, its seems reasonable to believe that a comparison of the attitude of the early leaders with the attitude of the average present-day church member might help to bring some sanity and poise into present-day thinking." By the end of the book, however, he wrote, "Once again this is not a sectional matter; North and South, East and West, the Christian Church conforms to caste"; ibid., 16, 292.

167. Ibid., 19. Historical scholarship supports Weatherford's perspective here. Indeed, historians have recognized the "biracial" nature of churches in the antebellum period. See John B. Boles, ed., *Masters & Slaves in the House of the Lord: Race and Religion in the American South, 1740–1870* (Lexington: University Press of Kentucky, 1988), esp. 1–2.

168. W. D. Weatherford to Mable Gillespie, November 28, 1958, folder 3429, Weatherford Papers.

169. Weatherford, *American Churches and the Negro,* 21.

170. Ibid., 248.

171. Frank P. Graham, introduction, ibid., 11–12.

172. Weatherford, *American Churches and the Negro,* 283.

173. Ibid., 286, 295, 296.

174. Ibid., 291; emphasis in original.

175. W. D. Weatherford to B. J. Hardwood, December 12, 1956, Record Group no. 9, box 1, folder 8, W. D. Weatherford Sr. Collection.

176. Ibid.

177. Weatherford, *American Churches and the Negro,* 300.

178. W. D. Weatherford to A. B. Cash, August 28, 1956, folder 3513, Weatherford Papers.

179. The Southern Manifesto, a document signed by the vast majority of southern senators and congressmen challenging the *Brown* decision, was issued on March 12, 1956. Weatherford did not make his agreement with the Christopher Publishing House until September 18, 1956. Weatherford was clearly aware of the Southern Manifesto and had even been in correspondence with Abingdon Press as a possible publisher and considered Senator John Sparkman of Alabama as a candidate for writing a preface. The editor at Abingdon Press advised against Sparkman's taking this role because he had signed the Southern Manifesto. See Emory Stevens Bucke to W. D. Weatherford, September 10, 1956, folder 3813, Weatherford Papers.

180. W. D. Weatherford to Benjamin Mays, March 11, 1957, box 1, folder 9, Weatherford Sr. Collection.

181. Benjamin E. Mays to W. D. Weatherford, May 16, 1957, box 1, folder 9, Weatherford Sr. Collection.

182. W. J. Faulkner, review of *American Churches and the Negro,* in *Chicago Defender,* August 3, 1957, clipping in folder 3671, Weatherford Papers.

183. Paul Green to W. D. Weatherford, March 26, 1957, box 1, folder 8; and Guy B. Johnson to W. D. Weatherford, August 13, 1957, box 1, folder 9, both in Weatherford Sr. Collection; and George S. Mitchell to W. D. Weatherford, June 26, 1959, folder 3831, Weatherford Papers.

184. H. L. Puxley, review of *American Churches and the Negro,* in *International Review of Missions* (January 1959), clipping in folder 3671, Weatherford Papers.

185. Ibid.

186. W. D. Weatherford to Cleveland E. Dodge, December 10, 1956, box 1, folder 7, Weatherford Sr. Collection.

187. See Weatherford to Harwood, December 12, 1956, box 1, folder 8; Weatherford to Dodge, December 10, 1956, box 1, folder 7; and Weatherford to Mays, March 11, 1957, box 1, folder 9, all in Weatherford Sr. Collection.

188. W. D. Weatherford to F. D. Patterson, November 28, 1958, folder 3437, Weatherford Papers.

189. Ibid.

190. See James McBride Dabbs, *The Southern Heritage* (New York: Alfred A. Knopf, 1958). For correspondence between Weatherford and Dabbs, see W. D. Weatherford to James McBride Dabbs, January 8, 1959; James McBride Dabbs to W. D. Weatherford, January 10, 1959; and W. D. Weatherford to James McBride Dabbs, March 3, 1959, all in folder 3828, Weatherford Papers.

191. For information on Dabbs see Egerton, *Speak Now against the Day,* 551–52; and Bruce Clayton and John Salmond, *Debating Southern History: Ideas and Action in the Twentieth Century* (Lanham, Md.: Rowman and Littlefield, 1999), 63–64.

192. See King, "Letter from Birmingham Jail." It is unclear how King would have viewed Weatherford, specifically whether he would have classified him as one of the "white moderate[s]" of this time. In many ways, though, Weatherford fit the mold of the gradualist that King criticized.

193. Weatherford to Patterson, November 28, 1958, folder 3437, Weatherford Papers.

194. Ibid.

195. Frederick D. Patterson to W. D. Weatherford, December 31, 1958, folder 3437; George S. Mitchell to W. D. Weatherford, June 9, 1959, folder 3831; and W. D. Weatherford to George S. Mitchell, June 26, 1959, folder 3831, all in Weatherford Papers.

196. For the younger Mitchell, see Egerton, *Speak Now against the Day*, 129, 133.

197. W. D. Weatherford to Christopher Publishing House, January 29, 1965, folder 3878, Weatherford Papers. In this letter he appealed to the publishers to reprint his book, suggesting that perhaps they put a statement on the book's cover that said "WHAT HAS CIVIL RIGHTS DONE TO YOUR CHURCH? This book will help you decide what you should do."

198. W. D. Weatherford to Grayson Kirk, March 14, 1964, folder 3873, Weatherford Papers.

199. Richard L. Stevens, memorandum, April 10, 1964, folder 3873, Weatherford Papers.

200. W. D. Weatherford to Flora M. Rhind (Rockefeller Foundation secretary), March 7, 1964, folder 3874, Weatherford Papers.

201. Ibid.

202. William Bagwell, "The Pitiful State of Negro Education in Western North Carolina," February 20, 1962, folder 3855, Weatherford Papers.

203. William Bagwell to George Abbott, January 4, 1962; William Bagwell to W. D. Weatherford, April 13, 1962; and George A. Abbott, memorandum to "Council Member," May 1, 1962, all in folder 3855, Weatherford Papers.

204. W. D. Weatherford to Paul Anthony, November 5, 1965, folder 3669a, Weatherford Papers.

205. From March 21 to 25, 1965, Martin Luther King Jr. and approximately 25,000 others participated in a march to Montgomery, Alabama. A few Berea College students took part in this event, and Weatherford's personal secretary at the school at the time made the following inquiry of Weatherford: "What do you think of the situation and will King's encouraging people not to buy Alabama-made products effect the ACIPCO? Knowing the negro as you do, and knowing the Alabama people, do you think this procedure of marching and demonstrating is good or bad?" Weatherford's response—if he made one—does not remain, but it is likely he would not have wholeheartedly approved. See Elizabeth Wyckoff to W. D. Weatherford, March 29, 1965, folder 3571, Weatherford Papers; and David R. Goldfield, *Black, White, and Southern: Race Relations and Southern Culture, 1940s to the Present* (Baton Rouge: Louisiana State University Press, 1990), 164–67.

206. Rachel and Herman Schilling to W. D. Weatherford, February 7, 1965, folder 3886, Weatherford Papers. Also included in this letter was the program from the dinner.

207. This issue remains a debated point among historians. The extent to which personalism influenced King's thought and activism has been called into question by the historian David L. Chappell. See David L. Chappell, *A Stone of Hope: Prophetic Religion and the Death of Jim Crow* (Chapel Hill: University of North Carolina Press, 2004), 52–54.

208. King, "Letter from Birmingham Jail."

209. "Weatherford Hails Appalachia Efforts," *Charlotte Observer,* December 2, 1966, clipping in folder 3747, Weatherford Papers.

210. Ibid.

6. Bringing a Revival to the Mountains

1. John Herbert Roper, *Paul Green: Playwright of the Real South* (Athens: University of Georgia Press, 2003); and Charles S. Watson, *The History of Southern Drama* (Lexington: University Press of Kentucky, 1997), 99–121.

2. "Berea Will Mark Centennial Year," *New York Times,* June 19, 1955.

3. W. D. Weatherford to Paul Green, May 14, 1953, Record Group no. 9, box 1, folder 8, Weatherford Sr. Collection; emphasis in original. It appears Weatherford chose not to pursue a "Race Drama" largely because he was interested in what a play highlighting white Appalachians could do to bring support for the school and the region. African American concerns remained secondary, but Weatherford still had these on his mind. In 1964 he corresponded with Green about the possibility of "writing a great Negro Drama—which would dramatize the 300 years of Negro struggle for his place in America." Though it never materialized, Green apparently supported this project. See "Notes by W. D. Weatherford, 3/21/64," Weatherford Family Papers.

4. Wilson, *Berea College,* 83.

5. Ibid., 84.

6. Ibid., 77–81.

7. Ibid., 147.

8. See "Notes by W. D. Weatherford, 3/21/64," Weatherford Family Papers.

9. W. D. Weatherford to Elizabeth Wyckoff, November 25, 1960, folder 3553, Weatherford Papers. Humbly, Weatherford responded, "But I will trade for just an efficient advocate of the mountains." Schweitzer was a theologian and physician born in Alsace in 1875 (the same year as Weatherford). Known for his study of the "historical Jesus," he worked the greater part of his life as a medical missionary in Gabon, Africa. He was awarded the Nobel Peace Prize in 1953. See Albert Schweitzer, *The Quest of the Historical Jesus* (1906; repr., Minneapolis: Fortress Press, 2001), vii–ix.

10. "Notes by W. D. Weatherford, 3/21/64," Weatherford Family Papers.

11. Weatherford, "Growing Up in Weatherford, Texas," Weatherford Family Papers.

12. Dykeman, *Prophet of Plenty,* 52–56.

13. "Notes by W. D. Weatherford, 3/21/64," Weatherford Family Papers.

14. See "Berea College Progress Report," June 1963, folder 3499, Weatherford Papers; and Loyal Jones, "The Surveys of the Appalachian Region," *Appalachian Heritage* 4 (Spring 1976): 37.

15. Wilson, *Berea College*, 116.

16. W. D. Weatherford, untitled speech, 1939, folder 2688, Weatherford Papers.

17. Ibid.

18. W. D. Weatherford to Thomas E. Jones, January 10, 1945 [1946], folder 3312, Weatherford Papers.

19. Francis S. Hutchins to W. D. Weatherford, February 19, 1944, folder 3365; and Charles Ward Seabury to Francis S. Hutchins, April 10, 1945, folder 3366, both in Weatherford Papers.

20. See Bruce Barton to William A. McRitchie, October 19, 1955, folder 3409, Weatherford Papers; and "Bruce Barton, Ad Man, Is Dead; Author, Former Representative," *New York Times,* July 6, 1967. Barton was also famous for his rendering of Jesus of Nazareth's story in *The Man Nobody Knows* (1925), which highlighted Jesus's business skills and masculinity. For more on Barton, see Richard M. Fried, *The Man Everybody Knew: Bruce Barton and the Making of Modern America* (Chicago: Ivan R. Dee, 2005).

21. See "Bruce Barton's Pet Enthusiasm," folder 3458, Weatherford Papers.

22. Ibid.

23. Barton to McRitchie, October 19, 1955, folder 3409, Weatherford Papers.

24. W. D. Weatherford to Katharine H. Baker, November 16, 1950, folder 3371, Weatherford Papers.

25. Richard B. Drake, *A History of Appalachia* (Lexington: University Press of Kentucky, 2001), 20–21.

26. See "Talk by Dr. Willis Duke Weatherford (age 85) to Catholic Bishop Waters (and others) of the Raleigh, NC Diocese and Glenmary Missionary Order," ca. 1961–62, sound recording, SC-OR-500-001-A, Special Collections and Archives, Berea College; and "Statement mailed to Wilma D., Nov. 17, 1966," folder 3761, Weatherford Papers.

27. Ronald D Eller, *Uneven Ground: Appalachia since 1945* (Lexington: University Press of Kentucky, 2008), 13–15. For more on Appalachia see Thomas Kiffmeyer, *Reformers to Radicals: The Appalachian Volunteers and the War on Poverty* (Lexington: University Press of Kentucky, 2008); John C. Inscoe, "The Discovery of Appalachia: Regional Revisionism as Scholarly Renaissance," in *A Companion to the American South,* ed. John B. Boles (Malden, Mass.: Blackwell, 2002), 369–86; Drake, *History of Appalachia;* and Randal L. Hall, *Mountains on the Market: Industry, the Environment, and the South* (Lexington: University Press of Kentucky, 2012).

28. Eller, *Uneven Ground,* 16–20.

29. Ibid., 37.

30. Ibid., 23–25. For the Great Migration see Milton C. Sernett, *Bound for the Promised Land: African American Religion and the Great Migration* (Durham: Duke University Press, 1997).
31. Eller, *Uneven Ground*, 25.
32. Roy E. Proctor and T. Kelley White, "Agriculture: A Reassessment," in Ford, *The Southern Appalachian Region*, 87.
33. Eller, *Uneven Ground*, 29.
34. Ibid., 28.
35. Ibid., 31.
36. Drake, *History of Appalachia*, 121.
37. See John C. Campbell, *The Southern Highlander and His Homeland* (1921; repr., Lexington: University Press of Kentucky, 1969), vii; and Jones, "Surveys of the Appalachian Region," 26.
38. Jones, "Surveys of the Appalachian Region," 27–29.
39. Ibid., 29.
40. Kiffmeyer, *Reformers to Radicals*, 20.
41. See Jones, "Surveys of the Appalachian Region," 26, 35–36.
42. Eller, *Uneven Ground*, 41.
43. W. D. Weatherford to Francis S. Hutchins, June 26, 1953, folder 3397; W. D. Weatherford to Francis S. Hutchins, January 19, 1954, folder 3404; and W. D. Weatherford to Mrs. Stanley R. McCormick, November 23, 1954, folder 3406, all in Weatherford Papers.
44. Laurence G. Avery, ed., *A Southern Life: Letters of Paul Green, 1916–1981* (Chapel Hill: University of North Carolina Press, 1994), 527.
45. In 1961 Green was unable to attend Weatherford's eighty-sixth birthday party but wrote to its organizer: "Please convey to him sincere regrets and my heart-full of admiration and love for him as always. He is a wonderful man and I can always draw a bead on some of his values when I consider how much poorer the world would be if he had not been"; Paul Green to James W. Sells, November 28, 1961, folder 3848, Weatherford Papers. For another letter attesting to Green's respect for Weatherford, see Paul Green to W. D. Weatherford, October 31, 1962, folder 3857, Weatherford Papers.
46. See Paul Green, *Wilderness Road: A Symphonic Outdoor Drama* (New York: Samuel French, 1956), [iii].
47. See Avery, *A Southern Life*, 544; Paul Green to Ted Cronk, November 26, 1954, folder 3403; and W. D. Weatherford to James Cannon, October 25, 1954, folder 3402, both in Weatherford Papers. Indeed, Green went ahead and drafted this version of the play until Berea's President Hutchins vetoed the plan.
48. Francis S. Hutchins to W. D. Weatherford, December 4, 1954; and Francis S. Hutchins to Paul Green, December 4, 1954, both in folder 3404, Weatherford Papers.
49. Julia F. Allen to Francis S. Hutchins, May 28, 1952, folder 3382; and Elizabeth S. Peck to Francis S. Hutchins, December 5, 1954, folder 3404, both in Weatherford Papers.

50. Allen to Hutchins, May 28, 1952, folder 3382, Weatherford Papers.

51. Wilson, *Berea College,* 157.

52. "Play Dares South to Face Problems," *New York Times,* June 30, 1955. For more information on the play and Berea's centennial activities, see "Berea Will Mark Centennial Year," *New York Times,* June 19, 1955.

53. Avery, *A Southern Life,* 553; W. D. Weatherford to Paul Green, July 6, 1955, in the Paul Eliot Green Papers, Southern Historical Collection, UNC.

54. Dykeman, *Prophet of Plenty,* 201.

55. Paul Green to W. D. Weatherford, November 3, 1967, box 1, folder 8, Weatherford Sr. Collection.

56. Weatherford to Cannon, October 25, 1954, folder 3402, Weatherford Papers.

57. Ibid.

58. The play did not run on these evenings.

59. W. D. Weatherford to William J. Baird, June 5, 1956; W. D. Weatherford to Earl Brewer, January 7, 1956; and W. D. Weatherford to Arthur Bannerman, March 21, 1956, all in folder 3512, Weatherford Papers; emphasis in original.

60. See W. D. Weatherford, "The Southern Appalachian Studies: Their Final Form and Potential," *Mountain Life and Work* 35 (Winter 1959): 27.

61. W. D. Weatherford to Henry S. Randolph, September 29, 1956, folder 3517, Weatherford Papers.

62. "Report of Southern Appalachian Studies," January 1962, folder 3577a, Weatherford Papers.

63. Weatherford, foreword to Ford, *The Southern Appalachian Region,* [v].

64. Weatherford, "The Southern Appalachian Studies," 27–28; and "Berea Gets $250,000 to Make Study of Southern Appalachian Mountains," *Pinnacle,* January 14, 1958, clipping in folder 3482, Weatherford Papers.

65. "Editorially Speaking," *Pinnacle,* March 7, 1961, clipping in folder 3493, Weatherford Papers.

66. Jones, "Surveys of the Appalachian Region," 37–38.

67. Ford, *Southern Appalachian Region,* vi.

68. Ibid.

69. Jones, "Surveys of the Appalachian Region," 38.

70. Ibid., 39.

71. See Thomas Ford, "Weatherford Award Speeches," 1974, sound recording, AC-OR-169-002, Special Collections and Archives, Berea College.

72. Ibid. A University Press of Kentucky editor, Bruce F. Denbo, also noted that "the approach Dr. Weatherford took to this subject would not be the one which would prevent serious criticism from scholars"; Bruce F. Denbo to Thomas R. Ford, May 2, 1960, folder 3546, Weatherford Papers.

73. Ibid.; and Thomas R. Ford to W. D. Weatherford, May 5, 1960, folder 3546, Weatherford Papers.

74. Thomas R. Ford to W. D. Weatherford, May 28, 1960, folder 3546, Weatherford Papers.

75. Ibid.

76. See W. D. Weatherford and Wilma Dykeman, "Literature since 1900," in Ford, *Southern Appalachian Region*.

77. Wilma Dykeman to W. D. Weatherford, March 7, 1964, folder 3874, Weatherford Papers.

78. Eller, *Uneven Ground*, 43.

79. Ibid., 43.

80. Ibid., 41.

81. Dykeman, *Prophet of Plenty*, 219–21.

82. "Invasion from the Mountains: Poverty the Main Spur Driving Migrants to North," July 20, 1959, clipping from unidentified newspaper; Mary Ellen Wolfe, "Mountain Leaders Working to Keep Their People from Moving North," *Dayton Journal Herald*, July 22, 1959, clipping; and Evelyn S. Stewart, "Hill People—Proud and God-Fearing," *Detroit Free Press*, July 31, 1959, clipping, all in folder 3604b, Weatherford Papers.

83. W. D. Weatherford, "Publication and Uses of Materials, Together with a Study of Agencies That May Be Interested in Implementing These Studies" (ca. 1961), folder 3593, Weatherford Papers.

84. Eller, *Uneven Ground*, 53–54.

85. Drake, *History of Appalachia*, 173.

86. Quoted in Eller, *Uneven Ground*, 54.

87. Ibid., 59, 72.

88. Ronald D Eller, "*Night Comes to the Cumberlands: A Biography of a Depressed Area*, Harry Monroe Caudill," in *Poverty in the United States: An Encyclopedia of History, Politics and Policy*, ed. Gwendolyn Mink and Alice O'Connor (Santa Barbara: ABC-CLIO, 2004), 507.

89. Ibid.

90. Eller, *Uneven Ground*, 66–67; and Drake, *History of Appalachia*, 174.

91. Drake, *History of Appalachia*, 174–75.

92. Jean Haskell Speer, "Appalachian Regional Commission, *The Tennessee Encyclopedia of History and Culture*, http://tennesseeencyclopedia.net/entry.php?rec=28 (accessed April 30, 2016).

93. Drake, *History of Appalachia*, 175.

94. "Notes by W. D. Weatherford, 3/21/64," Weatherford Family Papers.

95. W. D. Weatherford to Elizabeth Wyckoff, January 9, 1961, folder 3556; W. D. Weatherford to John J. Sparkman, January 27, 1961, folder 3555; W. D. Weatherford to John J. Sparkman, January 30, 1961, folder 3555; and W. D. Weatherford to Charles R. Younts, October 14, 1961, folder 3560, all in Weatherford Papers.

96. Weatherford to Younts, October 14, 1961, folder 3560, Weatherford Papers.

97. Ibid.

98. "Notes by W. D. Weatherford, 3/21/64," Weatherford Family Papers.

99. Weatherford and Brewer, *Life and Religion in Southern Appalachia*, ix, 68.

100. W. D. Weatherford to Mrs. G. H. Myers, March 3, 1959, folder 3436, Weatherford Papers. See also "Talk by Dr. Willis Duke Weatherford (age 85) to Catholic Bishop Waters (and others) of the Raleigh, NC Diocese and Glenmary Missionary Order," ca. 1961–62, sound recording.

101. Loyal Jones, interview by the author, November 4, 2009, Berea, Ky.

102. "Notes by W. D. Weatherford," Weatherford Family Papers.

103. W. D. Weatherford to Wilma Dykeman, November 8, 1966, folder 3593, Weatherford Papers.

104. Ibid.

105. For studies of Appalachian Christianity, see Loyal Jones, "Mountain Religion: The Outsider's View," in *Religion in Appalachia: Theological, Social, and Psychological Dimensions and Correlates,* ed. John D. Photiadis (Morgantown: West Virginia University Center for Extension and Continuing Education, 1978), 401–7; Deborah Vansau McCauley, *Appalachian Mountain Religion: A History* (Urbana: University of Illinois Press, 1995); Loyal Jones, *Faith and Meaning in the Southern Uplands* (Urbana: University of Illinois Press, 1999); and Bill J. Leonard, ed., *Christianity in Appalachia: Profiles in Regional Pluralism* (Knoxville: University of Tennessee Press, 1999).

106. Jones, *Faith and Meaning in the Southern Uplands,* 210.

107. Jones, "Mountain Religion," 406.

108. See "Talk by Dr. Willis Duke Weatherford (age 85) to Catholic Bishop Waters (and others) of the Raleigh, NC Diocese and Glenmary Missionary Order," ca. 1961–62, sound recording.

109. W. D. Weatherford to Elizabeth Wyckoff, January 8, 1961, folder 3556, Weatherford Papers.

110. W. D. Weatherford to the Bay Foundation, May 3, 1965, folder 3564; W. D. Weatherford to George Esser, November 16, 1965, folder 3565; and W. D. Weatherford to Robert Walker, February 21, 1966, folder 3573, all in Weatherford Papers.

111. Weatherford to Esser, November 16, 1965, folder 3565; and Weatherford to Walker, February 21, 1966, folder 3573, both in Weatherford Papers. For more on the North Carolina Fund, see Robert R. Korstad and James L. Leloudis, *To Right These Wrongs: The North Carolina Fund and the Battle to End Poverty and Inequality in 1960s America* (Chapel Hill: University of North Carolina Press, 2010).

112. George H. Esser to W. D. Weatherford, April 8, 1966, folder 3572, Weatherford Papers.

113. W. D. Weatherford, "One Answer to Appalachia," *Berea Alumnus,* May 1964, 6, folder 3502, Weatherford Papers. For an earlier consideration of this question, see Thomas R. Ford to W. D. Weatherford, July 5, 1960, folder 3546, Weatherford Papers.

114. Weatherford, "One Answer," 6, folder 3502, Weatherford Papers.

115. Ibid.

116. Ibid. Weatherford's idea seems very similar to an approach outlined by

Thomas R. Ford in 1960. See Ford to Weatherford, July 5, 1960, folder 3546, Weatherford Papers.

117. Beverly Wolter, "Appalachia Poverty and a Work Service: Dr. Weatherford Offers a Plan," *Winston-Salem Journal and Sentinel,* July 18, 1965, clipping in folder 3747, Weatherford Papers.

118. Ibid.

119. See "The Appalachian Dozen," ca. 1968; "List of Supplemental Publications for Inspiration and Information on the Appalachian Mtns."; and "A Full Commentary on Appalachian People and Problems," all in folder 3594, Weatherford Papers.

120. "The Appalachian Dozen," folder 3594, Weatherford Papers.

121. Wilma Dykeman to W. D. Weatherford, January 15, 1960, folder 3548; W. D. Weatherford to Wilma Dykeman, June 4, 1960, folder 3548; W. D. Weatherford to Wilma Dykeman and James Stokely, January 28, 1964, folder 3874; Elizabeth Wyckoff to W. D. Weatherford, July 12, 1965, folder 3571; and Elizabeth Wyckoff to W. D. Weatherford, September 6, 1965, folder 3571, all in Weatherford Papers.

122. Wilma Dykeman, untitled speech at Weatherford Convocation, August 28, 1965, folder 3763b; and W. D. Weatherford to Elizabeth Wyckoff, February 8, 1959, folder 3541, both in Weatherford Papers. See also Dykeman and Stokely, *Seeds of Southern Change.*

123. Loyal Jones, interview by the author, November 4, 2009, Berea, Ky.

124. See Wilma Dykeman, *The French Broad* (New York: Holt, Rinehart, and Winston, 1955); and Dykeman and Stokely, *Neither Black nor White.*

125. "Berea College: Board of Trustees Meeting, October 24, 1969," folder 3457a, Weatherford Papers.

126. Dykeman to Weatherford, January 15, 1960; and Weatherford to Dykeman, June 4, 1960, both in folder 3548, Weatherford Papers.

127. Weatherford to Dykeman and Stokely, January 28, 1964, folder 3874; and Wilma Dykeman to W. D. Weatherford, February 1, 1965, folder 3569, both in Weatherford Papers.

128. Weatherford to Dykeman and Stokely, January 28, 1964, folder 3874, Weatherford Papers.

129. "List of Supplemental Publications," folder 3594; Dykeman, untitled speech at Weatherford Convocation, August 28, 1965, folder 3763b; and "A Full Commentary on Appalachian People and Problems," folder 3594, all in Weatherford Papers.

130. "List of Supplemental Publications," folder 3594, Weatherford Papers.

131. Dykeman, *Prophet of Plenty,* [v].

132. Ibid., 6; Wilma Dykeman to W. D. Weatherford, December 11, 1966, folder 3897, Weatherford Papers; and Wilma Dykeman Stokely, "Dr. Weatherford: Prophet of Plenty Dies," *Asheville Citizen* (n.d.), clipping, Record Group no. 3.06, box 1, Willis Duke Weatherford Jr. Collection, Special Collections and Archives, Berea College, Berea, Ky.

133. Not surprisingly, Weatherford and Dykeman were also interested in having this biography used in schools in Appalachia as a textbook. See Wilma Dykeman to W. D. Weatherford, September 6, 1969, folder 3915, Weatherford Papers.

134. Wilma Dykeman to W. D. Weatherford, June 1, 1966, folder 3573, Weatherford Papers.

135. Dykeman, *Prophet of Plenty*, 1.

136. Weatherford to Dykeman and Stokely, January 28, 1964, folder 3874; Elizabeth Wyckoff to Wilma Dykeman and James Stokely, October 1, 1964, folder 3874; and Elizabeth Wyckoff to W. D. Weatherford, July 12, 1965, folder 3571, all in Weatherford Papers.

137. Dykeman, *Prophet of Plenty*, 6.

138. W. D. Weatherford to Wilma Dykeman, November 15, 1966, folder 3573, Weatherford Papers.

139. Francis S. Hutchins to Bruce Barton, January 6, 1954, folder 3404; and W. D. Weatherford to Martha W. Pride, March 8, 1966, folder 3455, both in Weatherford Papers.

140. "Schedule of Visits to Schools in Western North Carolina," 1958, folder 3483; "Report of W. D. Weatherford," January 27, 1950, folder 3462; form letter to students, 1952, folder 3385; W. D. Weatherford to Mrs. Max C. Fleischmann, November 20, 1953, folder 3395; and Hutchins to Barton, January 6, 1954, folder 3404, all in Weatherford Papers.

141. W. D. Weatherford to Harry M. Arndt, October 29, 1959, folder 3433, Weatherford Papers.

142. See form letter to students, 1952, folder 3385; and Weatherford to Fleischmann, November 20, 1953, folder 3395, both in Weatherford Papers. Weatherford seems to have been true to his word that he wanted only financially disadvantaged youth to attend Berea. In 1959, after finding out that twin boys he had helped gain admission to Berea had "considerably more money" than he thought, he urged the Berea admissions director to investigate their resources. See W. D. Weatherford to Allan Morreim, January 8, 1959, folder 3436, Weatherford Papers.

143. Calvin Jackson Thomas to Allan Morreim, August 14, 1953, folder 3392, Weatherford Papers.

144. "Students Enrolled in Berea College from Buncombe County, North Carolina," 1956, folder 3419, Weatherford Papers.

145. Letter to unknown recipient, April 29, 1957, folder 3427, Weatherford Papers.

146. Ibid.

147. George Brosi, "Versatile Is Billy Edd Wheeler," *Appalachian Heritage* 36 (Winter 2008): 20–23. This issue had a special section focused on Wheeler.

148. Ibid., 21.

149. Billy Edd Wheeler, interview by the author, September 8, 2009, Black Mountain, N.C. See also W. D. Weatherford to Billy Edd Wheeler, September 25, 1961, folder 3854, Weatherford Papers. Weatherford wrote, "I am deeply con-

cerned that you shall have the fullest opportunity, for I think you have some real genius and I'd like to see it expressed."

150. W. D. Weatherford to Emily Ann Smith, February 7, 1962, folder 3445, Weatherford Papers.

151. Billy Edd Wheeler, interview with the author, September 8, 2009.

152. "Report on Shoes and Clothing Expenditures," April 13, 1964; Elizabeth R. Wyckoff to Claude R. Collins, January 6, 1964; and Mary Phillips Kirby-Smith to W. D. Weatherford, February 2, 1964, all in folder 3563, Weatherford Papers.

153. Kirby-Smith to Weatherford, February 2, 1964, folder 3563, Weatherford Papers.

154. Ibid.

155. W. D. Weatherford to Francis S. Hutchins, January 10, 1964, folder 3449, Weatherford Papers. William A. Hammond was a businessman from Xenia, Ohio.

156. Elizabeth Wyckoff to Gilbert Osofsky, August 5, 1965, folder 3453, Weatherford Papers.

157. "Notes by W. D. Weatherford," Weatherford Family Papers.

158. Wilson, *Berea College,* 161–77.

Conclusion

1. "Weatherford, Sr. Dead after Many Years of Service," *Pinnacle,* March 7, 1970, clipping in Record Group no. 9, box 1, folder 1, Weatherford Sr. Collection.

2. See Weatherford gravestone, YMCA Blue Ridge Assembly, Black Mountain, N.C. See also Paul M. Limbert, "A Synopsis of the Life and Times of Dr. W. D. Weatherford," August 1979, 7, Record Group no. 9, box 1, folder 2, Weatherford Sr. Collection.

3. For an obituary for Julia McCrory Weatherford, see "Sunday Services at Blue Ridge for Mrs. Weatherford," *Black Mountain News,* October 10, 1957, clipping in folder 3747, Weatherford Papers.

4. Degree citation, June 6, 1955, Record Group no. 9, box 1, folder 1, Weatherford Sr. Collection.

5. Rupert B. Vance to "Committee on Honorary Degrees," October 27, 1961, folder 3854, Weatherford Papers.

Bibliography

Archives and Manuscript Collections

Amistad Research Center, Tulane University, New Orleans
Alrutheus Ambush Taylor Papers

Berea College Special Collections and Archives, Berea, Ky.
Sound recordings
Willis Duke Weatherford Jr. Collection
Willis Duke Weatherford Sr. Collection

Blue Ridge Assembly, Black Mountain, N.C.

East Carolina Manuscript Collection, J. Y. Joyner Library, East Carolina University, Greenville, N.C.
Lucy Cherry Crisp Papers

W. L. Eury Appalachian Collection, Special Collections, Appalachian State University, Boone, N.C.
Cratis D. Williams Papers

Fisk University, Franklin Library Special Collections and Archives, Nashville
Charles Spurgeon Johnson Papers
Thomas Elsa Jones Collection

Kautz Family YMCA Archives, University of Minnesota, Minneapolis
Biographical Records, W. D. Weatherford
Channing Tobias Papers

Microfilm Collections

Mary McLeod Bethune Papers: Bethune Foundation Collection, Daytona Beach, Fla.
George Washington Carver Papers, Tuskegee Institute Archives, Tuskegee, Ala.

Personal Family Papers

Culbreth Family Papers, Waynesville, N.C.

Southern Historical Collection, Wilson Library, University of North Carolina at Chapel Hill

Paul Eliot Green Papers
Howard Anderson Kester Papers
Katharine Du Pre Lumpkin Papers
Samuel Chiles Mitchell Papers
Anne Queen Papers
Willis Duke Weatherford Papers

Southern Oral History Program interviews
John Hope Franklin
Charles M. Jones
Don West
Louise Young

Special Collections and University Archives, Vanderbilt University Library, Nashville

Alumni Relations (Willis Duke Weatherford)
Robert Burns Eleazer Papers
John Egerton Papers
Vanderbilt Alumnus

Weatherford Family Papers, Far Horizons, Black Mountain, N.C.

Weatherford Public Library, Weatherford, Tex.

Weatherford family vertical file

Periodicals

Blue Ridge Voice
Chicago Defender
The Crisis
New York Age
New York Times

Interviews by the Author

Bryan, G. McLeod. July 14, 2010, Winston-Salem, N.C.
Hibbard, C. Roger. May 1, 2008, by telephone.
Jones, Loyal. November 4, 2009, Berea, Ky.
Weatherford, Anne. September 11, 2009, Black Mountain, N.C.

———. March 16, 2010, by telephone.
Wheeler, Billy Edd. September 8, 2009, Black Mountain, N.C.

Books and Articles Authored or Edited by W. D. Weatherford

Weatherford, W. D. *American Churches and the Negro: An Historical Study from Early Slave Days to the Present.* Boston: Christopher Publishing House, 1957.

———. *Analytical Index of De Bow's Review.* Santa Barbara: Privately published, 1952. First published in 1922 by Williams Printing Co. (Nashville).

———. "Changing Attitudes of Southern Students." *Journal of Negro Education* 2 (April 1933): 147–50.

———. *Christian Life, a Normal Experience: A Study in the Reality and Growth of Christian Experience.* Nashville: Smith and Lamar, 1916.

———. *College Problems.* 3 vols. Nashville: Publishing House of the M. E. Church, South, 1907–9.

———, ed. *Educational Opportunities in the Appalachian Mountains.* Berea, Ky.: Berea College, 1955.

———. *Fundamental Religious Principles in Browning's Poetry.* Nashville: Smith and Lamar, 1907.

———, comp. *Interracial Cooperation: A Study of the Various Agencies Working in the Field of Social Welfare.* N.p.: Interracial Committee of the War Work Council of Y.M.C.A., [1920s].

———. *Introducing Men to Christ: Fundamental Studies.* New York: Association Press, 1911.

———. *James Dunwoody Brownson De Bow.* Charlottesville: Historical Publishing Co., 1935.

———, ed. *Lawlessness or Civilization—Which? Report of Addresses and Discussions in the Law and Order Conference, Held at Blue Ridge, N.C., August 4th, 5th, and 6th, Nineteen Hundred and Seventeen.* Nashville: Williams Printing Co., 1917.

———. *The Negro from Africa to America.* New York: George H. Doran, 1924.

———. *Negro Life in the South: Present Conditions and Needs.* New York: Association Press, 1910.

———. *Personal Elements in Religious Life.* Nashville: Publishing House of the M. E. Church, South, 1916.

———. *Pioneers of Destiny: The Romance of the Appalachian People.* Birmingham, Ala.: Vulcan Press, 1955.

———. *Present Forces in Negro Progress.* New York: Association Press, 1912.

———. "Race Relationship in the South." *Annals of the American Academy of Political and Social Science* 49 (September 1913): 164–72.

———, ed. *Religion in the Appalachian Mountains: A Symposium.* Berea, Ky.: Berea College, 1955.

———. *Songs of Southern Colleges and Old Southern Melodies.* Nashville: Southern Students Secretaries of YMCA, 1913.

———. "The Southern Appalachian Studies: Their Final Form and Potential." *Mountain Life and Work* 35 (Winter 1959): 27–30.
———. *Studies in Christian Experience*. Nashville: Methodist Evangelistic Material, 1962.
———, ed. *A Survey of the Negro Boy in Nashville, Tennessee*. New York: Association Press, 1932.
———. "Training of Social and Religious Workers." *Journal of Social Forces* 2 (January 1924): 211–12.
Weatherford, W. D., and Earl D. C. Brewer. *Life and Religion in Southern Appalachia: An Interpretation of Selected Data from the Southern Appalachian Studies*. New York: Friendship Press, 1962.
Weatherford, W. D., and Charles S. Johnson. *Race Relations: Adjustment of Whites and Negroes in the United States*. 1934. Reprint, New York: Negro Universities Press, 1969.

Secondary Sources

Ahlstrom, Sydney. *A Religious History of the American People*. New Haven: Yale University Press, 1972.
Anderson, James D. *The Education of Blacks in the South, 1860–1935*. Chapel Hill: University of North Carolina Press, 1988.
Antone, George Peter, Jr. "Willis Duke Weatherford: An Interpretation of His Work in Race Relations, 1906–1946." Ph.D. diss., Vanderbilt University, 1969.
———. "The Y.M.C.A. Graduate School, Nashville, 1919–1936." *Tennessee Historical Quarterly* 32 (Spring 1973): 67–82.
"At Home and Afield: Hampton Incidents, Addresses," *Southern Workman* 40 (October 1911): 589–92.
Avery, Laurence G., ed. *A Southern Life: Letters of Paul Green, 1916–1981*. Chapel Hill: University of North Carolina Press, 1994.
Barrows, Edward Flud. "The Commission on Interracial Cooperation, 1919–1944: A Case Study in the History of Interracial Movement in the South." Ph.D. diss., University of Wisconsin, 1954.
Bartley, Numan V. *The New South, 1945–1980*. Baton Rouge: Louisiana State University Press, 1995.
———. *The Rise of Massive Resistance: Race and Politics in the South during the 1950s*. Baton Rouge: Louisiana State University Press, 1969.
Baskervill, William Malone. *Southern Writers, Biographical and Critical Studies: Sidney Lanier*. Nashville: Barbee & Smith, Agents, 1896.
Bauerlein, Mark. *Negrophobia: A Race Riot in Atlanta, 1906*. San Francisco: Encounter Books, 2001.
Becker, Anja. "Southern Academic Ambitions Meet German Scholarship: The Leipzig Networks of Vanderbilt University's James H. Kirkland in the Late Nineteenth Century." *Journal of Southern History* 74 (November 2008): 855–86.

Bellamy, John Stark. "If Christ Came to Dixie: The Southern Prophetic Vision of Howard Anderson Kester, 1904–1941." Ph.D. diss., University of Virginia, 1977.

Blight, David W. *Race and Reunion: The Civil War in American Memory.* Cambridge: Belknap Press of Harvard University Press, 2001.

Boles, John B., ed. *A Companion to the American South.* Malden, Mass.: Blackwell, 2002.

———. "The Discovery of Southern Religious History." In *Interpreting Southern History: Historiographical Essays in Honor of Sanford W. Higginbotham,* edited by John B. Boles and Evelyn Thomas Nolen, 510–48. Baton Rouge: Louisiana State University Press, 1987.

———, ed. *Masters & Slaves in the House of the Lord: Race and Religion in the American South, 1740–1870.* Lexington: University Press of Kentucky, 1988.

———. *The South through Time: A History of an American Region.* 3rd edition. Volume 2. Upper Saddle River, N.J.: Pearson Prentice Hall, 2004.

Boles, John B., and Evelyn Thomas Nolen, eds. *Interpreting Southern History: Historiographical Essays in Honor of Sanford W. Higginbotham.* Baton Rouge: Louisiana State University Press, 1987.

Bone, Winstead Paine. *A History of Cumberland University, 1842–1935.* Lebanon, Tenn.: Author, 1935.

Bowne, Borden Parker. *Personalism.* 1908. Reprint, Norwood, Mass.: Plimpton Press, 1936.

Brightman, Edgar Sheffield. *Is God a Person?* New York: Association Press, 1932.

Brosi, George. "Versatile Is Billy Edd Wheeler." *Appalachian Heritage* 36 (Winter 2008): 20–23.

Brundage, W. Fitzhugh. *The Southern Past: A Clash of Race and Memory.* Cambridge: Belknap Press of Harvard University Press, 2005.

Bryan, G. McLeod. *These Few Also Paid a Price: Southern Whites Who Fought for Civil Rights.* Macon, Ga.: Mercer University Press, 2001.

Campbell, John C. *The Southern Highlander and His Homeland.* 1921. Reprint, Lexington: University Press of Kentucky, 1969.

Capeci, Dominic J., Jr., and Jack C. Knight. "Reckoning with Violence: W. E. B. Du Bois and the 1906 Atlanta Race Riot." *Journal of Southern History* 62 (November 1996): 727–66.

Cecelski, David S., and Timothy B. Tyson, eds. *Democracy Betrayed: The Wilmington Race Riot of 1898 and Its Legacy.* Chapel Hill: University of North Carolina Press, 1998.

Chappell, David L. *Inside Agitators: White Southerners in the Civil Rights Movement.* Baltimore: Johns Hopkins University Press, 1994.

———. *A Stone of Hope: Prophetic Religion and the Death of Jim Crow.* Chapel Hill: University of North Carolina Press, 2004.

Chatfield, E. Charles. "The Southern Sociological Congress: Organization of Uplift." *Tennessee Historical Quarterly* 19 (December 1960): 328–47.

Clayton, Bruce. *The Savage Ideal: Intolerance and Intellectual Leadership in the South, 1890–1914.* Baltimore: Johns Hopkins University Press, 1972.

———. "Southern Critics of the New South, 1890–1914." Ph.D. diss., Duke University, 1966.

Clayton, Bruce, and John Salmond. *Debating Southern History: Ideas and Action in the Twentieth Century.* Lanham, Md.: Rowman and Littlefield, 1999.

Cobb, William H. *Radical Education in the Rural South: Commonwealth College, 1922–1940.* Detroit: Wayne State University Press, 2000.

Combs, Sara Trowbridge. "Race Reform in the Early Twentieth Century South: The Life and Work of Willis Duke Weatherford." Master's thesis, East Tennessee State University, 2004.

Conkin, Paul K. *Gone with the Ivy: A Biography of Vanderbilt University.* Knoxville: University of Tennessee Press, 1985.

———. *When All the Gods Trembled: Darwinism, Scopes, and American Intellectuals.* Lanham, Md.: Rowman and Littlefield, 1998.

Culley, John Joel. "Muted Trumpets: Four Efforts to Better Southern Race Relations, 1900–1919." Ph.D. diss., University of Virginia, 1967.

Curtis, Susan. *A Consuming Faith: The Social Gospel and Modern American Culture.* Baltimore: Johns Hopkins University Press, 1991.

Dabbs, James McBride. *The Southern Heritage.* New York: Alfred A. Knopf, 1958.

Degler, Carl N. *The Other South: Southern Dissenters in the Nineteenth Century.* 1974. Reprint, Boston: Northeastern University Press, 1982.

Dorsey, Allison. *To Build Our Lives Together: Community Formation in Black Atlanta, 1875–1906.* Athens: University of Georgia Press, 2004.

Doyle, Don H. *Nashville in the New South, 1880–1930.* Knoxville: University of Tennessee Press, 1985.

———. *Nashville since the 1920s.* Knoxville: University of Tennessee Press, 1985.

Drake, Richard B. *A History of Appalachia.* Louisville: University Press of Kentucky, 2001.

Duberman, Martin. *Black Mountain: An Exploration in Community.* New York: Dutton, 1972.

Du Bois, W. E. Burghardt. "Does the Negro Need Separate Schools?" *Journal of Negro Education* 4 (July 1935): 328–35.

———. *The Souls of Black Folk.* Chicago: A. C. McClurg, 1903.

Dunbar, Anthony P. *Against the Grain: Southern Radicals and Prophets, 1929–1959.* Charlottesville: University Press of Virginia, 1981.

Dykeman, Wilma. *The French Broad.* New York: Holt, Rinehart, and Winston, 1955.

———. *Prophet of Plenty: The First Ninety Years of W. D. Weatherford.* Knoxville: University of Tennessee Press, 1966.

Dykeman, Wilma, and James Stokely. *Neither Black nor White.* New York: Rinehart, 1957.

———. *Seeds of Southern Change: The Life of Will Alexander.* New York: W. W. Norton, 1962.

Eddy, Sherwood. *A Century with Youth: A History of the Y.M.C.A. from 1844 to 1944.* New York: Association Press, 1944.

Edwards, Ethel. *Carver of Tuskegee.* Cincinnati: Psyche Press, 1971.

Egerton, John. *A Mind to Stay Here: Profiles from the South.* New York: Macmillan, 1970.

———. *Speak Now against the Day: The Generation before the Civil Rights Movement in the South.* New York: Alfred A. Knopf, 1994.

Eller, Ronald D. *Uneven Ground: Appalachia since 1945.* Lexington: University Press of Kentucky, 2008.

Ellis, Ann Wells. "The Commission on Interracial Cooperation, 1919–1944: Its Activities and Results." Ph.D. diss., Georgia State University, 1975.

Ellis, Mark. *Race Harmony and Black Progress: Jack Woofter and the Interracial Cooperation Movement.* Bloomington: Indiana University Press, 2013.

Eureka! A Century of YMCA Blue Ridge Assembly. [Black Mountain, N.C.]: [YMCA Blue Ridge Assembly], 2005.

Flynt, Wayne. *Alabama Baptists: Southern Baptists in the Heart of Dixie.* Tuscaloosa: University of Alabama Press, 1998.

———. "'Feeding the Hungry and Ministering to the Broken Hearted': The Presbyterian Church in the United States and the Social Gospel, 1900–1920." In *Religion in the South,* edited by Charles Reagan Wilson, 83–137. Jackson: University Press of Mississippi, 1985.

———. "One in the Spirit, Many in the Flesh: Southern Evangelicals." In *Varieties of Southern Evangelicalism,* edited by David Edwin Harrell Jr., 23–44. Macon, Ga.: Mercer University Press, 1981.

Folger, Dagnall Frank. "A Comparison of Two Methods for Training Secretaries of the Young Men's Christian Association." Ph.D. diss., Yale University, 1931.

Ford, Thomas R., ed. *The Southern Appalachian Region: A Survey.* Foreword by W. D. Weatherford. Lexington: University of Kentucky Press, 1962.

Franklin, John Hope. *Mirror to America: The Autobiography of John Hope Franklin.* New York: Farrar, Straus and Giroux, 2005.

Franklin, John Hope, and Alfred A. Moss Jr. *From Slavery to Freedom: A History of Negro Americans.* 6th ed. New York: McGraw-Hill, 1988.

Fried, Richard M. *The Man Everybody Knew: Bruce Barton and the Making of Modern America.* Chicago: Ivan R. Dee, 2005.

Gilmore, Glenda Elizabeth. *Defying Dixie: The Radical Roots of Civil Rights, 1919–1950.* New York: W. W. Norton, 2008.

———. *Gender and Jim Crow: Women and the Politics of White Supremacy in North Carolina, 1896–1920.* Chapel Hill: University of North Carolina Press, 1996.

Gilpin, Patrick J., and Marybeth Gasman. *Charles S. Johnson: Leadership beyond the Veil in the Age of Jim Crow.* Albany: State University of New York Press, 2003.

Glen, John M. *Highlander: No Ordinary School, 1932–1962.* Lexington: University Press of Kentucky, 1988.

Godshalk, David Fort. *Veiled Visions: The 1906 Race Riot and the Reshaping of American Race Relations.* Chapel Hill: University of North Carolina Press, 2005.

Goggin, Jacqueline. *Carter G. Woodson: A Life in Black History.* Baton Rouge: Louisiana State University Press, 1993.

Goldfield, David R. *Black, White, and Southern: Race Relations and Southern Culture, 1940s to the Present.* Baton Rouge: Louisiana State University Press, 1990.

Green, Paul. *Wilderness Road: A Symphonic Outdoor Drama.* New York: Samuel French, 1956.

Hair, William Ivy. *Carnival of Fury: Robert Charles and the New Orleans Race Riot of 1900.* Baton Rouge: Louisiana State University Press, 1976.

Hall, Jacquelyn Dowd. "The Long Civil Rights Movement and the Political Uses of the Past." *Journal of American History* 91 (March 2005): 1233–64.

———. *Revolt against Chivalry: Jessie Daniel Ames and the Women's Campaign against Lynching.* New York: Columbia University Press, 1979.

Hall, Randal L. *Mountains on the Market: Industry, the Environment, and the South.* Lexington: University Press of Kentucky, 2012.

———. *William Louis Poteat: A Leader of the Progressive-Era South.* Lexington: University Press of Kentucky, 2000.

Hammond, Lily Hardy. *In Black and White: An Interpretation of the South.* Edited by Elna C. Green. 1914. Reprint, Athens: University of Georgia Press, 2008.

Harper, Keith. *The Quality of Mercy: Southern Baptists and Social Christianity, 1890–1920.* Tuscaloosa: University of Alabama Press, 1996.

Harrell, David Edwin, Jr., ed. *Varieties of Southern Evangelicalism.* Macon, Ga.: Mercer University Press, 1981.

Harrison, Gilbert. *A Timeless Affair: The Life of Anita McCormick Blaine.* Chicago: University of Chicago Press, 1979.

Harvey, Paul. *Freedom's Coming: Religious Culture and the Shaping of the South from the Civil War through the Civil Rights Era.* Chapel Hill: University of North Carolina Press, 2005.

———. *Redeeming the South: Religious Cultures and Racial Identities among Southern Baptists, 1865–1925.* Chapel Hill: University of North Carolina Press, 1997.

Hersey, Mark D. *My Work Is That of Conservation: An Environmental Biography of George Washington Carver.* Athens: University of Georgia Press, 2011.

Hill, Samuel S. *Southern Churches in Crisis Revisited.* Tuscaloosa: University of Alabama Press, 1999.

Holden, Charles J. *The New Southern University: Academic Freedom and Liberalism at UNC.* Lexington: University Press of Kentucky, 2012.

Hopkins, C. Howard. *History of the Y.M.C.A. in North America.* New York: Association Press, 1951.

———. *John R. Mott, 1865–1955: A Biography.* Grand Rapids, Mich.: William B. Eerdmans, 1979.

———. *The Rise of the Social Gospel in American Protestantism, 1865–1915.* New Haven: Yale University Press, 1940.
Israel, Charles A. *Before Scopes: Evangelicalism, Education, and Evolution in Tennessee, 1870–1925.* Athens: University of Georgia Press, 2004.
Jones, Loyal. *Faith and Meaning in the Southern Uplands.* Urbana: University of Illinois Press, 1999.
———. "The Surveys of the Appalachian Region." *Appalachian Heritage* 4 (Spring 1976): 25–42.
Journal of Religious Thought 2 (Autumn–Winter 1945): 1–59.
Kean, Melissa. *Desegregating Private Higher Education in the South: Duke, Emory, Rice, Tulane, and Vanderbilt.* Baton Rouge: Louisiana State University Press, 2008.
Kester, Howard A. "Radical Prophets: A History of the Fellowship of Southern Churchmen." (1974). (Unpublished manuscript; photocopy in author's possession; original in possession of Nancy Kester Neale, Asheville, N.C.)
Ketchell, Aaron K. *Holy Hills of the Ozarks: Religion and Tourism in Branson, Missouri.* Baltimore: Johns Hopkins University Press, 2007.
Kiffmeyer, Thomas. *Reformers to Radicals: The Appalachian Volunteers and the War on Poverty.* Lexington: University Press of Kentucky, 2008.
K'Meyer, Tracy Elaine. *Interracialism and Christian Community in the Postwar South: The Story of Koinonia Farm.* Charlottesville: University Press of Virginia, 1997.
Korstad, Robert R., and James L. Leloudis. *To Right These Wrongs: The North Carolina Fund and the Battle to End Poverty and Inequality in 1960s America.* Chapel Hill: University of North Carolina Press, 2010.
Krueger, Thomas A. *And Promises to Keep: The Southern Conference for Human Welfare, 1938–1948.* Nashville: Vanderbilt University Press, 1967.
Leonard, Bill J., ed. *Christianity in Appalachia: Profiles in Regional Pluralism.* Knoxville: University of Tennessee Press, 1999.
Lewis, George. *Massive Resistance: The White Response to the Civil Rights Movement.* London: Hodder Arnold, 2006.
Liles, Deborah. "Inventing the Past: How Historiography Contributes to Deceptions in Small Communities." Paper presented to Parker County History and Heritage, Weatherford, Tex., January 19, 2010. (Photocopy in author's possession.)
Link, William A. *The Paradox of Southern Progressivism: 1880–1930.* Chapel Hill: University of North Carolina Press, 1992.
Logan, Rayford W. *What the Negro Wants* (With a New Introduction and Bibliography by Kenneth Robert Janken). 1944. Reprint, Notre Dame: University of Notre Dame Press, 2001.
Lomax, John A. *Adventures of a Ballad Hunter.* New York: Macmillan, 1947.
Lorence, James J. *A Hard Journey: The Life of Don West.* Urbana: University of Illinois Press, 2007.

Lovett, Bobby L. *The African-American History of Nashville, Tennessee, 1780–1930.* Fayetteville: University of Arkansas Press, 1999.

Luker, Ralph E. *The Social Gospel in Black and White: American Racial Reform, 1885–1912.* Chapel Hill: University of North Carolina Press, 1991.

———. *A Southern Tradition in Theology and Social Criticism, 1830–1930: The Religious Liberalism and Social Conservatism of James Warley Miles, William Porcher Dubose, and Edgar Gardner Murphy.* New York: Edwin Mellen Press, 1984.

Lumpkin, Katharine Du Pre. *The Making of a Southerner.* 1946. Reprint, Athens: University of Georgia Press, 1991.

Mackintosh, Barry. "George Washington Carver: The Making of a Myth." *Journal of Southern History* 42 (November 1976): 507–28.

Martin, Robert F. "Critique of Southern Society and Vision of a New Order: The Fellowship of Southern Churchmen, 1934–1957." *Church History* 52 (March 1983): 66–80.

———. *Howard Kester and the Struggle for Social Justice in the South: 1904–77.* Charlottesville: University Press of Virginia, 1991.

———. "A Prophet's Pilgrimage: The Religious Radicalism of Howard Anderson Kester, 1921–1941." *Journal of Southern History* 48 (November 1982): 511–30.

May, Henry F. *Protestant Churches and Industrial America.* New York: Harper & Brothers, 1949.

Mays, Benjamin E. *Born to Rebel: An Autobiography.* New York: Charles Scribner's Sons, 1971.

Mazzari, Louis. *Southern Modernist: Arthur Raper from the New Deal to the Cold War.* Baton Rouge: Louisiana State University Press, 2006.

McCauley, Deborah Vansau. *Appalachian Mountain Religion: A History.* Urbana: University of Illinois Press, 1995.

McConnell, Francis John. *Borden Parker Bowne: His Life and His Philosophy.* New York: Abingdon Press, 1929.

McCulloch, James E., ed. *Battling for Social Betterment: Southern Sociological Congress, Memphis, Tennessee, May 6–10, 1914.* Nashville: Benson Printing Co., 1914.

———, ed. *The Call of the New South: Addresses Delivered at the Southern Sociological Congress, Nashville, Tennessee, May 7 to 10, 1912.* Nashville: Brandau-Craig-Dickerson Co., 1912.

———, ed. *The Human Way: Addresses on Race Problems at the Southern Sociological Congress, Atlanta, 1913.* Nashville: Brandau-Craig-Dickerson Co., 1913.

———, ed. *The South Mobilizing for Social Service: Addresses Delivered at the Southern Sociological Congress, Atlanta, Georgia, April 25–29, 1913.* Nashville: Brandau-Craig-Dickerson Co., 1913.

McDonough, Julia Anne. "Men and Women of Good Will: History of the Commission of Interracial Cooperation and the Southern Regional Council, 1919–1954." Ph.D. diss., University of Virginia, 1993.

McDowell, John Patrick. *The Social Gospel in the South: The Woman's Home Mis-*

sion Movement in the Methodist Episcopal Church, South, 1886–1939. Baton Rouge: Louisiana State University Press, 1982.

McGerr, Michael. *A Fierce Discontent: The Rise and Fall of the Progressive Movement in America, 1870–1920.* New York: Oxford University Press, 2003.

McGuinn, Henry J. Review of *A Survey of the Negro Boy in Nashville, Tennessee,* in *Journal of Negro Education* 2 (April 1933): 216–18.

McMurry, Linda O. *George Washington Carver: Scientist and Symbol.* New York: Oxford University Press, 1981.

Meier, August, and Elliott Rudwick. *CORE: A Study in the Civil Rights Movement, 1942–1968.* 1973. Reprint, Urbana: University of Illinois Press, 1975.

Miller, Francis Pickens. *Man from the Valley: Memoirs of a 20th-Century Virginian.* Chapel Hill: University of North Carolina Press, 1971.

Miller, Robert Moats. *Harry Emerson Fosdick: Preacher, Pastor, Prophet.* New York: Oxford University Press, 1985.

Mink, Gwendolyn, and Alice O'Connor, eds. *Poverty in the United States: An Encyclopedia of History, Politics and Policy.* Santa Barbara: ABC-CLIO, 2004.

Mixon, Gregory. *The Atlanta Riot: Race, Class, and Violence in a New South City.* Gainesville: University Press of Florida, 2005.

Mjagkij, Nina. *Light in Darkness: African Americans and the YMCA, 1852–1946.* Lexington: University Press of Kentucky, 1994.

Moorland, Jesse Edward. "The Young Men's Christian Association among Negroes." *Journal of Negro History* 9 (April 1924): 127–38.

Morgan, William H. *Student Religion during Fifty Years: Programs and Policies of the Intercollegiate Y.M.C.A.* New York: Association Press, 1935.

Moton, Robert Russa. "The Negro's Debt to Lincoln." *Southern Workman* 51 (1922): 329–34.

Myrdal, Gunnar. *An American Dilemma: The Negro Problem and Modern Democracy.* 2 vols. New York: Harper & Brothers, 1944.

National Association for the Advancement of Colored People. *Thirty Years of Lynching in the United States, 1889–1918.* New York: N.A.A.C.P., 1919.

Novick, Peter. *That Noble Dream: The "Objectivity Question" and the American Historical Profession.* New York: Cambridge University Press, 1988.

Peck, Elisabeth S. *Berea's First 125 Years: 1855–1980.* Lexington: University Press of Kentucky, 1982.

Photiadis, John D., ed. *Religion in Appalachia: Theological, Social, and Psychological Dimensions and Correlates.* Morgantown: West Virginia University Center for Extension and Continuing Education, 1978.

Pilkington, Charles Kirk. "The Trials of Brotherhood: The Founding of the Commission on Interracial Cooperation." *Georgia Historical Quarterly* 69 (Spring 1985): 55–80.

Poteat, Edwin McNeill, Jr. *Coming to Terms with the Universe: A Study in the Philosophy of Religion for the Semi-Sophisticated.* New York: Association Press, 1931.

Powell, William S., ed. *Dictionary of North Carolina Biography*. Chapel Hill: University of North Carolina Press, 1994.
Putney, Clifford. *Muscular Christianity: Manhood and Sports in Protestant America, 1880–1920*. Cambridge: Harvard University Press, 2001.
Rauschenbusch, Walter. *Christianity and the Social Crisis*. New York: Macmillan, 1907.
———. *Christianizing the Social Order*. New York: Macmillan, 1912.
———. *The Social Principles of Jesus*. New York: Association Press, 1916.
———. *A Theology for the Social Gospel*. New York: Macmillan, 1917.
Richardson, Joe M. *A History of Fisk University, 1865–1946*. 1980. Reprint, Tuscaloosa: University of Alabama Press, 2006.
Robbins, Richard. *Sidelines Activist: Charles S. Johnson and the Struggle for Civil Rights*. Jackson: University Press of Mississippi, 1996.
Robertson, Nancy Marie. *Christian Sisterhood, Race Relations, and the YWCA, 1906–46*. Urbana: University of Illinois Press, 2007.
Rodgers, Daniel T. *Atlantic Crossings: Social Politics in a Progressive Age*. Cambridge: Belknap Press of Harvard University Press, 1998.
Roper, John Herbert. *Paul Green: Playwright of the Real South*. Athens: University of Georgia Press, 2003.
Salmond, John A. "The Fellowship of Southern Churchmen and Interracial Change in the South." *North Carolina Historical Review* 69 (April 1992): 179–99.
Schulman, Bruce J. *From Cotton Belt to Sunbelt: Federal Policy, Economic Development, and the Transformation of the South, 1938–1980*. Durham: Duke University Press, 1994.
Schweitzer, Albert. *The Quest of the Historical Jesus*. 1906. Reprint, Minneapolis: Fortress Press, 2001.
Scott, Anne Firor. *The Southern Lady: From Pedestal to Politics, 1830–1930*. 1970. Reprint, Charlottesville: University Press of Virginia, 1995.
Sernett, Milton C. *Bound for the Promised Land: African American Religion and the Great Migration*. Durham: Duke University Press, 1997.
Setran, David P. *The College "Y": Student Religion in the Era of Secularization*. New York: Palgrave Macmillan, 2007.
Shedd, Clarence P. *Two Centuries of Student Christian Movements: Their Origin and Intercollegiate Life*. New York: Association Press, 1934.
Singal, Daniel Joseph. *The War Within: From Victorian to Modernist Thought in the South, 1919–1945*. Chapel Hill: University of North Carolina Press, 1982.
Smith, David Paul. *Frontier Defense in the Civil War: Texas' Rangers and Rebels*. College Station: Texas A&M University Press, 1992.
Sosna, Morton. *In Search of the Silent South: Southern Liberals and the Race Issue*. New York: Columbia University Press, 1977.
Southern, David W. "*An American Dilemma* Revisited: Myrdalism and White Southern Liberals." *South Atlantic Quarterly* 75 (Spring 1976): 182–97.

Stricklin, David. *A Genealogy of Dissent: Southern Baptist Protest in the Twentieth Century.* Lexington: University Press of Kentucky, 1999.

Taylor, Alrutheus Ambush. *The Negro in South Carolina during Reconstruction.* Washington, D.C.: Association for the Study of Negro Life and History, 1924.

———. *The Negro in Tennessee, 1865–1880.* Washington, D.C.: Associated Publishers, 1941.

———. *The Negro in the Reconstruction of Virginia.* Washington, D.C.: Association for the Study of Negro Life and History, 1926.

Tindall, George Brown. *The Emergence of the New South, 1913–1945.* Baton Rouge: Louisiana State University Press, 1967.

Torrence, Ridgely. *The Story of John Hope.* New York: Macmillan, 1948.

Trawick, A. M., ed. *The New Voice in Race Adjustments: Addresses and Reports Presented at the Negro Christian Student Conference, Atlanta, Georgia, May 14–18, 1914.* New York: Student Volunteer Movement, 1914.

Van Dusen, Henry P. *God in These Times.* New York: C. Scribner's Sons, 1935.

Watson, Charles S. *The History of Southern Drama.* Lexington: University Press of Kentucky, 1997.

Webb, Clive, ed. *Massive Resistance: Southern Opposition to the Second Reconstruction.* New York: Oxford University Press, 2005.

Welch, J. Edmund. "The Y.M.C.A. Graduate School of Nashville." *Forum* (March 1969): 13–16.

West, Connie. Willard Uphaus illustration and caption. *Appalachian Heritage* 36 (Fall 2008): 5, 50.

White, Ronald C., Jr. *Liberty and Justice for All: Racial Reform and the Social Gospel (1877–1925).* 1990. Reprint, Louisville: Westminster John Knox Press, 2002.

White, Ronald C., Jr., and C. Howard Hopkins. *The Social Gospel: Religion and Reform in Changing America.* Philadelphia: Temple University Press, 1976.

Wiebe, Robert H. *The Search for Order: 1877–1920.* New York: Hill and Wang, 1967.

Wilson, Charles Reagan, ed. *Religion in the South.* Jackson: University Press of Mississippi, 1985.

Wilson, P. Whitwell. "The Projectile from the South." *Association Men* (October 1925).

Wilson, Shannon H. *Berea College: An Illustrated History.* Lexington: University Press of Kentucky, 2006.

Witherspoon, Joe B. *Weatherford College: Enlightening the Frontier, 1869–1986.* [Texas?]: n.p., 1986.

Woodson, Carter G. "A Rejoinder to Dr. Tobias." *Chicago Defender,* July 30, 1932.

———. Review of *The Negro from Africa to America,* in *Journal of Negro History* 9 (October 1924): 574–77.

Woodward, C. Vann. *Origins of the New South, 1877–1913.* Baton Rouge: Louisiana State University Press, 1951.

———. *The Strange Career of Jim Crow.* New York: Oxford University Press, 1955.

Online Sources

The Handbook of Texas Online, https://tshaonline.org/handbook.
King, Martin Luther, Jr. "Letter from Birmingham Jail," http://abacus.bates.edu/admin/offices/dos/mlk/letter.html.
Laura Spelman Rockefeller Memorial Fund on the Rockefeller Center Archive website, www.rockarch.org/collections/rockorgs/lsrmadd.php.
Tennessee Encyclopedia of History and Culture, https://tennesseeencyclopedia.net.
Traughber, Bill. "The History of Vanderbilt Athletics, part 1," August 27, 2008, http://vucommodores.cstv.com/genrel/082708aaa.html.

Index

Page numbers in *italics* refer to illustrations.

Ackley, S. A., 254n195
African American education: Weatherford's views of, 136, 153–54
African American educational institutions: employment of whites at, 152–53; relationship of the YMCA Graduate School with, 129–30, 131–36; Weatherford's visits to as YMCA student secretary, 45. *See also* Fisk University
African American farmers, 60
African Americans: attendance at Blue Ridge, 71–72, 74, 82, 84–92; development of black protest in the 1930s and 1940s, 172–74; limitations and achievements of Blue Ridge's work in race relations, 110–13; in Nashville, sociological surveys of, 140–41; in Nashville in the late 1890s, 20; paternalism in Weatherford's views of, 57–58, 60; racial policies at Blue Ridge and (*see* racial policies at the Blue Ridge Association); racial policy at the YMCA Graduate School, 128–29; racism in Weatherford's views of, 54, 55–56, 60–61; response to Weatherford's *Negro Life in the South*, 57–58; seating issue at the 1914 National Conference of Charities and Corrections, 65; segregation laws and, 13; servants at Blue Ridge, 78–79; in Texas in the late 1890s, 13; visiting professors at the YMCA Graduate School from Fisk University, 129–30; voting requirements, 52, 167, 291n108; Weatherford's disapproval of radical blacks, 54; Weatherford's relations with while at Vanderbilt, 22, 24; Weatherford's views of in *Negro Life in the South*, 52–56; Weatherford's views of in *Present Forces in Negro Progress*, 59–61
African American soldiers: founding of the CIC and, 67–69
African American students: at Berea College, 187–88; collegiate YMCA and, 45; delegates at Blue Ridge, 91; summer student conferences, 58–59, 123, 245n38; Weatherford's relationship with at Fisk University, 158–63; YMCA Graduate School and, 122–24, 132
African American women: racism in Weatherford's views of, 55–56
Agricultural Adjustment Administration, 172
Alexander, Gross, 28
Alexander, Will W., 68, 72, 90, 99, 123, 254n195
Allen, Julia F., 195
Alpha Tau Omega, 21
American Cast Iron Pipe Company (ACIPCO), 135–36

American Christian Ashram, *103*
American Churches and the Negro (Weatherford), 6, 149, 176–81, 182
American Dilemma, An (Myrdal), 167–68
American Missionary Association (AMA), 152
Ames, Jessie Daniel, 168–69
Anderson, Hans P., 44
Anthony, Paul, 183
Appalachia: 1956 interdenominational meeting at Berea College to discuss religious conditions in, 197–98; conditions in and outmigration from in the mid-twentieth century, 193–94; *Life and Religion in the Appalachian Region* by Weatherford and Brewer, 203–4; missionaries and reformers, 194–95; national concern for in the 1950s and 1960s, 200–203; Weatherford and the 1958 regional survey of, 198–200; Weatherford and the issue of government-support payments, 206–7; Weatherford on federal and state aid to, 202–3; Weatherford on the "religious crisis" in, 196–97; Weatherford's advocacy for, 5, 195, 196–98, 213–14; Weatherford's "Appalachian Dozen" project, 207–10; Weatherford's charity work in, 213; Weatherford's connections to, 190; Weatherford's gradualist approach to change and, 188–89; Weatherford's paternalistic views of, 189; Weatherford's *Pioneers of Destiny*, 192; Weatherford's recruitment of students from western North Carolina, 210–11, 213; Weatherford's views of mountain churches, 204–6
"Appalachian Dozen" project, 207–10
Appalachian Governors' Conference, 203

Appalachian Regional Commission (ARC), 202
Appalachian Shepherd, The (Hendricks), 207
"Appeal to the Christian People of the South, An" (CIC declaration), 84
"Applied Anthropology" courses, 124–28
Area Redevelopment Act (1961), 201
Arkansas, 172
Armour, Mildred, 159
Asheville Area Council on Human Relations, 183
Asheville School for Boys, 41
Association Press, 251n152
Atlanta Race Riot of 1906, 52
Atlanta University, 152, 154
Ayer, Perley F., 195

Baber, Ray Erwin, 138–39
Ballou, T. P., 137
Basis of Ascendancy, The (Murphy), 62
Baskervill, William M., 21, 24, 190
"Battle of Concho Creek," 12
Berea College: 1956 interdenominational meeting to discuss religious conditions in Appalachia, 197–98; American Missionary Association and, 152; history of integration at, 187–88; honorary doctorate awarded to Weatherford, 218; Southern Appalachian Studies and the regional survey of Appalachia, 198; Weatherford and the play *Wilderness Road,* 187, 195–97; Willis Weatherford Jr. as president, 4, 214; Weatherford offered presidency in 1919, 115, 190–91; Weatherford's fund-raising for, 192–93; Weatherford's gift establishing the Weatherford and Hammond Mountain

Collection, 213; Weatherford's involvement with after 1946, 5, 166, 187, 188–90; Weatherford's involvement with before 1946, 4, 190–92; Weatherford's recruitment of students from western North Carolina, 210–11, 213; YMCA-YWCA Southern Student Conference, 108
Bergthold, John W., 71, 89, 91, 111
Bethlehem Center (Nashville), 123, 274n49
Bethune, Mary McLeod, 91
Bigart, Homar, 202
Bingham School, 41
black farmers, 60
Black Mountain (NC), *85*
Black Mountain College, 74, 97–99, 107
Blue Ridge Assembly, 99, 107–8
Blue Ridge Association for Christian Conferences and Training: African Americans in attendance, 71–72, 74, 82, 84–92; anonymous threats against, 81; black servants at, 78–79; as Blue Ridge Assembly, 99, 107–8; as Blue Ridge College, Incorporated, 97–99; George Washington Carver's visits to, 4, 71–72, 87–91; Commission on Interracial Cooperation and, 84, 85; conferences on race at, 63, 83–84; context of southern segregation and racism, 75; financial troubles, 94–95, 97, 99; focus on white students at, 76; William Frost and, 190; growth and regional influence of, 80; influence on participants and their views of race, 93–94; interracial student conferences and, 104–5, 106–7, 108; overview of Weatherford's work at, 3–4; policy of freedom of speech at, 80–81; race relations and (*see* race relations and the Blue Ridge Association); racial policies at (*see* racial policies at the Blue Ridge Association); Southern College of the YMCA summer courses, 80; southern criticism of, 105–6; Southern Student Conference, 41–43, 76, *77;* student working staff, 76, 78, 79–80; training for YMCA secretaries during World War I, 68; uniqueness as a place to talk about race, 4, 74–75, 83; Weatherford and the creation of, 41–43, 69; Weatherford offers to resign from in 1929, 96; Weatherford's burial at, 215; Weatherford's departure from, 99; Weatherford's educational goals and principles for training YMCA leaders, 75–76; Weatherford's personal and health problems in the 1920s, 95–96; Weatherford's purpose in creating, 72; Weatherford's retirement home, 166; Yale Divinity School and, 145–46, 283–84n206; YMCA Graduate School's purchase of in 1933, 96–97; YMCA Graduate School summer session, 4, 120–21, 145–46
Blue Ridge Board of Directors, 96
Blue Ridge College, Incorporated, 97–99
Blue Ridge Committee for the Southern Student Conference, 82–83
Blue Ridge Voice, 80, 94–95
Booker T. Washington Hall (Blue Ridge Association), 79
Boston University, 30
Bowne, Borden Parker, 30–31
Brewer, Earl D. C., 198, 203–4

Brightman, Edgar Sheffield, 31, 141, 142
Brockman, Fletcher, 18, 19
Brown, James, 201
Brown, O. E., 137
Browning, Robert: Weatherford's appreciation for the work of, 25; Weatherford's dissertation and book on, 28–30
Brown v. Board of Education, 112, 177
Bryan, G. McLeod, 180
Bryan, William Jennings, 76
Buncombe County (NC), 211
Burwell, Millard, 129
Buttrick, Wallace, 254n195

Campbell, John C., 194
Campbell, Olive Dame, 194
Camp Highland Lake, 107
Cannon, James, 196, 197
capitalism, 7, 8
Carnegie-Myrdal study on race, 167–68
Carroll, Luan Traudt, 122
Carver, George Washington, *73;* first meeting with Weatherford, 1, 18–19; Jim Hardwick and, 87–88, 93; impact of the 1924 Blue Ridge visit, 93–94, 111, 112; visits to Blue Ridge, 4, 71–72, 87–91
Cashin, Lillian E., 129
Caudill, Harry Monroe, 201–2, 210
"Celtic Thesis," 192
Charlotte Observer, 184–85
Chesnutt, Charles Waddell, 127
Chicago Defender, 180
China, 66
Christian Century, 180
"Christian Imperative and Race Relations" conference, 169–71
Christianity: *American Churches and the Negro* (Weatherford), 176–81, 182; as the frame for Weatherford's response to interracial student conferences, 108; the limits of Weatherford's liberalism and, 8–9; social gospel tradition, 7–8, 228–29n24, 228n21, 230–31n28; Weatherford's crisis of faith while at Vanderbilt, 26–28; Weatherford's dissertation on the Browning and, 28–30; Weatherford's notions of faith in work with YMCA, 36; Weatherford's published devotional studies, 47–48; Weatherford's rational defense of, 46–47; Weatherford's views of Appalachian churches, 204–6; Weatherford's views of Christian doctrine, 241–42n158. *See also* religion
"Christianity in Race Relations" (Mordecai Johnson speech), 92
Christian Life, a Normal Experience (Weatherford), 47–48
Christopher Publishing House, 177
CIC. *See* Commission on Interracial Cooperation
Citizens' Councils, 177
civil disobedience, 184
Civil Rights movement: development of black protest in the 1930s and 1940s, 172–74; Weatherford's efforts in school desegregation, 183–84; Weatherford's racial liberalism and, 149–50
Clark, Frances, 159
Cleveland H. Dodge Foundation, 181
Club IV, 22
Coble, Ruth, 143
College Bulletin, 39
collegiate YMCA. *See* YMCA student movement
Colored Work Department (YMCA), 45

Coming to Terms with the Universe (Poteat), 141–42
Commission of Southern Universities on the Race Question, 63
Commission on Interracial Cooperation (CIC): Blue Ridge Association and, 84, 85; impetus for the creation of, 67–68; program as an interracial organization, 67, 68–69; Southern Regional Council and, 168–69; Weatherford and the founding of, 3, 67–68, 254n195
Commonwealth College, 74
Comte, Auguste, 26
Conference of Southern Mountain Workers, 194
Conference of the Southern Mountains, 194, 195
Conkin, Paul, 20, 32
Conner, Jerome A., 125
"Constructive Message of Blue Ridge, The" (Weatherford), 80–81
Couch, William T., 174
Council of the Southern Mountains, 198, 200–201, 206
Cragmore School for Girls, 99
Crisis (NAACP magazine), 63
Crum, Mason, 56
Culbreth, James Marvin and Elizabeth "Bess," 52

Dabbs, James McBride, 181–82
Dark Princess (Du Bois), 127
Darwin, Charles, 30
Davis, Jackson, 58
Day Law (KY), 188
De Bow's Review, 277n98
Defying Dixie (Gilmore), 75
Denbo, Bruce F., 200
desegregation. *See* school desegregation
devotional studies: published by Weatherford, 47–48
Dillard, James Hardy, 63

Dillard University, 152
Divine Comedy (Dante), 25
Doyle, Don, 123, 141
Drake, Richard B., 192
"dual civilizations" idea, 66, 150
Du Bois, W. E. B., 53, 54, 127, 152
Dunbar, Anthony, 75
Dunbar, Paul Laurence, 61, 127
Dunning School, 164
Durham, Plato, 254n195
Durham Manifesto, 168, 174
Dykeman, Wilma: biography of Weatherford, 207, 208–10, 225–27n19; interview with Patricia Johnson on Weatherford, 160; relationship with Weatherford, 200, 207–10; on Weatherford's muscular Christianity, 49; on Weatherford's racial liberalism, 149

Eagan, John J., 135, 254n195
Eagan Plan, 135
Economic and Social Problems and Conditions of the Southern Appalachians (USDA), 195
Economic Opportunity Act (1964), 202
education. *See* African American education; liberal arts education
Edwards, Ethel, 88
Egerton, John, 69–70, 172
Eleazer, Robert Burns, 68
Eliot, George, 2, 25, 26
Eller, Ronald D, 193–94
Emerson, Cora. *See* Reese, Cora
Emory College, 49
England, Martin, 4, 112
Eppse, Merl R., 132

Farm School, 41
Faulkner, Josephine, 159–60
Faulkner, W. J., *155,* 159, 160, 175, 180

Fellowship of Reconciliation, *103*
Fellowship of Southern Churchmen, 229n26
Fentriss Coal and Coke Company strike, 142
First Annual Institute of Religion (Howard University), 169–71
Fisk University: academic reputation of, 155; black professors invited to the YMCA Graduate School, 129–30; employment of whites at, 152–53; founding of, 152; impact on Weatherford's racial liberalism, 175; relationship with the YMCA Graduate School, 129–30, 131–32, 136; Weatherford's employment at, 5, 147, 152, 153–66; Weatherford's fundraising, 156–57; Weatherford's outreach to the black community, 158; Weatherford's relationship with students and faculty, 158–64; Weatherford's retirement from, 164–66; Weatherford's teaching and faculty positions, 157–58
Fisk University Quartette, 83
Folger, Dagnall F., 142, 143, 146
Ford, Thomas R., 198, 200
Ford Foundation, 5, 198
Fosdick, Harry Emerson, 76
Franklin, John Hope, 153
Frazier, E. Franklin, 129
freedom of speech: at Blue Ridge, 80–81
French, Arden, 108–9
French Broad, The (Dykeman), 207
Frost, William Goodell, 188, 190, 194
Fulton, John E., 22, 24
Fundamental Religious Principles in Browning's Poetry (Weatherford), 28–30

Gaines, Lloyd L., 172–73
Gaines v. Missouri, 172–73
gender: race relations at Blue Ridge and, 90–91, 92–93
George Williams College, 116
Gillean, Lucy, 122
Gilmore, Glenda, 75
God in These Times (Van Dusen), 142
Gore, Al, Sr., 167
gradualism: in the approach to race relations at Blue Ridge, 110–11; in Charles Johnson's views of race relations, 165; Weatherford's courses on race relations at the YMCA Graduate School and, 126; in Weatherford's views of race relations, 5–6, 8, 110–11, 126, 165, 217
Graham, Frank Porter, 4, 48, 112, 162, 178–79
Grayson, Betty, 161
Great Depression, 172
Green, Paul, 180, 187, 195, 196, 299n45
Gregg, Abel, 101

Hall, Jacquelyn Dowd, 173–74
Hamilton, Dave, 105
Hammond, Lily Hardy, 61, 241n153
Hampton Institute, 107, 152
Hancock, Gordon Blain, 168
Hardwick, Jim, 87–88, 93, 146
Harmon, Nolan, Jr., 175
Harris, Joel Chandler, 61
Hart, Albert Bushnell, 62
Hart, Mrs. Henry, 122
Harwood Endowment Fund, 181
Hawthorne, Nathaniel, 25
Haygood, Atticus Greene, 240n153
Haywood White Sulphur Springs Hotel, 41
Heath, Mary, 125
Hendricks, Garland, 207
Highlander Folk School, 74, 229n26
Highsmith, Agnes, 146

Holland, Curtis, 159
Home Betterment League, 62
honorary doctorates, 218
Hope, John, 52, 92
Horton, Myles, 4, 142
House behind the Cedars, The (Chesnutt), 127
Houston, Charles Hamilton, 172–73
Howard University conference (1943), 169–71, 174
"How to Enlist the Welfare Agencies of the South for Improvement of Conditions among the Negroes" (Weatherford address), 64
Human Way, The (Southern Sociological Congress), 63
Hume, Fred, 50
Hutchins, Francis S., 189, 191, 195, *209*
Hutchins, William J., 156

In Black and White (Hammond), 61
Ingersoll, Henry, 47
In Memoriam (Tennyson), 25, 27
intermarriage: Weatherford's views on, 285n12
International Committee (YMCA): support for the student movement, 38–39
International Review of Missions, 180–81
International Student Secretaryship for the Southern and Southwestern States (YMCA), 44. *See also* YMCA student secretary for the south
interracialism: gradualist and progressive views of, 110; Weatherford's views of, 109, 110
interracial organizations. *See* Commission on Interracial Cooperation
interracial student conferences, 104–5, 106–10, 182–83

Introducing Men to Christ (Weatherford), 47–48
Is God a Person (Brightman), 142

Jackson, Thomas "Stonewall," 55
Jews, 142–43
Jim Crow: 1943 Howard University conference and, 169–71; failure of "separate but equal," 52; prevalence in the South in the early 1900s, 75; racial policies at Blue Ridge and, 100–102; Weatherford's evolving views of, 174–76
Johnson, Charles Spurgeon: as an invited speaker at the YMCA Graduate School, 131, 132, 142; conflicting views with Weatherford on racial concerns, 164–65; as president of Fisk University, 153, 164; *Race Relations* text coauthored with Weatherford, 124, 164–65, 168
Johnson, Guy B., 180
Johnson, James Weldon, 67, 129, 142
Johnson, Lyndon B., 202, 203
Johnson, Mordecai, 91–92, 111
Johnson, Patricia, 160
Jones, George H., 89
Jones, Loyal, 198–99, 204, 205, 207
Jones, M. Ashby, 254n195
Jones, Richard, 24–25, 27
Jones, Thomas E., 129, 131, 162, 164
Jones, Thomas Jesse, 254n195
Jordan, Clarence, 4, 74, 112
Journal of Negro Education, 140–41, 154
Journal of Negro History, 57
Julius Rosenwald Fund, 130, 131

Kennedy, John F., 201, 202, 203
Kentucky: school segregation in, 188
Kern, Paul B., 175–76
Kesler, John Louis, 137
Kester, Alice, 142

Kester, Howard, 4, 89–90, 93–94, 106, 112, 142
King, Ed, 109
King, Martin Luther, Jr., 182, 184, 296n205
King, Richard H., 254n195
Kings Mountain Student Conference, 58–59, 91, 106, 245n38
Kirby-Smith, Mary Phillips, 213
Knudson, A. C., 31
Kohn, Herbert, 142
Koinonia Farm, 74–75, 112, 229n26

Lake Geneva Student Conference (YMCA), 1, 18–19, 40
Lanier, Sidney, 25
Laura Spelman Rockefeller Memorial Fund, 130
Law and Order Conference on lynching, 63
Lee, Robert E., 55
Lee School for Boys, 95
Legal Defense Fund (NAACP), 175
"Letter from Birmingham Jail" (King), 184
liberal arts education: Weatherford's belief in for African Americans, 136, 153–54; in Weatherford's gradualist approach to change in Appalachia, 189; YMCA Graduate School and, 119, 120
liberal Christianity: Weatherford and, 32–33
libraries: Weatherford's "library" on African American culture, 61–62; YMCA Graduate School special collection of documents related to African Americans, 131–32
Life and Casualty Insurance Company of Nashville, 145
Life and Religion in the Appalachian Region (Weatherford & Brewer), 203–4, 207

Lincoln, Abraham, 83
literature: Weatherford's "Appalachian Dozen" project, 207–10; Weatherford's appreciation for, 25–26
Locke, Alain, 127
Logan, Rayford, 174
Lovejoy, Arthur O., 98
Loventhal, Lee, 143
Lumpkin, Katharine Du Pre, 4, 88–89

March on Washington Movement (MOWM), 171, 173, 174
Marshall, Thurgood, 172–73
Martin, E. F., 126
Martin, Mercedes, 159
materialism: versus personalism, 30
Mathews, Shailer, 33
Mays, Benjamin, 149, 180, 185
McConnell, J. Paul, 140–41
McCormick reaper, 131
McCrory, Julia Pearl, 95–96. *See also* Weatherford, Julia Pearl
McGrew, John H., 122–23
McGuinn, Henry J., 140–41
McKay, Claude, 127
Menafee, Martin, 90
Messing, Frederick B., 137
Methodist Abingdon-Cokesbury Press, 175
Methodist church: Bethlehem Center in Nashville, 123, 274n49; Vanderbilt University and, 19, 20; Weatherford ordained in, 44, 236n75, 246n50; Weatherford's early involvement with, 13–14; Weatherford's vision of racial progress and, 175–76
Middlemarch (Eliot), 2
Miles, A. B., 137
Miller, Francis Pickens, 112
Mims, Edwin, 137
Mississippian, 105–6

Mitchell, George S., 182
Mitchell, Samuel Chiles, 137
modernists, 32
Montreat-Anderson College, 94
Montreat Southern Student Conference, 41, *42*, 56
Moody, Dwight L., 40
Moorland, Jesse, 57, 58
Morton, Helen, 104–5
Moton, Robert Russa, 65, 86–87, 127, *133*, 134, 254n195
Mott, John R., *42*, 43, 44, 66–67, 141
Mount Hermon School, 40
Murphy, Edgar Gardner, 62, 66, 241n153
muscular Christianity, 3, 22, 36, 48–49, *50*
Myrdal, Gunnar, 167

Nashville (TN): African American population in the late 1890s, 20; Bethlehem Center, 123, 274n49; sociological surveys of African Americans in, 140–41; Weatherford's relations with African Americans, 22, 24; Weatherford's southern identity and, 34, 36; YMCA Graduate School and, *116*, 118
National Association for the Advancement of Colored People (NAACP), 172–73, 175
National Conference of Charities and Corrections, 65–66
National Social Science Honor Society, 141
National Student Council of the YWCA, 104–5
National Students' Summer School (YMCA), 18–19
Negro from Africa to America, The (Weatherford), 131, 164

Negro Life in the South (Weatherford), 52–59, 62, 131, 154, 181
New Deal, 172
New York Carnegie Corporation, 167
New York Times, 196
Night Comes to the Cumberlands (Caudill), 201–2, 210
nonviolent resistance, 171
North Carolina: school desegregation and, 183; Weatherford's recruitment of students for Berea College, 210–11, 213
North Carolina Fund, 206
Northfield Student Conference (YMCA), 40

Ober, Charles Kellogg, 43
Odum, Howard, 139–40, 168–69
Office of Economic Opportunity (OEC), 202
Old South: Weatherford's southern identity, 33–35, 36

"parallel civilizations" idea, 66, 150
Parker, J. A., 105
Parker County (TX), 12–13
paternalism: in Weatherford's views of African Americans, 57–58, 60; in Weatherford's views of Appalachia, 189; in Weatherford's worldview, 217
Patterson, Frederick D., 135, 181, 182
Peabody College, 19
Peoples, A. J., 95
Personal Elements in Religious Life (Weatherford), 207
personalism, 17, 30–32
Personalism (Bowne), 31
Phelps-Stokes Fund, 130–31, 181
Phi Beta Kappa, 21
philanthropic foundations: funding of the YMCA Graduate School and, 130–31

Phillips, A. L., 42
Phillips, Rachel, 125, 126
philosophy of religion, 17
Pierrel, Gren O., 102
Pi Gamma Mu, 141
Pioneers of Destiny (Weatherford), 192, 207
Plessy v. Ferguson, 173
poll taxes, 167, 291n108
positivism, 26
Poteat, Edwin McNeill, Jr., 141–42
Poteat, Gordon, 166
Poteat, William Louis, *42,* 76
premillennialism, 242n158
Present Forces in Negro Progress (Weatherford), 59–61, 131
President's Appalachian Regional Commission, 201
Progressivism: belief in environmental factors in human conditions and change, 61; overview, 51–52; Southern Sociological Congress, 62–66; views of interracial student conferences, 110; Weatherford's courses on race relations at the YMCA Graduate School and, 125–26; Weatherford's writings on race relations and, 52–61
Prophet of Plenty (Dykeman), 207, 208–10, 225–27n19
Putney, Clifford, 48–49
Puxley, H. L., 180–81

Race Distinctions in American Law (Stephenson), 62
race relations: 1943 Howard University conference and, 169–71; absence of self-critical thinking in Weatherford, 185–86; assessment and legacy of Weatherford's career, 215–17; Atlanta Race Riot of 1906, 52; backlash against southern liberals, 71–72; Blue Ridge Association and (*see* race relations and the Blue Ridge Association); Carnegie-Myrdal study on race, 167–68; development of black protest in the 1930s and 1940s, 172–74; development of Weatherford's liberal views, 18–19; evolution of Weatherford's racial liberalism, 18–19, 150–52, 166–72, 174–76, 185 (*see also* racial liberalism); following World War I, 67–69; importance of the YMCA in, 67–70; overview of Weatherford's involvement in, 3; Progressivism and Weatherford's writings on, 52–61; Southern College of the YMCAs and, 69; Southern Sociological Congress and, 62–66; Weatherford and the Commission on Interracial Cooperation, 67–69; Weatherford's 1914 Asian trip, 66–67; Weatherford's "Applied Anthropology" courses at the YMCA Graduate School, 124–28; Weatherford's efforts in the 1960s, 182–85; Weatherford's personalism and, 32; Weatherford's study of in *American Churches and the Negro,* 176–81, 182; Weatherford's views of religion as the foundation for improving, 64; Weatherford's views on intermarriage, 285n12; Weatherford's work in and writings on while YMCA secretary, 49–70
Race Relations (1934 textbook), 124, 164–65, 168
race relations and the Blue Ridge Association: African Americans in attendance at Blue Ridge, 84–92; Blue Ridge as a unique space to speak about race, 4, 74–75, 83;

George Washington Carver's visits and, 4, 71–72, 87–91, 93–94, 111, 112; conferences on race, 83–84; gender and, 90–91, 92–93; impact of funding issues on, 81–83; impact on its participants, 93–94; individualized approach to change, 76; limitations and achievements of, 110–13; overview and significance of, 4; Weatherford's leadership in and commitment to, 4, 69

Race Relationship Fund (YMCA), 58–59

race riots: Atlanta Race Riot of 1906, 52; prevalence in the South in the early 1900s, 75; "Red Summer" of 1919, 67

racial liberalism: absence of self-critical thinking in Weatherford, 185–86; evolution of Weatherford's views, 18–19, 150–52, 166–72, 174–76, 185; Weatherford's views in the 1950s and 1960s, 149–50

racial policies at the Blue Ridge Association: criticism of, 99–100, 105–6; Abel Gregg's praise of, 101; guidelines prepared by the Blue Ridge Assembly, 107–8; impact of funding issues on, 81–83; interracial student conferences and, 104–5, 106–7, 108; North Carolina segregation laws and, 100–102; regarding accommodations and eating, 94, 102–4

racial policy: at the YMCA Graduate School, 128–29

racial violence, 75

racism: belief in race as a determinant of behavior, 61; in Weatherford's views of African Americans, 54, 55–56, 60–61

Randolph, A. Phillip, 171, 173, 174, 175
Raper, Arthur F., 140
Rauschenbusch, Walter, 7
Ray, J. J., 97
"Red Summer, The," 67
Reese, Cora, 161–63
religion: 1956 interdenominational meeting at Berea College to discuss religious conditions in Appalachia, 197–98; ecumenical approach at the YMCA Graduate School, 142–43; as the foundation for improving race relations in Weatherford's views, 64; as a key motivator in Weatherford's thought and actions, 7–8; the limits of Weatherford's liberalism and, 8–9; Weatherford and personalism, 30–32; Weatherford and the philosophy of, 17; Weatherford's crisis of faith at Vanderbilt, 26–28; Weatherford's dissertation on religion and Browning's poetry, 28–30; in Weatherford's gradualist approach to change in Appalachia, 189; Weatherford's views of Appalachian churches, 204–6; Weatherford's views of religious doctrine, 241–42n158. *See also* Christianity

"Religion the Common Basis of Co-operation" (Weatherford address), 64

Religious Workers' Conference for the Appalachian Mountains, 197–98
Rice, John Andrew, 97–98
Ring and the Book, The (Browning), 25
Robert E. Lee Hall (Blue Ridge Association), *79,* 83
Rockefeller, John D., Sr., 43, 57, 130
Rollins College, 97–98
Roosevelt, Theodore, 71
Rosenwald, Julius, 60

Roy, V. L., 92–93
Royal Customs College, 66
Russell Sage Foundation, 194

Sanders, Herbert W., 97, 143
Sanford, Terry, 183
Sartor Resartus (Carlyle), 25
Schilling, Rachel, 184
school desegregation: *Brown v. Board of Education* and, 177; Weatherford's efforts in, 183–84
school segregation: in Kentucky, 188; Weatherford's views of, 54, 151–52
secular humanism, 26
segregation: 1943 Howard University conference and, 169–71; *Brown v. Board of Education* and, 177; development of black protest in the 1930s and 1940s, 172–74; division among southern liberals over, 169; "dual civilization" idea, 66; prevalence in the South in the early 1900s, 75; southern radicals who questioned, 75; Weatherford's approval of, 54, 55–56, 65–66, 151–52; Weatherford's evolving opposition to, 174–76, 179
segregation laws: racial policies at Blue Ridge and, 100–102; rise of, 13
Shedd, Clarence, 123
Sinclair, William A., 54
slavery, 13
social gospel tradition, 7–8, 228–29n24, 228n21, 230–31n28
sociological surveys, 140–41
Souls of Black Folk, The (Du Bois), 53, 127
Southeastern Division of War Work (YMCA), 68
Southern Appalachian Region, The (1958 survey), 198–200, 207
Southern Appalachian Studies (SAS), 198–200

Southern College of the YMCA: degrees and programs offered, 121–22; location, *116;* mission of, 115; overview of Weatherford's involvement with, 4–5; summer courses at Blue Ridge, 80; Weatherford's work on race relations and, 69. *See also* YMCA Graduate School
Southern College YMCA Camp, 95
Southern Conference on Human Welfare, 167, 172
Southern Co-Operative League for Education and Social Service, 62
Southern Heritage, The (Dabbs), 181, 182
Southern Highlander and His Homeland, The (Campbell), 194
southern identity: Weatherford and, 33–35, 36
southern liberalism: assessment and legacy of Weatherford's career, 215–17; backlash against, 71–72; the development of Weatherford's liberal views, 11, 17–19, 22, 24, 25, 32, 36; division over segregation, 169, 174; importance of the YMCA's work in race relations, 69–70; radicals who questioned segregation, 75; southern liberals defined, 223n4; Weatherford and the limits of, 8–9; Weatherford's approach to reform and, 5–6; YMCA Graduate School and, 117, 146–47
Southern Manifesto, 177, 295n179
Southern Regional Association of Boys' Work Secretaries, 128
Southern Regional Council, 168–69
southern society: Weatherford's gendered view of, 55
Southern Sociological Congress, 3, 62–66, 141

Index   333

Southern South, The (Hart), 62
Southern Student Conference. *See* YMCA Southern Student Conference
Southern Tenant Farmers' Union (STFU), 172
southern tradition: Weatherford's appeal to in *Negro Life in the South*, 55
Springfield College, 115–16
State Normal College at Natchitoches (LA), 92
Stephenson, Gilbert Thomas, 62
Stokely, James, 207
Story of the Negro, The (Washington), 62
Story of the Negro Retold, The (Woodson), 164
Stuart, Jesse, 207, *208*
Students' Christian Association, 38
Studies in Christian Experience (Weatherford), 207
Survey of the Negro Boy in Nashville, Tennessee, A (McConnell), 140–41

Tagore, Rabindranath, 25
Talladega conference, 106, 268n220
Tall Woman, The (Dykeman), 207, 208
Taylor, Alrutheus Ambush, 162, 163–64
Taylor, Alva, 132, 138, 142
Tennessee Agricultural and Industrial State Normal School (A and I), 123, 132, 136
Tennessee State University, 132
Theobold, Robert, 206
Thread That Runs So True, The (Stuart), 207
Tillett, Wilbur F., 31
Tobias, Channing, 58, 129
Torrence, Edgar, 147
Tracy McGregor Fund, 157
Trawick, Andrew Marcus, 34, 35
Trawick, Arcadius McSwain ("A. M."), 58, 59
Trawick, Lula Belle, 34–36, 52
Trotter, William Monroe, 54
Turner, Lorenzo, 129
Tuskegee Institute, 86, 87, 132, 134–36

"Uncle Remus" books (Harris), 61
University of Arkansas, 47
University of Iowa, 46
University of Michigan, 38
University of Mississippi, 105–6
University of Missouri, 173
University of North Carolina at Chapel Hill, 112, 218
University of North Carolina Press, 174, 175
University of Virginia, 38
Up from Slavery (Washington), 61, 62, 127
Uphaus, Willard E., 138
U.S. Department of Agriculture, 195
U.S. Supreme Court, 112, 173, 177

Vance, Rupert, 198, 218
Vanderbilt, Cornelius, 236n67
Vanderbilt School of Religion, 120, 137
Vanderbilt University: origin of, 236n67; problems in the late 1890s, 20–21; student body composition in the late 1890s, 20; Weatherford's decision to enroll at, 19–20; Weatherford's crisis of faith at, 26–28; Weatherford's graduate work at, 3, 24–28, 239n128; Weatherford's introduction to personalism at, 31–32; Weatherford's preparation for, 16; Weatherford's relations with African Americans at, 22, 24;

Vanderbilt University *(cont.)* Weatherford's southern identity and, 34, 36; Weatherford's study of Appalachian literature, 190; Weatherford's undergraduate education and life at, 21–24; YMCA Graduate School and, 120, 137, 143–44
Van Dusen, Henry P., 141, 142
voting requirements, 52, 167, 291n108

Wake Forest College, 166
Walton, Lester, 86
War Work Council (YMCA), 68
Washington, Booker T., 54, 61–62, 71, 127, 132, 134
Watkins, George W., 91
Watkins, Lucile, 126
Weatherford (TX), 11, 12–13, 232–32n3, 233n17
Weatherford, Anne, 35
Weatherford, Felix, *16*
Weatherford, John, *16*
Weatherford, Julia Pearl (née McCrory), 95–96, 139, 147, 215, 217–18
Weatherford, Margaret Jane Turner, 11–12, 15–16, 234n32
Weatherford, Robert, *16*
Weatherford, Samuel Leonard, 11–12, 14–15, 19, 232n3, 232n11
Weatherford, Samuel Leonard, Jr., 12
Weatherford, Willis, Jr., 4, 95, 146, 214
Weatherford, Willis Duke: 1943 Howard University conference and, 169–71; absence of self-critical thinking in, 185–86; activities with the Southern Sociological Congress, 63–66; *American Churches and the Negro,* 176–81, 182; appreciation for literature, 25–26; approval of segregation, 54, 55–56, 65–66; assessment and legacy of, 215–18; Berea College and (*see* Berea College); birth and early life, 11–15, 233–34n29; books on race and race relations, 52–61 (*see also* race relations); Carnegie-Myrdal study on race and, 167–68; coauthor of *Race Relations* with Charles Johnson, 124, 164–65, 168; conflicting views with Charles Johnson on racial concerns, 164–65; connections and advocacy work for Appalachia, 190, 195, 196–98 (*see also* Appalachia); crisis of faith while at Vanderbilt, 26–28; death and funeral of, 215; development of Blue Ridge Association, 41–43 (*see also* Blue Ridge Association for Christian Conferences and Training); devotion to reading, 46; "dual civilization" idea and, 66, 150; Wilma Dykeman's biography of, 207, 208–10, 225–27n19; John Eagan and, 135; early involvement with the YMCA, 3, 18, 21; education at Weatherford College, 15–18; employment at Fisk University, 147, 152, 153–66 (*see also* Fisk University); evolving views on racial liberalism, 18–19, 150–52, 166–72, 174–76, 185 (*see also* racial liberalism); first meeting with George Washington Carver, 1, 18–19; *Fundamental Religious Principles in Browning's Poetry,* 28–30; gradualism in the racial views of, 5–6, 8, 110–11, 126, 165, 217; historical and scholarly accounts of, 6–7; honorary doctorates received, 218; interracialism and interracial student conferences, 108–9, 110,

182–83; lessening of faith in the YMCA in the 1950s, 205; liberal Christianity and, 32–33; limitations and achievements of Blue Ridge's work in race relations, 110–13; the limits of southern liberalism and, 8–9; marriage to Julia Pearl McCrory, 95–96, 139, 147, 215, 217–18; marriage to Lula Belle Trawick, 34–36, 52; at the Montreat Student Conference center, 42; Robert Moton and, 87, *133*, 134; muscular Christianity and, 3, 22, 48–49, *50;* NAACP and, 175; opinion of Black Mountain College, 98; ordained in the Methodist church, 44, 236n75, 246n50 (*see also* Methodist church); overview of life and career, 1–5; personal and health problems in the 1920s, 95–96; personalism and, 30–32; personality and outlook of, 2–3; on the phases of his career, 284–85n3; philosophy of religion and, 17; policy of free speech at Blue Ridge and, 80–81; Progressivism and, 51–62; published devotional studies, 47–48; radical southern groups supported by, 229–30n26; relationship with Wilma Dykeman, 200, 207–10; relationship with father, 14–15; relationship with mother, 15–16, 234n32; religion as a key factor in the thoughts and actions of, 7–8; retirement home at Blue Ridge, 166; southern identity of, 33–35, 36; southern liberalism and approach to reform, 5–6; Southern Regional Council and, 168–69; Jesse Stuart and, *208;* Vanderbilt University and (*see* Vanderbilt University); views of black education, 136, 153–54; views of Martin Luther King Jr., 184; views of religious doctrine, 241–42n158; Billy Edd Wheeler and, 211, 213; Carter Woodson and, 164; writing style of, 29; YMCA Graduate School and (*see* YMCA Graduate School); as YMCA student secretary for the south (*see* YMCA student secretary for the south)

Weatherford College, 15–18
Weidensall, Robert, 38–39, 40
Weil, J. B., 143
welfare: Appalachia and, 206–7
Wesley Hall (Vanderbilt University), 21
West, Don, 4, 112, 138
West, Tom, 50
Westside Row (Vanderbilt University), 22
West Virginia, 201
What the Negro Thinks (Moton), 127
What the Negro Wants (essay collection), 174
Wheeler, Billy Edd, 211, 213
White, Carl, 124
white women: students at the YMCA Graduate School, 122; Weatherford's gendered view of white womanhood, 55
Whitsell, Fannie, 17
Wilderness Road (Green), 187, 195–97
Wilder strike, 142
Williams, E. P., 159
Williams, Robert, 101, 102
Wilson, Jim, 17
Wingfield, Robert, 22
Winston-Salem Journal and Sentinel, 206
Wishard, Luther, 38–39, 40, 43
Wolter, Beverly, 206
Woodson, Carter G., 60–61, 163–64

Work, John M., 129
World Student Christian Fellowship, 112
World War I: African American soldiers and racial tensions following, 67–69
World War II: development of black protest and, 173–74; impact on Appalachia, 193
Wunsch, W. R., 107
Wyckoff, Elizabeth, 213

Yale Divinity School, 145–46, 159, 283–84n206
Yale University, 118
YMCA: Association Press, 251n152; colleges for training YMCA workers, 115–17 (*see also* Southern College of the YMCA; YMCA Graduate School); Colored Work Department, 45; founding and growth of, 37–38, 243–44n3; impact of Weatherford's *Negro Life in the South,* 58–59; importance in race relations, 67–70; International Committee support for the student movement, 38–39 (*see also* YMCA student movement); Race Relationship Fund, 58–59; response to the Atlanta Race Riot of 1906, 52; summer student conferences (*see* YMCA summer student conferences); War Work Council, 68; Weatherford's early involvement with, 3, 18, 21; Weatherford's lessening faith in the 1950s, 205
YMCA Graduate School: degrees and programs offered, 121–22; ecumenical approach at, 142–43; faculty, 136–40, 143; financial problems and closing of the Nashville facility, 143–45; funding from northern philanthropic foundations, 130–31; impact of, 146–47; importance to southern liberalism, 117; mission of, 115; National Social Science Honor Society and, 141; overview of Weatherford's involvement with, 4–5; purchase of Blue Ridge in 1933, 96–97; racial policy toward African American guests, 128–29; relationship with African American educational institutions, 129–30, 131–36; sociological surveys of African Americans in Nashville, 140–41; special collection of documents related to African Americans, 131–32; special lecturers and the intellectual community at, 141–42; summer session at Blue Ridge, 4, 120–21, 145–46; Vanderbilt University and, 120; Weatherford and African American students at, 122–24; Weatherford and the establishment of, 118–20; Weatherford's "Applied Anthropology" courses on race relations, 124–28; Weatherford's decision to accept the presidency of, 117–18; Weatherford's personal challenges and difficulties as president, 147–48; Weatherford's vision and goals for, 117, 119–20; Weatherford's workload and personal life stresses, 139; white women students, 122; Yale Divinity School and, 145–46. *See also* Southern College of the YMCA
YMCA Southern Student Conference: Blue Ridge Association, 41–43, 76, 77 (*see also* Blue Ridge Association for Christian Conferences and Training); George Washington

Carver's visits to, 87–91; early settings for conferences, 41; interracial student conferences, 104–5, 106–10

YMCA student movement: Charles Ober and, 43; origins and growth of, 38–39; success and growth in the early 1900s, 5, 44–45; summer student conferences and conference centers, 40–43 (*see also* YMCA summer student conferences)

YMCA student movement in the south: impact of the Civil War on, 39–40; student conferences and conference centers, 41–43 (*see also* Blue Ridge Association for Christian Conferences and Training); Weatherford as secretary (*see* YMCA student secretary for the south)

YMCA student secretaries: Luther Wishard, 39; YMCA colleges and, 115–17; YMCA Graduate School and, 118–20, 146–47 (*see also* YMCA Graduate School)

YMCA student secretary for the south: Weatherford's 1914 Asian trip, 66–67; Weatherford's attendance at the Kings Mountain student conference, 59; Weatherford's beliefs and goals, 36; Weatherford's development of Blue Ridge and, 41–43; Weatherford's "library" on African American culture, 61–62; Weatherford's muscular Christianity, 3, 48–49, *50;* Weatherford's published devotional studies, 47–48; Weatherford's quick rise to the position of, 43–44; Weatherford's rational defense of Christianity, 46–47; Weatherford's responsibilities and focus in the early years, 45–51; Weatherford's success and reputation, 47–48; Weatherford's training for YMCA secretaries during World War I at Blue Ridge, 68; Weatherford's work in and writings on race relations, 49–70

YMCA summer student conferences: African American students and, 58–59, 123, 245n38; Chesapeake Summer School, 123; development of conference centers, 40–43; interracial student conferences, 104–5, 106–10, 182–83; Kings Mountain, 58–59; National Students' Summer School at Lake Geneva, 1, 18–19, 40; origins of, 40. *See also* YMCA Southern Student Conference

YMCA-YWCA Southern Student Conference, 108, 109

Young, Louise, 143

YWCA Southern Student Conference, 76, *77*

Zerfoss, Karl, 146

New Directions in Southern History

Series Editors
Michele Gillespie, Wake Forest University
William A. Link, University of Florida

The Lost State of Franklin: America's First Secession
Kevin T. Barksdale

The Civil War Guerrilla: Unfolding the Black Flag in History, Memory, and Myth
edited by Joseph M. Beilein Jr. and Matthew C. Hulbert

Bluecoats and Tar Heels: Soldiers and Civilians in Reconstruction North Carolina
Mark L. Bradley

Becoming Bourgeois: Merchant Culture in the South, 1820–1865
Frank J. Byrne

Willis Duke Weatherford: Race, Religion, and Reform in the American South
Andrew McNeill Canady

Cowboy Conservatism: Texas and the Rise of the Modern Right
Sean P. Cunningham

A Tour of Reconstruction: Travel Letters of 1875
Anna Dickinson (J. Matthew Gallman, ed.)

Raising Racists: The Socialization of White Children in the Jim Crow South
Kristina DuRocher

Lum and Abner: Rural America and the Golden Age of Radio
Randal L. Hall

Mountains on the Market: Industry, the Environment, and the South
Randal L. Hall

The New Southern University: Academic Freedom and Liberalism at UNC
Charles J. Holden

Entangled by White Supremacy: Reform in World War I–era South Carolina
Janet G. Hudson

Bloody Breathitt: Politics and Violence in the Appalachian South
T. R. C. Hutton

Cultivating Race: The Expansion of Slavery in Georgia, 1750–1860
Watson W. Jennison

De Bow's Review: The Antebellum Vision of a New South
John F. Kvach

Remembering the Battle of the Crater: War as Murder
Kevin M. Levin

My Brother Slaves: Friendship, Masculinity, and Resistance in the Antebellum South
Sergio A. Lussana

The Political Career of W. Kerr Scott: The Squire from Haw River
Julian Pleasants

The View from the Ground: Experiences of Civil War Soldiers
edited by Aaron Sheehan-Dean

Reconstructing Appalachia: The Civil War's Aftermath
edited by Andrew L. Slap

Blood in the Hills: A History of Violence in Appalachia
edited by Bruce E. Stewart

Moonshiners and Prohibitionists: The Battle over Alcohol in Southern Appalachia
Bruce E. Stewart

The U.S. South and Europe: Transatlantic Relations in the Nineteenth and Twentieth Centuries
edited by Cornelis A. van Minnen and Manfred Berg

Southern Farmers and Their Stories: Memory and Meaning in Oral History
Melissa Walker

Law and Society in the South: A History of North Carolina Court Cases
John W. Wertheimer

Family or Freedom: People of Color in the Antebellum South
Emily West

CPSIA information can be obtained at www.ICGtesting.com
Printed in the USA
BVOW08*0913171016

464546BV00013B/7/P